The 20th Century Legal Philosophy Series

VIII

THE FRENCH INSTITUTIONALISTS
Maurice Hauriou, Georges Renard, Joseph T. Delos

20TH CENTURY LEGAL PHILOSOPHY SERIES: VOL. VIII

THE FRENCH INSTITUTIONALISTS
Maurice Hauriou, Georges Renard, Joseph T. Delos

Edited by Albert Broderick

Translated by Mary Welling

Introduction by Miriam Theresa Rooney

HARVARD UNIVERSITY PRESS
CAMBRIDGE, MASSACHUSETTS
1970

© Copyright 1970 by the President and Fellows of Harvard College
All rights reserved
Distributed in Great Britain by Oxford University Press, London
Library of Congress Catalog Card Number 76-99514
SBN 674-32125-1
Printed in the United States of America

GENERAL INTRODUCTION TO THE SERIES

by the Editorial Committee

This book is one of the 20TH CENTURY LEGAL PHILOSOPHY SERIES, published under the auspices of the Association of American Law Schools. At this annual meeting in December, 1939, the Association authorized the creation of a special committee "for the purpose of preparing and securing the publication of translations on the same general lines as the Modern Legal Philosophy Series, sponsored by this association at the annual meeting thirty years ago . . . the materials to represent as nearly as possible the progress of Continental legal thought in all aspects of Philosophy and Jurisprudence in the last fifty years." The members of the committee were John H. Wigmore (Northwestern University), honorary chairman, Jerome Hall (Indiana University), chairman, Edmond N. Cahn (New York University), Lon L. Fuller (Harvard University), George W. Goble (University of Illinois), Edward A. Hogan, Jr. (Hastings College of Law), Josef L. Kunz (University of Toledo), Edwin W. Patterson (Columbia University), Harold G. Reuschlein (Villanova University), and Max Rheinstein (University of Chicago).

Whereas the earlier series was a very daring venture, coming, as it did, at the beginning of the century when only a few legal scholars were much interested in legal philosophy, the present series could be undertaken with considerable assurance. In 1909 only a few of the leading law schools in this country included Jurisprudence in their curricula, and it was usually restricted to the Analytical School. By 1939 Jurisprudence was being taught in many law schools, and the courses had been broadened to include not only Analytical Jurisprudence, but also the Philosophy and the Sociology of Law. The progress in logical theory, ethics, and social science between 1909 and 1939 was without doubt an important factor in the expansion of Jurisprudence. In 1939 there was not only the successful precedent of the earlier series, now completely out of print, but also the known rise of a substantial body of interested readers, including students and practicing lawyers as well as professional scholars. This thoroughly admirable change, especially in the English-speaking countries, has been widely recognized as productive of a great enrichment of Anglo-American law. The Modern Legal Philosophy Series has been justly credited with a major part of that influence by making readily available the Continental jurisprudence of the last century.

The primary task of the legal philosopher is to reveal and to maintain the dominant long-run influence of ideas over events, of the general over the particular. In discharging this task he may help his generation to understand the basic trends of the law from one generation to the next, and the common cultural ties of seemingly disparate national legal systems. He may, again, create from these common ideal goods of the world's culture general theories, beliefs, and insights that will be accepted and used as guides by coming generations. The works of great legal philosophers not only serve the needs of the practitioner and other utilitarian ends; they also contribute abundantly to our theoretical knowledge. Indeed, in a deeper sense, we have come to understand the superficiality of setting utility against theory. The day is past when jurisprudence can defensibly be regarded as a curious hobby or as "merely cultural" in the sense that the fine arts contribute to the rounded education of a gentleman at the Bar. The issues are now correctly formulated in terms of whether one wishes to be a highly competent lawyer or a technician. Since the question, thus put, is obviously rhetorical, it is but another mode of asserting the considered judgment of those best qualified to pass on such matters, that the science and philosophy of law deal with the chief ideas that are common to the rules and methods of all positive law, and that a full understanding of any legal order therefore eludes those whose confining specialties keep them from these important disciplines.

The recent revival of interest in American history also reminds us emphatically that the great Fathers of the Republic, many of them lawyers, were men of universal intellectual outlook. They were as thoroughly grounded in French thought as in English. Grotius and Pufendorf were almost as widely read as the treatises on common law. Indeed, Jefferson and Wilson, to select two of the many great lawyers who come to mind, were able philosophers and social scientists. They apparently regarded it as essential to the best conduct of their professional careers to study philosophy and, especially, jurisprudence, Jefferson remarking that they are "as necessary as law to form an accomplished lawyer." The current movements in politics and economics have raised innumerable problems which, just as in the formative era of the Republic, require for their solution the sort of knowledge and skills that transcend specialization and technical proficiency. They call for a competence that is grounded in a wide perspective, one that represents an integration of the practitioner's technical skills with a knowledge of the various disciplines that bear directly on the wise solution of the present-day problems; and these are by no means confined to public affairs—they equally concern the daily practice of the private practitioner. With many such legal problems, with methods relevant to sound solutions, with the basic ideas and values involved, the eminent legal philosophers whose principal works appear in this series have been particularly concerned. If it seems to some that the literature of jurisprudence is rather remote from the immediate practical problems that occupy the attention of most lawyers, it is necessary to reassert our primary dependence for the solution of all such problems upon theory—a truth that has been demonstrated many times in the physical sciences but which holds, also, in the realm of social problems. The publication of such a series as this rests on the premise that it is possible to discover better answers than are now given many problems, that a closer approximation to truth and a greater measure of justice are attainable by lawyers, and that in part, at least, this can be brought about through their greater sensitivity to the relevant ideals of justice and through a broader vision of the jurisprudential fundamentals.

In the General Introduction to the first series it was noted, "The value of the study of comparative law has only in recent years come to be recognized by us. Our juristic methods are still primitive, in that we seek to know only by our own experience, and pay no heed to the experience of others." As nations are drawn closer together by forces not wholly in human control, it is inevitable that they should come to understand each other more fully. The legal institutions of any country are no less significant than its language, political ideals, and social organization. The two great legal systems of the world, the civilian and the common law, have for some years been moving toward what may become, in various fields of law, a common ground. The civilian system has come more and more to recognize actually, if not avowedly, the importance of case law, whereas the common law system has been exhibiting an increasing reliance on legislation and even on codes. In a number of fields, such as commercial law, wills, and criminal law, there is so obvious an agreement of substantive principles as to make uniformity a very practical objective. While economic interests will undoubtedly provide the chief stimulus to that end, in the long-range view the possibility of focusing the energies of leading scholars and lawyers, the whole world over, on the same problems is the most inviting ideal of all. The problems of terminology, legal methods, the role of precedent, statutory interpretation, underlying rationale, the use of different types of authority, the efficacy of various controls and their operation in diverse factual conditions, the basic issues concerning the values that are implemented—these and innumerable other fundamental problems of legal science and philosophy may and should receive collaboration on a scale never before attainable. The road to the attainment of these objectives is not an easy one, but if any such avenue exists it is surely that indicated by the best literature in jurisprudence.

These fundamentals are also invaluable aids to better understanding of one's own law. On the side of insight into legal methods and substantive doctrines alone, the gain is immeasurably great. The common lawyer, at least until very recent times, was wont to accept a rigorous adherence to the rule of precedent as axiomatic in any modern system. He was apt to regard the common law through Blackstonian eyes; and he can hardly be said to have been even initiated into the criticism of statutes from other perspectives than those required by an unquestioning acceptance of the primacy of case law. The gains should be no less great as regards organization of the substantive law. A century and a quarter ago John Austin remarked that the common law was a "mess." Although much progress in systematization has been made since that time, we still have a great deal to learn from our civilian friends—particularly from those who have attained wide recognition for their jurisprudential analyses of the common problems of modern legal systems. In addition, there is that vast illumination to be had from the discovery that other advanced legal systems, representing cultures of high achievement, sometimes apply to the solution of many problems different rules of law and even different basic doctrines than does our own. What better avenue to sound criticism of our legal system, what easier road to its early enrichment than by way of intimate knowledge of the innumerable ideas, some identical with our own but otherwise enunciated, some slightly divergent, others directly opposite, that are supplied so generously in the works of legal philosophers!

With the above objectives in view, the Editorial Committee, appointed early in 1940, took up its task. For almost a year it engaged in active correspondence with practically all the legal philosophers in the United States, with many European, including English, legal philosophers, and later on, when the committee decided to include in the series a volume devoted to Latin American jurisprudence, with legal philosophers of Latin America. Similar activities centered on the engagement of translators qualified to translate works of jurisprudence into readable English. Anyone who has undertaken such translation will realize the difficulties involved, and the high competence required. The committee was able to set rigorous standards in this regard because of the presence in the United States of an exceptionally able group of European legal scholars, some of whom had for many years been well versed in the English language.

In making its selection of works for inclusion in this series, the Editorial Committee has been guided in part by the originality and intrinsic merit of the works chosen and in part by their being representative of leading schools of thought. The first series, the Modern Legal Philosophy Series, has made available some of the work of nineteenth-century European legal philosophers—including Ihering, Stammler, del Vecchio, Korkunov, Kohler, and Geny. That series and other publications had brought Duguit to the English-reading public. In 1936 the Harvard University Press published a translation of Ehrlich's *Fundamental Principles of the Sociology of Law.* The present century has also seen the rise of a number of brilliant legal philosophers who have attained wide recognition. Among those whose inclusion in this series was clearly called for were Max Weber, Kelsen, Petrazycki, Radbruch, the French Institutionalists, chiefly Hauriou and Renard, the Interests-Jurisprudence School centering around Heck, and others. The opinion of the committee as to these men was abundantly confirmed by the numerous communications received from legal philosophers of many countries, and the chief problem was to decide which of their works should be translated. But distinction in jurisprudence is not confined to a few writers, and any choice solely on the basis of scholarly merit would be enormously difficult, if not impossible. The committee, like its predecessors, sought "to present to Anglo-American readers, the views of the best modern representative writers in jurisprudence . . . but the selection has not centered on the notion of giving equal recognition to all countries. Primarily, the design has been to represent the various schools of thought" (General Introduction to the Modern Legal Philosophy Series). Some schools of thought have been much more productive than others, especially those of Legal Positivism and Sociology of Law, which number many able representatives. Without further presentation of the numerous phases of this problem, it may be stated that the committee, whose members represent various legal philosophies, has endeavored to make the best selection possible under the conditions of its appointment, the objectives set before it, and the rigorous restriction resulting from the size of the series.

The success of such a project required considerable assistance of many kinds, and the committee is pleased to acknowledge the abundant aid extended to it. Our greatest debt is to the late John H. Wigmore, whose broad experience as Chairman of the Editorial Committee of the Modern Legal Philosophy Series was placed at our disposal, and who advised us frequently on many problems that arose in the initial stages of the work. As Honorary Chairman of this Committee until his death on April 20, 1943, he participated in many of its conferences and took an active and highly important part in launching the project and assuring its success. It was Mr. Wigmore who, in the early uncertain days of the enterprise, interested his former student, a Trustee of Northwestern University, Mr. Bertram J. Cahn, and Mrs. Cahn to contribute a substantial sum to defray the expenses of translation. The publication of the series involved the expenditure of a considerable amount of money and would have been impossible had not the committee also received a substantial subsidy from Harvard Law School. No less a debt does the committee acknowledge to the authors who contributed their work and, in some instances, their close personal collaboration. The translators have earned the committee's admiration for their splendid achievements in the face of serious obstacles and with very little financial assistance to ease their task. We of the committee wish, also, to give our hearty thanks to the many legal philosophers, American, Continental, English, and Latin American, who made valuable suggestions and encouraged us by their interest in the project. They are far too numerous to be named, as are those persons in various positions, some of them rather humble ones, who lightened our tasks by their kindly aid. Finally, the committee acknowledges the special help given by Harvard Law School, the University of San Francisco Law School, Columbia University Law School, and Indiana University Law School. Each of the first two schools provided at its own cost a member of its faculty to serve as a translator, as well as stenographic assistance, and the other schools provided considerable stenographic, clerical, and other help. To each of the above persons and institutions the committee gives its grateful thanks for assistance, without which the publication of this series would not have been possible.

CONTENTS

xi

PREFACE

Represented here are the three principal scholars of what is known as the school of French Institutionalists, which enjoyed its heyday in the decade before the outbreak of World War II. The designation "school" is somewhat misleading, for the writings of these men do not share the same theoretical starting points or methodologies. The theme around which the volume centers is Maurice Hauriou's "theory of the institution," to which Georges Renard and Joseph T. Delos both gave distinctive elaboration. In an age when the terms "personal" and "institutional" have come into conflict, the designation "institutionalist" for these writers is likewise misleading, for Hauriou, Renard, and Delos are all three "personalist" philosophers of law. The fundamental aim of law, they agree, is to "constitute" a society, or societies, into "a social whole of personalities." Hauriou's emphasis in this phrase, derived from Grotius, rests on the last word—"personalities." The strategy of law is to foster integrated, fully realized human individuals by creating balances (*équilibres*) in social groups, which promote personal freedom and counteract de facto human tendencies to the abusive exercise of power. Institutions are led by men—men who will supply them the spark of creativity, the deliberation of wisdom, the more so as their society has afforded a climate suitable to their personal enlargement.

Not everything written by these men makes their personalism clear. For a time Hauriou placed such emphasis on the "objective" elements in law that Georges Gurvitch saw in Hauriou a kinship with his own notion of the "normative fact," a kind of sociological positivism. Gurvitch noted with sadness a shift in Hauriou's thought after 1916, which he charged to a late seduction of the jurist by thomistic doctrine. In fact, the change in Hauriou's emphasis derived not from thomism (with which there is little evidence he was truly familiar), but from his preoccupation after 1912 with the study of sovereignty and of French constitutional law. The Italian positivist jurist Norbert Bobbio has written that even if Hauriou *qua* philosopher were a thomist, Hauriou *qua* sociologist and lawyer "is not more thomist than positivist or individualist or liberal."

Renard and Delos are without question thomists, which is of significance to an appraisal of their institutional writings. In his 1942 study of the thomistic theory of social justice, William Ferree stressed the incompleteness of St. Thomas' social doctrine and singled out Pope Pius XI's Encyclical Quadragesimo Anno of 1931 and Georges Renard's *La théorie de l'institution* as commencing to fill the gap. In fact, this papal document in its institutional analysis also drew upon the work of Hauriou. But the point made by Ferree is that theological theory seized the work of the institutionalists to complete its design, rather than institutional theory drawing upon thomistic philosophy. Further evidence of the impact of institutional ideas on theology is seen in Pope John's celebrated Letters *Mater et Magistra* and *Pacem in Terris*.

A very limited hearing has been given these French scholars by jurists in common law countries. In part this may be explained by the lack of an English version of their writings. Some American sociologists of continental origin (Florian Znaniecki and Nicholas Timasheff) have fairly appraised their work. But when noticed at all by academic lawyers, they have been subjected to grotesque misrepresentation. To Ivor Jennings, Hauriou's work as much as Renard's rested upon "the Catholic rationalism of St. Thomas." Roscoe Pound read "neo-scholastic institutionalism" as pronouncing with a single voice that "the state is its own justification." Wolfgang Friedman saw Hauriou's "idée directive" as fostering "the collective as against the individual," much like "the mysticism of Fascist theory." And most recently, Julius Stone, while exculpating the institutionalists from these neo-fascist implications, has contrasted the "natural law institutionalism" of Hauriou and Renard with the "empirical positivist" version of institutionalist theory constructed by Santi Romano, Hauriou's Italian comtemporary. In the light of current preoccupation with institutional considerations, I would like to suggest a basis for their relevance to contemporary American studies.

Hauriou's institutional work passed through distinct phases. The first phase (1907–1910) emphasized purely objectivist considerations. The second phase (1916–1925) was both objectivist and subjectivist —in the sense that it put stress on creativity in members of institutions, as well as on the objectivist factors. The final "personalist" phase came largely in Hauriou's post-1925 writings. In fact, its clearest expression is in Hauriou's as yet unpublished "Introduction à l'étude du droit." Renard and Delos, in contrast, show personalist and natural law accents throughout their institutionalist writings.

Because Hauriou's work is more complex than any of the other institutionalist writers and yet fundamental to an understanding of their new insights, a large part of this book, and of these introductory remarks, is devoted to him. If clarity were indeed the supreme juristic virtue, the palm would go to Renard and Delos. Hauriou, continually revising his theories, saw no such clarity in things, and his texts often reflect his uncertainties.

Hauriou was led to revise his earlier "objectivist" version of the institutional theory by his realization that it failed realistically to account for the creative force in society, which he would not accept as a pure reaction to an externalized *conscience collective* (Durkheim) or *masse des consciences* (Duguit). Departing from his earlier emphasis on institutions as embodiments of social ideas, in the post-1915 versions Hauriou emphasized the individual initiative or creative ideas that brought new enterprises into being and guided their development. These new enterprises earned the full right to be called "institutions" (in this special sense) only when they were organized in a certain way, with separate powers, and when the idea of the enterprise was actively shared by its organs and members (*communion*). But he recognized that many a would-be "institution" was striving to achieve a particular idea, without having actually reached it. Thus, the institution was always admixed with imperfections and conflicts. In fact, throughout his institutional theory Hauriou defined institutions as being internally balanced by conflicting forces, and he conceived this conflict as itself an element of the stability of the institution. Hauriou recognized that the "ideas of enterprise" of which an institution might consist were as varied as human creativity and social development itself.

Unlike Renard, Hauriou never explicitly postulated a hierarchical state in which lesser institutional orders were conceived as inherently subordinate to the state governmental norms. Either a unitary condition or a pluralistic one was within the range of possibilities for a social institution. Despite his great interest in the theory of the state, Hauriou was identifying characteristics that he conceived of as being applicable in some way to any type of durable organized group—club, business, hospital, university, or church. He argued that an institution which achieved an internally balanced organization, purpose-directed, and with purpose-shared-by-members durability did have a certain call upon the state for recognition as a legal person. But he never denied that it was within the province of the state (or any superior legal order) to deny it recognition. In a sense, the institution was *de droit,* but the state (even "rightly"—as when there were too many such organizations in that line of enterprise) might deny it recognition.

Hauriou viewed law not as mere *loi,* but as *droit.* He did not, however, view *droit* as normally juridically superior to the *loi* of a legal order. That is, a rule of *loi* that was clearly applicable to the facts would prevail. He argued that there were levels of law, and that there might be general principles of law which the arrangements of a given legal system might accept as superior to mere legislation. These views have since been accepted by the Conseil d'État. Although the Conseil d'État, as well as many French jurists, have resisted the notion that this development constitutes a "natural law" accretion, in at least one sense it does. But this concession hardly justifies the dismissal of Hauriou's institutional theory, even in its final stages, as a "natural law version" (Stone). It would be more accurate to argue that Hauriou's institutional theory in its last version was cast in an ideal mode to answer the question, How can one identify a democratic-liberal type of social organization?

Hauriou's later preference as a jurist was to represent a legal system in terms of legal persons with rights and duties, whereas his emphasis in his earlier institutional writings was upon objective situations. One reason for Hauriou's final preference for the *droit subjectif* (rights and duties) approach was, perhaps, his final preference for a "personalist" theory of law, using the fully developed human person as the model for the idealized institution. However, the right-duty terminology is still current among many positivist jurists and has no special connotation of a natural law doctrine. The question arises as to what happens when the "idea" of one institution conflicts with the "idea" of another institution. Hauriou would answer that, from the standpoint of positive law, this may often depend on the institutional arrangements or ideas of the particular jurisdiction where the question is raised. In this sense Hauriou, as much as Santi Romano, is a jurist of positive law.

Hauriou also rejected the "will" theory of law. He was concerned primarily with the content and not the form (norm) of legal rules. He thus had to search for guides to the direction that law should take. One guide was his notion of "directing ideas" or "leading ideas," which became an integral part of his theory of the institution. Hauriou has been criticized for an overemphasis on law as a conceived purposeful means of achieving articulated and clearly perceived objectives. In fact, however, Hauriou recognized that at any moment in a group's history it was possible through investigation of objective data, primarily of institutional phenomena, and through reflection, to ascertain the central ideas of a given society. These ideas were not necessarily perceived in their present specificity in the founding days. Often time subjected them to elaboration and refinement. The history of "due process of law" is a case in point. Renard was helpful here in suggesting that the "ideas" were "themes for development."

Hauriou's interest in psychological factors, considered as social science data dealing with conduct, is evident from his earliest writings. In this respect he was writing against the tide of Durkheim and his school, which stressed social factors. Remarkably early among jurists, Hauriou emphasized the significance of unconscious factors in man's makeup. He considered that a psychologically realistic view of man's conduct, which it was law's role in part to guide or control, demanded attention to the data of human emotions and of moral inadequacies (such as the tendency to abuse power), to a consideration that man often acts from intuition rather than logic, and to an awareness that beliefs (of whose formation no empirical account has yet been given) hold a large place in man's psyche. Hauriou did not himself furnish empirical studies in support of these conclusions, although the possibility of testing them empirically seems more within the reach of social science today than when Hauriou wrote. Hauriou was nevertheless convinced that these insights were the fruit of human experience. His idea of man accorded with Montesquieu's and Acton's in placing major emphasis on man's weakness, and giving as the chief social evidence for that weakness man's persistent historical abuse of power. Hauriou thus concluded that the function of law was to organize society so as to protect it against such abuse —by forming objective situations, institutions, *équilibres*.

In his later writings, as I have already stated, Hauriou stressed that individual initiative and creativity play a crucial role in social and legal development. While the social milieu has a great effect upon men, man is not totally a reflection of this milieu. A doctrinal presentation of society, or of the legal system, which leaves out of account either the "objective" (control) or the "subjective" (initiative) factor is thus incomplete.

Hauriou commenced the development of his institutional theory of law from a consideration not of legal rules, but of social institutions, the most prominent of which was the state itself. To Hauriou, social institutions hinged on certain leading ideas in process of realization. To realize these ideas, the organization of the group took place along functional lines. From the elements of the organization charged with a regulative task—legislature, court, administrators —legal rules emerged. If "properly" conceived, they were directed toward the achievement of the leading ideas. In the instance of the state, the basic idea was to provide a milieu of order, freedom, and justice. The general ideas could take different forms in different states. In addition, particular states could provide for a different relative emphasis, as well as additional leading ideas (economic, political, or religious). The general legal theory of Hauriou thus might be conceived of as hospitable to a host of different types of society and social views.

In the final development of his institutional thought, Hauriou retained elements of his earlier institutional theory, but he was no longer content to furnish a neutral approach to law and society that would accommodate diverse philosophical, political, and social ideas. He frankly proposed a special philosophy of law that may be more appropriately styled "personalist" than "institutional."

In every organized society, or in any society in process of organization, wrote Hauriou, there is "a perpetual dialogue between the power of command and that of subjection," which constitutes its essential function. But this dialogue should be set within a frame of reference that gives the basic end of law as "instituting society in the interest of persons." This aim involves first preserving peace, but it also means organizing the particular society as a "social whole of personalities." The law, conceived as the complex of legal arrangements, whether constitutional, legislative, judicial, or administrative in origin, "will see in every human being a complete personality with all juridical capacities—slaves and women as well as free men." In addition, Hauriou proposed that "the impersonal collective powers which exercise governmental power in the society will be personified and thus led to the juridical measure of personality, in order to be able to establish, even in the affairs of government, more liberty and justice." To "institute" such a society was the proper task of law, argued Hauriou. This task was distinct from either morals or statecraft. "To institute (*in statuo*)," he insisted, meant "to establish within, by internal resources." And "to institute a social organization" consisted in "infusing within it an internal principle of life," or as Terence wrote, "To implant in its heart a more lively affection."

No longer was Hauriou content to generalize from data. He made clear that on the lofty plane of ultimates between the society and the individual, the individual, and his freedom and equal treatment among his fellows, now had paramount value. Individuals did not live alone; they worked out their human existence in groups. But advantage to the group, properly conceived, in Hauriou's view, redounded to the benefit of the members. The "personalist" element thus became the ultimate critical principle of Hauriou's thought.

The deferred articulation of Hauriou's philosophical preference was deliberate. Time and again, he wrote that his first concern was to deal with the data at hand and to propose theories of law and the state that were consistent with this data. This positivistic tone persisted, though somewhat less resonantly, in his 1925 tract essay on the theory of the institution. But in another sense the postponement of the final philosophical formulation was a consequence of two additional factors: Hauriou's only casual attention to the specifics of the problem until his last years, and his lack of satisfaction with both traditional and contemporary natural law formulations.

It is true that Hauriou's final views of the end of law were never published. But the much revised manuscript of his "Introduction à l'étude du droit," from which they come, and their prominent place in its pages, give assurance that they represent the culmination of his jurisprudential thought. From the date in 1927 when Hauriou was introduced by Gurvitch to Grotius' phrase, "a social whole of personalities," he made it his own. His gloss upon the phrase shows him to be the first modern "personalist" philosopher of law.

What difference does it make in the organization and presentation of a legal system to accept Hauriou's personalist view of law? Clearly it involves a doctrinal organization of the materials with the traditional notions of legal "person" and "rights." It also places the stress on law's creative function: the doctrinal study of law is used to direct purposefully the "institutionalization" of society with the specific view, beyond maintaining order, of fostering individual liberty in the sense of accenting options for personal, or private institutional, action. Hauriou's view thus identifies a place both for creative action on the part of individuals within the national and private institutions, and for the establishment of a milieu of balanced and objective situations (institutions and rules of law) to control the exercise of that creativity. Finally, it is based on a particular—personalist—view of man and his relation to society, which rests on few preconceived ideas and continually seeks an increasing knowledge of man and society from the experience derived from societies past and present.

Hauriou's special version of sociological jurisprudence is founded on his view that man as a species is relatively fixed, and that the task of the positive juridical order is to infuse "justice into the organizations created by brute force," and to transform them "into sustaining institutions." The procedures by which law is to accomplish this end are chiefly by establishing "objective balances" within organized groups and by "the corporate personification of institutions."

What possible guidance in solving concrete problems of law would Hauriou find in the almost meaningless breadth of his natural law (stable species) concept? To François Geny natural law was a given, a separate moral source with readily ascertainable answers to which law might, in certain circumstances, turn for the solution to its problems. Hauriou, on the contrary, did not conceive of natural law as a set of moral answers. To him, its answers were often as much in doubt as those of the law itself. Hauriou sought from natural law the answer to another question: How had the general concepts of justice and human liberty worked themselves out under concrete circumstances at various times and places? His view of human history was not one of constant progress, but of a series of cycles representing advance and regression. Yet he felt that the facts of history, to which he turned for his evidence, indicated a constant, if slow, overall advance. In seeking content for the general ideas of justice and liberty, and for natural law, he therefore turned to what he called the "classic" models. By this he did not mean the "classical" constructs of human thought, but the "classical" replicas of human action. These action models were not a priori "oughts," but concrete evidences of what man was capable of achieving because "in the nature of things" he had achieved them. For Hauriou, it was not their widespread acceptance that recommended the study of laws or a legal system as "classic"; it was rather that they most adequately approached the ultimate goals of law and human society, as he conceived them. The constant challenge to law and society is to match, and even surpass, the achievements of these "classic" models.

From his early sociological work Hauriou was struck by the significance of individual differences (as well as likenesses) of men in society. He was early attentive to peculiarly individuating aspects of human psychology, such as the emotions and the subconscious (before Freud had brought it to the fore). Like so many in France in the first two decades of this century, he came under the influence of Henri Bergson's stress upon intuition and *création de nouveau*. He was attracted by the notion (which empirical studies in anthropology and psychology have since made fashionable) of different cultural and personal types. He indulged in some crude intuitions of national types as explanations of differences between French and English institutions. He was more attracted by the individualistic, "vitalist" psychology that enjoyed a vogue at the turn of the century than by the intonation of Durkheim's rigorous sociologism that man is a "social product." In the psychological notion of shared "ideas" he found the central notion that would serve as his bridge from the individual to the social. He joined with Duguit in his objective, if not his approach, that is, to curb the power of "the governors" over "the governed." His opposition to Duguit's formula of the *masse des consciences* as identifying the rule of law was based, in part, on the havoc that it might wreak upon a dissenting minority.

Yet Hauriou's liberal views were not egalitarian. The special educational advantages given to more promising students and the special privileges afforded to educators and officials in France were justified, he maintained, by the national necessity to develop an elite, which was the prerequisite for a successful democratic state. His theme of "minority power" embraced the notion that the small percentage of citizens who served as governors (executives, legislators, administrators) of the French state was an elite. Hauriou boldly styled the French state as "patricio-plebeian," and pronounced the role of the "majority power"—that of the electors—as being more realistically one of control.

Hauriou does not fit into that species of contemporary personalist who exaggerates the value of individual freedom and personal development at the expense of organized society and its institutions, which are merely tolerated as a necessary environment for personal development. His lasting concern with the study of institutions is convincing on this point. His "personalism" constitutes a culmination rather than a rejection of his earlier work. Nor can Hauriou be placed with those philosophers who are preoccupied with the psychological at the expense of the sociological and anthropological evidence of social determinism. Although he rejected Durkheim's exclusive primacy of the social, he was at home with many aspects of Durkheim's work that have since received wide acceptance among behavioral scientists, as well as philosophers and theologians. To his philosophical rejection of the notion that there exists an elaborate moral code (under the rubric of natural law or any other name), Hauriou anticipated farflung reactions among Christian philosophers in this generation. As a prophet of the presently evolving interdisciplinary cooperation in dealing with behavioral problems, he would have found a basis for his personalist philosophy in the extensive empirical studies in personal and social psychology, political, religious, and legal sociology, anthropology and ethics that have developed since his day.

Hauriou's "personalities" within a "social whole of personalities" consist in both individual and collective personalities. The well-ordered, just, free, human being who has realized his full potential is conceived of as more than an individual; he is a personality. In an analogous manner, argued Hauriou, "Personification is the way by which social organisms endowed with collective powers are instituted." Personified organisms, both human and collective, are perceived as "a centralization of ordered powers which obey a rule, both a rule of reason and a rule of instinct." In stating that law "institutes" these collective social organisms, Hauriou meant that law "orders them toward an objective of order and justice." More properly, law "reorganizes and reforms them, because the social institutions . . . are first organized by individual initiatives." As an example, he noted occasions when legislation had brought about reforms in private stock corporations because of the danger posed by their operations to public credit or private investors. American legislation with respect to securities, exchanges, investment companies, and public utility holding companies in the 1930's are a familiar illustration of Hauriou's point.

It is clear that Hauriou was not a follower of one form of "traditional" natural law doctrine. He rejected the notion of a body of immutable rules as well as the view that law basically represents reason in any scientific (logical) sense. His stress upon the "artistic" function of law mediating between a fundamental dualism (justice and order), his allowance for intuition, his reliance upon the fruit of experience rather than the logical elaboration of absolutes—all these factors negate any suggestion that his postulation of a human species, or his search in history for "natural law models," committed him to a traditional systematic view of natural law.

Like Helmut Coing, Hauriou in his personalism postulated the individual as the end of law over the state, although he perceived the inevitable interrelationship between the individual and the group. His pessimistic individualism, stressing abuses of power, seemed to be verified in "the nature of things" as known by human experience. But pessimistic individualism is hardly an empirical discovery; it is a philosophical one.

Certain emphases in contemporary jurisprudence reveal a concern with questions to which Hauriou early called attention. Although I cannot here determine whether contemporary jurists dealing with these questions have been affected by Hauriou's thought, his continuing relevance is confirmed by his early concern with problems such as decision-making, the reunion of law and politics, the role of creativity, discretion, and flexibility in the judicial and administrative process (including an excess of what has been called "dueprocessitis"), the legal system as an institution, centralization versus decentralization in public administration, the need for an interdisciplinary approach to the study of law (widened to include philosophy), the need to develop internal safeguards against administrative abuses (witness the widespread current attention to the Ombudsman approach), the need to acknowledge the place of policy in law-making (judicial as well as legislative), and finally, the task of the jurist to "construct" a new order aimed at securing human dignity.

The contemporary American jurist with whom it would be most interesting to compare Hauriou is Myres McDougal of the Yale Law School. Together with Harold Lasswell, a political scientist, McDougal has been pursuing the interdisciplinary approach to law, with a special emphasis on the interrelationship of law and politics, and the significance of approaching law from the standpoint of institutions. McDougal's work on the place of policy in law-making, his exploration of the content of community goals, his attempt to explicate in the light of sociological evidence the value of "human dignity," and his definition of the jurist's role as to construct a society in the image of a "human dignity" determined through empirical research, are so strikingly like Hauriou's thought as to suggest an intellectual kinship. The apparent link between them is the French international jurist Georges Scelle, to whom McDougal acknowledges a debt. Scelle was an "institutional" thinker who admittedly borrowed from Hauriou, and from Léon Duguit as well.

Other jurists pursued strands of Hauriou's thought in the decade that intervened between his death and World War II. Selections from the most creative of these "institutionalists" are offered here. They include key writings of Georges Renard and Joseph T. Delos, and an introduction to institutionalist thought by Jean Brèthe de la Grassaye. Renard, like Hauriou a scholar and teacher in public law, made deliberate extensions and new applications of Hauriou's central insight that an "institution"—in the sense of an organization—was best understood as a leading idea or set of ideas guiding the organized enterprise established to secure its achievement. Among Renard's most important contributions are his stress on institutional "ideas" as "themes for development," his identification of the "institution" as the "category of movement," his perception that "institutions" may be distinguished from one another by the degree of "intimacy" among their members (a library needs rules, whereas a truly fraternal, intimate, face-to-face group has less need of them).

Renard also strove explicitly to set institutionalist thought within the perspective of thomistic philosophy. Many feel that Renard forced too strongly the kinship between Aquinas and Hauriou, whose debt to Plato and Bergson seemed more striking. But Renard frankly told us that he struck out on his own beyond Hauriou.

Delos, a scholar and professor in both law and theology, made the first conscious effort (later picked up by Renard) to expand Hauriou's analysis of the "institution" into an "institutional" theory of law. That this effort was not successful in the sense of being immediately taken up by other scholars is not surprising, for pre-World War II France was almost as uncongenial to natural law inflections as it is today. Even the other embryo institutionalist writers preferred to follow Hauriou's more restrained published views than those of either Renard or Delos.

Contemporary accents on personalism and phenomenology in philosophy, on institutions in sociology, and on the possible relevancy of natural law in jurisprudence give a new interest to examining these French institutionalist writers of just a generation or two ago, who dealt with the fabric of law and institutions. They were conscious of being engaged in what is now freely termed an interdisciplinary endeavor, with no pretense that it was value-free.

For this edition, lengthy footnotes from the original writings have occasionally been abbreviated or eliminated. Significant deletions from the authors' main texts are indicated by ellipses, and are sometimes further clarified in editor's footnotes, which are enclosed in brackets.

This volume's existence is owing primarily to the labors of the translator, Sister Mary Welling, O.P., of Nairobi, Kenya, whose fresh, incisive style is evident throughout. Its publication in the 20th Century Legal Philosophy Series owes much to the persistent interest of Dr. Miriam Theresa Rooney, who has furnished the Introduction. Interest in France in such a work was first stimulated in 1963 when Professor Michel Villey invited publication in the *Archives de philosophie du droit* of a brief article of mine, which elicited suggestions from French jurists as to which Institutionalist writings would be most appropriate for translation. Throughout the years of preparation of this work, during which all the writings of Hauriou, Renard, and Delos were examined, I enjoyed the strong cooperation of Joseph T. Delos himself, of André Hauriou of the University of Paris (son of Maurice Hauriou), Jean Brèthe de la Grassaye of the University of Bordeaux, and Bernard Geny (nephew and former student of

Georges Renard), a judge on France's supreme administrative court, the Conseil d'État. In addition, each of these jurists prepared original interpretative studies for this book. Georges Vedel and Georges Burdeau of the Faculté de Droit of Paris, Jacques Maury and Pierre Hebraud of the Faculté de Droit of Toulouse, and Felix Senn of the University of Nancy were generous in their comments and advice. Appreciation is due to the Rockefeller Foundation for a grant in legal and political philosophy, which made it possible for me to spend most of the year 1962–1963 on research in France. I am grateful to the late Henry M. Hart, Jr., of Harvard Law School, as well as to H. L. A. Hart of Oxford and Jerome Hall of Indiana University, for lengthy discussions of "institutionalism" from a common law point of view. Critical readings of the final translations were offered by Brèthe de la Grassaye (on Hauriou), Bernard Geny (on Renard), and by Delos himself. A helpful preliminary translation (not used) of Renard's *La philosophie de l'institution* was prepared by Sister Aquiline Petit, O.P., of Barry College, Miami, Florida.

Special thanks are due to Joseph T. Delos and to the heirs of the other authors and to their publisher, Éditions Sirey, Paris, for permission to translate the writings here, and to Marcel Waline of the Faculté de Droit of Paris for permission to include his perceptive study of Maurice Hauriou. It is appropriate to call attention to the contributions made to this work by a 750-year old "institution," the Dominican Order. Two of the three authors whose works are translated—Renard and Delos—are Dominicans, as are the translator and the editor.

This volume is dedicated to an American legal scholar whose professional life closely paralleled that of the founder of French institutionalist thought, who like Hauriou was a superb legal craftsman, a searching and productive scholar, a creative thinker about the law, and an inspiration to three and a half decades of law students, of whom I am happy to have been one—the late Henry M. Hart, Jr.

Columbus School of Law
The Catholic University of America
Washington, D.C.   ALBERT BRODERICK, O.P.
September 1969

INTRODUCTION   by Miriam Theresa Rooney

The new awareness manifested in twentieth century thought finds distinctive legal expression in the work of the French Institutionalists. Their perspectives range from man's activity within his social groups to the environmental conditions that limit his constructive efforts. In order to comprehend the "radical perspectivity" of their work, a comparison with contemporary developments in philosophy is as necessary as is a comparison with the writings of other jurists. Although the diction of the Institutionalists may sometimes seem as old-fashioned as the language of the Napoleonic Code that they taught, their insights into current problems spring out of a scientific methodology that is not notably different from the methodology in current use in the social sciences. Their originality of viewpoint marks a unique advance over traditional modes of expounding the law.

Although Maurice Hauriou, Georges Renard, and Joseph Delos are grouped together under the designation of French Institutionalists, since they are the principal developers of "the theory of the Institution," their outlook is not primarily theoretical but, in fact, quite practical. The emphasis is upon observation. Novelty marks their manner of combining observations of human behavior, methodological advances in interpreting those observations, and the changing provisions of modern law, especially in its constitutional, administrative, civil, and eventually international, branches.

Briefly, the French Institutionalists reject an exclusive conceptualism. The empirical method of science and technology, which directs many other twentieth century activities, influences the trend of their thought. Their thought has not created institutions; rather, the phenomena of the existing institutions under observation have shaped their thought. As professors of constitutional law, they confronted the practical task of reconciling legitimacy in government with the actual law-giving habits prevailing in nineteenth- and early twentieth-century France. The sources of law and the maintenance of authority were brought into especially sharp focus during the

1

centennial years of the French Revolution, when Dean Maurice Hauriou was just beginning his professional career. The old imperialist tradition had been effectively replaced by the goals of *liberté, égalité, fraternité,* but the forms of applying the Code in practice showed few corresponding changes. The radically new procedure of the Conseil d'État, allowing an individual to sue on claim of abuse of power by a government official, was a major innovation in professional practice. Maurice Hauriou was quick to see the potentialities of this procedure and at once began his life-long collection of notes upon decisions (*arrêts*) of the Conseil d'État. He became so outstanding an authority on the *Droit Administratif,* as well as on the *Droit Constitutionnel,* that his reputation as a jurist might rest on these subjects alone, even had he not devised the theory of the Institution. His intellectual struggles at rationalization in the fields of both Constitutional and Administrative Law in fact led to the formulation of his theory. The practical application of the theory is not limited to public law, however, but can be extended into branches of private law, wherever the orderly behavior of people can be observed. Deeds, contracts of agency, partnerships, trusts, corporation charters, treaties, and comparable groupings that involve people, can all be explained in terms of the Institution when its implications are understood. Being both humanistic and concrete in its application, the theory of the Institution avoids the excesses of positivism on the one side, and of idealism on the other; it yields a middle way of operation, which is essentially realistic.

What the Institutionalists actually do is to shift the focus in law from concepts to percepts. By saying, in effect, "Look; see; this is the way it is," they reject assumptions, no matter how long-established. Like the scientists who invented lenses to maximize the capabilities of natural eyesight, these jurists have discovered in the phenomenon of the Institution an instrumentality that discloses how men, when working together, generally proceed in accordance with accepted rules. Nonetheless, a spontaneity in legal behavior becomes apparent which had been lost to view in formal systems.

Contemporary philosophy shows a similar freshness of viewpoint. Edmund Husserl, for example, calls his method Phenomenology; Maurice Merleau-Ponty retains the label of Existentialism; while Adrian van Kaam combines something from both perceptions in writing about the Existential foundations of psychology. Taking into account the data obtained through the use of telescopes and microscopes, they note the multiplicity of perspectives that are possible by shifting the focus. Because they have written since Albert Einstein demonstrated the importance of perspective, as well as perception, in learning about the universe out there, their view of reality is referred to as "radical perspectivity." The term "perspectivity" indicates the increasing awareness in contemporary thought that man's knowledge is primarily perceptivistic. By "radical perspectivity" is meant the continual multiplication of methods and viewpoints, from which may be developed the increasingly wide variety of perspectives essential to a scientific, theoretical integration of hypothetical constructs postulated upon perspectivistic research. Perspectivity is denominated "radical" insofar as it substitutes multiple percepts for a single or one-method approach to the formation of concepts in the learning process.

The implications of radical perspectivity in law may be exemplified briefly in the expansion of the "best evidence" rule and the rejection of hearsay. The best evidence rule has regularly been relied on to place on record the specific phenomena that were actually observed. For instance, in answering a question the witness is generally limited to testimony that begins with an assertion about an event that is purported to have taken place, such as, "I saw." Hearsay, on the contrary, is the repetition of what someone else asserted as true, whether or not he saw the situation at issue with his own eyes; and with rare exceptions, such testimony is excluded. The significance of radical perspectivity is therefore not novel but has been acknowledged for centuries. The innovative aspects are its application to current problems of apprehension through use of the scientific method.

In rejecting the prevailing conceptualist jurisprudence, the French Institutionalists do not espouse a frontier position for its own sake. Instead, Hauriou somewhat obscurely, but Renard and Delos clearly, maintain that their position is based on natural law foundations and fully consistent with the philosophical principles of Thomas Aquinas. Georges Renard, in particular, wrote at length professing his adherence to Thomism no less than to the theory of the Institution. For readers whose knowledge of the Thomistic position in relation to modern scientific method is itself based on hearsay rather than on first-hand examination of the development of St. Thomas' thought, the disassociation of radical perspectivity, as found in the theory of the Institution, from the proverbial conceptualism of many teachers and defenders of the natural law position, may appear scarcely credible. A careful reading of the literature on both views, however, will show that natural law is not displaced in the Institutionalist view, but rather, the conceptualist view of natural law.

Natural law may be conceived of as an earlier term used to describe what the Existentialists now speak of as the human condition. Modern sociology takes a similar position when it points out that each person is born into an ongoing universe and an established social culture. His development is affected, and indeed limited, by that environment and that culture, whether it be the geographic area, the family, the group, or the nation. The means of coping with his native environment is conveyed to each person by a local language, which in turn becomes his principal way of expressing his adjustment, his perceptions, and his inferences, gained from experience. In effect, this view inverts the order maintained by René Descartes (*I think, therefore I am*), which once dominated French thought, and accords primacy of place to being, or existence. Then, within the limitations or conditions of his being, man is distinguished from the rest of existence by his capacity for thought (*I am a human being, therefore I think*). After men reach this take-off point, cultural experiences ordinarily lead in different directions. It is not possible, therefore, to generalize about any single Existentialist position, or to attribute identical views to all adherents. It is only necessary to develop the order of priorities to the point where primacy is accorded to being or existence, in order to equate the basic Existentialist viewpoint with that of the realistic view of the nature of the universe, or natural law. Notwithstanding the divergences that may occur beyond this point, the views of Thomists, Institutionalists, and some prominent Existentialists appear to be in agreement that, in the acquisition of knowledge, existence of the world comes first, awareness of that world comes next, and only then does man's thought about the world become important.

The next step in the learning process, after recognition that a universe exists outside the mind whether or not a person is aware of it, involves the perception of phenomena, or the shape in which aspects of the environment, or nature, are encountered. Here again Thomists, Institutionalists, and some Existentialists and Phenomenologists appear to agree that sense perception is primary in the learning process. As St. Thomas expresses it, nothing is in the mind that is not first in the senses. Although sense perception involves tactile and other experiences besides seeing, the visual phenomena appear most compelling today. Especially since the advent of high-powered lenses, phenomena of the physical environment have provided innumerable fields for observation and application of the scientific method in the measurement of similarities and variations. Human intervention through choice of perspective is possible, as is the imposition of a pattern or framework upon physical phenomena. In the social, or human, environment a phenomenon may take on the appearance of a structure—or an institution. Apparently no change is required in the method of observation. Encounter or confrontation with environment, whether physical or social, is dependent upon perception first. Unless a phenomenon is clearly seen, and its shape contrasted with other shapes, clarification of its significance is unlikely to follow, and comprehension may not be achieved.

In the next stage after the perception of phenomena, two paths exist for further progress. One is the natural capability of the mind for abstraction and generalization. On this point the conceptualists lay heavy weight—so heavy, indeed, that the learning process has often been thrown out of balance, and progress in knowledge has been impeded. The other path, employing the scientific method of observation and experiment, suggests that phenomena may be interchanged, or even manipulated, through slight shifts in perspective or insight. It is here that human constructs may be arranged to lead to a reshaping of aspects of the environment. Through the transposition of natural shapes for useful goals, participation in creativity becomes possible to a limited degree. Inventions may therefore be introduced in the social order no less than in physics and chemistry. Since methodical observation of human behavior has scarcely commenced in law, the possibilities for reshaping structures suitable for the human encounter still lie ahead. It is especially for the future that the theory of the Institution holds considerable promise.

One important element of Hauriou's theory is his use of the word "idea." Traditionally, since Plato's time, the notion has generally been taken for granted that the human mind gives shape to matter for purposes of comprehension, which puts special emphasis on the concept in the learning process. Furthermore, to the human mind has been attributed the capability of formulating a purpose or objective, also called an idea, which may appear desirable. Energies can therefore be directed toward such a goal. Overloading the idea with this sort of content has often led man to attribute to the Creator of the universe man's own limited views of the desirable, which are then spoken of as divine attributes. This presumptuous ideology has been more likely to result in the creation of a God in man's own image than to show the universe as the Creator has actually created it. It constitutes an inversion of the natural order. To see life steadily and to see it whole, as the poet says, may call for heroic courage. At the very least, humility must replace arrogance. Through the method of radical perspectivity, one can avoid the inversion of the natural order that has often followed the unwarranted overloading of the concept in the learning process. By restricting the word "idea" to that minimum level of abstraction needed for intelligibility, the undue exaggeration implied in the term "conceptualism" can be reduced. There is nothing in the Hauriou theory that would tend to eliminate concepts. On the contrary, the distinctly human ability to derive meaning through percepts prevents the Hauriou attention to phenomena from becoming merely mechanical, or subhuman, as crude behaviorism has tended to become. The theory of the Institution, through its recognition of the importance of the idea, restores a necessary balance between percepts and concepts and thereby supplies a corrective for overemphasis on either aspect. In the Hauriou theory of the Institution a philosophically integrative factor for law is proposed, which undertakes to reconcile man and environment without unduly minimizing the value of either.

Although Maurice Hauriou began to publish his views in the 1890's, not until 1925, four years before his death, did the most complete formulation of his theory become available in print. In the 1925 issue of the *Cahiers de la nouvelle journée*, no. 4, Hauriou gave his clearest definition of the theory of the Institution, and at this point Georges Renard picked up the threads and began to weave his own speculations into the original pattern. The juridical core of the Institution according to Renard nevertheless remains in Hauriou's innovative thinking about law, society, the constitution of government, and its administration.

Maurice Hauriou's views were already becoming known beyond the borders of France during his lifetime. Translations had been made into Spanish in 1927, into Russian in 1929, and into Chinese in 1933. His viewpoint gave rise to doctoral dissertations in the Dutch language at Nijmegen in 1945 and at Leyden in 1954. In France, a number of distinguished jurists contributed to the *Mélanges* published in his honor by his own Faculty at Toulouse in 1929, and other learned commentaries may be found in professional journals published since his death. As may be seen from the Bibliography to this book, however, items in the English language are few. The need for documentation and analysis in this area is long overdue.

Like Hauriou, François Geny perceived the inadequacy of the static approach to positive law in meeting the needs of changing practices or behavior observed in the people. His experimentation with the scientific method, however, did not lead him to accord priority to percepts as such, and he did not himself adopt the theory of the institution. Instead, in his rejection of extreme conceptualism,

he retained the prevailing intellectual emphasis on the human capacity for abstraction in the learning process, placing his reliance
on the creative capacity of the human mind in its interpretive function to bridge the gaps between the authoritative Code and the
ongoing ways of the people. By doing so, he introduced the notion
of process, development, or growth in law, which tended to displace
the conceptualist adherence to immutability. Geny's view of creative
intellection amounted to a repudiation of Descartes' formula quite
as fully as did Hauriou's, for they shared a recognition of the actu-
ality of natural law as essentially realistic rather than conceptualistic.
Through his introduction of the scientific method as an improvement
upon the rigidities of the syllogism, his substitution of a dynamic
perspective for law instead of the prevailing static view, and his
recognition of the existing law of nature, not through concepts but
through *donnés* or "givens" of human existence, Geny provided a
fresh stimulus in modern juridical thinking. In fact, his own work
on juridical interpretation constituted the sort of bridge he had
visualized as desirable in advancing from the old forms to the new.
Recognition of the innovative character of his thought was accorded
in the Common Law world with the start of reconstruction after
World War I, when Justice Benjamin Cardozo cited his writings at
several points in his series of lectures given at Yale Law School, *The
Nature of the Judicial Process.*

At the University of Nancy in France the Faculty of Law not only
depended upon François Geny to lecture on the French Civil Code,
but also looked to Georges Renard for lectures on the sociological
aspects of public law. Renard had married Geny's young sister and
undoubtedly was aware of the originality of Geny's work. Renard
nevertheless preferred the prospect for public law presented by
Maurice Hauriou at Toulouse, for unlike Geny, he adopted the theory
of the Institution. Renard was no mere imitator, however. He significantly amplified the theory of the Institution along philosophical
lines, as the selections in this book make clear.

Born in 1876, Georges Renard was twenty years younger than
Maurice Hauriou and fifteen years junior to François Geny. Whereas
Hauriou and Geny were pioneers in proposing innovations in juridical thought through patiently evolved arguments, Renard was known
for his quick appraisal of the merits of progressive ideas, for his
ardent advocacy, and for his oratorical gifts as shown in his university lectures—even when, at the close of World War II, the number of students in his sociology classes at the Dominican House of
Studies at Le Saulchoir, near Paris, were greatly reduced. His youth-

ful enthusiasm for improving on the work of outstanding thinkers of his time won for Renard a unique place among the French intellectuals who were erecting the framework for twentieth century thought.

In order to understand Renard's particular genius, one must recall the circumstances that conditioned his achievement. When Renard was quite young, Pope Leo XIII's famous Encyclical Letter of 1891, *Concerning New Things (Rerum Novarum)*, was issued. Soon after, a group of young men who had accepted the leadership of Marc Sangnier (1873–1950) proposed a program of social, economic, and political reform, which they believed would implement some of the papal recommendations. With the Sillonists, Georges Renard found an outlet for his enthusiasms. The movement lasted from 1894 to about 1910. Unhappily, before any reforms could become well established, they aroused criticism among the traditionalists and conceptualists. Indeed, the full implications of Pope Leo's guidelines were not widely welcomed in conservative circles at the time they were published, nor for years afterward, being considered naïvely impractical, if not theoretically socialistic, in their revolutionary impact. The opposition to progressive ideas took many forms. In politics, it defeated the young Sillonists. In theology, it aimed at the distinguished founder of the American Paulist Congregation, Father Isaac Hecker, who became a victim of misinformation in France, largely because of linguistic difficulties and inaccurate translations and reports. Headlined as the "Americanist Heresy" in French journals, the episode assumed inflammatory proportions, documented by Thomas McAvoy in a paperback published by Notre Dame University Press in 1963. In philosophy, the conservatives became aroused to the point of demanding papal condemnation of "modernism." The condemnation was proclaimed in 1907 by Pope Pius X. In essence, however, the Leonine reforms survived, receiving subsequent approval in Encyclical Letters, such as *Forty Years After (Quadragesimo Anno)* by Pope Pius XI in 1931 and *Pacem in Terris* by Pope John XXIII in 1963. The form in which efforts at implementation had been presented, rather than their substance, had alarmed those not fully prepared by training to distinguish truth from fallacy or to build constructively. The effect of the criticisms and eventual condemnation was to postpone for years the formulation of clear proposals for needed reforms, especially in science and government. For the young men like Renard, who were eager to make improvements, the years from 1895 to the beginning of World War I must have been both frustrating and confusing. It was some time before their energies could be refocused in more hopeful directions.

Among sensitive intellectuals who were also loyal adherents of the Catholic faith, the period was especially difficult. Conscious that they had something important to contribute, they were nevertheless discouraged from articulating it. Eventually, Renard's enthusiasm was revived by Maurice Hauriou's juridical perceptions and his efforts at formulating the theory of the Institution.

Not until 1920 did Renard's name begin to appear in law books in connection with his faculty appointment at Nancy. The 1920 volume *Notions très sommaires de droit public français* reveals his professional concern with public law, which was also Hauriou's field of specialization. By 1929 Renard had achieved sufficient recognition to join the two dozen distinguished jurists, including François Geny, Louis LeFur, and Léon Duguit, who contributed to the *Mélanges Maurice Hauriou.* And in 1930 he published his treatise on *La Théorie de l'Institution,* which undertook to locate Hauriou's theory of the Institution within a broader philosophical framework. By 1934 two more titles appeared. One is a short reprint from the *Révue des sciences philosophiques et théologiques,* XXIII, entitled *Thomisme et droit social, à propos de l'idée du droit social de M. Gurvitch.* The other book is entitled *L'Institution fondement d'une rénovation de l'ordre social,* in which the author states, "Je tiens mon 'institution' pour une adaptation du thomisme." In 1939, just before World War II began, interrupting the publication and circulation of French juridical treatises abroad, Georges Renard combined his speculations on the relations between the theory of the Institution and Thomistic philosophy in a volume entitled *La Philosophie de l'Institution,* which did not become known in the United States until 1948. The philosophical insights that led Georges Renard to find common ground between the system of Thomistic philosophy and the theory of the Institution can be attributed to his understanding of realism and the learning process. It is in epistemology, at the stage of percepts rather than concepts, that Thomistic philosophy, natural law, and the theory of the Institution share common ground.

While Hauriou was writing at Toulouse, and Renard at Nancy, a third law professor, Louis LeFur at Paris, was also struggling to reconcile modern French law with juridical realities. His interest in the law of nations and its basic relationship to the realism of the natural law foundations is revealed in a preface he wrote for the 1929 publication of *La Société internationale et les principles du droit public,* by Joseph T. Delos. The Delos book was well received in a world that was groping for a rational solution to the complex problems of international relations, inherited by modern democratic governments from the royal rulers who had once dominated any agreements in the international law system. Translated into English and published in Dublin in 1932, the book also appeared in excerpts in a Spanish edition, published in Mexico in 1944. The author's views were also introduced into French Canada in 1943 and 1944, during a resident lectureship in Montreal and Quebec. Directing his attention to the relationships that exist between nations, society, civilization, public law, the political order, and international law, Delos found in the notion of the Institution a phenomenon common to all. He utilized this perception to build a rational system of public order in the international field, and thus became the third member of the original group identified as the French Institutionalists.

The development of the theory of the Institution—formulated at first in public law or the governmental field by Hauriou; enriched in its theoretical relationships through localization within the system of realistic philosophy by Renard; and extended to meet the needs of international relationships by Delos—did not cease to expand after World War II. In fact, its significance has been considerably enhanced. Not only have jurists like Achille Mestre and René Clemens, adopted it, but it has also been utilized to provide new insights in the quest for peace. Especially noteworthy is a book by Gerard Herberichs, published in Paris in 1964, entitled *Théorie de la paix selon Pie XII*. As a member of the staff of the Council of Europe, Herberichs has doubtless been confronted with many practical problems in the international law field. In his search for help in solving some of the questions without precedent, he eventually looked for guidance to the work of Pope Pius XII and the resolution of some of his diplomatic tasks. As a basic theory became apparent, documentation was sought. Consultation with distinguished jurists in contemporary Europe, especially in Holland, led Herberichs to the writings of the French Institutionalists. The resulting book is roughly divided into two parts, the first being a summary of the Pope's statements, the second being an outline of the French Institutionalist theory, with an indication of the similarity between the two views. From the analysis it would appear that the application of the theory of the Institution to international law made by Delos in 1929 is even more relevant a third of a century later. Furthermore, the tests of practical diplomatic experience seem to strengthen rather than disprove the value and validity of the theory. As worked out in the Delos book, the theory found some practical recognition when the author was appointed Adviser to Jacques Maritain, the Ambassador of France at the Vatican. As presented in the Herberichs book, the theory is available in the daily functioning of the Council of

Europe, besides enjoying the recommendation of Professor Charles de Visscher of Louvain, formerly the Belgian judge on the International Court of Justice, whose emphasis on realities rather than concepts in international law has been widely acclaimed.

The theory of the Institution, as developed from experiences in French law, has been matched to some extent by comparable advances in Germany and England. The juridical scholarship nourished at the German universities in connection with the century-long project of drafting the German Civil Code was expanded into the modern comparative law field largely because of the universal outlook of Max Weber, who became deeply impressed by the basis for comparison provided by the phenomenon of the Institution. Between the French and German Institutionalists no direct derivation is apparent, however, perhaps because the French were consciously realistic in their approach to natural law, while the German scholars were more influenced by the prevailing idealism of Kant or Hegel. The Weber emphasis on power appears to draw upon the voluntarism of Kant's juridical theory and is thus contrary to the more democratic view of the French Institutionalists.

In England, Sir Henry Maine's books mention institutions frequently. The author had at first been dismayed by his experience as a government official in India, where he found the people law-abiding because of their observance of local customs, notwithstanding their lack of familiarity with the Common Law system and its methods of enforcement, which he had been taught to uphold in his training at the Inns of Court. Impressed by his first-hand observation of the functioning of institutions in the maintenance of order, Maine read widely upon his return to England, looking at the working of institutions in Ireland before the Common Law system had been imposed, and eventually investigating the development of legal institutions in international law, where there was no sovereign in the Austinian sense. Because of this broad outlook, Sir Henry Maine became in fact the founder of comparative law studies in the Common Law world.

An entirely different approach brought Frederick William Maitland, the incomparable historian of the English Common Law, to note the pervading phenomenon of the institution in medieval England. In endeavoring to trace the roots of the established court system, Maitland found institutions everywhere that were indigenous with the local population. Whether he looked to shires or to manors for ways of settling disputes over persons or property, he discovered consistent evidence that the law arose with the people and not from reliance upon the king, except when appeals were made from local judgments. The imperialist notion of the derivation of law, common on the continent of Europe, was manifestly absent in medieval England. In the early days of the Common Law, the king, when acting as an appellate judge in the search for justice, was said to be, in Maitland's phrase, a man who actually walked the earth on his own two feet, and definitely not the abstract concept referred to today as the Crown. In other words, a realism was discoverable in the local law of England in the Middle Ages, even in the Norman era, which seems to have been lost in modern times. Maitland, in pursuing his quest for actualities, found support in the researches of Paul Vinogradoff, the Russian scholar who had worked with the German jurists and found their theorizing to be highly conceptualistic. Vinogradoff became increasingly convinced of the importance of local institutions in locating the sources of law. Another writer, familiar with German juridical speculations, whose rejection of conceptualism appealed especially to Maitland, was Otto von Gierke. They shared a common interest in the modern legal entity known as the corporation, and repudiated the reasoning by analogy that treated the corporation as a fictitious person. The German philosophical expression *als ob* (as if), was replaced in their thinking by the method used in Phenomenology, which has become familiar through the expression "piercing the corporate veil." In other words, the corporation is founded upon a reality, which is in fact an organized group of people, and these people are real persons, not quasi-persons nor fictions. The shape that the corporation takes is a phenomenon for purposes of recognition. The behavior of people as perceived in the phenomenon, not the abstract corporate structure, is the subject-matter of law. In rejecting the conceptualism implicit in the prevailing Germanic philosophy, Maitland found added support in von Gierke's insight into the natural law, and he made available excerpts from the von Gierke writings by translating them into English. Von Gierke, Maitland, and the French Institutionalists, in holding fast to perceptions rather than to conceptions of the way people behave, find common ground in the actualities of the existing universe, formerly spoken of as the law of nature or the natural law.

In the United States, incipient efforts have been made to observe systematically the behavior of people as they operate under legal rules. During the 1920's Professor Underhill Moore at Yale reported in detail on human behavior when directed by traffic regulations, and also observed practices in the transfer of funds through the use of bank checks. A research institute for the expansion of such observations of legal behavior was established at Johns Hopkins University by a group advocating a "new realism" in legal studies, but the enterprise was terminated for lack of financial support at the beginning of the Depression in 1929. In more recent years, the methods of radical perspectivity have been utilized to some extent in analyses of court administration, the results being stored in computers for subsequent retrieval and utilization.

The theory of the Institution, as disclosed in the views expressed by the French writers in the following pages, is built on observation—the observation of the external behavior of people, acting together, in more or less formally organized groups, leading to a manifest result, which may or may not be consciously recognized as a goal. The activity which is perceived has a spontaneous quality, arising out of the ways of the people, and is therefore indigenous. When the behavior under observation is repeated under similar circumstances or conditions, it becomes known as customary, habitual, or regular. Regularity, or governance by rules that are accepted, known, and anticipated, gives rise to the legal order. The important feature is that law arises from the very nature of man. It is therefore democratic in essence, and limited in its direction by the conditions of the existing universe. These conditions constitute the *données* or "givens" of the human condition in the juridical order.

Institutions, as phenomena subject to observation, take a particular shape from the groups who constitute them. They are essentially human. They affect the behavior of people exclusively. They are not primarily imperialistic in origin. They do not relate directly to property nor to the material aspects of the environment. In other words, institutions exist apart from the power assumed by any state. The theory of the Institution, therefore, presents a view of the legal order that necessarily rejects the theory of law as primarily command. The shared "idea" is paramount.

Association of the notion of law exclusively with externals of human behavior seems innovative to those who have been habituated to justify law on the basis of the command theory, or to those who place emphasis on motive or intent. The view, however, is not new. It was so well known in Thomas More's time that the consummate jurist who had been Lord Chancellor of England relied upon it when on trial for his life. Charged with subversive intent, he pointed out that evidence of intentions, whether perjured—as at his trial—or not, was inadmissible, for as he said, it was never the law of England to punish a man for his thoughts.

The method of radical perspectivity, when introduced to the juridical order, among people already drawn together through the methods of science and technology, would seem to provide a common ground upon which the code practice of Europe and the case law of the Anglo-American system could become more closely unified in the resolution of both private and public law problems. In its contemporary application, it already appears to promise reconciliation between law, sociology, life sciences, and philosophy. Perhaps the sterile debates of the last century between positivism and the outdated conceptualistic interpretations of the natural law can now be turned in a more hopeful direction. Radical perspectivity would seem to avoid the undue exaggeration of individualism on one side and socialism on the other, and to restore a realistic understanding of law seriously lacking in modern times. The French Institutionalists, in demonstrating the value of clear perceptions in the learning process and the place of insight, have also opened a new outlook for law school studies, which may tear down the artificial barriers existing in the universities and inaugurate a new awareness of the importance of the legal order in human development.

The Sociological Theory of the Institution and French Juristic Thought   by Jean Brèthe de la Gressaye

To measure the newness of Maurice Hauriou's social ideas against the background of the French juridical milieu, one must first recall the predominant tendencies before him in French juristic thought, then point out the juridical consequences of the theory of the institution, and finally inquire how it has been received by French jurists.

THE INDIVIDUALIST CONCEPTION OF LAW AND SOCIOLOGY

Throughout the nineteenth century, the ideas of Jean Jacques Rousseau and the French Revolution led jurists to conceive of social relationships under the schematic form of a collection of autonomous individuals, related by private ties, and together forming a single society, the political society. According to this conception, individuals, born free and equal in law, are invested with natural rights inherent in their person, of which the principal ones are liberty and property, and by means of which they can acquire other rights if they so wish. These are subjective rights, that is, attributed to the individual, connected with his juridical personality, and consisting in a power of will, whose effects are sanctioned by the state. For the individualists, the relationships of individuals among themselves constitute private law, and the relationships of individuals with the state constitute public law.

Private law is founded principally upon contract, since man, being free, can be bound only by his will. Marriage is a contract; so is the corporation[1] or the association, just like a sale or a lease. An agreement is the law of the parties. The law of the state can limit the autonomy of the individual will only exceptionally, for reasons of public order; its essential aim is to ensure the coexistence of the rights of individuals. Nonimperative laws[2] are simply the expression

1. [Société. See Glossary—hereafter referred to as "G."]
2. [I.e., permissive.]

15

of what is presumed to be the will of the parties, but these laws are general, whereas contracts produce effects only between the parties.

Public law is constructed to a great extent upon the same individualist bases. The state is a moral person, endowed, like physical persons, with subjective rights, powers of will. These powers derive from the sovereignty of the people, which is expressed in the political constitution and the laws of parliament. The constitution and laws are expressions of the general will of the people to which each individual has adhered in advance by virtue of the social contract, so that it is still by contract that the law binds citizens. This sovereignty knows only one limit: the rights of man, public liberties, and civic rights. In international relations the sovereignty of the state is absolute; it is limited only by the obligations that it has voluntarily contracted in international agreements. However, the Administration is not subject to private law for its contracts, its responsibility, and its executive actions; it enjoys the prerogatives of public power,[3] and is liable to suit only in special courts of justice.[4]

Citizens' relationships with the state are of the same nature as the relationships of individuals with one another, except that they are rooted in inequality because of the sovereignty of the state.

A fortiori, the relationships between members of a private corporation or association are treated as relationships of individual to individual: the members are not subject to the managers' authority, as they voluntarily adhered to contractual charters[5] and named agents to run the common business. Even such a recent development as the collective labor agreement falls into the category of contracts: it is a voluntary agreement by which employers assume the obligation of guaranteeing certain conditions of work to their employees. Finally, the notion that private groups have moral personality is a legal fiction, since subjective rights are powers of will, and there is no collective will. What is more, bodies that are intermediary between the individual and the state may exist only by exception, by a concession on the part of the state.

In like manner, the statist conception of German juristic thought at the end of the nineteenth century was still voluntarist and subjectivist, but only to the benefit of the state. The state is the creator of every right, individuals themselves have only those subjective rights that the sovereign state wishes to recognize in them.

This whole conception of law—individualist or statist—was vio-

3. [*Puissance publique.* G.]
4. [The administrative courts ascending to the Conseil d'État.]
5. [*Statuts.* G.]

lently attacked from 1901 on by Léon Duguit, Dean of the Faculté de Droit of Bordeaux.[6] For him, the state has neither personality nor will, and the individual has no rights, natural or positive. No one has subjective rights, powers of will. There are only objective situations, of government, official, owner, determined by the juridical rule.[7] All law[8] is objective. And the juridical rule has its source in the society. Inspired by the sociology of Auguste Comte and of Émile Durkheim, Léon Duguit argued that the primordial social fact in juridical matters is social solidarity. A rule of custom or an economic rule becomes a juridical rule, obligatory under the threat of social constraint, when the observation of this rule is indispensable to the sustenance and development of social solidarity. But while Durkheim claimed that juridical rules are conceived by the collective conscience of the society, Duguit, rejecting this myth,[9] said that it is the mass of individual consciences[10] that has the sense of what social solidarity requires in a given country at a given time. The human will contents itself with expressing this imperative of society by juridical acts. A law is a juridical act that has no more value than a contract. It is distinguished from contract only by its *form:* it is a collective act, a multitude of unilateral declarations of will converging toward the same object; and by its *effects* it is an act-rule, creating a juridical situation that is general, abstract, and permanent; whereas a contract is a subjective act, creating a juridical situation that is concrete, particular to the contracting parties, and temporary.

Hauriou rose up against objectivism as well as subjectivism. Against Duguit, he wished to show that juridical rules are secondary, for they only limit the powers of individuals and of institutions, which are sources of life and of action. Against Durkheim, he insisted

6. Duguit, *L'état, le droit objectif et la loi positive* (Paris, 1901); *Traité de droit constitutionnel,* 3rd ed. (Paris, 1927).

7. [*La régle de droit* and *droit objectif* were to Duguit identical in meaning: "a rule of conduct that imposes itself upon individuals living in society, a rule the respect for which is considered at a given moment by a society as a guarantee of the common interest, and a violation of which provokes a collective reaction against its author." Léon Duguit, *Manuel de droit constitutionnel,* 2nd ed. (Paris, 1911), p. 1.]

8. [*Droit,* i.e., rightful law, which for Duguit was the only valid law. See G.]

9. [See Duguit, *Traité de droit constitutionnel,* I, 81.]

10. [*La masse des consciences.* G. As has been recently stressed, "English requires two words—'conscience' and 'consciousness'—to translate *conscience . . .* The French term *conscience* means three things: internalized sanctions, awareness, and perceived culture." Paul Bohannan, "*Conscience Collective* and Culture," in Kurt H. Wolff, ed., *Essays on Sociology & Philosophy by Emile Durkheim et al.* (New York, 1964), pp. 78–79. Duguit specifically rejected Durkheim's notion that there was a *conscience collective.* He substituted for it the concept of a *masse des consciences individuelles,* a kind of consensus. See Duguit, *Traité de droit constitutionnel,* I, 81.]

that the social milieu is inert, without creative force. To the German theorists he retorted that the state is itself subject to law. He was more reserved with regard to individualism, for his theory of the institution is balanced by his belief in the value of an individualist social order. One must not lose sight of this dualism.

THE THEORY OF THE INSTITUTION AND ITS JURIDICAL CONSEQUENCES

Hauriou does not speak of society in general, nor does he deal exclusively with the political society; he considers the diverse social or corporate institutions which together constitute society. Private groups are, for him, institutions by the same right as the state. And unlike the sociologists, who put unorganized groups (races, generations, social classes) and organized groups (public collectivities, private corporations or associations) on an equal footing, he regards only the latter, the juridical groups, as the creators of law.

Hauriou's conception of the institution is intellectual and psychological. The fundamental element is not the will but the directing idea, which explains the foundation of the institution, its duration, the juridical powers of its organs. However, the will has a role subordinate to the idea. This role is manifested by the power to act of the founders and organs in the service of the idea. Hauriou adds an original element, the phenomenon of consciousness: the manifestations of communion between the members and the organs, by which the idea, assumed principally by the organs, passes into a subjective state in the individual minds of the members. This phenomenon has the effect of strengthening the cohesion and unity of the group, and of having the group's direction ratified by the consent of the members. Although the mother-idea of the institution is objective, the personal role of individuals in the creation and life of a social body is nonetheless paramount. Hauriou rejects both Durkheim's collective conscience and Duguit's mass of individual consciences. The founders of a social body discover an idea and adopt it, the members adhere to it, the organs serve it. The institution is a collectivity that lives by the activity of individuals. But it surpasses them; it is durable, permanent, hence its name (status, state). The persons involved in it succeed one another; the institution subsists, as long as the idea has partisans. And to endure, it adapts itself to the changing conditions of life: it can modify its rules in order to remain faithful to the idea.

This sociological analysis of the institution has juridical consequences, which were remarked by Hauriou himself and by his disciples.

(1) *The unity of public law and private law.* Whether an institution is public or private, one finds the same elements in it: directing idea, organization, authority, permanence; and in the authority are found three powers, legislative or regulatory, executive, repressive (the penal law of the state, the disciplinary law of the Administration over its officials or of private institutions over their members).

(2) *The opposition between institution and contract.* Not even private institutions, which are optional and therefore voluntary, come from a contract between their members. For Hauriou, as for Duguit, the foundation of a corporation or an association is the result of a collective juridical act, of a fund of unilateral concordant declarations of will. The deliberations of general assemblies, like those of parliamentary or administrative assemblies, are also the fruit of a concurrence of wills tending toward the same object. The charters or regulations of private institutions have the generality and the permanence of laws or administrative regulations. While the parties to a contract are equal, the members of an institution, even a private institution, have submitted themselves to the authority of the organs.

(3) *The division of law according to social relationships.* Interindividual law has the object of regulating the relationships of individual to individual (whether physical or moral), relationships that are established between persons not as belonging to the same social body but to satisfy their respective interests, on the basis of equality, of commutative justice. *Institutional* or *corporate* law has the object of regulating the relationships that are established among the members of the same social body, to realize the idea that is the good of all, on the basis of the authority of the organs, in virtue of social justice.

This division of law is superior to the classic division between private law and public law, because it recurs within each of these two branches: public law is essentially corporate, but in administrative law there are also relationships of the interindividual type between the Administration and private persons (contracts, responsibility); private law regulates the relations between individuals (property, obligation, responsibility), but also the corporate relations between members of a family, of an enterprise, of a corporation or association.

Corporate law is itself divided into two branches: *statutory law,* which has the object of determining the constitution of the institution (state or private group) and the individual rights of the members; and *disciplinary law,* the object of which is to reprove by punishment the acts of the members that would trouble the order proper to the institution, thus hindering it from realizing its idea.

(4) *The institution, source of law.* Not only is the state the general source of a country's positive law, but each institution, even each private institution, forms for itself its own distinctive law, under the form of charters, regulations, collective labor agreements, within the framework traced out by the laws of the state. The institution has juridical autonomy; so that law is not derived exclusively from the state but is composed of a plurality of superimposed juridical orders: the law of bodies distinct from the state, national law, international law.

(5) *The reality of moral personality.* Institutions can be created freely: there are corporate liberties as well as individual liberties. And institutions have full right to juridical personality. They have an objective reality, not because they are the seat of a collective will, for there are only individual wills, but because the idea that animates them passes into the conscious minds of organs and members, and psychological consciousness is the mark of personality. To be a person is to be conscious of one's being. Every institution is then by itself a moral person, and by nature demands juridical personality.

Must one push further in developing the notion of institution so as to conceive of a *general theory of law* that would be entirely institutional? Joseph T. Delos[11] advanced this idea by suggesting that every juridical act, whether it be the foundation of an institution, a law, or a contract, has the same structure, a will in the service of an idea: the mother-idea of the institution, the idea of the legislator, and in contract the exchange of two equivalent things, what jurists call the *cause* of the contract, which is objective, that is, distinct from the individual motives of the contracting parties. But however true this analysis may be, the institutional charter, which would be reduced to a single element of the institution (the idea), would concern only juridical acts, the sources of law, and not the content of law, the substance of the rules.

Georges Renard[12] leaned toward an institutional theory of law, by

11. ["The Theory of the Institution"] *Archives de philosophie du droit et de sociologie juridique,* 1931. pp. 97–153.
12. *La théorie de l'institution,* 1930.

which he simply meant that law is composed of several juridical orders: the order of the state, the ecclesiastical order, the international order, and the inferior orders that are proper to the diverse particular institutions.[13] Here again, it is a question whether we can limit ourselves to a single aspect of law, the ordering of rules according to their institutional domain.

Hauriou himself framed a response to this question, and it is a negative one. Although throughout his successive studies on the institution, he seemed to see it everywhere in law, during the last years of his life he felt the need of re-establishing the balance between the individual and society, between the individual and the social end of law.[14] Law is intended, not exclusively for the social institution, but also for the individual person. In fact, the social order of civilized, laboring, sedentary peoples is an individualist order established for the individual good of man, because personal interest, and even the speculating spirit of the entrepreneur, is the indispensable drive behind productive work. Hauriou even went so far as to conclude, not without some exaggeration of the merits of capitalism, that the historic experience of the success of occidental civilization, with its individualist basis, is the revelation of a definitive social truth, a truth of natural law, with the reservation that personal interest must be made moral by Christian ideas. For individualism is fallible, it can degenerate into egotism, into the exploitation of the services of one's fellow man. It is certain that he gave first place to the rights of the individual. The institution is only the second element of the social order, an objective element that simply tends to assure the duration of social life. Law, seen under its essential aspect, its end, is then not entirely institutional: it is for the good of the person and for the good of society. The truth is simply that Hauriou's synthesis builds law upon two bases: social institutions and individual rights.

THE DESTINY OF THE THEORY OF THE INSTITUTION

Maurice Hauriou's ideas have been favorably received in France, if not in every juridical milieu, at least by jurists who are concerned with the social order. Among *sociological jurists,* Georges Gurvitch[15] found that some of Hauriou's conceptions were very much like his

13. [Analogy as applied to legal orders.]
14. *Précis de droit constitutionnel,* 1st ed., 1923; "L'ordre social, la justice et le droit;" *Revue trimestrielle de droit civil,* 1927; *Précis de droit constitutionnel,* 2nd ed., 1929.
15. *L'idée de droit social* (Paris, 1932).

own: the institution is what he called a *normative fact* since it is
a source of juridical rules; institutions create multiple juridical orders; social law is distinct from interindividual law. Gurvitch, who,
like most sociologists, was inclined to make man entirely dependent
on society, regretted only that Hauriou had ultimately leaned toward
an individualist social order. Furthermore, the theory of the institution has been warmly received by the Semaines Sociales de France,[16]
the organ of the Catholic social school, because it corrects the evils
of the excessive individualism of the French Revolution by its concern for social justice whose object is the common good of the society; because it rehabilitates intermediate bodies, especially professional groups, which Catholic social thinkers see as one of the foundations of the social order, guaranteeing justice and peace between
capital and labor; and finally because the theory of the institution
does not sacrifice the person to society. However, the last jurist
disciple of Durkheim's school, Henri Lévy-Brühl,[17] passed over the
theory of the institution in silence.

    In the area of general theory of law, Jean Dabin,[18] in his classi-
fication of rights, noted *corporate rights,* powers of the institution
and individual rights of its members. In *L'introduction générale à
l'étude de droit,* 1948, written by me in collaboration with Marcel
Laborde-Lacoste, we ourselves adopted the distinction between interindividual law and corporate law, admitted the plurality of juridical
orders, and recognized the reality of moral persons. And I have
presented my conception of the institution in my article "Institution," published in *Répertoire Dalloz de droit civil* in 1952, and
again in my study on corporate law.[19]

    The authors of *public law,* even though Hauriou was one of their

16. [The Semaines Sociales de France have convened one week each year since 1904
(with the exception of the war years), rotating among the different French cities. Each
year a particular social theme is singled out for investigation from the standpoint
of the social sciences and Catholic social teaching. Renard and Delos on several
occasions gave papers at these Semaines Sociales (See Bibliography). The leading
French précis of labor law recently attested to the influence of these meetings on
contemporary Frency social developments: "This criticism of the autonomy of the
will [the supposed equality of condition of employer and worker] has been chiefly
the work of juridical socialism and of the Catholic jurists of the movement of the
Semaines Sociales de France, who have brought together the traditional teaching of
the Church on contractual justice." André Rouast and Paul Durand, *Droit du travail,*
3rd ed. (Paris, 1963), p. 26. See Eugène Duthoit, *Rénovation française. Apport des
Semaines sociales* (Paris, 1942).]
    17. *La sociologie juridique* (Paris, 1951).
    18. *Théorie générale de droit* (Brussels, 1944), pp. 59ff; *Le droit subjectif* (Brussels,
1960).
    19. "Droit corporatif," *Annales du droit et des sciences politiques,* Louvain, 1960.

own, have not rallied to the theory of the institution. Marcel Waline is almost the only one to have found it just and fruitful,[20] and he did not use it again in his treatise on administrative law.[21] Even though the disciplinary power appeared clearly in Hauriou as the property of every institution, the French authors of administrative law have claimed that this power, recently recognized in the associations of the liberal professions, is delegated to them by the state, and that consequently these associations are organizations of public law.

Among the authors of *private law,* the theory of the institution has been respected by those who had not been convinced by the contractual conception of social groups. André Rouast and Paul Durand have explained the juridical functioning of the enterprise, the labor union, the collective labor agreement, by the notion of institution,[22] as I have also done myself.[23] And I have had the satisfaction of seeing the Cour de Cassation[24] interpret in this sense the shop rule, the disciplinary power of the head of an enterprise,[25] and the splits of labor unions.[26] Finally, thanks to the theory of the institution, Alfred Légal and I have identified corporations, associations, labor unions, enterprises, and professional groups.[27]

20. "Les idées maîtresses de deux grands publicistes français, Léon Duguit et Maruice Hauriou," *Année politique française et étrangère* (1930). [But see Georges Burdeau, *Traité de science politique* (Paris, 1949–1957), esp. II, 238ff; Marcel Prelot, *Institutions politiques,* 3rd ed. (Paris, 1963), pp. 39ff, and *La science politique* (Paris, 1963), pp. 85ff; and Suzanne Bastid, "Place de la notion d'institution dans une théorie générale des organizations internationales," in *L'évolution du droit public: études en l'honneur d'Achille Mestre* (Paris, 1956), pp. 43ff. All these authors show an interest in Hauriou's theory of the institution, which was stimulated at Paris by Hauriou's former colleague, Professor Achille Mestre, of the Faculté de Droit.]

21. [See Waline, *Droit administratif,* 9th ed. (Paris, 1963).]

22. *Droit du travail,* 3rd ed. (Paris, 1963). [These authors recognize that the "patronal enterprise in fact constitutes an institution, and one can justify by the theory of the institution anomalies that cannot be explained by the theory of contract." They add, however, that "the contract of work conserves a role in the organization of labor relations, and one must rather associate the two ideas of contract and institution." *Droit du travail,* p. 403. See also Michel Despax, *L'entreprise et le droit* (Paris, 1957), and Gabriel Roujou de Boubee, *Essai sur l'acte collectif* (Paris, 1961).]

23. "Syndicats professionnels," in Emmanuel Vergé and Joseph Hamel, eds., *Répertoire Dalloz de droit social et du travail* (Paris, 1961), II, 637–662; "Comités d'entreprise et délégués du personnel," *Répertoire Dalloz de droit social* (1960), I, 519–536; "Convention collective de travail," *Répertoire Dalloz de droit civil* (Paris, 1951), I, 1071–1078; and "Les caractères juridiques des corporations," *Études agricoles d'economie corporative* (1942).

24. [The highest court of French civil law.]

25. See my article, "Le pouvoir disciplinaire du chef d'entreprise," *Droit social* (1960), pp. 633–638.

26. See my note, *Recueil Dalloz* (1960), pp. 14ff.

27. *Le pouvoir disciplinaire dans les institutions privées* (Paris, 1938).

But commercial lawyers have had difficulty in admitting that corporations, even joint stock companies, are not contractual.[28] And civil lawyers persist in interpreting moral personality as a notion of pure juridical technique; they fail to see any social reality in it.

Generally speaking, the authors of private law, who are accustomed to constructing law upon the basis of physical persons, have been disconcerted by the institution. The very name adopted by Hauriou has baffled them, because for them juridical institutions are bodies of rules established around a central subject: property, for example, or mortgage.[29] But when the legal historians study political, administrative, financial, and ecclesiastical institutions, they encounter bodies of rules as well as social bodies: families, communes, trade unions, administrations, states, churches, religious orders. Besides, Hauriou had made himself perfectly clear by distinguishing between *institution-things*, juridical rules, and *institution-persons*, social bodies.[30] May the interest now shown in the United States in the theory of the institution further convince French jurists of the value of the ideas of this great jurist-sociologist who renewed the science of law.

---

28. Joseph Hamel and Gaston Lagarde, *Traité de droit commercial*, I (Paris, 1959). However, see Georges Ripert, *Aspects juridiques du capitalisme moderne* (Paris, 1946), no. 39, and especially Jean Gaillard, "La théorie institutionnelle et le fonctionnement des sociétés anonymes," Thesis, Lyon, 1932.

29. Paul Roubier, *Théorie générale du droit,* 2nd ed. (Paris, 1954), no. 3, and treatises by Léon Julliot de la Morandière, *Droit civil* (Paris, 1960); Henri and Léon Mazeaud, *Leçons de droit civil,* 2nd ed. (Paris, 1959); and Gabriel Marty and Pierre Raynaud, *Droit civil,* I (Paris, 1961).

30. [See Maurice Hauriou, The Theory of the Institution and the Foundation, below.]

Maurice Hauriou—A Memoir   by André Hauriou

The life of Maurice Hauriou is inseparable from his work. The steps of his scientific career and the bibliography of his writings together form the conducting wire of his biography.

Maurice Hauriou was born August 17, 1856, at Ladiville in Charente, and died March 12, 1929, at Toulouse. He was admitted to the staff of the Facultés de Droit after an examination in which he took first place. In 1883 he was named Professor of the History of Law at the Faculté de Droit of Toulouse; then in 1888, Professor of Administrative Law; and finally in 1920, Professor of Constitutional Law. In 1906 he became Dean of this Faculté, to which he dedicated the remaining years of his life.

On April 22, 1931, a bust of Maurice Hauriou was placed in the gardens of the Faculté de Droit of Toulouse. At this ceremony Hauriou's successor, Dean Charles Cesar Bru, displayed copies of his work, which included: eleven editions of the *Précis de droit administratif*, published between 1892 and 1927 (a new edition about every three years); two editions of the *Principes de droit public,* 1910 and 1916; two editions of the *Précis du droit constitutionnel*, 1923 and 1929; a volume that appeared in 1896 on *La science sociale traditionnelle; Leçons sur le mouvement social*, 1899; a book on *La souveraineté nationale*, 1912; his licentiate thesis, "Du terme en droit romain et en droit français," Bordeaux, 1876; his doctoral thesis, "Étude sur la *condictio*—Des contrats à tître onéreux entre époux," 1879; several articles on the "theory of the institution;" forty-four articles on diverse subjects, which appeared in reviews of public law, metaphysics, and economics; 370 case notes on decisions of the Conseil d'État and the Tribunal des Conflits, which appeared in the monthly publications of Sirey from 1892 to 1929 and have since been collected in three volumes (*Notes d'arrêts sur décisions du Conseil d'État et du Tribunal des Conflits*, Paris, 1929). In addition, he wrote an "Introduction à l'étude du droit," a monument of the philosophy of the spirit of the law, which was left unfinished but is soon to be published.

Dean Hauriou left his study in Toulouse only to enter another at Nonac in Charente, where he spent summers with his family. Throughout his life he never ceased to develop his mind in the liberal arts and in science, in both of which disciplines he held bachelor's degrees. In his *Leçons sur le mouvement social,* for example, he sought to transpose the system of thermodynamics to the study of societies. Thus, the ensemble of his work should be considered as issuing from a mind in unceasing evolution, to which history and contemporary events brought constructive elements, and which was always, as Hauriou himself affirmed, "directed toward the real, directed toward the present." He spent the first hour of every day in meditation so that, as he used to say, "ideas could visit him."

In 1881 four young men were preparing for the national *agrégation* in law at Bordeaux: Léon Michoud, who died prematurely, Léon Duguit and Hauriou, who fought one another with alacrity all their lives, and Joseph Berthélemy, who became Dean of the Faculté de Droit of Paris. Berthélemy once reminisced: "When we were preparing together for the tests of the *agrégation,* Roman law and civil law engrossed our attention. Hauriou was a first-rate Romanist, formidable in argumentation, and the lectures in civil law that he gave at the conference made it easy to foretell the brilliant success that he won."

One special characteristic of Hauriou's thought consisted in its use of dialogue. Professor Pierre Hebraud, who was his pupil, writes: "When Maurice Hauriou was in the presence of an idea, he wanted to submit it to an intellectual trial. Hence the rapid views that are only an experimental sounding . . . that were thrown out to the reader only to observe his reaction. You enter into his game and respond to his plan only to slip when at first sight these views do not seem to fit together. Nothing in this procedure compromises the fundamental soundness of what comes through the trial purified. And, in compensation, what impetus you often get from these flashing illuminations of perspectives among which is suddenly opened up the way you have been looking for and on which you will go forward." He sought through a dialogue, with his students and his readers, to uproot bits of error from a truth that had not yet been refined.

In a letter of June 14, 1923, Hauriou affirmed that the "theory of the institution" was the great concern of his life, and that it is, in essence, bound to the idea of God. He asked at another time: "Where do we human souls come from and where do we return to after having been plunged for a short time into phenomena? We come from the supernatural and so does the entire civilization that we create." He completed Descartes' thought in this way: "If instead of *I think,* he had said: I think of God, therefore God is, therefore I am. . . his intention would have been better understood."

In the same way, the theme of "balance in movement," the foundation of his work, is bound to religious and metaphysical presuppositions. Professor Achille Mestre, who studied under Hauriou and was profoundly influenced by him, writes: "It is very remarkable that these two great public lawyers (Duguit and Hauriou), who start out from such different points of view, are in agreement on the essential point that a juridical work has value only if it is based upon truths of an order that surpasses pure technique. The doctrine of the juridical rule, of the social reaction, and of the juridical act is based in Duguit upon a monist philosophy. The entire work of Hauriou is established upon a fundamental dualism that he boils down to the irreducible opposition of matter and form." In *La science sociale traditionnelle* Hauriou wrote: "the spirit and the body of man constitute a contradictory dualism. Psychical facts are the antithesis of physical and biological facts."

His doctrine of the soul's modes of activity, insofar as they concern society, is essentially traditional: "Desire, belief, will, correspond to the Being, the Word, the Spirit of the Christian Trinity." But there is a secular analogy: "The executive power stands for the very being of the state; the legislative power is the thought of the state expressed in law; the judicial power, if it understands its mission well, is an ever-present social will, charged with harmonizing the law in all its applications with the constitution of the state."

Hauriou's key ideas on public law and constitutional law developed during the course of his long tête-à-tête with administrative law. In 1888, despite Léon Aucoc and Édouard Laferrière, French administrative law was still very disorganized. In the Facultés they taught an enumeration of rules that were poorly coordinated and sometimes difficult to justify. In a few years the young professor sifted out a number of ideas that would help to make French administrative law an ordered and coherent whole. For example: the action of administrative authorities should be understood as "an enterprise of management carried out in the interest of the public"; this enterprise is conducted by means of the power that is at the disposal of the Administration, "the public power"; but this power, which in France is not subject to the jurisdiction of the ordinary courts, "instituted" itself progressively, in the sense that the Administration gradually obliged itself to act only in the public interest and in order to realize a public good.

Of course, this "institutionalization" of power was not achieved by a "subjective self-limitation"; that is, the Administration did not "institute" its power solely by the tension of its will. On the contrary, it moderated its power and submitted to the idea of service, of public utility, of public good by a series of "objective self-limitations," by establishing procedures or mechanisms capable of opposing barriers to what was often excessive in its power: the procedure of executory decision, which is the separation of the moment of decision from the moment of execution; the appeals in litigation that are brought before the administrative courts, and in particular the appeal for *excès de pouvoir.*

In his studies in public law and constitutional law Hauriou resumed these diverse reflections on the importance of "power," on the phenomena of objective self-limitation and "institutionalization of power," and on the importance of ideas and beliefs. Of course, he enriched his earlier reflections with many new discoveries: for example, the idea that the liberty of individuals is, in essence, a "power" of the same nature as that of the state, and that it can therefore strike a balance with the "public power." But the orientation of his thought remained the same: acceptance of the complexity of reality; awareness of the ambivalence or, more exactly, the fundamental dualism of socio-political phenomena and consequently of juridical phenomena; search for the balance that should subtend these same phenomena or situations; and dialogue with the ideas that spur on the progress of civilization, with power and with liberty.

An extensive analysis of Hauriou's ideas would go far beyond the scope of this biography. But on the human level, what seems an excellent résumé was by Georges Vedel in 1931, then the young President of the Law Section of the General Association of Students at Toulouse, and in his turn Dean of the Faculté de Droit of Paris: "I remember the joyful astonishment we experienced when, at the word of such a professor, the majestic perspectives of public law— which we had expected to be rather grim—opened up before us. The law, which we had thought of as an ardous technique, with its mysterious rites and language, enclosed in traditionally dusty codes, was revealed to us as a science surprisingly close to life and in unceasing contact with the great questions that confront the human mind. What chiefly struck our minds, which were not yet very open to purely juridical considerations, was that prodigious faculty of synthesis, that constant liaison which Dean Hauriou established between law and the great social, moral, or philosophical concepts. It is mainly thanks to him that we have understood that law is not a logic exercised on texts—although the jurist must have texts and logic—but a science of man, I was almost going to say a part of the humanities, which, as such, can be passionate, and which, in the words of the Latin poet, should not remain foreign to us."

Georges Renard—A Memoir   by Bernard Geny

To present Georges Renard to American or European readers means first of all to recall his life. For, although some men may have no significant existence outside their work, either because they lived in an ivory tower or because they lead a professional career and a life of meditation simultaneously but independently, other men put into their intellectual works the struggles and ideals of youth, the experience of maturity, and the reflections of later life. No one fits better in this second group than Georges Renard. No one has more to gain from a disclosure of his life, which was largely spent in active combat for noble causes. To comprehend the full resonance of his thought on the theory of the institution, which was his chief interest, let us then first consider his life. It will exhibit a richness that will explain the originality of his intellectual position on the problems that he tackled.

Renard's life fell into three distinct periods: the militant Christian democrat, the professor, and the Dominican religious. Although their harmonious liaison does not break the fundamental unity of a single existence, each period has its own characteristics and bequeaths to the following period the best of its harvest.

Georges Renard belonged to the generation that reached the age of twenty-five at the beginning of the century. This was the time of the *Sillon*, when generous hearts, who kept the sad memory of the closing of convents and schools, resolved to carry the message of Christ to the people and to restore, by public opinion and suffrage, the bases of a democracy in conformity with their ideals. Among such people as these, Georges Renard mixed when he came to Paris with his young wife to prepare for the *agrégation de droit*. A champion of the people, an admirer of Marc Sangnier and Paul Renaudin, he was attracted by everything in this movement: its objectives and means, the warm comradeship of its members, and the disinterestedness of their activity. From the Latin Quarter where he studied to the quarter of the Rue Haxo or the Moulin Vert, he learned not only the art of speaking to the people but chiefly the art of understanding and sharing their aspirations, of appreciating their material and moral distress, of finding a way to their hearts. However, an intelligence such as his could not subscribe to a vain demagoguery, and if, like some of his leaders, he looked for the sensitive point of his audience, he undoubtedly appealed to their most noble and generous sentiments. His direct, incisive style, his art of gripping the imagination by images, sallies, or anecdotes, were drawn from these contacts with the crowd, but with a crowd that he knew how to raise to his level.

The fate of the *Sillon* is well known. After having received certain marks of favor and the encouragement of a solemn audience at the Vatican in 1903, this movement aroused a growing storm of alarm. Some were worried that its bonds with the Church were becoming more and more slack; others feared that a tendency toward social leveling would open the way to political socialism; still others denounced an excessive openness to the non-Catholic world, in contradiction to the aims professed by the movement. On May 25, 1910, a pontifical letter, paternal in tone but firm in content, condemned the *Sillon*. With an admirable spirit of submission, the Sillonists obeyed. By this time Georges Renard had returned to Lorraine, his native province. At Nancy the pontifical instructions were faithfully followed, and Nancy's *Semaine Religieuse* published the letter of submission of the "Sillon Lorrain." It was signed: Georges Renard.

Such was the first stage of the life of the author of *La théorie de l'institution*. In this period, although he had thought a great deal and faced the most diverse audiences, he had not yet expressed the depth of his thought.

The second stage began after the war of 1914–1918, especially in 1920 when Renard was named Professor of Public Law at Nancy and devoted himself entirely to this scientific work and teaching. He brought to his task the richness of a varied experience. His contacts with the people, with the bar, which he had not abandoned, and with the ecclesiastical spheres, led him to a higher view of the problems of law and of morality in action, for which he instinctively sought a synthesis. He was by nature repulsed by juridical positivism, despite his admiration for [Raymond] Carré de Malberg; his mind was too lucid to adhere to an uncontrolled subjectivism. He found in the objective doctrines, especially Hauriou's, the echo of his own interests and the elements of a synthesis that he aspired to achieve. From his recent past he kept an almost "visceral" fidelity to liberal ideas and a profound faith in the eminent dignity of the human person, while his reason told him of the necessity of reserving substantial powers to the state in order to harmonize activities in the framework of the common good. But while Léon Duguit and his school sought the bases of the state's function in a de facto solidarity immanent in human society, while Hauriou himself conceived of the juridical order as a position of balance between individual liberties and a supreme authority delegated to the organs of the state, Georges Renard, developing a hypothesis of Hauriou's, ordered the theory of the institution around the idea of ends and raised the juridical order to the ontological plane by presenting it as the reflection of a thought that presides over the very order of creation. So the hue and cry went up that he dehumanized law! He crushed the will! He enslaved the state to natural law! A threefold sacrilege that his critics found difficult to pardon.

Those who knew him during this time noted the vigor of his convictions. In his eloquence there was much of the ardor of the prophet, tempered by a profound courtesy and a mastery of words. If his thought was sometimes stinging, his expression was never wounding. But like a true prophet, he was not satisfied to be right; he had to convince. And he would have thought his effort insufficient if it had been addressed only to the elite of legal philosophers. To reach a wider public, he for some years took advantage of the series of public conferences instituted by Nancy's Faculté de Droit to present the essentials of his theories to an audience that was enlightened but not made up of specialists. In the little books drawn up by him from these conferences one grasps the essential form of his talent and the vivacity of his thought. The lecturer of popular circles is there with his mischief, his humor, his anecdotes. But the thinker follows the same path and climbs by degrees as high as he can take his audience.

Finally, a third period marked this ardent and eventful life. Plunged into grief by the accidental death of his wife, Georges Renard, to whom God had given no children, sought consolation in the religious life. The Dominican Order was willing to receive him. Previously, as his works indicate, Professor Renard had already extended his studies to the field of theology. In thomistic philosophy he had found elements of a doctrine of the common good and of a highly spiritual conception of the juridical order that provided a support for his own ideas. After entering the Dominicans, he grew all the more convinced that the doctrines of public law and the teachings of theology could be fruitfully synthesized. He now completed the evolution of the ideas that had been at the center of his teaching and published, under the habit of the Friars Preachers and with the approbation of his order, his "Philosophy of the Institution" in which the plane of juridical systems was penetrated by spiritual ideas. *La philosophie de l'institution* came out in 1939. This was the year the war began. Georges Renard would not see it end in his lifetime.

Such is the figure who is presented in this book through selections from his works. Certainly, in a collection of the thought of the French authors who have worked on the theory of the institution, his name and his contribution could not be omitted. The place he holds among them is paramount. His lifelong attachment to the idea merited such treatment.

But does this mean that his thought had, and still has today, all the influence it should? As often happens, the superficial lines of a face make the most lasting impression; the peculiarities and audacities of a thought discourage later generations after the dynamism of the master has disappeared. In this respect the theory of the institution as presented by Renard has suffered somewhat. First of all, most of Renard's works are courses of lectures that were published just as he delivered them. The magnetic eloquence, the wit, the startling and brilliant digressions that captivated his audience, lose their magic power on the printed page. His works need editing. Second, the frequent use of Cartesian logic and the postulates of faith and theology turn a certain number of minds away from paths the author nimbly climbs. These difficulties are explained by the man's career, by his militant past, by his religious affinities, and by an incomparable temperament against which the struggle of reason was often violent. But, having acknowledged this, what richness and what teaching Renard has left us! And how right he has been proven by what for him was the future and for us is the present!

In conclusion, I should like to offer just two examples of extensions of his thought that he would have been happy to see, could he have witnessed the intellectual and political evolution of this century. Of course, I do not pretend that either of these two manifestations of contemporary thought draws its source directly from Georges Renard's writings, or from those of any other theorist of the institution. But it seems to me that their appearance and development fits in too well with the ideas of the author of *La philosophie de l'institution* for us not to see them as a proof of the fecundity of his thought and the sureness of his views.

The first of these examples comes from a man who, in one respect, followed the opposite path from that of Georges Renard. Teilhard de Chardin, a religious and mystic by vocation, incorporated in his spiritual life a synthetic philosophy based upon scientific experience.

All of his work tends to show that at the point of civilization so far reached, the progress of humanity, in an impulse that might make it cross a new ontological stage, is being accomplished by a concentration of social and economic structures, by the expansion, multiplication, or deepening of collective facts of consciousness, in a word, by an intense development of the institutional phenomenon. While he sees in this development the continuation, on another level, of a natural law of elevation of the human consciousness in relation to the complexity of the matter that serves as its support, he fastens this natural law to a point of attraction that is situated outside the sensible world and which, for the Christian, can only be God. Expressed in another language, founded on another domain of knowledge, this view supports the hypotheses of the jurist and the philosopher of the institution. Without a doubt, Georges Renard would have welcomed it as the confirmation of his own thought.

The other example is the one presented on the international level today by the society of occidental and especially European states. The study that Renard devoted to the problems of international law makes it easy to imagine what new chapters he would have added to his writings if he could have witnessed the construction of the edifice slowly rising on our old continent. European economic integration and its political implications, born, on the French side, of the tenacity and lucidity of a great Christian democrat, agrees too well with his own conceptions for him to have hesitated an instant in recognizing it as a verification of his most cherished ideas.

The collection presented here is not just an homage to three men who have enriched and orchestrated, each in his own way, a common theme of reflection. Its dissemination in the Anglo-Saxon world invites one to make an examination of conscience. What do we owe to institutional philosophy? What have we done with this heritage? Is there still time to make these talents bear fruit? I hope that after having read these works, some young legal philosophers in the Anglo-Saxon, Latin, or Germanic world will feel inspired to use the materials. I hope that such young men will discriminate what ought to be preserved in these texts, underscore the imperishable truths they contain, and succeed in completing a work that is one of the richest fruits of faith conjoined to a profound understanding of the needs of humanity.

The Evolution of the Institutional Conception of

Positive Law—A Backward Glance

by Joseph T. Delos

The authors whose most significant texts have been chosen for this volume formed neither a school, nor an academy, nor a clique. Independent of one another and in their respective universities, they launched their investigations into the nature of the positive law that they were teaching. But the paths that they cleared proved to be convergent and led them to profess a similar conception of positive law, one that has given them the name of "institutionalists."

Without anticipating the judgment that the reader will form about the value of the doctrine, it will surely be permissible for one who has participated in this current of investigations in the most modest way, compared to Hauriou, Renard, and other of their contemporaries, and who continues to believe in the fecundity of the ideas and methods it has brought to light, to explain, in a brief summary, the foundation and import of a conception of positive law that fully restores its institutional character.

This current of thought cannot be properly understood unless one first accepts a resolutely objective point of departure. Positive law should be considered as a fact, a reality, an object, offered to our observation. To describe it is the first task of juridical science. This work of verification will bear upon one or several branches of law, in one state, in several, or in a complete cycle of civilization, according to the intellectual taste of the jurist.

But this verification is simply a work of documentation. The picture of the state of positive law that it reveals will perhaps suffice for the judge on the bench, who controls the conformity of acts and situations with the law in force; but the academic jurist will not be satisfied with it. He is compelled by vocation to investigate the nature of the object of his science, its method, the place that it holds in the hierarchy of the human sciences. The institutionalist doctrine of law was born of the need for an answer to these questions.

Our research was launched under the impulse of a twofold intellectual drive: the need to correct the current doctrines which, in giving positive law an essentially rational and moral explanation, failed to consider its objective reality; and the need to make use of the findings of sociology, for its bonds with juridical science appeared evident.

In referring to the rationalist conceptions of positive law that we encountered at the beginning of our research, I am not alluding to the School of Natural Law and of the *Jus Gentium*[1] (which had already been repudiated), but to certain sequels to it after it had been abandoned. This school originated from a tendency initiated by Grotius in the seventeenth century. It spread, grew, and asserted itself victoriously for almost two centuries. Its rationalism had a double aspect. First, the philosophy detached nature and natural law from every bond with an order transcendent to them. It secularized or laicized, so to speak, the conception of natural law that had been inherited from Christianity and ancient thought. Reason gained self-sufficiency.

Second, nature and natural law were taken as the ultimate foundation and immanent order of states and human societies. Thus, philosophical abstraction and universal reason were substituted for history and experience. Sociology had no place at all.

This rationalism inevitably spread from the domain of philosophy to that of positive law. To each being, rights were attached that were inherent to its nature. Reason defined these rights, deducing them from the particular nature. Thus, positive law sometimes appeared as a fragment detached from the law of nature (a case in point was the *jus gentium*), and sometimes it was derived by way of a syllogism from natural law, its ideal prototype.

As a matter of fact, this philosophical and juridical rationalism led to voluntarist positivism. Although it started out with an abstract consideration of the data[2] inscribed in nature, and elaborated by reason, it wound up by canonizing the will of the legislator, that is, the will of the state. Positive law was a work of reason, but of the commanding reason: the commanding reason par excellence was the reason of the state.

1. The literature on this current of thought is abundant. I shall content myself with referring, for its origins, to Paul Hazard, *La crise de la conscience européenne* (Paris, 1935); and to his *La pensée européenne au XVIIIème siècle,* 2 vols. (Paris, 1946).

2. [The French word here, *donnés,* is a term that was put into circulation by François Geny. Throughout this volume it is translated as "data." However, data does not perfectly express the French idea. For an explanation of Geny's meaning, see the Glossary.]

These positions had long been abandoned by academic lawyers when the institutionalist movement was born. But their sequels, under the form of rationalism and of voluntarism, continued to clutter the paths of juridical thought.

We are indebted to several great jurists for the vigorous effort they made during the second quarter of the twentieth century both to conquer juridical positivism and to temper the excesses of a conception of positive law that was exclusively rational and moral. We owe much to the authors who reintroduced into modern doctrine a truer idea of natural law, an idea that was liberated from eighteenth century rationalism and from the sarcasms of nineteenth century positivism. Their victory over this positivism seems to have been decisive. They have shown that every legal norm, every juridical system, is necessarily bound to principles of a higher ideal; that the order set up by positive law is always established with reference to a rational and moral conception—philosophical or metaphysical —of society and human relationships; that an aspect of law escapes us if we do not consider it in the light of the moral principles inspiring it.[3]

At the same time, these authors realized that abstract rationalism was incapable of explaining the formation of positive law. Hence, François Geny, in his remarkable studies on *Science et technique en droit privé positif,* showed that juridical activity works upon a fourfold datum: real, rational, historical, and ideal.[4] Louis Le Fur supported this view, and showed that the general principles of natural law could be transposed to positive law and to its concrete applications only if reason worked upon—scrutinized and probed into— the diverse historical and economic data of law.[5] But none of these jurists went further.

The lacuna that remained in their conception of positive law was just as apparent as their victory over positivism was complete. An essential part of legal theory had yet to be constructed. To argue that positive law results from the encounter of an idea with reality, from the union of a rational datum with a factual datum—economic,

3. "Positivism, in law as elsewhere, has the merit of having recalled the importance of the observation method, but it is absolutely incapable of providing directing principles. It is not without reason that it has already long been treated as a myopic philosophy." Louis Le Fur, *La théorie du droit naturel depuis le XVIIIème siècle et la doctrine moderne* (Paris, 1928), p. 5.

4. François Geny, *Méthode d'interprétation et sources en droit privé positif. Essai critique,* 2 vols. (Paris, 1898); *Science et technique en droit privé positif. Nouvelle contribution à la critique de la méthode juridique,* 4 vols. (Paris, 1914–1924).

5. In addition to his work already cited, see Le Fur, *Les grands problèmes du droit* (Paris, 1937).

political, or social—is all very true. But how does this encounter come about? What does their amalgam consist in? How does positive law proceed from it? And what light does it throw on the nature of positive law?

Because they failed to answer these questions, these restorers of a theory of law legitimately founded upon moral conceptions and natural law were not able to finish their task and to present a complete doctrine of positive law. They remained—in a sense in spite of themselves—with a conception that gave positive law merely a rational and moral existence.

To profess, for example, that law is composed of three elements: a command, pronounced by reason; an end, constituting a juridical good to be attained or a juridical evil to be avoided; and a sanction —or again, and more precisely, to define law as "a determination of the rights of juridical persons, worked out in conformity with the common good by a qualified authority and eventually guaranteed by the application of positive sanctions"[6]—is to state a number of most important truths; but it is to grasp positive law only in its rational and moral reality—as an order, a rule, a measure of the situations and acts of the members of a society. This conception of law satisfies the requirements of the moralist. He need only know what situations are legitimate, what others illegitimate, and what acts are in conformity with the law, which is itself the interpreter of the common good. But the jurist of positive law has his own requirements. They exceed those of the moralist. For the jurist, positive law is order, rule, and measure, but it is also a constituent element of the social body, within which it fulfills a function. This function is essential to it, belonging to its nature. So the debate passes to the sociological plane.

The institutionalist conception has profited by the great advance that sociology experienced in the first half of the twentieth century. At the same time it has had to guard against the presumptions of this science, which momentarily grew too proud: One thing should be noted at once. Sociology provides a point of departure for the investigations of the jurist who questions the nature of positive law; but of itself it cannot provide the answer. It is essentially descriptive. It observes social facts. It analyzes them. It classifies them. There ends its proper role. It relates the special characteristics of the juridical system in force in a society. It notes the social factors that have conditioned this system's development. It records the changes that

6. Le Fur, *Les grands problèmes du droit*, pp. 106–107.

its application effects in the behavior of men. These are simply works of description. At any rate, they have the advantage of underscoring the sociological function of the positive juridical rule.

This rule is properly a form of society. Consider an example. The juridical norms that regulate the buying and selling of property in a society determine the condition of goods (some are declared transferable and in commerce, others untransferable and outside of commerce) and the status of persons (some are recognized as capable of possessing and acquiring, others incapable or subject to certain incapacities). Thus, the reciprocal position of goods and men is established, legitimate transactions are defined in advance, and a situation is determined that is both social and juridical. The norm of positive law gives the social body a new form, the juridical form. It transforms a human society into a juridical society. In other words, the positive juridical rule is itself a sociological fact and an element of the construction of society.

The institutional character of the positive juridical rule is now coming into focus. It is not an injunction, addressed by a subject who has authority to another subject who owes obedience. Nor does it establish between juridical subjects a juridical relationship that would be directly and exclusively interindividual. It is a complex. It rules and measures the relationships that proceed from a certain juridical subject (physical or moral person) and which go, as to their term, to a certain other juridical subject, but which pass through an object, whose role is essential. The object specifies the relationships of the subjects. It determines them. It qualifies them. In the example cited above, the relationships are established between the subject-seller of the property and the subject-buyer; but their relation is qualified, determined by its object: the possession of the property against the remission of a price. This exchange is the objective element, the *medium rei* that takes its place between the two persons. The will of the subject-seller and that of the subject-buyer meet in an object, which determines them. Such is the internal structure of positive law. It is not, properly speaking, the rule of the relationships of individual to individual, of person to person, but the rule of the relationships of subjects with an object, of subjects with one another by reason of an object. In our analysis we have taken an example from private law, but we would have chosen one from any branch of law—private or public, internal or international.

No doubt it will be remarked that if such is the structure of the juridical act, it is no different from any other societal act. We readily concede this. What is more, we underscore the importance of this observation. It illustrates the liaison that exists between the science of positive law and sociology. But over and above this there is a specific characteristic that differentiates the norm of law from every other societal fact, that distinguishes the positive juridical institution from every other institution; in short, that distinguishes the science of law from sociology.

From the sociologist's point of view, every object—every good, every end—that requires a collaboration among men in order to be attained can become the principle of a social institution. The co-operation of the men concerned simply needs to perpetuate itself, stabilize itself, organize itself, that is, to fix permanent ways and means by which the men can attain the end that groups them together. In a word, the collaboration needs to institute itself. This is the way the many social institutions of the economic, political, cultural, and religious domains are born.

But the juridical norm and system have this proper quality: their "object" contains an "ideal" element—the idea of what is just for the society in which the juridical rule is promulgated. The fact or situation that, in an historic moment and in concrete conditions, is considered as "what is just," the *quod justum,* is the mother-idea of the positive juridical institution.

We do not mean justice as an abstract and universal concept, as a philosophical or metaphysical principle. We mean the *quod justum,* the abstract idea of justice as professed here by concrete individuals in a specific society. The form that it takes in their minds, the force of attraction that it exercises, the role that it plays in the ordering of social relationships depend on many individual and social contingencies. The *quod justum* is that justice whose realization the society considers as its good, the common good of its members.

Now the institutional nature of the positive juridical rule is in sharp focus. By means of this rule, the idea of justice is instituted. We mean that this idea is professed by a particular society, that it is part and parcel of the society's mentality, that it feeds its dynamism, and what is more, that this notion of the just is provided with the ways and means of assuring its realization in the social body. By ways and means we refer to the actual ordering of the relationships of the members of the society, the creation of procedures, and the putting in place of the instruments—even the material ones— necessary for this realization.

Does this mean that justice as realized by positive law loses its transcendence? Does justice depend on the fluctuations of societies, and does it undergo the reversals of the collective mentality? Is the jurist of positive law exposed to Pascal's irony: "Truth this side of the Pyrenees, error beyond! The farce of justice bounded by a frontier"?

The justice of positive law is nothing of the sort. The object of the juridical institution, the *quod justum,* has a face turned toward the social body. The social body has its eyes fixed on this *quod justum,* adopts it as a good, institutes it in society's midst. But the *quod justum* also has a face turned toward transcendental values, and it invites one to rise up to their consideration. The *quod justum* leads the jurist of positive law to the threshold of a new science, whose object is no longer the historical conditions of social life, but values of the spirit: ethical, philosophical, metaphysical. Positive law does not acquire its whole significance, or have its whole import and its whole truth, until the jurist sees in it a point of departure for rising up to the idea of the just in itself. If the jurist refuses, he does not simply diminish his humanist culture; he frustrates his very science. This science contained an invitation, and the invitation has not been accepted. It asked for a higher light, and this light has been denied it.

In closing this brief summary, I must not fail to note that the institutionalist doctrine makes a synthesis of all the truths scattered throughout the diverse theories of law. It does not lump them together arbitrarily. It does not practice a superficial syncretism. It provides a principle of synthesis.

It convinces the partisans of juridical positivism that an ideal, intentional, rational element resides at the heart of positive law—a reference to philosophical or metaphysical values that the jurist cannot exclude from his preoccupations without disregarding the internal demands of his object.

The institutionalist conception proves to be in full agreement with the doctrines that, in reaction to positivism, have called attention to the dependence of positive law upon rational law and natural law. But it has filled in the lacunae and the vacuum that they left in the theory of law. It has shown how the liaison is made between a rational datum and an historical datum, how a moral rule becomes a social institution, transforming a human society into a juridical society. It has provided the positive juridical norm with the sociological element that belongs to it by nature, and without which it cannot be distinguished from a normal rule.

The alliance between the institutional conception of law and sociology is evident. The long-neglected function of positive law as a form of society has been restored to it. But just as the institutionalist conception enables us to distinguish the science of positive law from that of morality, while establishing an hierarchical bond between them, so also it maintains the specific character of the science of law in relation to sociology, and assigns to each its place in the hierarchy of knowledge. Sociology is descriptive. The science of positive law is normative, for it institutes justice in society and, without losing its proper character, pays tribute to ethics.

PART I   MAURICE HAURIOU

MAURICE HAURIOU   The Two Realisms

In all things it is very difficult to keep the just mean. The individualism of the eighteenth century and of the Revolution had been excessive, but now the reaction against it is also exceeding proper bounds. What is more, the doctrines of social law or of *droit objectif* (objective law)[1] tend to shock us much more quickly than had those of individual law, because we feel threatened in the depths of our being.

Duguit is one of the most vigorous leaders of the campaign for objective law, and also, we must say frankly, one of the most excessive. This was not so striking while his thought was evolving in the regions of public law, which lend themselves to objective perspectives. But with the book he brings us from his lecture tour in Argentina,[2] he penetrates into the regions of private law where the subjective point of view is dominant. His ideas, while they appear in sharper focus in this new milieu, also appear more troublesome and provoke more precise criticisms.

While our esteemed colleague, in his iconoclastic zeal, was working to smash only the moral personality of the state and the *droits subjectifs* (subjective rights)[3] of the public administrations, most jurists were not moved, because these icons did not mean much to them. But now he is hammering at more familiar effigies: the juridical personality of the individual, the subjective rights of man, liberty, individual property. This time jurists are going to be disturbed, not only in their working habits, but in their reflective convictions and

ED. NOTE: Translated from "Les deux réalismes," *Recueil de législation de Toulouse* (1912), pp. 1–10. Hauriou's philosophical commitment to "realism" led him to distrust an a priori monism that dispenses with "taking all the facts into consideration." A view of all the facts, he felt, and not just a few extrapolated beyond their worth in support of a predetermined position, leads one back to the "individualist tradition." These views are most tersely expressed in this essay directed against Léon Duguit in 1912.

1. [G.]

2. Léon Duguit, *Les transformations générales de droit privé depuis le Code Napoleon* (Paris, 1912).

3. [G.]

in their sentiments, and as there is quite a stir, they are going to need reassurance.

We should like to help them. We ourselves have worked for the rehabilitation of objective law, but in its own interest and in order not to compromise it, we censure these exaggerated theses. The restoration of objective law should not entail the sacrifice of subjective law. Each one of them has its own domain, and if these two laws have no logical point of reconciliation, a truly positive science of law, that is, one excluding any metaphysical preoccupation with logical unity, should content itself with the practical unity that is realized by social institutions.

I. Duguit's premise is that private law, which is for him not distinguished from public law, after having passed through a metaphysical stage, entered into the positive phase and since then has been moving rapidly and inevitably toward a complete objectivism. This means that everywhere the subjective notion of individual right will be replaced by the objective notion of social function. There will be no more rights to defend, there will be only functions to fulfill.

To establish this premise, Duguit examines a series of contemporary facts. But his readers will not fail to notice that in his observation of the contemporary tendencies of private law, he abuses that procedure which consists in drawing from a fact that is true in itself, but of limited import, unlimited consequences.[4]

There is no doubt that under diverse influences a certain socialization of private law has been taking place in the past few years. This slight withdrawal from individualism simply amounts to a rectification of the frontiers between social forces and individual forces, an oscillation that appears quite limited if one rises, as one should, to an observation of the age-old movements of these forces in battle. Duguit, with his absolutist spirit, sees in this movement a definitive sweep of evolution, an irremediable defeat of individualism. Let the reader judge.

From the very meager case law on the abuse of rights that warns us that the individual right of property is limited by a certain concern for its social function, and from the fact, which we have known for a long time, that it is not absolute, he concludes, *ultra probata,* that individual property no longer exists as a subjective right, that it exists only as a social function.[5]

---

4. There is a critical study of this juridical individualism which, unlike Duguit's, is balanced, and consequently convincing, in an excellent thesis from Dijon by Emmanuel Gounot, published under the title *Le principe de l'autonomie de la volonté en droit privé* (Paris, 1912).

5. Duguit, *Les transformations générales,* p. 166ff.

From the theory of the declaration of will and because it was sanctioned in part, with respect to proof, by the German civil code,[6] and also from the multiplication of contracts of adhesion that incontestably mark an offensive reaction of the social institution against contract, he concludes quite simply that the reign of contract is over.[7]

From the situation that houses of worship found themselves in after the law of separation[8]—a situation that provides us with an example of affectation of property, and which is certainly curious and interesting, as we have pointed out ourselves, but exceptional and transitory, for jurists on all sides are trying to reconstruct the subjective rights of ministers of religion—Duguit draws what he calls a striking example of the evolution of juridical conceptions on property.[9] Well, what is most striking in this example is very certainly the effort that is being made to recreate a subjective right in this objective situation. But Duguit does not see this effort and, according to an expression that he loves, "the objection does not hit the mark."

You see his procedure and what it consists in: exaggeration, an incomplete observation of things, the prejudice that sees only one side of reality when there are several, the obnoxious tendency to take the exceptional for the normal.

Many currents of ideas could be pointed out that show that individualism still prevails in the regions of private law: for example, the theory of the juridical relationship, which is still dominant there; for example, the tendency to the individualization of punishment in penal law. And it is provocative, to say the least, to note that at the very time when Duguit, in South America, was combatting the Latin tradition of subjective private law, in North America an Anglo-Saxon, a judge of the Supreme Court of the United States, was advising his fellow citizens to turn toward this same Latin tradition condensed in our civil code, as representing a superior juridical culture.[10]

So the facts are complex and, for a good observer, the two tendencies, the individualist and the social, balance each other. There has always been and there will always be something of the social function beside the individual right, something of the social institution

6. [The Bürgerliches Gesetzbuch (German Civil Code) was drafted over the period 1874–1896. It was passed by the Reichstag and promulgated by the Emperor in 1896, and took effect January 1, 1900.]

7. Duguit, Les transformation générales, pp. 86ff, 106ff, 121ff.

8. [See Maurice Hauriou, Principes de la loi du 9 décembre 1905 sur la séparation des églises et de l'état (Paris, 1906).]

9. Duguit, Les transformations générales, p. 175.

10. Charles F. Beach, Le droit civil en Amerique (Paris, 1912).

beside contract, but also always something of the individual right beside the social function and something contractual beside the social institution. There is a duel of antagonistic forces here like that of the earth and the sea. The ocean beats against the shore continually, but it always finds a shore to meet it. Atlantis has disappeared, tomorrow Holland might sink beneath the waves, God forbid! but continents would still remain, not to mention the volcanic islands and the new Alps that might spring up.

II. Truly, in Duguit's controversies, facts appear only to provide rather mediocre illustrations of a priori ideas. He is convinced a priori that subjectivism, or to speak the language everyone understands, individualism, is condemned by science as being a sort of supernatural metaphysic. He applies Auguste Comte's theory of the "three stages" to law and, besides, he applies it badly.

Law, according to Duguit, has passed through a theological age, then a metaphysical age, and finally, in our time, it has entered an age of positive knowledge. And this is perfectly true. But it is false to believe that because the methods of knowledge have changed, the forces that act in law have changed. Yet this is what Duguit believes. He claims that because the knowledge of law has become positive, the individualist forces in law have disappeared. He claims, therefore, that the individualist forces that have been acting in law up to now were due to the metaphysical manner in which law was studied. He confuses the methods of knowledge with the social forces that are to be known.

It would not be difficult to show that in the system of the theologians of the Middle Ages—for example, in St. Thomas Aquinas's *Summa*[11]—we find a complete social construction, with *droit subjectif* and *droit objectif;* everything is there, only it is envisaged from a theological point of view. Similarly it might be shown that in the system of the metaphysicians of the modern epoch[12]—for example, in a Spinoza, a Leibnitz, a Malebranche, a Hegel—we also find a complete social construction, with its objective elements as well as subjective; everything is there, only it is envisaged from a metaphysical point of view. The presumption is, therefore, that in the system of positive social science, when it is complete, we shall

11. [*Summa Theologiae.*]
12. [Cf. Michel Villey, "Law and Values—a French View," 14 *The Cath. Univ. of Amer. L. Rev.* 158, 160 (1965): "In France when we speak of modern thought, we mean the thought that is derived from the 16th and 17th centuries. We still depend on this philosophy. We are educated under its influence. It dominates our thinking."]

also find, envisaged from a positive point of view, individualist forces as well as objective forces. Everything will be there.

It is true that the system of positive social science is not yet complete. But while we are waiting for its completion, it would be more in keeping with the true scientific spirit to remain on the reserved side. The true realism is to have a preoccupation for taking all the facts into consideration.

On page 176 of his book Duguit confesses: "Some well-meaning friends, some flattering disciples sometimes tell me that I am the head of the realist school in France"; and he denies it with modesty. He is wrong to deny it, even though one must generally mistrust flattering disciples and chapel atmospheres. He is the head of a certain realist school; but in social matters there are two realisms, the good and the bad, and the one that he practices is not good.

This realism of his consists in taking into consideration, under the label of objective facts, only the collective factors of social organization: interdependence of men, division of labor, social function, etc., and none of the individualist factors, under the pretext that they are only ideas. This narrow realism was that of sociology in its beginnings, about twenty years ago; like all young sciences, it was constructed on a restricted base and appeared exclusive at first. For one thing, although calling upon observation, it chose the facts that best lent themselves to observation; for another, because it was constituted in opposition to those traditional disciplines, the moral sciences, which had instinctively adhered to the dogma of liberty, it took the contrary tack and excluded as metaphysics not only the premise of liberty, but the facts produced by the belief in liberty.

Duguit has obviously remained in this first period of sociology, but while his ideas have been crystallizing there, the growing science has been evolving. Furthermore, the science is not confined to one school. You need only peruse the very numerous reviews, in France and abroad, that currently deal with sociology, directly or indirectly, to see that the investigation of facts has expanded tremendously. It has been noted that while individual ideas, perhaps, may not be objective facts, *currents of ideas* are objective social facts. Fouillée has contributed much to this progress by his striking formula of idea-forces. A current of ideas, that is, an idea that animates a party, a people, a succession of generations, any collectivity whatsoever, very obviously becomes a social force. History has come to the rescue; every kind of history reveals the power of collective currents of ideas: the history of religion, the history of manners, the history of law, literary history. The history of public law shows how currents of ideas influence legislation, and this is surely an objective social fact. The famous English public lawyer, Dicey, has written a whole book on the relationships between law and opinion.[13]

Well, there are currents of individualist ideas. They are collective and objective as currents of ideas, but their tendency and their ends are individualist. Dicey shows exactly how the current of ideas of Benthamist individualism influenced nineteenth-century English legislation.

From the positive point of view, the question of the "individual" and the "social" proves to be reinscribed upon currents of ideas; some of them have individualist ends and others have social ends; both realize society and law. By their very opposition they keep each other in a certain state of balance. But this purely practical combination, while neutralizing certain of their effects, does not destroy either one of them; on the contrary, it utilizes both.

Individualism, which is the foundation of the commerce of private life, is nothing other than a vast and profound current of ideas with individualist ends that took birth in remotest antiquity and that has not ceased to flow up to our time throughout the most diverse civilizations. Since the distant time of Hammurabi, through the civilizations of Chaldea, Egypt, Greece, Rome, modern Europe, in pagan countries as in Christian, justice has been sought in private relationships by the reconciliation of individual liberties. This is the premise of the *jus gentium* of the Romans, that of the natural law of the seventeenth and eighteenth centuries, that of the French Revolution, in a word, the premise that, counterbalanced by objective institutions, has produced what up to now has been called human civilization and progress.

But this premise, under the form of a current of idea-forces, translated into legislation and into facts, is an objective social fact. Nothing could be more objective. And if Duguit does not wish to take it into consideration in his observations and if he does not wish to take into consideration this other fact, that the current of individualist ideas of private life has been associated up to now with what men call civilization and progress, he is no realist.

Thus, a little sociology turns one away from the individualist tradition and a lot of sociology leads one back to it. After having appeared revolutionary, sociology becomes conservative.

The old dualism of social mechanics and individual liberty that

13. [A. V. Dicey, *Lectures on the Relation Between Law and Public Opinion* (London, 1905; 2nd ed., 1914).]

the moral and political sciences used to admit metaphysically and a priori, is now being rediscovered by sociology a posteriori in a discursive manner and by the method of observation, as the tendency of currents of traditional ideas associated with the fact of civilization and of progress.

However new Duguit's radical ideas may appear in law, they are already outmoded in sociology where scholars are more atuned to nuances; so the catastrophic prophecies with which he threatens individualism will not be realized. Very fortunately, besides, for the objective ideal of justice that he claims would replace the individualist ideal, namely, the unlimited growth of human interdependence and of social functions, would certainly be the gloomiest, the saddest, the most discouraging ideal under which human societies have ever lived. The unlimited growth of interdependence among men! Universal and reciprocal servitude! Oh Jean-Jacques, you who wished to free man from man!

MAURICE HAURIOU   The Notion of an Objective

Juridical Order Establishing Itself in Political Matters

CONCERNING THE JURIDICAL ORDER

Let us take as our fundamental definition of the public law that it orders the 'public enterprise'[1] with a view to liberty and justice by the creation of institutions and by the personification of the political institution. For the moment I shall leave aside the question of the personification of the political institution; this will be the subject of the following chapter.[2] Here I am concerned exclusively with the notion of a juridical order of the 'public enterprise' establishing itself objectively. I shall examine the following three propositions:

1. There is a juridical order separable from the political order of things and the objective of this juridical order is to introduce justice into the political order;

2. The juridical order can realize justice in political institutions only by introducing de jure situations into them;

3. These de jure situations must establish themselves.

The present section will be devoted to a development of the first proposition.

I. *Concerning the distinction to be made between the juridical order and the political order.* Law is no more a pure and simple

---

ED. NOTE: Translated from Hauriou, *Principes de droit public*, 2nd ed. (Paris, 1916), pp. 7–17. Despite the severe attacks that had been leveled against it by Léon Duguit, the German Herrschaft school (dating from Carl F. von Gerber, *Grundzüge eines Systems des Deutschen Staatsrechts*, 1st ed. [Leipzig, 1865]) was still, in Hauriou's view (*Principes de droit public*, 2nd ed., p. 5) the "dogmatic school par excellence" in public law. But he rejects both this school's ultrasubjective definition of public law, which explains the entire organization of the state by a decree of its own will, and Duguit's ultraobjective alternative, which repudiates the notion of the state as a personified institution. Instead, he opens his analysis of the principles of public law with an account of the establishment of a truly "objective juridical order."

1. [*La chose publique.* G. Cf. *Res publica.*]

2. [This chapter is not translated because Hauriou's later treatment of the question of personification appears in his "Theory of the Institution and the Foundation," translated below.]

conformity to the brute order in political affairs than it is in private affairs. No doubt, it does conform to the brute order in part, since it is designed to govern social relationships and social organizations in their brute state, but it does not conform entirely, for then it would not govern them. To govern means to impose a rule that is not confused with the reality ruled. It is true that the rule can be drawn from concrete life by operations of generalization and abstraction, but the opinion of jurists is that while the juridical rule[3] is drawn from reality, it is also inspired by a certain ideal of justice in contradiction to elements of this reality.

Law, then, is a conformity to an ideal, or at least idealized, order of things. It does not realize purely mechanistic conceptions of the universe, but rather conceptions that comprise teleology and liberty, and therefore that presuppose the triumph of the just over the unjust, of good over evil.

Actually, there are two possible conceptions of the world. One is that everything in it is enchained by determinant causes, that it is without purpose, and that therefore, if any order appears in it, this order will be amoral. This is the mechanistic conception. The other view is that everything is not enchained by strictly determinant causes, that the laws of nature have a certain contingency about them, that the world may have a purpose, and that therefore, if a certain order appears in nature, this order can have been willed, at least in part, and that it is the consequence of a choice between good and evil. This is the teleological conception that reserves a role for liberty and also sees in each of the elements of the world, not only in man, but even in the atom, a certain "degree of liberty."[4]

Clearly, this second conception is closer to that of jurists, and it leads us to the notion of a juridical order of things that undoubtedly can be determined in part by antecedents that escape the action of

---

3. [*La règle de droit.* G.]

4. This conception of the world is that of contemporary French philosophy, as it derives from *Jules Lachelier and Emile Boutroux* (see Lachelier, *Du fondement de l'induction* [Paris, 1871; 8th ed., 1924]; Boutroux, *La contingence des lois de la nature* [Paris, 1874; 3rd ed., 1898]; *L'idée de loi naturelle* [Paris, 1895]; Henri Poincaré, *Science et hypothèse* [Paris, 1902]). [Hauriou sees "a certain degree of liberty in the most necessary social institutions." Some form of taxation is clearly necessary once we assume a state government. But what form should the taxation take—direct or indirect taxes, proportional taxes or progressive taxes? "Here is liberty's role: the choice of means." Public health requires that dwelling places be sanitary: landlords are therefore obliged to keep them clean—"but they retain the choice of means. Thus the kind of necessity and the kind of liberty that are blended in social things could be summed up as the obligation of taking action with the *facultas solutionis.*" *Principes de droit constitutionnel,* 2nd ed. (Paris, 1929), p. 9, n. 1.]

the will, but in part also by the will and by moral concerns. According to a formula of Lachelier, "nature constitutes a whole the parts of which are in order," and what is true of the great whole of nature is also true of that more restricted whole that is of special interest to us: society. If we can say of society "that it is a whole the parts of which are in order or aspire to put themselves in order," then we should keep in mind that this putting into order can be, to a certain extent, willed, sought after, and pursued by the men who are members of society by a discernment of the just and the unjust.

II. *The objective of the juridical order is to introduce justice into the brute order by special methods.* Observe first of all that the juridical order does not tend to create social institutions that are exclusively its own, but simply tends to regularize and improve, if possible, the existing brute organizations.

The first edition of this book was criticized because its conclusions regarding the foundation of law were purely formal and because they did not involve any attempt to determine the positive content of justice: "What is the state? Its nature? Its objective? Its rights? The limits of its action? Its relationships with the Church? With the individual? With thought?" And there were other questions: "The state and the principle of association? The state and marriage? The state and property? Is there any question that public law does not touch upon? What is the philosophical and social point of view of the author? The bent of his thought? Individualist or collectivist? etc."[5]

My answer to these insistent reproofs is that it is well to do each thing in its own time. I do not deny the importance of natural law and of searching out the objectives of the state; besides, I have indicated the essential element, the realization of the civil regime by means of the political corporation, and I have taken sides on particular questions like that of the indissolubility of marriage. I have avoided a systematic examination of the question of natural law, which is only one of the elements of the juridical order, for I felt that the most urgent work was to reveal the juridical order as a whole in opposition to the order of brute realities. This work was urgent because the fashionable monist philosophies have abolished the sense of this opposition by obliterating the distinction between good and evil. I have taken the juridical order in the sense of positive

---

5. Georges Platon, *Pour le droit naturel, à propos du livre de M. Hauriou, Les Principes de droit public* (Paris, 1911). [In this work Platon had challenged Hauriou's account of the positive content of justice, and of the nature, end, and rights of the state.]

law because under this form it is destined in practice to oppose the brute forces of the political order.

I went then to the most pressing problem. I ran to the ramparts to wage the true battle for law, that is, the battle against amorality, the battle for the distinction between the just and the unjust. I left to others, or put off till later, the task of analyzing all the elements of the just. What monopolized my attention were the methods by which the positive juridical order succeeds in infusing justice into the organizations created by brute force and in transforming them into acceptable institutions. Among these methods, the two principal ones are: (1) objective balances,[6] as a way to de jure situations: (2) the corporate personification of institutions.

III. *The juridical order's first method of introducing justice into matters: objective balances, as a way to de jure situations.* The fundamental problem of public law is the transformation of de facto situations into de jure situations. Since, in public law, the fact is often the consequence of force, this is the problem of transforming situations of force into de jure situations. The problem is solved sophistically in the German maxim *might makes right.* The sophism consists in the implication that situations of force become, by themselves, without any further transformation and without the intervention of any elements other than force, de jure situations. Nothing could be more false. It has always been understood that situations of force can become de jure only by virtue of a further transformation or legitimization and that the principal agent of this legitimization is *duration in peace.* The peaceful duration of a state of things within a society allows one to presume that there has been an adaptation and an acceptance of this state of things, which transforms it into an *institution* subsisting by itself and not by force. This presumption itself rests upon the postulate that only things that have become good and just can be definitively established in society, for good is more stable and more coherent than evil.[7]

Duration in peace, then, is the indispensable condition of the legitimization of organizations created by force. But these organizations cannot endure in peace unless they become moderate and supple in such a way as to ease their adaptation to and acceptance by men.

The important factor is, therefore, the work of making brute forces

6. [Equilibres. G.]

7. On this point, see Johann C. Bluntchli, *Le droit public general,* trans. Armand de Riedmatten (Paris, 1881), bk. I, chap. viii, "Ordre de fait et ordre de droit," pp. 16ff.

moderate and supple. Such work is chiefly responsible for trans-forming an armed force, with its immediate and terrible violences,[8] into a political power that acts by juridical precepts before coming to violence: a great step forward. This work then continues to moder-ate the political power more and more.

The task of making force supple and moderate is already the work of the juridical system and the result of a first juridical method, which is the objective balance of powers. It consists essentially in separating a given force into several elements, in partially opposing one of these elements to the other in order to balance them, and in this way obtain both more duration and more moderation in the exercise of power. This process is certainly juridical, since in con-stitutional law it is called the principle of the separation of powers, and just as certainly it helps to transform the brute political power of the state into a juridical sovereignty.

In the next subsection we shall isolate the objective balance that seems to us the most important of all, the one that is called the *de jure state* or the *state submissive to the regime of law,* and that is simply the over-all balance of the political and juridical forces in the state, as established to the advantage of the juridical forces.[9] Here we shall limit ourselves to a glance at the phenomenon of objective balances in general.

The social balances in our modern political societies are innumer-able. First, we see the balance between national forces and foreign forces; it is founded either upon an equivalence of the forces proper to each country or upon systems of alliances that become counter-weights. The territorial frontiers mark the point where the com-promise is established; there one of the antagonistic forces says to the other: You shall go no further. Next, the governmental force within a country can find itself counterbalanced by the force of reaction of the citizens' protected rights. The central administration can be counterbalanced by decentralized local administrations. Within the governmental machinery itself balances can be created, such as those of the parliamentary government, separation of an executive organ and a legislative organ, sharing of powers between

8. [*Voies de fait.* G.]

9. [In the subsection referred to, which has not been translated here, Hauriou describes the "de jure state" as follows: "There is a de jure situation (*état de droit*) within a political domination (1) when the political power, which is at the same time juridical, subordinates itself to the rules of positive law that it has created; (2) when the law that comes from governmental decisions and the law that comes from customary adherences of subjects are balanced in a superior juridical form, which is legislation (*loi*)." *Principes de droit public,* 2nd ed., pp. 18–19.]

them, in a word, balance. And there are other even more fundamental balances, although they are neglected by constitutional law, such as the balances between political and economic forces, between the military and civil power, between public and private life, between public and private property, between the activity of the public administration and private activity.

These social balances serve to create moderation in power and to assure permanence to the group; they economize the life of the group by giving it rhythm like the escapement of a pendulum. From this point of view, the balances of the parliamentary regime are remarkable. After a general election a majority party arrives in Parliament with a certain energy, a certain amount of power, a certain credit from the country; the problem is not to let this majority dissipate all its energy in an instant and use up all its credit in a legislative passion. This problem is the point of parliamentary procedures, multiple readings of proposed laws, the obligation of a separate vote by the two Chambers, the interplay of interpellations, the intrigues in the lobby, the struggle of the minority against the majority. All these counterbalancing resistances of forces are so successful in delaying the vote upon laws that years will pass in debates, years that will be sterile from the viewpoint of legislative work but that enable the assembly to survive until its term expires. These debates, dealings, and bargainings will have economized its life. Generally an assembly will be worn out at the end of its four years; it will need to soak again in the electoral bath. But without the rhythm and pendulum of all these parliamentary balances, it would have been worn out in three months.

Balance is so necessary to the long duration of political organisms that, on analysis, one is certain to discover it in even the most rudimentary. There is no government of horde or tribe, however low on the political scale, that does not contain a counterweight, and this counterweight is what enables it to last. A Negro chieftain who cuts off his subjects' heads himself has a sorcerer beside him; a chief is no sooner surrounded by intimate companions, favorites, than he is embroiled in the rivalries of these favorites; if he has need of a minister, he immediately has to reckon with this minister. When in the fourteenth century the constitution of the French monarchy began to evolve in so different a way from that of the English monarchy, and from being semifeudal became absolute because the States-General could not succeed in creating a balance, did we not see the rise of that extraordinary political resistance of judicial Parliaments, founded on the pretext of registering ordinances, but actually serving the purpose of providing the lacking counterweight? And when in the eighteenth century the monarchy could no longer tolerate even the control of these Parliaments and broke their resistance, how speedily it went to its fall and, so to speak, to the end of its rope!

This need of enduring in stability and of slowing down the social parade stimulated the creation of social balances that economized power by expending it only drop by drop. But this economy of power had a very interesting aspect for individuals, which was called the *moderation of power*. Economized and distilled in this way, power proved to be less oppressive. In later epochs of civilization, when political balances are created with reflection, they are created with the set purpose of moderating power and consequently of guaranteeing liberty. This purpose is the great obsession of Montesquieu when he describes the English constitution and its separation of powers. But it is good to know that, while the *moderation of power* and the guarantee of liberty were the reflective aim of men when they established social balances, their instinctive motive was the need of *assuring duration*.

Moreover, the creation of the balances of the state regime[10] is observed only in political societies enamored of change; it is clearly a remedy for too swift a stream of innovations. All human societies are not equally prone to variation; that is, all are not equally alert or progressive. Bagehot has remarked also that there are, even among peoples who are disposed to change, periods of relative immobility and other contrasting periods of rapid transformations.[11] It is in the epochs breaking with ancient customs, in the epochs of crisis and renewal, that the balances of the state regime appear in order to reconstitute a sufficient stability and, by means of this stability, a sense of duration.

But in their turn, the balances of the state regime, by becoming exaggerated, can help to close a period of change. If they carry social regulation to excess, they tend to immobility, exhaust the faculty of transformation that is the very life of the system, and in attempting to prolong its duration, risk bringing it to an end.

Thus, the quest for stability by balances is itself confined to a just mean; there are societies that are so dead, so immersed in the torpor of custom, that the need for balances does not even make itself felt. When social transformations do occur, balances are created to slow down the movement; they spontaneously adjust themselves by utiliz-

10. [*Regime d'état*. G.]
11. [Walter Bagehot, *Lois scientifiques du développement des nations (Paris, 1873).*]

ing the resistances that every movement provokes in the milieu in which it develops; such balances are only balanced resistances. But if they in turn become exaggerated, the movement stops. A society that at first had no history, then a very agitated history, then a more regulated history, risks falling into a torpor like that of its beginnings. With this difference: the immobility of its beginnings was a sort of infancy full of promise and virtualities, whereas the immobility of its end is an old age. For the duration of peoples, like that of individuals, is an irreversible movement; the speed of the movement can be slowed down, but its inevitable direction and conclusion cannot be changed.[12]

12. The preceding ideas are somewhat analogous to the ideas Henri Bergson presented in his book *L'évolution créatrice* (Paris, 1907). I feel free to examine the comparison that ought to be made between the two conceptions because they come from two independent lines of development. My current studies on the state regime are simply a continuation of social studies, fragments of which I published in 1896, under the title *La science sociale traditionnelle,* and in 1899 under the title *Leçons sur le mouvement social.*

Here, if I can put it well, is how our positions are alike and how they differ. According to Bergson, nature would contain an *élan vital* that would be characterized by a continuous creation of new realities, and that would therefore create duration in its irreversible movement. It is well to observe that the notion of time or duration is, in fact, irreversible: duration goes from the past to the future, it has a direction that does not change; time is a river that flows and that cannot return toward its source. This direction is toward the new; always to create what is new is the property of time and also the property of life. On this point I agree with him. I also agree with him when he notes that in the mind of man intuition and instinct move in the direction of life by steps that historically precede the intellect, which has too geometric a gait. This recourse to instinct and to intuition is what I tried to organize under the name of recourse to social tradition or to social revelation in my *Science sociale traditionnelle:* I need not say that this was done without any philosophical pretension.

Now here is what a direct observation of the state regime seems to me to reveal as incompatible with Bergson's premises: (1) In the state men seem to be preoccupied not only with assuring the life of social systems insofar as it consists in a continual creation of new things, but also and above all with slowing down and regulating this flow of new things so as to provide a sense of stability, which is an indispensable good for social life. And so we have the right to wonder if the notion of time or duration can, in fact, be divorced from a certain notion of stability, without which duration would speed by so rapidly that it would vanish and would no longer constitute an adequate good for social life. In any case, what the law calls *goods (bona quod beant)*, things, objects of property, and also what it calls *institutions,* are all formed owing solely to stability. In other words, the creation of what is new by intuition and instinct seems to correspond admirably to what is irreversible in time, but it does not seem an adequate explanation of what is durable and stable.

(2) It is remarkable that stability is obtained in the state regime by balances of forces that are a utilization of the resistances that the social *élan* meets on its path in the milieu, a utilization that is essentially thought out and intelligent. This fact would lead us to think that the notion of duration and the relationships it has with life are more complex than they appeared to Bergson. He would have to explain how it happens that life needs, not only the flow of time, but also its relative stability, and even give first place to the benefits of stability, which is a product of intellectual reflection. If the problem were stated in philosophical terms we would see that the

IV. *Juridical technique's second method of introducing justice into matters: the personification of social institutions.* The harmonization of liberties, which is the objective of justice, is realized in the last analysis by the subjective considerations of individual minds; to have a sense of justice is the property of the mind of man. But, in social groups, collective forces are unleashed that are so brutal that they escape the control of the minds of individuals, even of governors, unless by a prodigious effort of organization the collective forces are themselves arranged after the fashion of a mind. This arrangement will make them more manageable and will subject their exercise to such reasonable procedures that it will be easy for individual minds to act upon them in the perspective of justice.

There you have the whole secret of the personification of social institutions: it is an application of the maxim *similia similibus.* You will protest that this is anthropomorphism,[13] but the result is good since it is to humanize social institutions, which are for men.

hypothetical superiority of instinct and intuition over the intellect rests upon a confusion between the historical order of appearance and the hierarchical order of values. In the historical order of appearance, we agree that instinct and intuition act before the intellect; but in the hierarchical order of values we are forced to admit that the intellect takes first place, since men still prefer stability to new creations.

The notion of stability achieved by a uniform movement of social transformations can, in a certain way, be attributed to Auguste Comte to whom we must always refer. He not only distinguished between the static and the dynamic, but also saw clearly that the two ideas must be combined and that stability can exist only within movement. In a very interesting passage he says: If the movement that carries along social systems does not obey laws, static laws themselves would disappear, which is impossible. (*Cours de philosophie positive,* 5th ed. [Paris, 1892], IV, 299–301; cf. Franck Alengry, *Essai sur la sociologie dans Auguste Comte,* [Paris, 1899], p. 155). On the other hand, I do not believe that we can attribute to him the premise of balances. Undoubtedly, he insists upon the dualism of the spiritual and the temporal power and he considers this dualism as a separation and a balance (*Considérations sur la pouvoir spriituel* [Mar. 1826], *Système de politique positive ou Traité de sociologie, instituont la religion de l'humanité,* IV, Appendix, [pp. 177–216], [Paris, 1854] 4th appendix). But in his general system he assures order by hierarchy and by the ascendancy of social science, rather than by balances of power (*Cours de philosophie posit.,* VI, 556, 559). [See recent republication of the 1877 English translation of Comte's *Système* by Richard Congreve and Henry Hutton (New York, 1968), pp. 618–644.]

13. [Cf. Marcel Waline, "Les idées maîtresses de deux grands publicistes français: Léon Duguit et Maurice Hauriou," *L'année politique française et étrangère* (June 1930). p. 60 (translated below), for a treatment of the charge against Hauriou of anthropomorphism.]

MAURICE HAURIOU   The Separation of the
Individual and the State

THE FOUNDATION OF INDIVIDUAL RIGHTS[1]

We give this section the unusual heading "separation of the individual and the state" not for the pleasure of coining a striking phrase, but because it seems to us to express the true import of the fact of individualism. Here again we are faced with one of those separations and one of those balances[2] that the state regime[3] draws from the natural movement of things, ingeniously turning to its advantage what could have been its ruin. We see the power of the human mind[4], so feeble and yet so great, rising up against the mass of the social organization and striking a balance with it. Of course, the separation is not complete, and the power of the social organization remains superior to that of the individual; but the antagonism is pushed very far.

Our consideration of individualism, which will be purely juridical, will bear on the following points: (1) the bases of the separation of the individual and the state, and consequently the juridical foundation of individual rights;[5] (2) the declarations of rights; (3) the positive characteristics of and the enumeration of individual rights.

ED. NOTE: Translated from Hauriou, *Principes de droit public*, 2nd ed. (Paris, 1916), pp. 491–503. In explaining the foundation of individual rights. Hauriou here resorts to an historical analysis in which he again applies his celebrated theory of balance. He distinguishes between rights that are morally justified and those that are recognized by the state, and he emphasizes the concept of risk as the price for gaining and maintaining rights, which is a retouched variation on a contribution of Rudolf von Ihering (see his *Der Kampf um's Recht*, 2nd ed. [Regensburg, 1872]).

1. Cf. Adhémar Esmein, *Éléments de droit constitutionnel*, 5th ed. (Paris, 1909), pp. 476–502; Léon Duguit, *Traité de droit constitutionnel* (Paris, 1911), II, 1–164.
2. [*Équilibres*. G.]
3. [*Régime d'état*. G.]
4. [*Conscience humaine*, i.e., the mind as both cognitive and volitive.]
5. [Only this point is translated.]

I. *The posture of the problem of individual rights.* To resolve the problem of the individual right raised up against the social right, we must begin by posing it adequately. We must presuppose certain facts that we could not go into without leaving the domain of law, such as the practical dualism of the individual and society. If the individual is not separable to a certain extent from society, or to put it the other way, if society is not separable to a certain extent from the ensemble of individuals, the problem of individual rights cannot be posed in acceptable terms, for it postulates a certain opposition between the individual and society. This opposition itself can exist only if, on the one hand, the individual possesses an autonomy that does not owe everything to society, and, on the other, the social organization is the product of a necessity of things that does not owe everything to individuals. Therefore, in formulating the elements of the problem in philosophical terms, we must not ignore the fact that they consist in a practical combination of a certain amount of individual free will and a certain social determinism.[6] We do not have to discuss these dualist elements, but merely to verify them. It suffices for us to know that there are at issue a power proper to the individual and a power proper to society and that the problem is to justify the transformation of these two proper powers into rights. To define the rights of the individual, then, we must also define those of the state.

II. *The rights of the individual, like the rights of society, result from the order that is realized by a balance of powers.* The balance of the two powers, individual and social, by virtue of the superior order it realizes, transforms these powers into rights and, at the same time, determines their measure. The error of most individualists has been to believe that individual rights can be justified solely by the value of the human individual.[7] A right is never born of a unilateral principle; it is realized only in a social group and in a practical balance. Moreover, if you take the individual as the sole source of his own rights, you are led by logic to conclude that he is the absolute

6. How, for example, can Duguit reconcile his chapter on individual rights, and indeed, the individualistic spirit that animates his entire book and for which he should be praised, with the affirmations by which, in order to establish social solidarity, he denies that there is any autonomy in the individual mind [*conscience*] and thus prohibits himself from separating it from society?

7. "The eminent dignity of the human person," in Henry Michel's phrase (*L'idée de l'état* (Paris, 1896), conclusion), is for all individualists, philosophers, or jurists the ultimate justification of the rights of the individual. In other words, to put it more or less in juridical form, some base this justification on man's power of will, others on the fact that man is the sole real being who is free and responsible (cf. Charles Beudant, *Le droit individuel et l'état* (Paris, 1891); Alphonse Boistel, *Philosophie du droit* (Paris, 1899); Esmein, *Éléments de droit constitutionnel*, p. 480).

source of all rights and to deny social rights, or at least to lose the way of recognizing them and to risk the most hazardous constructions to provide a basis for them, such as Rousseau's hypothesis of the social contract.

No doubt, in the French state born of the Revolution individual rights have great force; they seem to have even more than social rights. But this situation calls for much reflection. For one thing, in other civilized countries the scales are not so weighted on the side of individual rights; social rights have more play. This imbalance makes one wonder if, in France, we have not gone beyond the bounds and if our situation is not in fact still revolutionary. It is urgent then to find a basis for social rights that has the same value as the basis we give to individual rights, and at the same time to give individual rights a basis that, of itself, leaves room for the limitations they must receive from social rights. For another thing, there is no doubt that individual rights, even though they exist on their own, need to be defined by the government of the state and that they are limited by this definition. Conversely, apropos of the classical theory of the sovereignty of the state, our authors of constitutional law observe that this sovereignty is limited by individual rights.[8]

The only way out of this imbroglio is the theory of balance. If these powers limit one another, it is because they balance one another, and by thus creating order, they justify one another. I want to point out besides that the order realized by the balance of the power of individual wills and the power of the social organization is simply an objective interpretation of the premise of Locke's political contract, which, according to almost unanimous opinion, was the origin of the modern doctrine of individual rights.[9]

III. *Upon what bases has the balance of powers between society and the individual been established?* Here is the clearest way to picture the matter.

This balance, like all the others, was established historically; it passed through two phases, the first of which is anterior to the state regime. Of course, men never existed entirely apart from the state

8. Cf. Esmein, *Éléments de droit constitutionnel,* pp. 476ff, and the criticism of this idea in Duguit, *Manuel de droit public* (Paris, 1907), I, 472ff.

9. John Locke, *Second Treatise on Civil Government,* 135–142; the influence of Locke has been dominant in this matter, says Esmein, *Droit constitutionnel,* pp. 479, 495; to the same effect, Duguit, *Manuel de droit public,* I, 481; and Locke's ideas rest on the theory of the political contract, Otto von Gierke, Althusius (Breslau, 1880), pp. 91, 92, 113–118. [In his critical edition of Locke, *Two Treatises on Government* (Cambridge, 1960; 2nd ed. 1967), Peter Laslett lists in his introduction 96 books that were available to Locke at the time, but cautions about the lack of evidence to indicate how much Locke actually drew upon them.]

of society, then to enter it at a given moment. But there really was an historical epoch when men had the right to enforce justice themselves and yet were part of an extremely loose-knit society, which itself enforced justice on certain occasions but did not claim to define all the rights of individuals. This is our starting point. It is the first form historically assumed by the opposition between the individual and society; there were two powers on the scene, each of which had the right to enforce justice on certain occasions. This state of affairs would be contrary to society as we understand it today, society as the juridical centralization of the state has made it, but this state of affairs is compatible with a certain form of society, and no doubt it is what Rousseau understood by the state of nature.

Each power, then, enforced justice itself, the society on one side, represented by its chief, and individuals on the other, at least the powerful individuals, the heads of families, the heads of clans. But these individuals alone counted in this epoch. The capacity to enforce justice oneself was the ultimate foundation of rights. This situation permitted each power to define its own rights: society and the individual both had rights that balanced each other on the terrain of juridical autonomy.

After this first historical period of savage or barbarian societies, the centralization of the state regime evolved. Gradually individuals lost the right to enforce justice themselves and society centralized all juridical protection, but a new balance appeared, and consequently a new juridical foundation of individual rights.

However, we are going to have to distinguish between the justification of a right and the formal recognition of it by society, for once the individual has lost his juridical autonomy and thereby the power of defining his rights himself, these rights will have to be defined by the state. Very often they will be morally justified a long time before they are formally recognized by the state.

1. *An individual right is justified if it is, for the individual, a means of accomplishing at his risk and peril his social function and, at the same time, of completing his own personality.*

What now is the social function of the individual? The state assumes the responsibility of juridical protection, but leaves to individuals all the enterprises of material, intellectual, and moral life, especially all the initiative in economic production.[10] At their own

10. [It was such a passage, undoubtedly, that prompted a recent dismissal of Hauriou's theory of the institution as "too reminiscent of a time when the legislator was noninterventionist to be valuable today." Jean Romeuf, ed., *Dictionnaire des sciences économiques* (Paris, 1956), I, 615. But Hauriou amended his views on this score. See his *Précis de droit constitutionnel*, 2nd ed. (Paris, 1929), pp. 145–146.]

risk and peril, individuals are charged with animating society and nourishing it with ideas, works, and wealth, with looking after the interests of society while tending to their own interests. The function one serves justifies all the rights that are necessary to the accomplishment of the function, with reservations that will later be made. Therefore, just as society will have all the rights of domination that are necessary to serve its function of juridical protection, so too individuals will have all the rights that are necessary to serve their function as pioneers of society and as managers of enterprises in the interest of society.

If individual rights are defined as *liberties* and the rights of the state as *powers of domination,* it is because of the way men look upon the balance that is established between the individual and the state. They are primarily concerned with the functions that they think these two forces must serve. They see the individual as having to serve a function of initiative, enterprise, and individual risk; he will have rights that take the form of liberties because they will all more or less be modalities of the liberty of enterprise. They see the state as having to serve a function of protection and guarantee; it will have rights of domination and constraint that will be indispensable in performing its task well in a social milieu where all the individuals are not reasonable nor well-intentioned.

The point should be stressed here that rights are justified by the social function to be accomplished only if the individual accepts the responsibility of exercising them at his risk and peril. Responsibility is the necessary counterpart of the power contained in a right, and moreover, the state regime cannot allow the collectivity to assume the risks of individual enterprises.

We have already considered[11] the importance of the question of risks. We know that human societies, in proportion as they have been organized, have had to reckon with chance disasters, that is, with the collisions that inevitably occur between the social organization and the outside world. One of the most fortunate characteristics of the state regime lies in the attitude it has taken in this question. It leaves up to individuals the question of assessing among themselves the bad consequences of accidents, and thus avoids being disturbed itself by them. A collectivist organization would not so readily escape these disturbances, for in centralizing all enterprises, it would centralize all risks. In return, and in accord with the principle of justice that he who suffers the burdens should share the benefits, the state

11. [Hauriou, *Droit public,* 2nd ed. (Paris, 1916), pp. 435–436, not translated here.]

regime recognizes in the individual not only the rights or liberties indispensable to running the risks of enterprises, but also the right to property, that is, the right to appropriate inventions, discoveries, natural benefits, as well as the results of his labor.[12]

This attitude of the state regime toward the outside world has determined the situation of the individual in relation to the state. There is a reverberation here that no one seems to have grasped very well.

Finally, the idea should be stressed that it is the *individual* who needs to accomplish, at his risk and peril, his social function and who asks to be armed and equipped as an individual in order to complete his own personality. By the force of things, individual rights thus appear as a means of completing the liberty of the human person, at the same time as they are a means of accomplishing a social function. And while objectively the justification of a right will be in the social need to be satisfied, subjectively it will be in the consciousness the individual has of his need of this right for the total liberty of the human person.

2. *The question of the state's formal recognition of even justified individual rights* can be summed up in the following headings: (1) individual rights are formally ratified by the state regime only at the price of risks run to obtain this recognition;[13] (2) individual rights, even when ratified, are in themselves merely potential and are realized in the form of property only by risks run by the individual; (3) the realization of civil rights[14] is surrounded by new risks; and (4) still further risks are introduced by juridical technique.

The recognition and the guarantee of individual rights by the state is entirely upon the condition of a request made by the individual and of a risk run that proves the necessity of the right requested.

(a) History attests that the individual rights listed in the declarations of the rights of man, which, however, are mere potentialities, were formally ratified after many insurrections in which citizens risked and lost their lives to gain these rights, or after many sufferings patiently borne, or after many acts of confidence in society attested

12. The advantage of our position is that it explains how it happens that, by property, the individual has the right not only to the product of his work, but to the profit that is the free gift of a happy chance. Property itself, like all goods, is explained by considerations of function and risks.

13. [Cf. The Civil Rights Act of 1964 in the United States, and the background of its enactment.]

14. [*Droits en justice,* such as rights in the family, of property, of credit.]

by the works and enterprises undertaken by individuals because of their faith in social justice.[15]

From the liberty of juridical commerce that broke open the gate of the Roman city after the social war of 663 to the law of universal suffrage that the modern city owes to the people of Paris, to the barricades and skirmishes of 1830 and 1848, the list of martyrs to the cause of individual rights is long. And the most silent sacrifices are the most efficacious. It is by the trust placed in society in courageously accepting the burdens of life in common, and also by the renunciation of the right to a private enforcement of justice—a renunciation that is necessary to social peace—and by all the risks involved in this trust and this renunciation, that men have merited recognition of individual rights.

But one must understand that this accomplishment is not simply an historical coincidence; there is a relation of cause and effect. Society needs proof that an individual right, requested as an attribute of the human person, is really necessary to this person. There is no more convincing proof than the risk of life or fortune. When a subject risks his person to obtain his right, *he risks the whole to obtain a part,* which proves that this element seems indispensable to his personality.

Society consents, then, to recognize as well founded an individual right, or to put it more generally, what is called a social claim, only when the men interested in it show that they are ready to sacrifice their lives or, at the very least, their goods to obtain it.

And in the same way, vested individual rights are not assured forever; they need to be defended. Hostile forces are straining to suppress them. Society maintains them only insofar as the beneficiaries show themselves ready to risk in order to defend them. If these beneficiaries desert what Ihering calls the "battle for the right" and what we call the "risk for the right," their right is lost.

The strength of workers' claims does not come from the socialist theories, which are mainly just rallying signs, but from the capacity

15. [In an earlier passage (*Droit public,* 2nd ed., pp. 193–194), Hauriou elaborates on this theme: "The foundation of individual rights is the faith that the individual has in social life and the trust that the individual places in society by his undertakings." He cites borrowers and lenders of money, as well as the one who undertakes training for a specialized profession trusting in the division of work in the society, then adds: "Not only all pecuniary trust (*crédit*), but every enterprise, every speculation, every social function accepted, every profession chosen, fundamentally implies an act of confidence in the society, and it is this act of faith, brought to life in works, by risks actually run, that gives birth to individual rights."

of the working class for sacrifice and risk, and from the inability of the bourgeois class to run the same risks to preserve its prerogatives. The workers risk in order to have; the bourgeoisie have, and hesitate to risk for fear of losing what they have.

Society is not interested in the satisfactions of those who possess without running any risk, not even the risks of economic production (for there are *real* risks of capital just as necessary to group life as the *personal* risks of labor). It needs the enterprises of those who risk in order to acquire, because these are the enterprises that set its resources in motion. So it takes the side of those who risk in order to have and keeps them perpetually going by the lure of individual rights.[16]

(b) If we now observe that the individual rights recognized in men are only potentialities, as they have often been reproached for being, we see that in fact they can be transformed into real goods only by a risk run for the economic realization of these rights.

We are familiar with the condition of risk in the economic realization of rights. The right to individual property is inscribed in the declaration of the rights of man and is offered to all, but it will be realized only by one who has run the economic risks necessary to obtain the means of acquiring an object of property. The right to property is a potentiality that can only be realized by risk. The liberty of engaging in commerce and industry is offered to all, but to profit

---

16. I have no objection to recognizing that this theory of "risk for the right," as applied not to the justification of the individual right but to its formal recognition by the society, is a transposition of the "battle for the right" that Rudolf von Ihering launched in his book *Der Kampf um's Recht* (Vienna, 1872), translated in 1890 by O. de Meulenaere under the title *Le combat pour le droit*. I believe I can say that my theory puts Ihering's in focus.

The battle for the right is an expression that has the drawback of suggesting the ideas of success and force. For a right to be protected, must those who battle for it succeed because triumph reveals their force? Not at all. This battle involves something more than force; it involves the risk run. And the proof that the risk run and not the force expended merits the right is this: many insurrections have failed, many revolts have been overcome that have still led to capitulation of the society and recognition of the right. Happily the weak man often conquers the strong when he risks his life. And so, the recognition of the right is founded not on force but on risk, which is often sacrifice, and always responsibility, and which is therefore a moral element.

Ihering was very close to the truth, and in many passages we feel that he touched the true basis of individual rights, namely, that since the right is an integral part of the person, the individual must risk his whole person in order to earn and conserve his right. I will cite in the French translation pp. 9, 14, 18, 21, 36, etc; p. 21: "the plaintiff does not battle for the miserable object of litigation, but for an ideal objective, the defense of his very person and his sense of right"; p. 36: "in his right, each one having an interest defends the moral conditions of his existence"; and the whole history of Shylock, pp. 66ff.

by it, one must run the risk involved in industrial and commercial enterprise. Liberty of the press is open to all, but to profit by it, one must run the financial risk of founding a newspaper, etc. . . .

Thus, the state regime founded on individual liberty utilizes man's need of an ever greater liberty. And, with man, the need for individual rights boils down either to the passion for possessions to which these rights lead, or to the passion for game and adventure that we know is fundamental to him, perhaps as fundamental as the passion for possessions.

(c) Still more significantly, the legal system attaches to the juridical realization of rights special juridical risks over and above the economic risks. An owner or creditor can realize his right only at the price of risk and personal responsibility, and we can say that the enjoyment of vested rights is justified by the risks that accompany their exercise.

Notice, first of all, that society does not assume the task of realizing our vested rights for us; it is up to the individual to watch over them: *jura vigilantibus, dormientibus ossa.* Even in the prosecution of infractions, society takes vengeance only in its own quarrels; it is up to the victim to bring his private legal action. This individual responsibility for the juridical realization of vested rights is perilous; it constitutes a whole enterprise in itself with its own risks, because it ultimately ends in litigation.[17]

(d) If we had the leisure to investigate the technical construction of private law, we should see that the fundamental theories of personality, patrimony, and responsibility are closely coordinated with the postulate of risk as the basis of the juridical guarantee of rights. Here are some examples:

1. The principle, still in force under a very mitigated form, that the entire patrimony of a debtor is pledged to each one of his creditors[18] is an application of the idea that it is natural to risk and, consequently, to engage the whole in order to obtain a part.

2. The principle still in force that one has to run the risk of responsibility for debts *ultra vires* to acquire the entirety of an estate is an application of the same idea. And, no doubt, as a practical matter, responsibility *ultra vires* has been suppressed by the law exempting heirs from liability for debts exceeding assets, but this exemption

17. This condition of juridical risk in the realization of rights must certainly be very basic, for the public administration itself, in realizing its rights, is obliged to submit to it. The price of ignoring it is litigation and the responsibility for ill-founded executions (Cons. d'Ét., 27 fevr. 1903, *Zimmerman,* S. 1905.3.17 and note).

18. *Code civil,* art. 2092. [See Appendix.]

has corrupted the right of succession; since it is no longer justified by a special risk, its social utility grows steadily feebler.

3. The principle still in force that the risk of accident or error is imputed either to the owner of the thing or to the head of the enterprise is one of the justifications for the right of property; the many types of insurance available against fire, livestock mortality, accidents, etc., in attenuating the risks of property, have not strengthened its position from the social point of view. We need new risks that can be imputed to the property owner.

4. There is no other justification for interest paid on borrowed capital than the risk run by the lender. And so, in proportion as the organization of credit grows more secure, interest rates decrease. Right now the premium government securities no longer produce more than a meager interest. But if a war should break out, with all its risks, the interest rate would immediately rise again, etc.

If, on their side, the rights of the state are defined as powers of domination and constraint, and as authority, this is because the functions of protection and guarantee that the state assumes require such a definition. And the extent of the powers is measured by the need. In our time, when a new right is recognized in the state, whether it be the right of military conscription or the right to inspect work, it is always in the higher interest of defense, security, or police regulation, and this has also been the case in the past.

The Israelites accepted all the rights in kingship because they needed a king to wage their wars and to enforce justice among them. Thucydides recognized that the state regime relieves the citizens of the responsibility of watching over their security. Aristotle recognized that when the state took over the coinage and guarantee of money, the citizens were relieved of continual weighing and measuring.

The right to enforce justice, the right to wage war, the right to coin money, are thus for the state simply means of accomplishing a function of justice, a function of defense, a function of guarantee that the citizens very happily confided to the state in order to relieve themselves. And when the need for defense or protection does not seem so urgent, how quickly the citizens attack rights of the state that would seem incontestable at other times, for instance, the right of inflicting the death penalty, which has been under discussion now for a century.

The limitation of the state's rights of domination by the function of protection and of police regulation has become so much a part of the French scene that the state regime, in the contemporary individualist conception, must be considered as a simple management of the country. It would not be paradoxical to try to exemplify this conception by the image of a road system. The state regime would be a sort of park or great garden, where there would be works of art to facilitate traffic, large, well-sanded avenues, and numerous signs to indicate directions and precautions; this garden would be surrounded by walls and an army would stand by to ward off external enemies, while the police would maintain order within; there would also be theaters, concert halls, and libraries. As for individuals, they would walk about the avenues, for business or pleasure, taking care not to step on the flower beds.

This paradisiac conception is the logical outcome of the public regime that constitutes the basis of public life. If, in practice, the law of the state is reduced to a policing of the road system, it is because the nation is almost completely reduced to a public of individuals who rove through all the enterprises. And the hidden reason is that, owing to the progress of individualism and the flexibility of the social organization, man finds again, within the state, in addition to the benefits of civilization, the unrestrained ways of primitive life. He is still the eternal wanderer, the eternal nomad, the eternal adventurer. For a long time civilization imposed upon him a compact and very sedentary organization. He finished by bending this organization to his own ends, he made it his road surveyor and quartermaster; he will no longer crawl along in the forests, he will have roads; he will not only have solid roads through geographical spaces, he will have those open ways through the thickets of social relations that are the legal rules of the codes and also those luminous avenues that are the teachings of science. And because he loves movement above all, he will travel on all these ways, taking with him his possessions, which he is making ever more mobile.[19]

Under these images is hidden the more precise idea that the state regime is simply an existential milieu, not for an isolated individual but for an ensemble of individuals. But a milieu can be arranged, and the more it is arranged, the more useful it will be. Of itself a milieu imposes upon its inhabitants certain conditions of existence that are the counterpart of the conveniences it procures for them.

19. The contemporary tendency to movement, travel, tourism, mobility of wealth, and uniformity of living conditions in all countries could be invoked and utilized here. The rich individual, that is, the type whom all others tend to imitate, is in perpetual movement; sports, watering places, sea resorts, pleasure trains, booked tours have thus all become part of the customs of the bourgeoisie and the people. Let us add the travel owing to business affairs, the movement of government officials, and military service. The result is a kind of universal mobility.

A milieu can assimilate its inhabitants. But there is one thing a simple milieu cannot be, because this would be in contradiction with its nature: it cannot be completely authoritarian. The collectivity of the collectivists would no longer be a simple existential milieu for individuals because it would claim to have absolute authority over them; it would be a superorganism absorbing individuals. Here again, we see that collectivism is diametrically opposed to the state regime because its lack of respect for individual initiative leads it to force the collectivity beyond the stage of a simple existential milieu and beyond the simple powers of police and public service that the arrangement of this milieu entails.

MAURICE HAURIOU   The Special Guarantees of Individual Rights

Jurists have been slow to recognize the fact that the legislative power is even more dangerous to individual liberties than the administrative power. The reason for this slowness is that until very recently they have clung to Revolutionary illusions as to the true nature of this power. They liked to see in legislative law the expression of the general will, which they also misconstrued as a unanimous will; they saw in it, in Aristotle's phrase, dispassionate reason. And they left the legislative power confused with national sovereignty, capitalizing on the infallibility of this sovereignty.

These ideas have certainly changed. The discredit of Rousseau's paradoxes and the Revolutionary errors that they inspired, the political experience gained during the past century, a better understanding of the American doctrine on the limitation of legislative power, a closer analysis of the principle of national sovereignty—all these causes have enabled us to see the legislative power as it really is, that is, as *a majority governmental power*[1] subject to every sort of political seduction and most particularly to electoral pressures, a power that has already perpetrated many useless laws and some bad laws.

Guarantees of rights by a subjective self-limitation of Parliament. The Revolutionaries had already foreseen the danger, but they did not take sufficient precautions to ward it off. In addition to the declarations of rights, the first Revolutionary constitutions contained in their text a *guarantee of rights;* this was a clause in which the

ED. NOTE: Translated from Hauriou, *Précis de droit constitutionnel,* 2nd ed. (Paris, 1929), pp. 731–735. How are individual rights (liberties) protected against governmental encroachment once they have secured recognition? Hauriou here compares the protection given under the American and English systems with that afforded by French legal institutions.

1. [*Pouvoir gouvernemental majoritaire.* G.]

liberties enumerated in the Declaration were endorsed again and guaranteed *against the enterprises of the legislative power.* Constitution, September 3, 1791, title I, § 3: "The legislative power may make no laws that infringe upon and hinder the exercise of the natural and civil rights contained in the present section and guaranteed by the Constitution." This was a pledge not to suppress liberty. In virtue of this pledge the Chambers *were obliged to reject summarily, as unconstitutional, every legislative proposal tending to suppress a liberty.*

In a word, this was a system of subjective self-limitation of Parliament without the creation of any institution to assure the effectiveness of the self-limitation. This barrier did not suffice to stop the French Parliament, which does not feel that individual liberties are guaranteed by the Constitution, nor that a proposed restriction or even a suppression of individual liberty should be summarily rejected as unconstitutional.

It is true that the English Parliament, although sovereign, spontaneously respects individual liberties, but we shall wait in vain for the French Parliament to adopt the same frame of mind. It is not just a question of manners, as they often say, it is also a question of different juridical situations. We must not forget that England is a country of customary law, that individual liberties are protected there by ancient custom or *common law,*[2] and that this ancient custom is considered as forming the substance of the Constitution.[3]

Of course, the English Parliament makes written laws (*statute law*),[4] but it is not disposed to override custom, to which it knows all the electors are attached; nor are the judges, who have a great power of interpretation, any more disposed to abandon the platform of custom for that of written law; they refer written law to custom as much as they can. Clearly then, the forces of custom limit the English legislator in practice and do not limit ours, since we are in a country of written law.

Moreover, the Americans are also in a country of customary law; their individual liberties are protected by the same *common law,* yet they did not consider this guarantee sufficient, nor find it necessary to refer everything to the wisdom of the legislative power. As colonials of England, they had suffered too much from abuses of power on the part of the English Parliament to believe in the self-

2. [In English in Hauriou's text.]
3. A. V. Dicey, *Introduction à l'étude du droit constitutionnel, caractères veritables du droit constitutionnel,* trans. André Batut and Gaston Jèze (Paris, 1902), pp. 1ff.
4. [In English in Hauriou's text.]

limitation of parliaments. They gave themselves written constitutions; they protected their individual rights by these constitutions; they established the principle that the constituting power alone is sovereign, that all constituted powers, even the legislative power, are limited, and consequently that laws contrary to the Constitution must be denied effect as unconstitutional.

This principle has been organized by the Americans in a most practical way. They have conceded that a conflict between ordinary law and constitutional law comes under the jurisdiction of the ordinary judge, like every conflict of laws; that consequently, in any kind of legal action, any provision of law that is invoked and relevant to the action can be alleged to be unconstitutional and that the judge of the litigation is competent to decide this sort of interlocutory question. The unconstitutional provision is not annulled by the judge, but he refuses to apply it and, in practice, it is denied effect by his decision.

This is the *judicial control of the constitutionality of laws* that we have studied above.[5]

GUARANTEES OF INDIVIDUAL RIGHTS AGAINST THIRD PARTIES AND DE FACTO POWERS

1. *The guarantee provided by laws.* "Liberty consists in the power to do anything that is not injurious to another; therefore the exercise of the natural rights of every man has only those limits that are necessary to assure the other members of society of the enjoyment of these same rights. These limits can be determined only by law [*loi*]." So says the Declaration of Rights of 1789–1791, art. 4. Organic laws are, in effect, charged with determining the limits beyond which the liberty of some would become oppressive for others. This is the principle of what is called the *intervention of the legislator* in the relationships of private life or in economic relationships. This intervention is incessant, because circumstances are continually suggesting new ways of using a liberty that are injurious to others.

There is no more ancient liberty than liberty of contract, and there is none that, at first sight, seems to be more equal for all. Yet for a long time the legislator has been obliged to intervene in contractual situations to protect one of the parties against the other, to limit the rate in loans on interest, to forbid or limit sale with power of redemption, to forbid the establishment of any personal servitude whether

---

5. [*Droit constitutionnel,* 2nd ed., pp. 266ff, not translated here.]

or not it is bound to the possession of land and reminiscent of feudalism,[6] to forbid working contracts in perpetuity,[7] etc. This intervention is necessary because in reality the two parties to a contract rarely stand on equal footing; rarely are they able to discuss terms freely. Almost always one of the parties is in need, and the other lays down the law for him and tries to impose unconscionable terms upon him.

In our modern societies the industrial labor contract has become the most frequent occasion of legislative intervention. All of our industrial legislation, which constitutes the *Code industriel* today, was constituted by legislative interventions in the labor contract: limitation of working hours for children, women, adults; prohibition of work for children under a certain age and in certain industries; obligation of the weekly day off; obligation of pensions; a collective character imposed upon the labor contract, etc. During the entire nineteenth century the employer had imposed his terms upon the employees, and their liberty had to be defended against him. The day will perhaps come when the workers' unions will impose their terms upon the employer, and then the law will have to protect him against them.

We must then point to legislation as the principal protector of our liberties against the enterprises of others. Moreover, are we not aware that all our liberties are under the protection of laws, particularly penal laws, which safeguard us against crimes and torts, and alone enable us to enjoy our rights in peace.

2. *The guarantee provided by the administrative power.* The administrative power protects individual liberties by maintaining public order in the interest of the material peace that is indispensable to the exercise of any liberty. It protects them also by the fundamental principle that all constraint is centralized in the hands of the public power, that no individual, group, or enterprise can use any means of constraint against others unless he is an agent of the state or an administrative cog of the state or a concessionary of the state.[8]

3. *The guarantee resulting from the principle that no one has the right to take the law into his own hands.* This principle of the state regime means that no one has the right to proceed with a forced

6. *Code civil,* art. 686. See Appendix.
7. *Code civil,* art. 1780. See Appendix.
8. On the liberty of not joining a union, and on the currently nonobligatory character of the union, see Cass., June 22, 1892, S. 93.1.41. [On today's law in France, see Jean Brèthe de la Grassaye, "Syndicats professionnels," in Emmanuel Vergé and Joseph Hamel, eds., *Répertoire Dalloz de droit social et du travail* (Paris, 1961), II, 637–662].

execution against another without having obtained a judgment in court and without having a writ of execution from a ministerial officer. Moreover, the existing means of execution pertain only to material goods.[9] A firm jurisprudence should apply this principle to large enterprises and particularly to the electrical companies established with a blanket permission of free thoroughfare.[10] These firms have come to possess a de facto regional monopoly and dare to cut off the current from a consumer who does not wish to accept their new demands, to the jeopardy of his business and his industry. When you consider that a landowner does not have the right to evict by force a lessee who does not pay him, it is hard to understand how the owner of an electrical cable has the right to take the law into his own hands by cutting off his lessee's current.

9. Suppression of bodily constraint and imprisonment for debt in civil and commercial matters by the law of July 22, 1867.

10. [Régime de la simple permission de voirie sans cahiers des charges. See voirie in G.]

MAURICE HAURIOU Notes on Decisions of the Conseil d'État: The Tichit Case

Conseil d'État, March 1, 1912 (*Tichit*), Sirey 1913, IIIrd part, p. 137.

Sequel to the case of the strike of postal officials. The Conseil d'État puts the question on the terrain of the conflict of laws; distinction between fundamental laws and ordinary laws; the laws concerning the administrative hierarchy are not constitutional in form, but they are fundamental, and the powers of the judge allow him to prefer them to an ordinary law like that of April 22, 1905, art. 65.

The Conseil d'État: The law of April 22, 1905, art. 65, the decrees of April 23, 1883, November 9, 1901, June 9, 1906, and March 18, 1909, the laws of October 7–14, 1790, and May 24, 1872, being duly considered. According to the testimony of the head of the central telephone office and of the chief engineer, the petitioner Tichit publicly supported the strike and tried to induce his colleagues to do the same; therefore he was not justified in asking for an annulment of the decision attacked as having been made in violation of art. 65 of the law of April 22, 1905; Art. 1. The request is rejected.

March 1, 1912. Conseil d'État. Baudenet, *reporter;* Chardenet, *commissaire du gouvernement;* Raynal, *attorney.*

ED. NOTE: Translated from André Hauriou, ed., *Notes d'arrêts sur decisions du Conseil d'État et du Tribunal des Conflits publiées au Recueil Sirey de 1892 à 1928 par Maurice Hauriou* (Paris, 1929), III, 174 (*Tichit*) and III, 772 (*Esquieu*). Although others before him had published occasional commentaries on the decisions of the Conseil d'État, the supreme court of administrative law, Hauriou initiated the now accepted institution of *arrêtiste,* or commentator. From 1892 until his death in 1929, Hauriou selected one decision for comment each month, and these "Notes" were published by Sirey with the decisions of the Conseil d'État. A recent study by Jacques Fournier, "Maurice Hauriou, Arrêtiste," in *Études et documents* (1957), an authoritative

NOTE HAURIOU

Four years ago, in the *Winkell* case (Conseil d'État, August 7, 1909, S. and P. 1909.3.145; Pand. pér. 1909.3.145), we were also concerned with a strike of postal officials and with a refusal of the Conseil d'État to grant demands for annulment of the decisions to dismiss from office the employees involved in this activity, even though these demands for annulment were allegedly supported by the violation of art. 65 of the law of April 22, 1905, relative to the communication of the file.

It is interesting to return to this subject in connection with the *Tichit* case, because the Conseil d'État has drastically modified its formula. The decision remains the same, but the reasons adduced for it are very much changed. Whereas the *Winkell* decision was relatively long, the *Tichit* decision is remarkably brief; whereas in the *Winkell* decision the Conseil tried to analyze the situation of government officials, in the *Tichit* decision it no longer mentions this

publication of the Conseil d'État, evaluated these commentaries: "The work of the commentator is rated not only by its volume, but also, and primarily, by the influence that it exercises. And this influence is itself the result of an essential quality: discrimination. It is in the choice of decisions for comment and in the significance that he attributes to them that we can recognize the value of the commentator. From this point of view, the work of Hauriou defies all comparison. The entire [administrative] case law of the beginning of the twentieth century is known and evaluated today through the filter of his notes. His commentaries are inseparable from the decisions that they discuss. 'Conclusions Romieu; note Hauriou' is the label of the great decisions of this period" (pp. 156–157).

Two selections from this genre appear here as examples of Hauriou's juridical method. The first note, on the Tichit case, expresses Hauriou's view that there is a legitimate area for judicial control of ordinary legislation. This notion is of course a commonplace of American practice, but is still unacceptable in England and was, until recently, as strongly rejected in France. Hauriou's notes on *Tichit* and on *Winkell*, its direct precursor, have been interpreted by Benoît Jeanneau as prophetic of the post-World War II jurisprudence of the Conseil d'État with respect to "general principles of law *sans texte*" that may prevail even against specific conflicting legislation. Jeanneau, *Les principes généraux du droit* (Paris, 1954), pp. 150–152, 218–225.

The two cases are printed here just as they appear in the Sirey reports. First, the official citation of the case, then the summary or headnote, next the decision of the Conseil d'État, which ends with the listing of personnel appearing before the court. (The *commissaire du gouvernement* is not counsel for the government but a high independent official whose task is to present the state of the law on the issues, as he sees it, to the Conseil d'État.) Finally comes Hauriou's Note. The parenthetical data in the opening lines of the first note indicate the court, date of decision, and the three reports in which the case is published—*Recueil Sirey* (S), *Journal du palais* (P) and *Pandectes françaises périodiques;* the ensuing numbers refer to year, volume and page, respectively.

and limits itself to saying: "According to the testimony of the head of the central telephone office and of the chief engineer, the petitioner Tichit publicly supported the strike and tried to induce his colleagues to do the same; therefore he was not justified in asking for an annulment of the decision attacked as having been made in violation of art. 65 of the law of April 22, 1905."

Thus, before his dismissal, the petitioner Tichit was not given a chance to ask for communication of his file, although the terms of art. 65 of the law of April 22, 1905, absolutely require this procedure. From the moment the petitioner Tichit is found guilty of participation in a strike of government officials, he is no longer justified in asking for an annulment of his dismissal, despite the omission of the procedure of communication of the file. In other words, in this case there is no violation of art. 65 of the law of April 22, 1905, because, despite its apparent generality, this article does not apply to strikes.

And so, while in the *Winkell* case the Conseil d'État based its reasoning on the special situation of government officials and upon the incompatibility between the prerogatives this situation gives them and the right to strike, in our *Tichit* decision the Conseil d'État bases its reasoning solely upon the interpretation of art. 65 of the law of April 22, 1905, upon a question of interpretation of law (*loi*) and of violation of law (*loi*).

This shift in approach does not mean—mark well—that the Conseil d'État, weary of repeating the formula of the *Winkell* decision in all other cases of the same type that it has had to judge, decided to simplify it. When the Conseil d'État thinks it has found a good formula to solve a certain type of question, it does not change the formula but reproduces it in all the succeeding decisions . . . It changes its original formula only when it is not satisfied with the formula and wants to find a better one.

In our opinion the formula of the *Tichit* decision is better than that of the *Winkell* decision because it comes to grips with the real question, which is whether the failure to observe art. 65 of the law of April 22, 1905, in the case of dismissal of government officials for striking violated the law. This is the way we considered the problem in our note on the *Winkell* case, and we were led to the conclusion that, in reality, it was a case of the unconstitutionality of a law, that it would have been unconstitutional to apply the provision of art. 65 of the law of April 22, 1905, to the case of a strike of government officials, and that for this reason failure to have applied this provision did not violate the law.

We should like to take up this idea more fully, since the *Tichit* decision is not at all unfavorable to it.

The crux of the matter is to understand what we mean by the unconstitutionality of laws; for this expression has a narrow sense and a broad sense.

In its narrow sense, the unconstitutionality of laws presupposes that a distinction is made between two categories of laws that are not adopted in the same form, constitutional laws and ordinary laws, and that the laws in constitutional form are superior to the ordinary laws. The normal sanction of this distinction is that if, upon a given question, an ordinary law is found to be in contradiction with a law in constitutional form, the ordinary law must be declared inapplicable by the judge with jurisdiction of the litigation (see as illustration, Trib. d'Ilfov [Bucharest], February 2, 1912, S. and P. 1912.4.9; Pand. pér., 1912.4.9, with Barthélemy's note, and, on appeal, Cass. Roumania, March 16, 1912, S. and P. 1912.4.28; Pand. pér., 1912.4.28). This sanction is completely organized only in the United States of America.

The principle of the unconstitutionality of laws, thus understood, does not apply to our *Tichit* case, for the good reason that the French constitutional laws that are adopted in a different form from ordinary laws are very brief, dealing only with the interrelations of public powers. The organic laws of the public powers, notably the laws dealing with the administrative hierarchy and with public functions, which can be considered as being in contradiction with the right to strike of government officials, are, in form, ordinary laws. The law of 28 *pluviose*, year VIII, the fundamental text of administrative centralization, is, from the point of view of form, a law of the same type as art. 65 of the law of April 22, 1905, on the communication of the file, and, consequently, from the point of view of form, the two laws cannot be considered in opposition.

But the unconstitutionality of laws can be understood in a wider sense. Behind the formal idea of having constitutional laws that are adopted in a different way than ordinary laws so that they will have more solemnity and more value, there is the substantial idea that a hierarchy exists among laws, that some laws are fundamental and others are not, and that these ordinary laws must be subordinated to the fundamental laws. In other words, a legislative phenomenon is taking place in our time that we do not yet grasp very well because we are too close to it, but as time gives us perspective, we shall see it in all its clarity: a phenomenon of differentiation that is destined to segregate those laws that are fundamental from those that are not. This differentiation responds to a profound need of stability: everyday legislation must not be allowed to make spur-of-the-moment modifications in the organic principles upon which the state rests.

There are, then, fundamental laws, and there are, besides, constitutional laws properly so-called. Undoubtedly it would be good to give all fundamental laws the constitutional form; this formal guarantee would be of value to them. Some countries have done this, and they have very long constitutional laws. In France, very probably because we believed in the necessity of the absolute sovereignty of Parliament, and because we wished to tie it down as little as possible, we have preferred short constitutions.

What is more, the constitutional form is not the only guarantee for fundamental laws; there is also the guarantee of the principle that we might call the principle of *the speciality of laws*. What does this mean? This means that a law, made for a certain object and under a certain rubric, can be modified only by another law, made especially for the same object and under the same rubric, and that it cannot be modified by a provision slipped into a law the principal object of which would be foreign to it, for example, in a financial law. For anyone who knows how often, in the past few years, Parliament has used and abused reforms by way of the budget—and, consequently, made improvised and questionable reforms—the principle of the speciality of laws will appear particularly necessary. Indeed, it has just been affirmed by Parliament itself, in the military law of August 7, 1913 (*J. off.* of August 8), art. 2, in regard to fixing the number of men in active service. Parliament inserted in art. 2 the clause that the number of men in active military service can be modified in the future only "by special laws independent of financial laws." Of course, this is just a beginning, and the provision in the law is formal, which means that Parliament is tying its own hands; but it is a beginning, and if there is a sequel, that is, if such a provision is repeated, it will soon become a juridical rule, which could be applied apart from any legislative provision.

The procedure of rigid constitutions and the procedure of special laws are then, in our opinion, only instruments of form, used to distinguish in a certain way between fundamental laws and ordinary laws, and to prepare a solution for the conflicts that might occur between these two types of laws. But why not use a more direct and effective procedure: Entrust to the judge the responsibility of distinguishing fundamental laws, when the circumstances of a case reveal a conflict between the provisions of ordinary laws and the fundamental principles of the organization of the state? There would be no question of the judge's pronouncing a law null; he would need only refuse to apply it, or as in our case, refuse to recognize that it had been violated. The law would thus be denied effect only within the limits of the case litigated. Most often, moreover, this judgment would boil down to a simple matter of interpretation: a certain provision of an ordinary law would be declared inapplicable on a certain hypothesis, by reason of the impossibility of reconciling it with a certain fundamental law.

The task of making such decisions would not be given to a special court of justice; it would fall to the judge with normal jurisdiction of the case that has occasioned the conflict between the fundamental law and the ordinary law, as happens in the United States (see Berthélemy's note, § 2, under Trib. d'Ilfov, February 2, 1912, cited above). Consequently, it would fall sometimes to the civil judge, sometimes to the administrative judge. In the *Winkell, Tichit,* and other such cases, we believe that the Conseil d'État was faced with the conflict that exists between art. 65 of the law of April 22, 1905, which imposes a procedure for the dismissal of government officials, and the fundamental laws concerning the administrative hierarchy, which impose an immediate dismissal, without special procedure, in the case of a strike of government officials, in order to assure continuity of service, and that it resolved the conflict in favor of the fundamental laws. And we say this course must be continued.

There is an objection. Some claim that this procedure gives the judge a political power, which will politically limit the power of Parliament (see Esmein, *Éléments de droit constitutionnel,* 5th ed., p. 435; Duguit, *Traité de droit constitutionnel,* I, 159; Ferdinand Larnaude, *Bulletin de la société de législation comparée,* 1902, pp. 225–229). But this is an error that stems from an insufficient distinction between political powers and juridical powers. In a state that has a separation of powers, political power belongs only to one who has the authority to prevent a measure from becoming executory (see Montesquieu, *L'esprit des lois,* bk. 11, ch. 6, on preventive power). When a measure has become executory, it no longer concerns the political power; if it falls into the snare of a conflict, after or even before its execution, this is simply a juridical accident, and the judicial power, which by reason of the conflict will judge the consequences of its execution, or which will annul it before its execution with judicial forms, is simply a juridical power. The distinction between political and juridical corresponds to the distinction between the executive and the judicial power. The executive power has the task of rendering measures executory, the juridical and judicial power has the task of handling, from the legal point of view, the conflicts provoked by measures that have become executory.

A judge who refuses to apply a law on a given hypothesis does not prevent this law from becoming executory; he has no intention of checking Parliament in its right to legislate, nor the chief of state in promulgation. He is concerned with this law only after it has been passed; he does not even annul it. The Conseil d'État annuls executory administrative decisions, and no one says this makes it a political power. A fortiori, the judge who would refuse to apply an ordinary law, as contrary to a fundamental law, would not be performing a political act, since he would not even annul the ordinary law. He would not even declare the law inapplicable on every hypothesis; most often, he would declare it inapplicable only on certain hypotheses. He would merely be interpreting and applying the law, in the light of the idea that there is a hierarchy among laws, and that, from this hierarchy, conflicts can arise; he would classify laws once they are made, he would group them by categories, he would do the job of a museum curator or a librarian or an archivist, and he would follow the intentions of the legislator himself, for it obviously must be supposed that the legislator would implicitly admit the distinction between fundamental laws and ordinary laws.

For the same reasons, it is perfectly clear that in using this power of interpreting and cataloguing established laws into fundamental and ordinary, the judge would not commit any offense. Some jurists wave around a text of the *Code pénal,* which, in reality, applies to an entirely different thing; this is art. 127, § 1: "The following will be guilty of breach of office and punished by civic degradation: (1) judges . . . who interfere in the exercise of the legislative power, either by regulations containing legislative provisions, or by stopping or suspending the execution of one or more laws, or by deliberating about whether or not laws have been published or executed." The judge who resolves a conflict that arises in a given matter between a fundamental law and an ordinary law does not interfere in the exercise of the legislative power; he does not make a decision by regulation; he neither stops nor suspends the execution of a law. The law remains executory; the judge referees a conflict between two laws, and, in reality, one of the laws suspends the application of the other.

Anyway, what prevails over everything is an urgent need to assure the stability of institutions against the danger of modifications carelessly made by ordinary laws. It does not matter much whether this need is satisfied by the theory of laws in constitutional form or by the theory of fundamental laws. What matters is that some practical solution be found. We favor the theory of fundamental laws, as we have just explained it, because it does not require any modification of the organic laws; it does not oblige us to give them a constitutional form; it leaves to the judge the task of discerning the fundamental laws. This will be done slowly, progressively, with the tacit assent of the legislator. The Conseil d'État, in what concerns it, can establish a list of fundamental laws just as well as it has established a list of governmental acts.

The essential thing is to renounce the absurd idea that all laws are alike. For some time we have had the example of constitutional laws that are beyond classification. Now, in the military law of August 7, 1913, we have the example of provisions of laws that cannot be modified by budgetary legislation; we have recently encountered a distinction between laws that are imperative and others that are simply permissive or indicative (see Conseil d'État, January 26, 1912, *Blot,* S. 1913.3.17 and Hauriou's note). Why is there not also a distinction between fundamental laws and ordinary laws? In a certain way, a state that is taking the shape of a constitutional regime is a state that is elaborating its charter, and this charter must include all fundamental laws. Nothing says that the charter can be fixed only by laws in constitutional form, or that it can be fixed only by Parliament. The juridical powers should work in this as well as the political powers. It is a magnificent task for the judge.

MAURICE HAURIOU   The Esquieu Case

Conseil d'État, January 20, 1928 (*Esquieu*), Sirey 1928, IIIrd part, p. 49. The question of mixed schools. A misuse of power.

The Conseil d'État: The law of October 30, 1886, being duly considered. The provisions of the law of October 30, 1886, and notably articles 6 and 11, as well as the conditions in which it was elaborated and the objective for which it was made, clearly establish that the system of mixed schools was authorized only in order to avoid the burden of maintaining a school for girls and a school for boys in communes with insufficient resources, and not as a pedagogic system. It follows that when two schools already exist in one educational district, and consequently when considerations of economy are not relevant, these two schools must be used for the separate instruction of each sex. Therefore the departmental council of Lot in authorizing at Mauroux, in the same educational district, the coexistence of two schools, each to be used for children of both sexes but of different ages, and the minister of Public Instruction, in approving this decision, have used the powers conferred upon them by the said law of October 30, 1886, for a purely pedagogic objective, other than that authorized by the said law. Art. 1. The decision of the minister of Public Instruction dated February 16, 1925, is annulled.

January 20, 1928. Conseil d'État. Reinach, *reporter;* Rivet, *commissaire du gouvernement;* de Lavergne, *attorney.*

ED. NOTE: This second note was regarded by Jacques Fournier ("Maurice Hauriou, Arrêtiste," p. 162) as illustrating Hauriou's "touch of rigorism" on current morality, and his hostility to the fostering of "laxness" in public morals by administrators and courts. Its juridical interest derives chiefly from showing (in a nontechnical area) Hauriou's view of the jurist's function to interpret statutes within the framework of "the good" as made explicit by the received moral ideas of the national institution ("the state").

NOTE HAURIOU

This very important decision concerns the practice of mixed schools in primary education (girls and boys in the same class). It raises three questions: one involves pedagogy, another morality, and the third the interpretation of the law.

I. The pedagogic question comes up first, since it provoked the appeal for *excés de pouvoir* of which our decision is the conclusion. The Conseil d'État condemns the practice of mixed schools; but what induced the administrators of primary education to authorize and even to favor this practice?

First let us circumscribe the field of the debate. We must distinguish three categories of schools: (1) those of the communes of less than 500 inhabitants, which the law of October 30, 1886, allows to have a single school building and a single teacher's residence. For these schools the law itself authorizes the mixed school in principle (L. 1886, art. 11), on the condition, however, that it is directed by a woman teacher, who will have girls and boys under her direction; only by exception may a man teacher be authorized by the departmental council to direct a mixed school, on the condition that he be assisted by a woman sewing instructor (L. 1886, art. 6). In this first category of schools, and they are numerous since half the French communes have less than 500 inhabitants, there is no difficulty. We only note, and we shall return to this point, that in these communes with meager resources, the law authorizes mixed schools exclusively for reasons of economy.

(2) The second category of communes does not present any difficulty either. These are the communes where the population, which exceeds 500 inhabitants, is numerous enough not only for separate schools for boys and girls, but for two classes in each of these schools, one for the younger children, the other for the older ones. In these large communes there will be no mixed schools, and yet pedagogy will be satisfied, because the boys and girls can be classified according to their age.

(3) The seat of the difficulty is in the third category of communes, the ones that, having a population of more than 500 inhabitants, have constructed two school buildings and two residences for teachers; that, consequently, do not have the option of the mixed school, which is authorized only for communes with less than 500 inhabitants; but that do not have enough of a population to organize two classes of boys and two classes of girls. To these communes the fundamental

provision of article 6 of the law of October 30, 1886, directly applies: "The teaching is to be done by men teachers in the boys' schools, by women teachers in the girls' schools." They must have a boys' school where all ages are mingled, directed by a man teacher, and a girls' school where all ages are mingled, directed by a woman teacher.

This is the way the situation was understood and accepted by the teaching staff during the first years the educational laws were applied and, one might say, for a generation. Only then did a difficulty arise, an almost inevitable consequence of the new school constructions that amalgamated the girls' and boys' quarters in one building complex. There were inconveniences in sending unmarried men and women teachers into these joint schools to live in such immediate proximity; but on the other hand, there were advantages in giving these double posts to married couples who were teachers. Under the combined pressure of the preferences of the teaching staff and of the interests of good administration, almost all the joint schools with double posts were occupied by married couples during the second generation.

Then the pedagogic question came up. A husband and wife teach side by side, separated by a mere classroom wall; between them mutual confidence and understanding are assured; and their married state inspires confidence in the parents of their students. Instead of each one taking on a heavy class of children of all ages, why not lighten the burden by putting all the young children, boys and girls, together, in one class, and all the older children, boys and girls, in another class? Of course, the wife would take the younger class and the husband the older one. For recreations, the sexes would be separated: the girls would have their playground and would be supervised by the wife, and the boys would have theirs, supervised by the husband. The premises lend themselves to such combinations.

Some such attempts were made, timidly at first, in communes where parental disapproval was not anticipated. Then, when precedents had been established, the movement went ahead more boldly. Departmental councils of primary education authorized this practice, and the minister showed himself favorable to it as serving a pedagogic interest, without giving much consideration to its legal basis.

If you consider things only from the pedagogic point of view, you can easily imagine that given a large number of children of different ages and sexes, and given a limitation of two classes, it might be more advantageous to separate the children according to age, the sexes mingling, than to separate them according to sex, the ages mingling. In this way the burden would be lighter for the teachers and the benefit greater for the pupils. This would be very beneficial for education.

All the same, we might ask what, then, are the requirements of this education? For ages primary education has been given to children; for centuries it has been given to them in classes of mixed ages, and very satisfactorily. How does it happen that today the task seems so burdensome and almost impossible? Here we are touching the sensitive point. The conception of primary education is no longer what it used to be. Formerly, the program was to teach reading, writing, and arithmetic. Today, the program is to teach young children an encyclopedia of things: encyclopedia no. 1, on top of which comes the encyclopedia no. 2 of secondary education. Then, the primary school children must follow a regular course of studies from the ages of six to thirteen; during these seven years, there are special subjects for the youngest children, others for the middle ones, still others for the oldest; how can you keep these three classes going at once, all in the same room? Furthermore, an advanced section must be encouraged to prepare for the certificate of studies, created by the law of March 28, 1882, art. 6. How is this to be done?

The fault is not with the teaching staff. It is with the legislator, with those who inspire the educational laws, with those who formulate the programs of study. The traditional training in reading, writing, and arithmetic has been replaced by a cramming of heads with an encyclopedia of matters. The same error has been made in secondary education. But here it has had more serious effects, effects that far surpass the inconvenience of overloaded classes. It has uprooted the country people, made them misfits. On the rebound, it has increased the number of illiterate, for children have gotten used to listening to stories and readings about things and have refused to exert the personal effort it takes to learn how to read and write.

One can understand that the Conseil d'État was not very upset by the pedagogic question. It reflected that by aiming too high and doing too much, the legislators had unduly burdened the teaching staff, aggravated its task, and that after all, if they really wanted to, they could remove the burden. The difficulty with this perhaps was that when the current has begun to flow in one direction, one cannot make it turn back. There might be just one solution: to relieve the congestion of the primary school at the very lowest level by setting up a specialized staff for the youngest children, charged solely with teaching them to read, write, and count, and by limiting the educational obligation to this basic scholarship. But it is not our business to find legislative solutions. Let us get back to our decision.

II. Obviously it was not without urgent reasons that the Conseil d'État opposed a pedagogic practice in which the Administration had been so deeply involved. These reasons were drawn from public morality. The Conseil considered that morality came before pedagogy; and it judged that the mingling of sexes in one class was not very commendable from a moral point of view.

In taking this stand, the Conseil concurred with the traditional maxims of education, for, besides pedagogy, which is too exclusively preoccupied with teaching and instruction, there is moral education, which has its own requirements. One of the most important maxims of traditional education is this: *Maxima debetur puero reverentia,* that is, one must carefully avoid every occasion of arousing in the child the instinct of the species, which will wake up soon enough on its own. On this point, Freudianism—the excesses of which must be avoided, but which rests upon a basis of scientific experience— has come to confirm the traditional principles by showing that the awakening of the senses in the subconscious comes long before conscious perceptions. In a word, upon each child of school age we ought to imagine we see the label "Danger of Explosion." The only reasonable course is to avoid occasions, and it is very clear that mixed classes, instead of avoiding them, provoke them.

We know all the objections: "Girls and boys have plenty of other occasions of meeting one another, etc." Of course they do, but in life each one is responsible for what he can prevent. For what happens outside school, the administration is not responsible; in school, it is responsible if it does not take suitable precautions. "But in the communes of less than 500 inhabitants, the law itself is obliged to tolerate the mixed school, and these communes are numerous." Again, of course. But we know that this arrangement is for material reasons of economy; this is the best that can be done. Besides, in many of these communes there have long been and still are private schools for girls, the competition of which the administration has tolerated without any excessive tenderness, and which it ought to have blessed, for they have contributed indirectly to the acclimatization of the public school by giving satisfaction to fathers of families who, without their existence, would have vigorously protested against the mixed school.

And we must not try to shift the question over to the ground of manners under the pretext that manners have evolved, that what seemed shocking forty years ago does not seem so any longer. Let us not confuse manners with morality. Manners change, which does not mean that they become better, for there are bad manners. Morality does not change. It is not a question of whether the practice of the mixed school is shocking or not, but of whether it is good or bad. And this is why it is equally useless to argue upon a comparison with the manners of this or that foreign country; it is not a question of comparative manners, but of the morality to which we owe our civilization.

III. These moral concerns we have just developed do not seem to appear in our decision. None of the reasons adduced for it points to morality. All of them point to a misuse of power that consisted in putting a pedagogic interpretation on texts that should be interpreted solely as measures of economy. The mixed school was authorized by the law of October 30, 1886, articles 6 and 11, exclusively to permit communes with less than 500 inhabitants to economize on the construction and maintenance of school premises. To take advantage of these dispositions for a pedagogic objective is, on the part of the administration, to use powers that were conferred upon it by the law for an objective other than that authorized by the said law. This is a misuse of power by violation of the spirit of the law, but who does not see that this opposition established by the decision between the objective of economy of the law of 1886 and the objective of pedagogy hides a more profound opposition that the Conseil d'État does not reveal because the law of 1886 does not express it, but which is very much there although not expressed. Implicitly, the law of October 30, 1886, sides with morality against pedagogy in the mixed school question by the mere fact that it authorizes the mixed school only in communes that, in view of the scantiness of their resources, cannot do otherwise. The law of 1886 does not appear to take a stand on the question of morality, but actually it does, and as the Conseil d'État points out, this follows not only from its text, but also from the conditions in which it was elaborated and from the objective for which it was made. What was the sole objective of the educational laws of 1882–1886? To establish primary public education in all the communes, to establish it upon the principles that it be compulsory, free, and secular. There was no question of inaugurating new teaching methods, and above all great care was taken not to break with traditional morality. The substitution of lay teachers for religious created enough of an antagonistic atmosphere.

And there is no need to argue: "The Conseil d'État is appealing to ancient history; it interprets the law of 1886 according to the situation in 1886, but that is almost half a century ago. This method of interpretation is obsolete; the law should be interpreted according to the contemporary situation and present-day manners. The public school is now established, everyone is accustomed to it; the system of mixed schools is taking hold, our manners will get used to it. There would have been no trouble in applying an extensive interpretation of the law instead of this very restrictive interpretation."

Is this so sure? Morality does not change, even in half a century. The positivist error as to the progressive and inevitable disappearance of religions and religious moralities has, I think, been recanted. And events occur that make populations, if not more moral, at least more susceptible to morality. The war of 1914, and all that followed from it, was one of these events. Have you not noticed that the postwar Frenchman has more daring and keener awareness of his rights and liberties? There are regions and even provinces that are proving to be less long-suffering than in the past, and these are not the least sensitive to religion and religious morality; must we wage a war to impose the coeducational school on them? A poor battlefield and a sad crusade! The Conseil d'État, which has a governmental mind and which is a sort of collective man of state, has preferred to extinguish this potential firebrand before it started to burn, and it had great reason to do so: to govern is to foresee.

MAURICE HAURIOU   The Theory of the Institution

and the Foundation: A Study in Social Vitalism[1]

In law, as in history, institutions stand for duration, continuity, and reality; the process of their foundation constitutes the juridical basis of society and the state.

The juridical theory of the institution, which follows in the footsteps of historical reality, has been slow in taking form. It did not find its true place until the field had been cleared by the controversies over the social contract and over the objective and the subjective.

The dispute between the social contract and the institution is now settled. Rousseau had supposed that the social institutions existing in his time were corrupt because they were founded on sheer force and that they would have to be revivified by the social contract as an instrument of free consent. He had confused force with power.[2] Institutions are founded on power, but this power leaves room for a form of consent; if the pressure that power exerts does not amount to violence, the assent given by the subject is juridically valid: *coactus voluit, sed voluit*. Everyone agrees today that the social bond can only be analyzed as a *coactus volui* because it is natural and necessary.

ED. NOTE: Translated from "La théorie de l'institution et de la fondation," *Cahiers de la nouvelle journée*, no. 4 (1925), pp. 2–45. Hauriou's most original contribution to juristic thought, as most jurists agree, is his theory of the institution. Although its origins may be found in his *La science sociale traditionnelle* (1896), the first full-dress formulation did not appear until *Précis de droit administratif*, 6th ed. (1907). In 1925, after progressive revisions, he published this article in an obscure philosophical periodical, and it proved to be the most fully developed expression of his institutional theory, minor strokes were added in his last work, *Précis de droit constitutionnel*, 2nd ed. (1929).

1. [*Vitalisme social*. G.]
2. [*Pouvoir*. G.]

And so the institution came through this first ordeal triumphantly. But another was awaiting it: the controversy over the objective and the subjective. The first debate had led to a clarification of the degree of consent that is present in institutions; the second was to help determine the degree of their objectivity, that is, of their independent existence.

It would be useless now to return to the controversy over the social contract, but quite useful to consider the controversy over objectivity, which has not been entirely settled. The theory of the institution has reached maturity during this debate, and perhaps it has a solution to offer. Our account of this controversy will take the place of an introduction.

Some preliminary definitions are necessary. By *droit subjectif* jurists mean everything in law that depends upon the conscious will of particular subjects, for example, contracts and testamentary dispositions (called "last wills"); by *droit objectif* they mean everything in law that does not depend upon the conscious will of particular subjects and that therefore seems self-sustaining, for example, a juridical rule deriving from custom.[3]

If we go to the heart of the matter, we see that the juridical situations that seem self-sustaining are in reality bound to ideas that remain subconsciously in the minds of an undetermined number of individuals. Subconscious ideas are those that live in our memories without at the moment being consciously willed. They are the ideas that we have perceived, stored away, and then lost sight of. They live in us without our realizing it, and even influence our judgments and our acts, just as the presence of familiar objects reacts upon us. Subconscious ideas are objects that live within us.

And so the subjective depends upon our conscious acts of will, and the objective upon our subconscious ideas. With this in mind, let us begin our account of the dispute between *droit subjectif* and *droit objectif*.

Always and instinctively, jurists have admitted the coexistence of subjective and objective elements in the juridical system: juridical personality, subjective rights,[4] and juridical acts[5] constitute the first group; public policy[6] and what is called "regulation,"[7] that is, the

3. [*Règle de droit coutumiere*. G.]
4. [*Droits subjectifs*. G. In ordinary English usage, simply "rights." The continuing contrast here is with "*objective* rights," hence the literal translation.]
5. [*Actes juridiques*. G.]
6. [*Ordre public*. G.]
7. [*La réglementation*. G.]

whole gamut of laws, rules, and customs, constitute the second. This dualism, which corresponds to that of the conscious will and the subconscious idea is a wise compromise.

Toward the middle of the nineteenth century this compromise was repudiated by the organization of an ultrasubjectivist system, which provoked the formation of an ultraobjectivist system fifty years later. And so the dispute was on.

The subjectivist system was based upon juridical personality. It assimilated corporate moral persons, notably the personified state, to individual persons, and claimed that these persons and their wills were the support of all lasting juridical situations, even of the norms of juridical rules.[8] Some German authors—Gerber, Laband, Jellinek—in an attempt to force "regulation" within the subjectivist system, fancied they could assimilate juridical rules to acts of will of the personified state.

As far as legal rules were concerned, this notion was not new. Rousseau had already defined a law as the expression of the general will, which, in his thought, certainly signified the will of the personified state. But the notion had been confined to the domain of political philosophy, and it was imprudent of jurists to generalize it and to bring it into the domain of law. Strictly speaking, laws and rules elaborated by state organs might have been considered conscious acts of will of the state, or at least acts of will of the legislator or the government. But it was quite impossible to attribute customary rules[9] to the will of the state, for they are not the work of any state organ, and many of them are anterior to the era of the modern state. In the mid-nineteenth century the age of custom might well have seemed to be ending. In France custom had been abolished as a source of law by the *Code civil;* in Germany it seemed doomed. But this was just an illusion. Even in Germany it was going to return to the offensive at the time of the redaction of the new civil code; and in all the Anglo-Saxon countries under the name *common law*[10] general custom continued very much alive. The attempt of *droit subjectif* to monopolize all "regulation" was thus destined to fail.

8. [I.e., the individual laws were regarded as the continuing explicit or tacit expression of the will of the sovereign. Cf. John Austin, *The Province of Jurisprudence Determined,* ed. H. L. A. Hart (London, 1954), pp. 30–32.]

9. [See criticism of Austin's explanation by H. L. A. Hart, *The Concept of Law* (Oxford, 1961), pp. 44ff and 62ff; and Glanville Williams, "International Law and the Controversy Concerning the Word 'Law,'" *British Y.B. of International Law,* vol. 22 (1945), pp. 146–163.]

10. [English in original.]

There was another stumbling block. The state has not always existed. It is a political formation of a highly developed civilization. Human societies have lived very much longer under the regime of clans, tribes, and feudal seigniories than under state regimes. In these primitive formations either the law was customary or it came directly from the power of the ruler. In either case it was not the expression of the will of moral persons, who did not yet exist. Must it be said, then, that the law of the clan, or tribal law, or seignioral law were not true law, or to put it more simply, that before the appearance of the state, the juridical rule did not exist in any form?

Then we should have to go on to say that the juridical rule did not exist until the appearance of the moral personality of the state, for it would have to be an expression of the state's subjective will. But states generally go through a long period of political formation before their juridical personality appears; during this long period the law of the state would not have existed. This conclusion did not make Jellinek waver. He declared that questions about "the birth, life, and death of states belong only to history"; in other words, whatever is not a manifestation of will of the moral person-state does not belong to law.

The offensive directed by the subjectivist system against "regulation" backfired all the more against this system because it hid more than one weakness. It claimed to assure the continuity of juridical situations by having them sustained by juridical persons, but it did not have a good theory of personality. In an attempt to avoid the doctrine of fiction in regard to corporate persons, it gave every personality the *substratum* of a power of will (*Willensmacht*). But then it could not explain continuity in a convincing manner, for the power of will can be construed as discontinuous. Then, too, it fell into the snare of an insurmountable objection: it could not justify the personality recognized in the infant and the insane, who have no reasonable will.

Criticism had the game in its hands; a reaction was inevitable: a resurgence of the objective. By a sort of logic of things, the new system would gain a foothold in the area of "regulation" that had been so clumsily annexed to *droit subjectif*. This new system was Léon Duguit's system of the objective juridical rule.

The new thesis was just as absolute as the one it opposed. The ultraobjective was at swords' points with the ultrasubjective. The objective juridical rule, considered as a thing existing in itself, became the basis of all juridical existence, in place of the juridical person, which was now denied and rejected as a concept without value, not only in regard to corporate institutions but even in regard to individuals. Subjective rights lost their subjective center; all juridical efficacy was concentrated in the objective juridical rule. The acts of men could produce juridical effects only by their conformity to this rule. Moreover, the application of the objective juridical rule produced, in principle, only objective juridical situations, except when the rule itself admitted the intervention of individual acts that, with its permission, produced brief subjective situations.[11] Objective situations, by reason of their number and duration, took on a much greater importance than subjective situations and the subjective rights arising from them.

This system of objective law had not come alone. It had followed the auspicious tide of Durkheim's sociological system, which also made the objective supreme by ranking the social milieu above individuals. The kinship between Duguit and Durkheim is obvious. The juridical rule was itself only a product of the social milieu, a rule accepted as obligatory by "the mass of consciences."[12] The "mass of consciences" took over the direction of law in place of the "individual conscience."

This system is untenable because it overshoots the mark. Not content with making the objective juridical rule an element of continuity for social institutions, it claims to make it their formative element. But even if juridical rules are an element of conservation and duration for institutions, we cannot conclude that they are the active force in the creation of institutions. Here is the whole problem: we must know where in society the creative power lies; whether juridical rules create institutions, or institutions produce juridical rules owing to the power of government they contain. The system of the objective juridical rule collapses over this question of initiative and creation. To concede the creation of social institutions by the juridical rule would be to concede their creation by the social milieu, which is supposed to create the juridical rule itself. The error is glaring: the social milieu has only a force of inertia that finds expression in either a power of reinforcement of individual proposals when it approves them, or a power of opposition and reaction when it disapproves them; but of itself it has neither initiative nor power of creation. The social milieu cannot produce a creative juridical rule that, by hypothesis, would be anterior to what it was about to create.

11. [For example, an individual's (subjective) right of property in Blackacre.]
12. [*Masse des consciences*. G.]

Let us add, moreover, that if the social milieu were endowed with a creative power, the juridical rule would be a deplorable instrument of creation because it contains a principle of limitation. Juridical rules are transactional limits imposed upon the claims of individual and institutional powers. They are anticipated regulations of conflicts. The French Revolutionary definitions bring out this characteristic very clearly: "the exercise of the natural rights of every man has only those limits that are necessary to assure the other members of society of the enjoyment of the same rights; these limits can be determined only by law." And so the role of the legislator is that of a surveyor who places boundaries between fields of activity. The organic laws of individual liberties, the law of the press, the law of associations, the laws on the liberty of teaching, the many civil laws on the liberty of contracts or on the free use of individual property—even in those of their provisions that seem constructive —are in reality only boundaries and limits. Hence the traditional maxim of individualism: "Everything that is not forbidden by law is permitted"; or better, "Everything that is not forbidden by law and that is the work of an individual will is juridically valid."[13]

We shall return to these fundamental ideas later on; we have said enough about them for the moment. One can see what dangerous errors the system of the juridical rule contains. It would foster a principle that is diametrically opposed to the principle upon which individualism has always rested, asserting: "Everything that is not permitted by the juridical rule or everything that does not conform to a pre-existing juridical rule is juridically ineffectual." Aside from the clearly antiindividualist character of such a principle, we should notice its barrenness. All new creations of social practice would remain outside the law during an undetermined number of years; because they conform neither to the old juridical rule nor to a new juridical rule that would be born only when the social milieu is upset, they would remain in no man's land.

Here we touch the fundamental error of this entire system: taking reaction for action and duration for creation. The subjective elements are the creative forces in society; they furnish the action. The objective elements, the juridical rule, the social milieu, public policy, are merely elements of reaction, duration, and continuity. To attribute the role of one to the other is to turn the house upside down.

The ultrasubjective system and the ultraobjective system must be put back to back; one has mistaken action for duration and the other

13. [Declaration of the Rights of Man, articles 4 and 5.]

duration for action. Moreover, by a rather amusing coincidence, both have relegated to history important elements that they did not know how to fit within their juridical construction. The subjectivist system declared that the birth of states belongs only to history, which is to take the process of their foundation out of the domain of law. The objectivist system, on the other hand, had to admit that the formation of juridical rules belongs only to history since the rule has nothing juridical about it until it is accepted as obligatory by "the mass of consciences." And this development takes time.

On both sides, the process of foundation is left unaccounted for, the foundation of states as well as the foundation of juridical rules. The bases of law are thus excluded from law, for, as we have already observed, the basis of the state and the basis of the juridical rule are simply continued foundations, and everyone will readily admit that the bases of the state and the juridical rule are the bases of law.

By the logic that governs the movements of ideas, the theory of the institution and the foundation, which historically succeeds the subjectivist and objectivist systems, quite naturally took root in this matter of the foundation of institutions, which the two antagonistic systems had equally disclaimed. The essential object of this theory is to show that the foundation of institutions has a juridical character and that, from this point of view, the bases of juridical duration are juridical themselves. It has, moreover, profited by the controversy over the subjective and the objective: it accepts a certain dualism here, for it sees in this opposition not so much conflicting elements as different states through which a corporate institution or a juridical rule can pass, according to the moment.

The main lines of this new theory are the following: an institution is an idea of a work or enterprise that is realized and endures juridically in a social milieu; for the realization of this idea, a power is organized that equips it with organs; on the other hand, among the members of the social group interested in the realization of the idea, manifestations of communion occur that are directed by the organs of the power and regulated by procedures.[14]

There are two types of institutions, those personified and those not personified. In the first, which comprises the category of insti-

14. [This passage is the one most frequently quoted in general references to Hauriou's institutional theory: "Une institution est une idée d'oeuvre ou d'entreprise qui se réalise et dure juridiquement dans un milieu social; pour la réalisation de cette idée, un pouvoir s'organise qui lui procure des organes; d'autre part, entre les membres du groupe social intéressé à la réalisation de l'idée, il se produit des manifestations de communion dirigées par les organes du pouvoir et réglées par des procédures."]

tution-persons or constituted bodies (states, associations, labor unions,[15] etc.), the organized power and the manifestations of communion among the group members are interiorized within the framework of the idea of the work. After having been the object of the corporate institution, the idea becomes the subject of the moral person that comes into being in the constituted body.[16]

In institutions of the second category, which we can call institution-things, the elements of organized power and of manifestations of communion among the group members are not interiorized within the framework of the idea. These elements do exist in the social milieu, but they remain exterior to the idea. A juridical rule that has been established in a society is an institution of this second type. It is an institution because as an idea it is propagated and lives in the social milieu; but obviously it does not produce a corporate body that is proper to itself. It lives in the social body, for example in the state, by borrowing this body's power of sanction and by making use of the manifestations of communion that occur in it. A juridical rule cannot produce a corporate body because it is not a principle of action or enterprise but, on the contrary, a principle of limitation.

Institutions are born, live, and die juridically. They are born by acts of foundation that provide them with their juridical basis as long as they continue to exist. They live a life that is both objective and subjective, thanks to juridical acts of government and administration that are repeated and are bound together by procedures. Finally they die by juridical acts of dissolution or abrogation. Thus, they occupy time juridically, and the solid chain they constitute is intertwined with the lighter thread of transitory juridical relations.

We shall study only institution-persons or corporate institutions. We shall analyze their elements and observe their life. The same kind of study could be made for institution-things, especially for juridical rules. We do not have space here for this second exposition; we shall merely point out in passing the essential ways in which they differ from corporate institutions.[17]

The elements of every corporate institution are, as we have seen, three in number: (1) the idea of the work or enterprise to be realized

15. [*Syndicats*. G.]

16. [Hauriou here proposes that "the idea" itself is the subject in which the "moral personality" of the constituted body inheres. As the definition in the previous paragraph suggests, Hauriou conceives of "the institution" as "the idea"—an idea that has to some degree achieved exterior existence in a "work or enterprise."]

17. [Hauriou in fact never fully developed his institutional theory with respect to "institution-things."]

in a social group; (2) the organized power put at the service of this idea for its realization; (3) the manifestations of communion that occur within the social group with respect to the idea and its realization.

We should also recall that our institutions undergo a phenomenon of incorporation; that is, the element of organized power and the element of manifestations of communion among the group members are interiorized within the idea of the work. This incorporation leads to personification. It leads there all the more easily because in reality the corpus that results from the incorporation is itself a very spiritualized body; the group members are absorbed in the idea of the work, the organs are absorbed in a power of realization, the manifestations of communion are psychical manifestations. Since all these elements are more spiritual than material, this body is of a psycho-physical nature.

I. The most important element of every corporate institution is the *idea of the work to be realized* in a social group or for the benefit of this group. Every constituted body is formed to accomplish some work or enterprise. A commercial corporation is formed to put a business enterprise—that is, a profit venture—in action. A hospital is constituted to realize a charitable idea. A state is a body constituted to realize a number of ideas, the most obvious of which are summed up in the following formula: "a protectorate of a national civil society by a public power having a territorial jurisdiction, but distinct from territorial property, and thus leaving a great scope of liberty for its subjects."

The idea of the work to be realized, which may also be called "the directing idea of the enterprise," should not be confused with the notion of end, nor with that of function. The idea of the state, for example, is quite a different thing from the end of the state or the function of the state.

A first difference between the end of an enterprise and its directing idea is that the end can be considered as exterior to the enterprise, whereas the directing idea is interior to it. A second difference, tied in with the first, is that the directing idea includes a program of action and of organization for this action that far transcends the notion of end. When we say that the idea of the state is to protect the national civil society, the idea of protectorate suggests a prescribed organization and a prescribed program of action. But if we were talking of the end of the state, we should say that it is the protection of the national civil society, which merely suggests the idea of a result. The difference between program of action and result expresses quite well the difference between directing idea and end. It would not even be exact to liken the directing idea to the idea of the "end to be achieved," for the first denotes both the end and the means to be used to achieve it, whereas the idea of end alone does not denote the means.

Nor must the idea to be realized by an institution be confused with the function of this institution. The idea of the state far transcends the notion of the functions of the state. The function is only that part of the enterprise that is already realized, or at least already determined. But the directing idea also contains an undetermined and unrealized part that goes beyond the functional part. The separation of these two domains is striking in the state. There is the domain of function: the administration and a determined group of public services. Then there is the domain of the directing idea: the political government, which works in the undetermined area. And the fact is that the political government is of much more vital interest to citizens than the administration, which shows that what is undetermined in the directing idea has more influence over men than what is determined under the form of function.

The directing idea of corporate institutions other than the state cannot be reduced to the idea of a determined function either. For a long time our positive law was under the illusion that such a reduction was possible. Administrative law tried to restrict religious and charitable establishments to a determined functional activity so that they could not accept donations with conditions attached: a church-building fund was not allowed to accept a donation with the stipulation that it support a certain charity; a hospital was not allowed to accept a donation with the stipulation that it open a school, etc. Commercial law, in turn, tried to restrict business companies[18] to the functions determined by their charters, immutable as they were. When the great railroad companies built "Terminus" hotels in their stations, they were accused of going beyond their legitimate sphere of activity.

Larger ideas prevailed, and the "Terminus" hotels remained open. Business companies have been permitted to modify their charters to a great extent. The restriction imposed upon public establishments[19] has been recognized as a mere police regulation of the administration and a debatable one at that. Here again the undetermined character of the directing idea prevailed over the restriction to a determined function. The English have completely discarded

18. [Sociétés de commerce. G.]
19. [Établissements publics. G.]

the functional restriction for their business companies; in their view any company is entitled to undertake any sort of commercial venture, because its directing idea is profit.

The directing idea of the work, which thus transcends the notions of end and function, would be more accurately identified with the notion of object. The idea of the enterprise is the object of the enterprise, for the enterprise has the object of realizing the idea. The idea is so truly the object of the enterprise that the enterprise becomes objective and acquires a social individuality by means of and in the idea. For when the idea of the enterprise is propagated in the memories of an indefinite number of individuals, it comes to live an objective life in their subconscious—the *Bank of France,* the *city of Paris,* the *state* itself.

The idea will attract some closer adherents who will be especially interested in the success of the enterprise because they will be shareholders or subjects.[20] Even in this closer and more vitally interested group, the idea will ordinarily be in the objective state in the subconscious. Undoubtedly it will pass into the subjective state from time to time in conscious manifestations of voluntary acts, but this will be, in appearance at least, in a discontinuous manner, whereas the subconscious obsession with the objective idea will be continuous.

The objective idea will not be classified in every memory according to the same interpretation—that goes without saying. The idea, considered in itself, must be carefully distinguished from the subjective concepts through which it is perceived by individuals. Each mind reacts upon the idea and forms a concept of it. The eternal themes of passion at grips with duty or reason are not treated by Racine as they had been by Sophocles or Euripides. Racine's tragedies are neither acted nor understood in the twentieth century in the same way as they were in the seventeenth century. So it is with the ideal of justice; it has been understood in many different ways. But we cannot say that there is nothing lasting, nothing real, nothing objective in the idea of justice, any more than we can say this of the ideas of duty or love.

Despite the subjective gloss that each adherent gives to an idea of work that is propagated in the social milieu, it possesses an objective existence, and what is more, this reality enables it to pass from one mind to another and to be refracted differently in each mind without dissolving and disappearing.

20. [I.e., shareholders in a private corporation or subjects of a state, as the case may be.]

One must wonder if this objective character of the idea is native and fundamental to it. If the idea were the subjective creation of the mind of a particular individual, we could hardly conceive how it could acquire an objective character that would enable it to pass into another mind. Ideas that pass from one mind to another must have an objective nature from the outset. In reality, men do not create ideas, they simply find them. An inspired poet discovers an idea just as a miner discovers a diamond. Objective ideas exist beforehand in the vast world, incorporated in the things that surround us; in moments of inspiration we find them and free them of their slag.

These observations upon the native and fundamental objectivity of ideas must not divert us from studying the human group that, in a corporate institution, is interested in the success of the directing idea of the enterprise. There is no corporate institution without an interested group; the state has its subjects or citizens, the labor union its union members, the commercial corporation its shareholders. The formation of each group can be partly determined by the constraint of a power, but the ascendancy of the idea of the work and the interest the members have in its realization play a great role in that they explain the voluntary element in the support of these members. These interested members are adherents who run a personal risk in the success or failure of the enterprise.

This interested group, together with the governmental organs, is the bearer of the idea of the enterprise. In this sense we should recognize that the group of members of a state is also the group of subjects of the idea of this state. This observation gives the word "subject" a great depth of meaning: each person under the jurisdiction of a state bears within himself the idea of the state and he is the subject of this idea, because he assumes the risks and responsibility for its success. The subject of a state is, in a word, like a shareholder in the enterprise of the state. And this situation of the subject eventually results in his status as citizen, for if he is exposed to the risks of the enterprise, justice demands that he acquire a right of control and participation in its government.

This analysis of the characteristics of the interested group puts us in agreement with the ideas Michoud advanced in his *Théorie de la personnalité morale* of 1906, with this essential difference: the idea of the state or of the corporate enterprise, whatever it may be, is not borne by the interested group alone, but also by the governmental organs with their power. Hence, the idea of the state has at its service an autonomous power of government that is imposed upon the citizens themselves and in which they only participate.

II. The second element of every corporate institution is *an organized power of government* that is for the realization of the idea of the enterprise and that is at its service. This element is ordinarily called the organization of the institution, but organization must be interpreted as organized power: since power itself is a form of will and since institutional organs are envisaged as powers of will, this interpretation spiritualizes the human element of organization.

The bases of the organization of governmental power are entirely spiritual themselves. They can be reduced to two principles: the separation of powers and the representative regime.

Every separation of powers is a separation of competencies, which are spiritual things. In the separation of the modern state, the executive power has the inituitive competency of executory decision, the deliberative power has the discursive competency of deliberation, and the power of suffrage has the competency of assent. Of course, these competencies are entrusted to human organs, but the best proof that the organs are subordinate to the competencies is the plurality of organs that work in concert to exercise a single power: for the exercise of the executive power, the president of the republic and the ministers; for the exercise of the deliberative power, the two chambers; for the power of suffrage, the voters of a district.

Thanks to this separation of powers, which leads to an even greater separation of organs, governmental power is not just a simple force but a rightful power capable of creating law. These separations assure the supremacy of the competencies over the power of domination that the organs would tend to abuse without this precaution.

The principle of the representative regime responds to another need. The governmental power of a corporate institution must act in the name of the body; its decisions must be considered as those of the body itself. A body is nothing without its organs, and it wills only through them, but these organs must will for it and not for themselves. This difficult problem is solved by the representative principle, which rests entirely upon the idea of the work to be realized. This directing idea is supposed to be common to the organs of government and to the members of the group. The whole technique of representative organization consists in assuring in practice the reality of this common vision, continuously if possible, periodically at the very least.

The subordination of the ruling will to the idea of the enterprise can occur spontaneously in the proud consciousness of an absolute prince just as well as in the tractable consciousness of a minister subject to popular election. Election is not essential to the representative regime, but it is a natural element of its technique because it seems to guarantee a community of outlook between the governors and the members of the body.

The power of government of an institution does not always observe the attitude of docility and conformity that we have just outlined. The history of states and even of some private institutions teaches us that all too often ruling powers abandon their concern for the common good to follow selfish drives. But in the long view, this history proves two things: first, that the power of government is a spontaneous force of action and not just the fulfillment of function, since this force rebels against its function all too often; second, this history reveals the ascendant power of the idea of the work to be realized since slowly but surely and progressively, even in the state, the impetuous passions of governors have ended by submitting to its service. Constitutional mechanisms have certainly helped bring about this submission, but these mechanisms themselves either would not have been created or would have been useless if they had not been supported by a public spirit imbued with the idea of the state.

The voluntary submission of governors to certain directing ideas could be no better illustrated than by the example of the submission of military leaders to the civil power in modern states. This subordination of the armed forces, so contrary to the nature of things, could never have been effected by simple constitutional mechanisms. It is the product of a mentality created by the ascendancy of an idea, the idea of the civil regime joined to the idea of peace, considered as constituting the normal situation. As far back as 1896, in a chapter of my *Science sociale traditionnelle,* I pointed out this ascendancy that the directing idea has over the governmental power.[21] I called

21. [In *La science sociale traditionnelle* of 1896, Hauriou refers to "the fact of the redemption of social organizations," which he calls "the phenomenon of the institution": "Society itself, the family, marriage, property, universal suffrage, the republic are all institutions. True history has become the history of institutions. At the onset these institutions were provisional organizations, usually founded upon violence: marriage and the family were founded upon the seizure of the woman and the despotism of the male, property upon theft, universal suffrage and the republic—and royalty as well—upon many revolutions. But all this has been instituted, which means that the centuries and years have brought their alluvion of sacrifices, that these new organizations have been accepted, that those entrusted with power have understood the duties that are correlative to this power, that their power has become a function . . . Men have adjusted to these new organizations and they have adjusted to men. They have entered into the patrimony of common ideas. At first they had only a body, now they have a soul. They have understood their function and fulfilled it. They are no longer organizations, they are institutions, for to be instituted is to be given an internal principle, a soul, and what we have just described is the phenomenon of the *institution* . . . It is a fundamental social phenomenon" (pp. 188, 194, 193).]

it the *phenomenon of the institution*. And I underscored the characteristic of moral improvement in organizations founded upon power
that this notion presents.

III. There is one more element of the corporate institution for us
to put in place: the *manifestations of communion* among the members of the group and also among the governmental organs, either
in the idea of the work to be realized or in that of the means to be
used. This phenomenon of communion, to which we have already
alluded and owing to which the directing idea of the work passes
momentarily into the subjective state, must be studied in its phenomenal reality.

This element can be most clearly grasped in the great popular
movements that accompany the foundation of new political and
social institutions. The foundation of the communes in the Middle
Ages was accompanied by great moral crises that aroused populations to the cry "Communion, communion!" The formation of labor
unions at the end of the nineteenth century stirred up the same
movement for union among the working class. And without a doubt
the formation of states, at the time it took on the character of a
contagion, for example, about 1000 B.C., stirred up an analogous
movement; we have an echo of it in the book of Samuel, in the
passage where the Israelites "ask for a king."[22]

On a smaller scale, movements of communion appear at the
moment of the foundation of private institutions. Following a familiar pattern, the foundation of almost every institution is preceded
by meetings in which it is more or less enthusiastically acclaimed
in principle.

The functioning of institutions involves the same sort of com-
munions, especially under the regime of assemblies. Of course, not
all assembly meetings present such moving scenes as the Tennis
Court Oath or the night of August 4th,[23] nor do all realize such a
sacred union, but in a cooler way, the formation of any voting
majority always requires a union of wills.

These movements of communion cannot in any sense be analyzed
as manifestations of a collective conscience. It is individuals who
are moved by their contact with a common idea and who, by a
phenomenon of interpsychology, become aware of their common
emotion. The center of this movement is the idea that is refracted

22. [I Sam. 8:5: "Give us a king, such as other nations have, to sit in judgment over
us."]
23. [By the oath of the *Jeu de Paume* (Tennis Court Oath) of June 20, 1789, the
deputies of the third estate swore they would not adjourn before they gave a constitution to France. On the night of August 4, 1789, the constitutent assembly abolished
the feudal privileges.]

into similar concepts in thousands of minds and that stirs these minds into action. The idea passes momentarily into the subjective state in the thousands of individual minds that are united in it; these individuals invoke its name and it descends among them, adapted by them to the subjective state. This is the exact reality.

To analyze the phenomenon as the specter of a collective conscience, as the school of Durkheim has done, is to belittle the reality, for the collective conscience would be riveted to an average opinion in the social milieu, that is, in the mass of minds. On the contrary, the refraction of the same directing idea in a number of individual minds reserves to the superior minds the leading role in drawing conclusions for purposes of action. The two analyses are as far apart as the two explanations of the progress of civilization: by the action of the elite and by the evolution of the milieu alone. Communion in an idea is Ariel; the collective conscience, Caliban.

Communion in an idea includes an agreement of wills under the direction of a chief. It connotes not only intellectual assent but also the will to act and the initial step forward that, by reason of the risk assumed, engages the whole being in the common cause. In a word, this is a communion of action.

These agreements take on the importance of a special juridical process that we shall study in the following paragraph and that is the process of foundation.

IV. Corporate institutions undergo the phenomenon of incorporation, which leads them to the phenomenon of personification. These two phenomena are themselves dependent on a movement of interiorization that brings within the framework of the directing idea of the enterprise, first, the organs of government with their power of will, and then, the manifestations of communion of the members of the group. This *triple movement of interiorization, incorporation, and personification* is of major importance for the theory of personality. If we can verify the reality of this movement, we shall have verified the reality of moral personality, the basis of juridical personality, for we shall have established that the tendency to personification is natural. This will be established for individual persons as well as for corporate persons, because we must face up to the fact that today individual moral personality is as much contested as corporate moral personality.

This state of the question entitles us to use a new comparative method that involves an interplay of corporate and individual psychology. We shall use whatever introspection into individual psychology reveals in order to aid our analysis of corporate psychology, and conversely, we shall use the findings of corporate psychology in order to clarify the results of individual introspection.

The justification for this comparative method rests upon the postulates that society is a psychological work, that in this psychological work there is reciprocal action between the human mind and certain objective ideas that are the bases of institutions; that corporate personality is a social creation made, to a great extent, in the image of the human personality, but that, as it is made in a subconscious manner, it can reveal aspects of the human personality that conscious introspection does not reveal;[24] finally, that in corporate personality the details of organization are so magnified and as it were projected on a screen that they are easier to observe.

A. We shall establish, first of all, with the help of our comparative method, the reality of the triple movement of interiorization, incorporation, and personification, consequently, the reality of moral personality in the sense of its natural formation. Then we shall tackle another aspect of the question: we shall try to determine to what extent and in what manner the incorporated and personified institution assures its own duration and its own continuity, for, without doubt, incorporation and personification occur in order to obtain these results.[25]

As a type of corporate personality let us consider that of the state. The state is incorporated when it has reached the stage of representative government. At this stage a first task of interiorization has been accomplished: the organs of government, with their powers of will, act for the common good within the framework of the directing idea of the state. The state then possesses an objective individuality. In international law it becomes a Power that is all the more distinctive as the nation adheres to its government; not that the nation manifests active communion with the government, but passively it lets itself be led by the government. A representative government of this kind cannot permit any political liberty, that is, it cannot allow its citizens to participate in the government by election or any other way. It may be aristocratic. Still it will be representative, provided that it holds its course within the directives of the idea of the state.

The state is personified when it has reached the stage of political liberty with the citizens participating in the government. At this stage a second task of interiorization has been accomplished, for within

24. [This concept of the "evidence" furnished by institutions dates from Hauriou's early writings. See his *La science sociale traditionnelle*, pp. 187–196.]

25. [Three pages dealing with the psychology of the human personality have been omitted here.]

the framework of the directing idea, manifestations of communion among the members of the group now occur that intermingle with the decisions of the organs of the representative government (elections, deliberations of assemblies, referendums, etc.). Personification occurs because the manifestations of communion among the members of the group are subjective crises in which the directing idea of the state passes into the subjective state in the minds of its subjects.[26]

We should note that the stage of personification does not destroy the results of the stage of incorporation. Moral personality is added to the objective individuality of the body, but the latter does not disappear. For example, at the stage of incorporation the power of government is a minority power, at the stage of personification it is a majority power; the former is predominately executive, the latter predominately deliberative. But in reality the deliberative power of a majority, which marks the appearance of both political liberty and moral personality, will be combined with the executive power of a minority, which remains the appanage of corporate individuality.

If we transport to individual psychology the distinction of two stages, two states, and two modes of government that we have just analyzed, it will cast some light upon our interior life. There is, surely, in us a *discursive* government and an *intuitive* government. The discursive government directs us with all the din of publicity in the state of consciousness; the intuitive government directs us noiselessly during our sleep and, in a subterranean way, even in the state of consciousness.

Our discursive government is that of the moral person. It is the deliberative power of a majority. It admits of an internal political liberty: the participation of our basic psychical elements in this government. Undoubtedly the idea of this discursive power is to balance and control another power of government. What is this other power of government that needs to be controlled?

At this point the corporate analogy becomes valuable. This intuitive power that needs to be controlled is not of inferior order, it is not the power of instinct. On the contrary, it is a superior and very noble power, of great ability and lofty intelligence; it is the minority power[27] of the best psychical elements of the organism. But this "Council of the Ten"[28] must be controlled by the great publicity of

26. Cf. my work "Liberté politique et personnalité morale de l'État," *Précis de droit constitutionnel,* 1st ed. (Paris, 1923), appendix 2.

27. [*Pouvoir minoritaire.* G.]

28. [A Venetian secret council that had the right of control over the doge and was the instrument of political domination of the Venetian aristocracy.]

the deliberative power because intelligence itself needs to be controlled, the executive needs to be checked by a parliament, sometimes the members of parliament need to be checked by the sergeants at arms.

This restraint of the intuitive intelligence of the elite by the basic psychical elements of the mass gives the final touch to moral responsibility, the supreme characteristic of personality.

B. The reality of the historical development of the state in its movement of incorporation and personification, with the analogies this evolution reveals in the structures of individual and corporate personalities, would undoubtedly suffice to convince anyone that the personification of groups is a natural and spontaneous phenomenon. But the problem of the reality of moral persons is not the precise object of our endeavors here. Our precise object is to explain the duration and continuity realized in institutions by the phenomena of incorporation and grouping; it is therefore to explain the formation of institutions themselves, for, in short, why does an idea of a work or enterprise, in order to be carried out and perpetuated effectively, need to become incarnate in a corporate institution rather than remain in a free state in a given social milieu?

The solution of this fundamental problem can only be reached by distinguishing the stage of incorporation from that of personification and by observing in each the manner in which the continuity of the action of the directing idea is obtained.

1. In the *stage of incorporation* the continuity of the idea and its action has to be purely objective because, by hypothesis, we hold that no manifestations of communion among all the members of the group occur at this stage. The instructive history of the role of custom in the formation of the state, wherein we see the period of incorporation going on for centuries before a moral personality appears, teaches us that the continuity first established is that of a minority power and that it is very precarious.

In France, the first Capetians had kingly power only for life. The privileges that the reigning king had granted, that is, the juridical situations that he had created around his throne and that simply asked to continue, could have been revoked by his successor and had to be confirmed by him. The practice of "association to the throne," which was followed for two centuries, was a first mitigation in that the prince associated in the royal power during his father's lifetime was obliged to confirm the privileges granted by his father, at least for the beneficiaries who had approved his association. When the principle of heredity was accepted and the regular transmission of power assured, the juridical continuity of situations established upon this power was still not assured. Confirmations remained necessary with every change of reign, and they were not always granted because the hereditary prince considered himself an absolute master.

Then the legists[29] conceived the principle of legitimacy, that is, they recognized the idea that the devolution of power at the death of the king did not take place *jure successionis,* but in virtue of a fundamental law of the kingdom. Thus, the prince acceding to the throne received his power from the law together with all the charges with which the throne was customarily burdened. His liberty in dealing with established situations was now like that of a sort of landed heir. This *lex regia* is simply a form taken by the directing idea of the state that thus serves as a support exterior to the power. But, on the other hand, this long and persevering labor of the legists to obtain continuity of power and continuity of the action of power within the institution-kingdom reveals the importance of this action of an organized power for a continuing realization of the directing idea of the state. Only an organized power can create juridical situations and maintain them; and an idea of a work or enterprise cannot be socially realized unless juridical situations are created and maintained in and around it. Owing to the continuity of action of the organized power that results from incorporation, the incorporation of a directing idea in an institution establishes and maintains for this idea an ensemble of juridical situations among which it lives to great advantage.

2. The *stage of personification* opens new perspectives to the continuity of action of the directing idea because this idea here passes to the subjective state in the interior of the institution. First, we might ask how the continuity of a subjective action of the directing idea is established; second, what are the results of this activity.

The continuity of a subjective action of the directing idea within a corporate institution can be established only by proceeding from the initial manifestations of communion among the members of the group. As we have already seen, these manifestations are crises in which the directing idea passes to the subjective state in the conscious wills of the members. But straightaway an objection rears up that seems insurmountable: the manifestations of communion among the members of a corporate group appear to be very discontinuous.

These manifestations are sporadic, periodic at best; a succession of electoral consultations, of deliberations of assemblies, of public

29. [*Légistes.* G.]

meetings. They are but brief moments separated by long intervals, rapid flashes of light that fade away in the night.

For the directing idea to become the subject of the corporate moral person, however, it must be in the subjective state in a continuous manner. The moral subject seems continuous to us in the individual person, despite the way positive psychology analyzes states of consciousness as discontinuous unities, and also despite the interruptions of consciousness brought about by sleep and fainting. We must find an explanation that will enable us to pass from the discontinuous phenomena of states of consciousness to a continuity of the moral subject that is affirmed by our consciousness itself.

This explanation cannot be drawn from the fact that the changing series of states of consciousness would be bound together by the directing idea in its objective state, for such a continuity would not be subjective. But it can be drawn from the action of the power that is involved in all the acts of the conscious will where the directing idea has passed to the subjective state. Retroacting upon the past, just as it anticipates the future, this power throws bridges between the states of consciousness like the couplings thrown between railroad cars to establish the trembling continuity of an express.

In every conscious act of will there is a power involved. At any rate, there is a power involved in the manifestations of communion among the members of a corporate group, whether it be the executive power that intervenes in it or a deliberative, majority power that springs from it. The action of this power can be retroactive in the sense that it can regulate the present consequences of situations created in the past; and it can anticipate the future in the sense that it can regulate situations that will be created in the future. A law, the subjective work of the deliberative, majority power, is defined as a general rule, in the sense that it rules the future forever until it is either abrogated or modified.

When we consider this elasticity of the power that prolongs the effect of a subjective manifestation of will until it joins the next manifestation and that thereby realizes a subjective continuity, we can understand why the Germans were tempted to make the "power of will" (*Willensmacht*) the subject of moral personality. Their thesis is erroneous, however, because the "power of will," despite its elasticity, would not assure the soldering of the various manifestations of will if it were not in the service of a directing idea, for in what direction would it assure the continuity? The continuity in question here is that of a trajectory, and only the directing idea, in becoming subjective itself so as to enter into voluntary acts, can, by its own dynamism, determine the curve of this trajectory. The true subject of moral personality clearly remains, then, the directing idea of the work. The passage of this idea to the subjective state in the minds of the members of the group is assured both by the manifestations of communion and by the projections of the tentacles of the power that binds these manifestations together, a power that is partly in the will of the organs and partly in the directing idea itself.[30]

Thus, at the stage of personification, the corporate institution adds to the continuity of the idea in its objective state that was already realized at the stage of incorporation, the continuity of the same idea in its subjective state. What advantage will the directing idea derive from this new form of continuity? It seems to us that it will derive the threefold advantage of being able to express itself, to assume obligations, and to be responsible.

a. The directing idea of every enterprise tends to express itself subjectively. It expresses itself first in every institution by disciplinary or fundamental rules[31] that it hides within itself, so to speak. No doubt, these juridical rules become objective very quickly, but at the moment of their promulgation, they are really subjective acts of the will of the legislator who speaks in the name of the institution. No doubt, also, and this is more important, juridical rules do not have the precise object of expressing the positive content of the directing idea of the institution. What laws of the state, for example, precisely express the idea of the state? As we have already observed, juridical rules are essentially limits, they merely delineate the contours of things. But indirectly, in this delineation of contours, the positive content of the directing idea can be revealed to a certain degree. This consequence occurs most often in what concerns fundamental and constitutional rules.

But the highest forms under which the directing idea of an institution tends to express itself subjectively are not properly juridical. They are moral or intellectual, or, if they become juridical, they do so as higher principles of law.

30. This analysis of the subjective continuity of corporate personality was suggested to me by a remarkable work of Jacques Chevalier, professor of philosophy at the University of Grenoble, on the *Continu et le discontinu,* which I am most grateful to him for having sent me. It has been republished in the proceedings of the *Aristotelian Society, supplementary volume* IV (London, 1924), pp. 170–196. [It also appears in 15 *Cahiers de la nouvelle journée* (1929), pp. 7–29, a volume itself entitled *Continu et discontinu.* The republished version of Hauriou's article in 23 *Cahiers de la nouvelle journée* adds this note by Hauriou: "It now seems to me that there is an additional element of continuity in the intuitive consciousness of the members of the elite, a consciousness that is not produced by periodic crises but that really is continuous."]

31. [*Par des règles de droit disciplinaire ou statutaire.* G.]

For example, consider the *declarations of rights* that burst forth in America and then in France in the revolutionary crisis at the end of the eighteenth century. These declarations express the heart of the idea of the modern state in what concerns the individualist order that the state has the mission of protecting in society. They have remained "the principles of French public law." Thus, the largely indeterminate essence of the directing idea of the state defines itself progressively.

An even more significant example could be drawn from the history of the Church. The Christian idea, launched in the world to renew it by the redemption, contained, even after the message of Christ, a large part that was indeterminate. It is very instructive to examine, in the work of the progressive determination of the content of the idea and especially in the preservation of the continuity of the idea throughout successive determinations, the part that is due to the fact that the Christian idea has been incorporated in the institution of the Christian Church. This is the history of the Church and of dogma. Here the religious idea determines and expresses itself in articles of creeds, because the foundation of every religious idea is faith. How has the corporate continuity of the Church been able to facili-tate the development of dogma according to the true sense of the directing idea?

Once the Christian idea had been launched in the world, could it not have advanced there by itself, in freedom and in the state of objective truth? The misfortune is that objective ideas are perceived by men only through subjective concepts, so that Revelation, aban-doned to itself, would be in danger of sinking in the ocean of sub-jective interpretations and of heresies. The institution of the Church and the manifestations of communion that occur in a thousand ways within this institution and that are regulated by its government have made it possible to determine a common and official subjective interpretation of revealed truth. This official subjective interpretation constitutes Christian dogma and the Christian creed; it does not ex-haust the content of the objective idea since mysteries remain, but it affords the greatest guarantee of an exact approximation of this content and of the continuity of its action. This amounts to saying that a governmental action balanced by a communion of faithful is a guarantee of continuity in the subjective interpretation of the directing idea which is far superior to anything that free individual interpretation could offer.

b. In the second place, the subjective continuity of the idea allows the institution to assume obligations. It would be beyond our purpose here to enter into the juridical developments of the consequences of the capacity to assume obligations. We merely point out that the subjective personality of the state asserted itself on the occasion of the public debt and that the continuity of this debt could have thus been stretched out forever, opening the way for an impressive solidarity between successive generations. We also note that this capacity to assume obligations has become, for the state, the prerogative of using enormous resources of credit. The same advantages of this capacity to assume obligations can be found in every personified corporate institution.

c. Finally, the subjective continuity of the idea and moral personality bring the corporate institution into the domain of subjective responsibility, which is the counterpart of liberty. Here too juridical developments need to be provided, particularly on the application to the state and to corporate institutions of the principles of responsibility for fault. Despite the interest of these developments, we must confine ourselves to noting the fact that there is such an application.

All in all, the subjective continuity of moral personality completes and greatly enriches the effects of the objective continuity of a constituted body. Personality perfects incorporation. Together they assure in a powerful way the realization of the objective idea in the social milieu.

Now that we have considered the anatomy of corporate institutions, let us have a look at their physiology. Let us watch them live, observe their birth, their existence, and their death, and highlight their juridical reality in all these moments.

I. Corporate institutions are born by a process of foundation. Here we should distinguish between formal foundations and customary foundations. Since the elements of formal foundations are easier to see, we shall stick to them. There are two modalities of them: foundation by the isolated will of a single individual and foundation by the common will of several individuals. The first produces institutions of the category of *establishments* (hospitals, hospices, etc.), in which there is no permanent group of members to perpetuate the foundation, but instead, an affected patrimony.[32] The second ordinarily produces institutions of the category of *corporations* or *universitates*, in which there is a permanent group of members perpetuating the foundation. We just want to consider here the foundations by common will that produce corporate institutions.

32. [*Patrimoine affecté.* G.]

The field of activity of the founding process is larger than most people think because many foundations are obscured by other processes with which they are involved. Every time a contract, agreement, or treaty results in the creation of any sort of constituted body, we should recognize that a founding process has been mingled with the contractual process. If a stock corporation gives birth to a constituted body, it is because its articles, despite their contractual appearance, contain a foundation; for contract, of itself, can only produce obligations between the contracting associates, as in noncommercial societies. When Waldeck-Rousseau proposed his bill for a law on associations, these associations were to be purely contractual without any corporate character. But by the time this bill became the law of July 1, 1901, it had been transformed in that a founding process had slipped into the contract. In international affairs, states are created by treaties, although these treaties are contracts, for the same reason: a founding process is slipped into the contract by the founder-states. (E.g., states created by the peace treaties of 1919 and 1920 by the founding will of the great allied powers.)

The process of foundation by common will is composed of the following elements: (1) the manifestation of common will with the intention of founding; (2) the preparation of founding articles; (3) the de facto organization of the corporate institution; (4) the recognition of its juridical personality.

The manifestation of common will with the intention of founding is by far the most important element. It is the element of consensus and, consequently, the juridical basis, not only of the process of foundation but of the very existence of the constituted body, since this body is explained as a continuing foundation. As we do not aspire to exhaustive juridical explanations here, we shall consider only this element.

The manifestation of common will with the intention of founding implies many declarations of will coming from each of the members of the founding group. These declarations can be expressed simultaneously or separately, at intervals. They contain a common will, which is the will to found a certain work or enterprise, the directing idea of which is known by the founders. These manifestations of will, thus made in communion, form an aggregate of consents that produces the desired juridical effect, that is, it makes the foundation juridical. Two things call for explanation: the juridical effect of foundation and the formation of the aggregate of consents.

The juridical effect of foundation requires an explanation in the foundation by individual will as well as in that by common will.

How can these individual wills produce a social body? There is a surprising disproportion between cause and effect here: the duration of an institution will far surpass the longevity of its founders and their wills. We must understand that the organization into a social body and the duration of an institution are imputable not only to the will of the original founders but also to the special quality of the directing idea of the institution founded. This idea, in proportion as it becomes objectified in the social milieu, will keep on attracting new adherents who will be new founders in that they will continue the foundation. The original founders seem to have done more than they had power to do because they have planted in the social milieu a living idea that, once planted, develops by itself. They have done nothing more than property owners do every day when they plant vines or forests that certainly will outlive them and that will increase in value, owing to the collaboration of the earth, in striking disproportion to their effort. The justification of the individual liberty of foundation is of the same order as that of the right of property: man has the right to make use of the spontaneous collaboration of the social milieu just as he has the right to make use of the collaboration of the earth. The reasons that the state is too often hostile to the liberty of foundation are political: it fears the competition of spontaneous bodies. We do not have space here to pursue this theme.

The formation of the aggregate of consents that assures the con sensus in the foundation by common will, requires a longer explanation. Three factors concur in the formation of this aggregate: (1) unity in the object of the consents; (2) the action of a power; (3) the bond of a procedure.

Unity in the object of the consents is assured by the idea of the work, for this idea is the object and it is one. We have put enough stress upon the force of attraction of this object. This attraction is not sufficient in itself, however, to win a consensus; the manifestations of will with the intention of founding are not necessarily completely voluntary responses to this attractive power of the object. This is the error the German authors fell into when they analyzed the Vereinbarung,[33] which is what we shall call the founding com-

---

33. [The doctrine of the complex act in the form first proposed in Germany by Carl Binding, Die gründung des Norddeutschen Bundes, Festgabe für Dr. Bernhard Windschied (Leipzig, 1888), p. 69, later by Kuntze and Triepel in Germany and by Brondi and Borsi in Italy. See Hauriou, "L'Institution et le droit statutaire," pp. 155–158: "He [Binding] groups under the name of Vereinbarung all the hypotheses in which several declarations of will, identical in content, are necessary to produce a determinate juridical result; collegial pronouncements, decisions of a deliberative body, common exercise by several persons of a legislative or regulatory power (duality of chambers)." On this subject, see Gabriel Roujou de Boubée, Essai sur l'acte juridique collectif (Paris, 1961).]

munion, as an aggregate of parallel consents determined solely by the sameness of object.[34]

This is also the error of the social contract. In this sense Rousseau's social contract was already a *Vereinbarung,* for the contracting parties did not exchange different consents but expressed parallel consents all having the same object.

The truth is that the formation of the aggregate of consents is partly the work of a power and that the *liber volui* in it is strongly shaded by a *coactus volui.*

In the foundation of the state, which recurs under our very eyes with each revision of the constitution, the action of a political power is evident. First, more and more it is the governmental organs that take up the revision; what is more, they do so in obedience to a political majority. In the foundation of corporations, associations, labor unions, a great role is played by the deliberations of a general assembly of members where the opinion of a majority is decisive; unanimity is not required. No doubt, the dissidents can withdraw from the enterprise, but a thousand considerations prevent them from actually doing so, and these considerations show that a moral constraint weighs upon them. Furthermore, it is a fact that, when a private institution is about to be founded, the initiative is taken by one or several ringleaders who bring all sorts of influences to bear, and that many people, for one reason or another, cannot refuse their adherence.

The intervention of the element of power produces a twofold effect here. First, it unifies the consents. Even when the power is manifested by a majority vote of an assembly, we see the defeated minority, constrained and forced, accept the decision of the majority just by the fact that the minority members do not withdraw from the institution. Second, the decisions made have a juridical value in their own right, which is the mark of acts of a power. We must draw the conclusion that the "founding communion" is achieved by power as much as by consensus, and that the founders exercise a power. What is more, the foundation by individual will is very clearly the work of an individual power analogous to the act of a testator. The liberty of foundation is a private power, which partly explains the hesitations of the state in admitting its existence.

To the unity of object, to the action of a power, we must add the bond of a procedure. This is the exterior formal element that enables the founding process, despite its complexity and the succession of its moments, to acquire the unity of a juridical act. The internal

34. [See Hauriou, *Principes de droit public,* 1st ed. (Paris, 1910), p. 158, n. 1.]

elements of unity of object and action of a power do not suffice. Wherever the adherences can be successive, wherever the various formalities can be staggered, as, for example, the payment of a quarter of the subscribed capital, the arrangements for founders' shares in stock corporations, the series of shareholders' meetings, these manifold events must be bound together by a procedure. In the founding period of stock corporations, this procedure is provided for by the law.[35]

Further refinements now solicit our attention. Foundation is a subjective process; corporate institutions are born in a crisis of communion among the founding wills, in the course of which the idea of the work passes to the subjective state in the minds of the adherents. To the developments we have already furnished on this point we must add this: one can conclude from this subjective crisis that the moral personality of an institution is born at the same time as its corporate organization, but it would be going too far to conclude that the moral personality precedes and explains the corporate organization. This is the error the partisans of the ultrasubjectivist system commit when they explain the constitution of the state by the will of the moral person. This is also the error of the commercial lawyers who explain the whole procedure of foundation of stock corporations by the will of the moral person of the incipient corporation.

These errors hide a truth—that the idea of the work or enterprise exists from the beginning as the leaven that causes the dough to rise. But in these beginnings it cannot yet be equipped with a moral personality because it has no organs. In other words, it is begging the question to hold that the organs of a moral person are created by the will of this same person, since, until a moral person has organs, it has no will.

The truth is that the organization of the moral person is created from outside by the founders. The crisis of foundation is subjective *a parte condentium* only. When the moral person is created and the question concerns its government, then the crises of communion occasioned by this government will be subjective *a parte personae conditae*. If it were otherwise, there would be no difference between the constituent power and the governmental power.

II. In every case, the birth of corporate institutions results from a juridical process. Does their daily life involve acts of the same

---

35. In a brochure entitled *L'institution et le droit statutaire,* which I wrote in 1906 and which was very sketchy in all other respects, I dwelt upon the characteristic of "procedural" action that we find in the foundation of institutions. I shall not stress this aspect of the subject any further here. [See *Operation à procedure.* G.]

order? There is no doubt about the answer. All the acts by which a corporate institution conducts its life—deliberations of shareholders' meetings, decisions of the board of directors, decisions of the managing director—have a juridical character. In private institutions this juridical character is drawn from the basic statutes or the contract of association, and any action nullifying these acts must also be statutory or contractual. In public institutions, and notably in the state, the juridical character of the decisions by which the life of the government and that of the administration are conducted is drawn from the power that made them. And in France their nullity is pursued by a perfectly adequate action, which is the appeal for "abuse of power."[36] The analysis of public law is more exact here than that of private law. Everywhere, even in the corporations of private law, decisions are due to a power; they should be identified as manifestations of a power of decision and they should be subject to the possibility of a sort of appeal for abuse of power.

III. Although corporate institutions are made to last for a long time, they are perishable like everything that exists. Sometimes their death is caused by internal reasons—bad organization or deterioration of the idea; often, too, it is caused by external contingencies— the indifference or hostility of the social milieu. This death, in principle, has the shape of a juridical act: either institutions are suppressed by an exterior power, such as the partition of the Polish state in the eighteenth century in virtue of the agreements between Prussia, Austria, and Russia, or the suppression, by the revolutionary laws, of the corporate bodies and communities of the *ancien régime* in France, or the suppression and liquidation of nonauthorized religious congregations in virtue of the law of July 1st, 1901;[37] or institutions dissolve of themselves by a deliberation of the general assembly of their members.

These suppressions or dissolutions have juridical consequences with regard to the liquidation of goods. The corporate idea has made great progress in this area in the last century. At the beginning of the nineteenth century, it was decided without hesitation that the goods of a suppressed corporate institution belonged to the state and this decision was made in virtue of articles 539 and 713 of the *Code civil*[38] concerning the disposition of goods without an owner. At the present time, it is admitted that the articles of an institution can themselves regulate the fate of its goods in case of dissolution or

36. [*Excès de pouvoir*. G.]
37. [I.e., the law of associations. See Hauriou, *Principes de la loi du 9 décembre 1905 sur la separation des églises et de l'Etat* (Paris, 1906).]
38. [See Appendix.]

suppression, or they can confide the regulation of this disposition to a general assembly of members. Thus, institutions are allowed to make a sort of juridical testament.

These brief indications are sufficient for our purpose, which is simply to reveal the profoundly juridical character of the birth, life, and death of institutions, and not to give complete details of each act of the drama.

From these rather complex developments, numerous conclusions could be drawn. We shall limit ourselves to three: the first will concern the basis of continuity in society, in the state, and in law; the second will concern the reality of moral personality and juridical personality; and the third will concern the secondary role of the juridical rule.

I. We must certainly look to corporate institutions, the state among others, and to the process of foundation of these institutions, for the basis of continuity in social affairs. Because they live, and because they assure within and around themselves the continuity of their directing idea and its action, in both an objective and a subjective way, corporate institutions sustain around themselves by their power, all the juridical situations that are to endure. As they themselves owe their existence to a founding process that continues, it is to the amalgam of the three elements of this process—the directing idea, the power, the manifestations of consensual communion, elements that are reunited in the institution itself—that duration and continuity are due. We can set up these equations: (1) continuity equals institution and foundation; (2) institution and foundation equal directing idea, power, and communion.

II. On our way, we have verified the reality of moral persons by observing the naturalness of the phenomena of incorporation and personification in institutions. The import of the first observation was strengthened by a second: while incorporation realizes an objective continuity for the directing idea of an institution, personification, in turn, realizes a subjective continuity of the same idea, and the effects of the latter are added to those of the former. It seems impossible to push further the demonstration of the reality of moral personality. And the reality of juridical personality follows from this same demonstration, for it is simply a retouching and stylization of moral personality, and consequently it rests upon the same basis of reality.

III. Finally, the secondary role of the juridical rule in the juridical system as a whole seems to me to result from these developments.

The significant fact we pointed out above, that juridical rules, in their capacity as directing ideas, do not have enough life to organize around them a corporation of their own in which to express themselves, proves clearly enough that they are inferior to the directing ideas that do have enough life to incorporate themselves.

This striking comparison reminds us of the age-old truth that the important elements in the juridical system are the juridical actors—individuals and corporate institutions—because they are the living and creative personages, as much by the ideas of enterprises that they stand for as by their power to realize them. As for juridical rules, they only stand for ideas of limitation instead of incarnating ideas of enterprise and of creation.

In a world that wishes to live and act while harmonizing action with continuity and duration, corporate institutions, like individuals, are in the front rank because they represent both action and continuity. Juridical rules are in the second because, while they may represent continuity, they do not represent action.

The error that Léon Duguit made when he built his system of objective law was to stake everything on *droit objectif,* to stake everything on the juridical rule. The true objective element of the juridical system is the institution. It does contain a subjective seed that develops by the phenomenon of personification. But the objective element subsists in the corpus of the institution, and this corpus alone, with its directing idea and organized power, is far superior in juridical quality to the juridical rule. Institutions make juridical rules; juridical rules do not make institutions.

Let us keep the import of this article to just proportions. It is entitled "a study in social vitalism" and this is its whole pretension. Directing ideas, which are of a comprehensible objectivity since they pass from one mind to another by their own force of attraction without losing their identity, are the vital principle of social institutions. They communicate to institutions a distinctive life, as separable from that of individuals as ideas themselves are separable from our minds and capable of reacting upon them.

We do not go beyond the verification of this phenomenon. We refrain from investigating whether there is a substantial spiritual reality corresponding to this phenomenal objectivity of ideas. It would certainly be important to know if there is, for certain ideas could have more reality than others and thus could be nearer to the truth. This investigation of substantial reality belongs to the domain of philosophers. Since Georges Dumesnil, whose thesis on the *Rôle des concepts*[39] goes back more than thirty years, some philosophers have been working out the problem of the realism of ideas on new premises. We look to them for the metaphysical construction of this physics[40] that is the vitalism of social institutions.[41]

39. Georges Dumesnil, *Le rôle des concepts* (Paris, 1892). [Hauriou dedicated *La science sociale traditionnelle* to Dumesnil and Gabriel Tarde. Immediately following the passage in that work representing his first discussion of "the institution," Hauriou states, "The first idea for this section was borrowed from the remarkable thesis of G. Dumesnil, *Le rôle des concepts* (p. 187).]
    40. [*Physique*. G.]
    41. Jacques Chevalier, "L'idéalisme français au dix-septieme siecle," *Annales de l'Université de Grenoble* (1923).

MAURICE HAURIOU   Classical Method and Juridical Positivism

Law possesses a form and a matter.[1] Its form is that of rules and juridical acts; its matter is the content of these rules and acts, which in essence relates to human liberty conditioned by social order and justice.

The classical method attaches equal importance to both the form and the matter of law in the sense that it does not think either one can be absorbed in the other. It is dualistic, and simply seeks to strike a balance between form and matter.

Despite certain appearances, it seems that this balance ought to be established by a final predominance of the matter rather than the form. Of course, every new period of the history of law—especially where the law is codified—begins with formalism. At first jurists are preoccupied with the text of the law and the text alone. But as time goes on, a concern for the spirit of the law, which is simply its content of order and justice, victoriously supplants the preoccupation with the letter. This evolution is evident in all the developments of judicial decision,[2] but particularly in questions of illegality or unconstitutionality. However formal may be the notion of what is *illegal* or *unconstitutional* at the outset, it rapidly shifts over to the side of a material interpretation.

There is no better demonstration of this tendency than the history of the formation of *legitimacies*. In the development of their jurisprudence on the judicial control of the constitutionality of laws, American jurists have come to define unconstitutionality as a viola-

ED. NOTE: Translated from Hauriou, *Précis de droit constitutionnel,* 2nd ed. (Paris, 1929), Preface. In this preface to his last treatise, Hauriou puts his legal philosophy in sharpest focus. He contrasts Kelsen's scientific monism, which he identifies chiefly with the formal aspects of law, with his own sociological dualism, which considers as juridical the "matter" (content) of law as well as its "form."

1. [*Une forme et une matiére.* G. Note the special pejorative nuance often given "form" in these first paragraphs—"formal," "formalism.]
2. [*De la jurisprudence.* G.]

tion of substantial principles[3] of a *constitutional legitimacy* drawn
from the *common law,* and even to consider this *legitimacy of the
substance or matter* as above the text of the Constitution and suffic-
ing to declare unconstitutional a formally voted amendment to the
Constitution.[4]

An analogous phenomenon, in which we might see the play of
a sort of legitimacy of civil law, considered as common law, in
relation to administrative law, has occurred in the history of the
jurisprudence of our Conseil d'État. In matters of plenary jurisdiction,[5] where administrative law becomes a *parteien-recht* admitting private parties on an equal footing with the Administration, the
Conseil d'État quickly realized that it had to borrow many rules
from the common law. But, to safeguard the autonomy of administrative law, it imposed upon itself the working principle never to
apply these rules in the formal context given them by such-and-such
an article of the *Code civil.* What the Conseil d'État applies is not
the form but the matter, the content of order and justice. For example, in the judicial elaboration of the important theory of the administrative responsibility of public administrations for damages caused
in the carrying out of their public services, the Conseil d'État carefully avoided formally invoking articles 1382ff. of the *Code civil;*[6] if
it applies the rules of these articles, it does so because of the substantial principles that they contain.

An unprejudiced observation of the evolution of law reveals that
within a given period the emphasis shifts from form to substance
without ever actually sacrificing either element to the other. The
history of law is well aware of this canon, and the evolution of
Roman law reveals it with marked clarity: for example, when unjust
enrichment became the object of a "condictio,"[7] the matter of law
won a singular victory over the form.

3. [*Principes de fond.* G.]
4. [This strangely overconfident statement seems to have been derived from Édouard
Lambert.]
5. [*Plein contentieux.* G.]
6. [*Code civil,* art. 1382ff. See Appendix.]
7. [*Condictio.* See Justinian, Institutes, bk. IV, tit. vi. Of Actions, #15: "Actions in
personam in which a plaintiff claims that the defendant should give or do [something]
are called condictions. The word *condicere* in the old language means to give notice,
but today the word is applied to an action in personam in which the plaintiff claims
that something should be given to him, but incorrectly, for no formal notice is given
as in the old procedure." Trans. in R. W. Lee, *The Elements of Roman Law,* 4th ed.
(London, 1956), p. 461.]

If, at the present time, the predominance of substance over form seems less evident to many, it is because the current crisis of the moral sciences makes it difficult to see clearly the true bases of the legal system that was organized according to this predominance. Consider the system organized by the pandectists which rested upon the material notions of individual rights and the juridical person. This system had an internal order in which its parts were integrated, but upon what fundamental bases did it rest in the classical tradition that has transmitted it to us? We know all the less about it because these bases were merely implicit in the thought of our predecessors, and the contemporary flood of the critical spirit has brusquely swept us away from implicit modes of thought.

But everything that was implicit can be found again and made explicit by a patient work of reconstitution. We do not think we are mistaken in reconstituting, in the following propositions, the essential postulates of the traditional and classical system of the law of individual rights:

1. We must consider history in terms of civilizations.

2. There is an axial civilization superior to all others that is the occidental or Mediterranean civilization. It is on the side of truth and life, for one reason because there is only one truth, and for another, because it has become classical, that is to say human, which proves that humanity has recognized it as the true way.

3. This civilization was engendered by a great current of moral and social ideas, which has not ceased moving in the same direction since the beginning of the sedentary age. In this current of ideas, by successive alluvions, the matter of law has settled around a fundamental conception of social organization, which is that of a fallible and therefore relative individualism. Individualism means liberty; fallible individualism means the recognized necessity of conditioning this liberty by rules of conduct and social sanctions. Finally, individualism means a law that is based upon the juridical person and the individual right and a social order that is based upon individual enterprise.

This reconstitution of the classical thesis can be accepted by every man of mature reason who is free from philosophical prejudices. It was certainly presaged at the end of the last century in France by the promoters of the reform of juridical studies, all of whom were adherents of the school of the moral sciences. This important reform thrust our law schools toward the matter of law by expanding their curricula and transforming them into schools of juridical, politico-economic, and historical sciences. In the past few years the need of getting even closer to this matter of law has continued to concern our law schools, and spontaneously, here and there, they have organized studies in natural law.[8]

But as soon as any movement of ideas shows its colors, it provokes a reaction. At the same time that the science of law was expanding in the direction of its matter, some who were shocked by this expansion retreated toward a new formalism.

This tendency appeared first, in a sporadic fashion, in the *Règle de droit* of the Swiss Ernest Roguin, in the *Droit pur* of the Belgian Edmond Picard, and in the works of the Viennese public lawyer, Georg Jellinek. It took shape by joining forces with both the *formalist*[9] and the *objectivist*[10] systems of the *juridical rule,* and finally, it has just found its most rigorous and adroit formula in Hans Kelsen's system, which presents itself as a "juridical positivism."

Keenly aware that in itself law is irremediably complex, Kelsen directs his effort at simplification solely to the science of law or jurisprudence. His point of departure is that this science of law is not the science of an art indissolubly united to an artistic formulation, but that it is an ordinary science with knowledge alone as its object. Its proper object is the knowledge of the law that has already been created and the organization of the law into a system of purely technical and formal notions, carefully articulated. Any substantial element that is not itself enclosed within a form is excluded from this system.

All the elements foreign to form (moral ideas, preoccupations with social order and justice, natural law, etc.) are relegated to legal practice. Actually, legal practice, under all its modalities—legislative, judicial, administrative—creates law. The union of formal and substantial elements takes place in the work of creation. Science does not have to worry about this union, which it receives ready-made from practice, since by themselves, science and theory create nothing.

Kelsen's theory is clever if you admit his point of departure that jurisprudence is a pure science, and not the science of an art. But this point of departure is false, and no experienced jurist will admit

8. [Such studies appear to have been rare in the curricula of the law schools. Even at Nancy the philosophy of law courses of Geny and Renard were, for the most part, extracurricular.]

9. [Not otherwise identified by Hauriou.]

10. [The objectivistic system of Léon Duguit.]

it. Law is the *ars boni et aequi*,[11] and the science of law serves to illuminate this art.

Let us delve more deeply into Kelsen's theory. We cannot say that it suppresses the matter of law; it restricts itself to subordinating the matter to the form, that is, to recognizing the matter only when it is clothed in a form. At first sight, this method would not seem to make an appreciable change in the aspect of contemporary law, since so many formal rules have been established. However, it would foster more changes than you might believe, and we shall try to summarize them:

1. The jurist would be concerned only with the law already in existence; the perspectives of the creation of law would be closed to him. Consequently, his arguments could no longer be drawn from the considerations of order, justice, or morality that abound in the perspective of the *lex ferenda*.

2. Even in his commentary on the *lex lata* the jurist could only use arguments drawn from rules that have been formulated into positive laws: consequently, there would be no natural law, no natural obligation, no principle of justice.

This gap is so serious that Kelsen tries to mask it by the supposition of a *hypothetical constitution*,[12] which would include essential principles as yet unformulated. But this supposition presents a new dilemma: either the judge would not apply this hypothetical constitution, and then it would be nothing, or he would apply it, and then what would become of the logic of the system?—for this hypothetical constitution would be juridical matter without a form. But there is still another dodge. This hypothetical constitution would become a legislative program and would be quickly transformed into a positive constitution that would enumerate cases of unconstitutionality, illegality, abuse of power, etc., in other words, that would attempt to formulate the inexpressible.

3. In the system of law that this theory would teach, the traditional basis of law—individual rights and juridical personality—would be abandoned and replaced by the juridical rule (*règle de droit*) and juridical acts. The logic of the system would impose this substitution.

11. [See Hauriou, "L'ordre social, la justice et le droit," *Revue trimestrielle de droit civil* (1927), reprinted in 23 *Cahiers de la nouvelle journée* (1933), p. 48: "Justice has for its end the *aequum et bonum* of the jurisconsult Paul; it seeks to establish among men, in social relations as well as in individual transactions, the greatest equality possible in view of the Good."]

12. [Cf. the description of Kelsen's *grundnorm* in his *General Theory of Law and State* (Cambridge, 1945), pp. 395–396, and in *The Pure Theory of Law* (Berkeley, 1967), pp. 193–221.]

For the traditional basis is drawn from the matter of law,[13] its suggested replacement from the form; and we should have to pass from one pole to the other. It is rather like saying that after having turned toward the north pole since time immemorial, the magnetic needle is now going to turn toward the south pole. But we live in an age when such affirmations are not very surprising. And yet the welfare of society is at stake, for to abandon the individualist foundation of law is inevitably to abandon the individualist foundation of society.

4. Of course, the habits of mind that jurists acquire in using this purely formal science of law would reach into legal practice and notably into the judicial process; for it all hangs together. The separation that Kelsen conceives between the science and the practice of law is illusory, especially when it comes to judicial practice. We should soon see modifications in our system of evidence and, little by little, a return to strictly legal evidence. And why not? If the juridical rule is worthless unless enveloped in a legal form, why would evidence be worth anything if it were not clothed in a legal form? One cannot transfer with impunity the whole criterion of juridical value from the substantial to the formal. No more rules of justice, no more moral evidence! Anyway, the formalists complain, in criminal matters does not the moral evaluation of culpability by juries often lead to scandal? And then, this new approach would be so convenient, the protective forms would make life so easy for the judge! Behind these formalist systems lies an impetus that must not be concealed, an impetus of the instinct of the least effort. *Ecce iterum* Brid'oison: "the fo-orm, gentlemen, the fo-orm!"[14]

5. There is something still more disastrous: this jurisprudence, new style, would abdicate all concern for liberty and would fling itself toward every kind of servitude. This, not only because its exclusive preoccupation with created law would lead it to accept the *fait accompli* and because it would have to forego any criticism of laws that was not founded upon purely technical reasons, but also because in banishing morality, it also banishes liberty.[15] This sort of jurisprudence, since it has nothing to do with the creation of law (*droit*), would have no need for the liberty of individuals. If individual

13. [I.e., in Hauriou's view, there is an objective basis both to *droits subjectifs* and to juridical personality.]
14. [Brid'oison, a character in Beaumarchais' *Mariage de Figaro*, was a judge who was attached, above all, to the "fo-orme."]
15. [Hauriou later asserts that with Kelsen, "The primacy of liberty is replaced by that of order and authority." Hauriou, *Droit constitutionnel,* 2nd ed., p. 11.]

liberty does not create law, by a sort of spontaneous transposition of moral conduct, it is nothing.

This sacrifice of liberty is already perceptible in Kelsen's own presentation of his doctrine. But in the monograph of his disciple, Charles Eisenmann, on *Constitutional Justice and the High Court of Austria,*[16] it is exposed by a very significant detail: the denial of the right *to resist oppression,* which in the form of the right to a *fair hearing* constitutes a minimum of individual juridical autonomy unanimously admitted up to now by theologians, moralists, and jurists.

The exclusive preoccupation with a formal technical order and the elimination of morality and justice ally the Kelsenian error with the Maurrasian heresy. Maurras,[17] in the name of the ecclesiastical order, denounces the venom of the Gospel; Kelsen, in the name of the technical juridical order, denounces the venom of justice. These elements are disconcerting!

There you have the supreme prejudice, the prejudice of monism; there, also, the renunciation of classical humility. Classical thought, while appreciating the value of unity, knows how to bow down before the limits of human thought. The dualism of form and matter, irreducible for four thousand years of philosophy, is one of these limits for all those who are concerned with reality. But scientific pride prefers to ride upon a chimera. A monism of energy and form has been obstinately, and futilely, sought in the sciences for a century. Even in ultramodern physics, that of ions and radiations, matter resists, and the most passionate energists are forced to confess that the phenomenon of the quanta is still disclosing its existence.

16. [Paris, 1928. This volume has a preface by Kelsen. Charles Eisenmann is still a professor at the Faculté de Droit of the University of Paris.]

17. [Charles Maurras (1868–1952). Monarchist and opponent of democratic ideas, he was "head" (Maurice Pujo) of the rightist movement Action Française, and editor of the daily newspaper of that name from 1908. He was tried and convicted at Lyon in 1945 for communications with the enemy, and spent some time in prison. See Roy Pierce, *Contemporary French Political Thought* (London, 1966), pp. 11–23.]

MAURICE HAURIOU   The Social Order: The Formal

Organization of the Social Order Conceived as a

System Endowed with a Slow and Uniform

Movement. Institutions.

The social order appears to us to be a system endowed with a slow
and uniform movement.[1] An established social order, solicited by
the contrary appeals of forces of conservation and of change, inevitably goes over to the side of transformation, because the forces
of change are more active than those of conservation, and what is
more, because all life is in continual movement, so that social life
cannot escape the law of movement.

In order to understand the conditions of the *slow and uniform
movement* of an ordered social system, it will be useful for us to
observe the evolution of living organisms. There is no doubt that
these organisms are perpetually undergoing transformations that
affect all their parts and yet have respect for their form. Of course,
as these living organisms grow up from infancy to maturity and then
come to the decline of old age, the forms themselves undergo modifications; but the intensity of such modifications is not comparable
to the intensity of the molecular changes that the tissues undergo.

ED. NOTE: Translated from Hauriou, *Précis de droit constitutionnel,* 2nd ed. (Paris,
1929), pp. 71-77. In this brief analysis of the organization of the social order, taken
from Hauriou's last work, are expressed several of his fundamental concepts: the
reality of ideas, the place of balances in social organization, and the role of institutions.
The closing section, comparing the social order to an army column on the march,
is one of Hauriou's most enduring passages; it harks back, in this precise form, to
his *Le point de vue de l'ordre et de l'équilibre* (Toulouse, 1909), pp. 9-10.

1. [Earlier in this work (p. 34) Hauriou defined the social order as "An organization
of society on certain bases that is designed to give the best assurance of the subsistence
of the group and of the accomplishment of the enterprise of its civilization, and that
is also designed to obtain, by means of appropriate balances, the slow and uniform
movement of the ensemble of its social situations and relationships."]

In other words, the matter[2] of organisms is renewed by the circulatory flow with an extreme rapidity, while the forms remain relatively stable. Clearly then, if these living beings constitute systems that undergo transformations while remaining ordered, that is, while conserving their form, it is because they are organisms. And we must define organism as a system whose form subsists despite the continual renewal of its matter, *even when this form is or appears to be constituted only by balances of the matter itself and by a government.*

Groups or social systems will conduct themselves like living organisms provided they, like organisms, are organized. We shall, then, see social organisms traversing centuries even though their human matter and a great part of the social situations they contain have been renewed: because they have a government and because their essential balances have been maintained, their forms have survived. The problem to be studied, then, is the problem of social organization.

1. *Organization and institutions as conditions of duration of a social order endowed with a slow and uniform movement.* The sociologist who observes the phenomenon of social organization has an advantage over the physiologist who observes it in living organisms: if there are any elements of a psychical nature in social organization, they will fall under his observation, and we are going to see that there is no shortage of them.

First of all we must dispel a prevalent error: the explanation of social organization by the division of labor or by the differentiation of functions understood in the economic sense of the law of the least effort. Thirty years ago this explanation was considered valid for living organisms; I think it has been renounced. In any case, when it comes to social organization, the differentiation of organs and functions in the economic sense is a late phenomenon, not a primary one. The primary phenomena are of the political order: the appearance of a directing or founding center, of governmental organs, of governmental balances, and finally, of popular consent.

1. The role of the directing or founding center is to implant an idea in the social milieu: the idea of the organization to be created, considered as an enterprise to be realized. It entails a plan for this organization, and therefore contains in potency the form of this plan.[3]

2. [*Matière.* G.]
3. A directive center presides at the evolution of the cell and also at the evolution of the egg; I leave it to the biologists to discover if this center stands for an idea.

2. Organs appear that are to govern the organization, because the social organism has a government (just like the living organism). Either these organs have been prepared by the founding center, or they have spontaneously enlisted in the service of the enterprise. At the beginning there may be just one organ, and if this is the case, the government risks being despotic.

But throughout the steady stream of transformations, this government will maintain the order necessary for the subsistence of the organism's general form. Moreover, it governs in the name of the already created organization.

The appearance of the founding center and the governmental organs constitutes, if you like, a differentiation between governors and governed, but this differentiation is political in nature and has nothing to do with the division of labor.

3. A certain perfection of the governmental organization of the enterprise contributes powerfully in maintaining its form by creating balances: this perfection is the separation of organs and of powers (not the separation of functions). For example, the duality of magistracies in the Roman republic, even with *par potestas*,[4] created a balance within the form of the magistracies that helped to make this form endure. The same thing holds true for the duality of chambers in the parliamentary regime of modern nations. This balance enables the parliamentary form to endure by counteracting parliamentary abuses of power.

These balances of organs and powers subject the government of an institution to its function, that is, to realization of the enterprise as it is comprised in the directing idea. Only then do differentiations of functions appear; but not to any great extent, for politically speaking, an overdone specialization of functions is a bad thing.

4. Finally, as the organization completes and perfects itself by its internal balances, it becomes an object of approval, not only for the men it contains but also for all those who live within the social milieu. This approval bears upon the organization of the enterprise and especially upon the idea of the enterprise, which is the soul of the organization. At this point, which occurs rather early, the social organization becomes a *customary institution,* and its form is maintained not only by the action of the internal idea, not only by the action of its government, but also by the power of popular consent.

If we put together these characteristics of the *instituted social*

4. [*Potestas* in Roman law referred to the power of magistrates, all the rights and duties affecting a particular magistracy. Colleagues in a magisterial office had equal power (*par potestas*).]

organization, which is also the *incorporated institution,* we come to the following definition: A social organization becomes durable, that is, able to conserve its specific form despite the continual re- newal of the human matter it contains, when it is *instituted,* that is, when (1) the directing idea that is in it from the moment of its foundation has succeeded in subordinating to itself the governmental power, owing to balances of organs and of power, and (2) this system of ideas and balances has been ratified in its form by the consent of the members of the institution and of the social milieu as well.

To sum up, *the form of the institution, which is its durable element, consists in a system of balances of powers and of consents con- structed around an idea.*[5]

From this point of view, ideas not only shape the world, they sustain it and enable it to endure. Beside the currents of ideas and of opinion, which are often forms of change, we find ideas of enter- prises, which are forces of duration.

Institutions rest so much upon the force of ideas that certain peoples and races are incapable of possessing institutions because they are too insensitive to ideas. One can see that the institution of the state, which is fundamental in the sedentary age,[6] is taken seri- ously only by certain races, and that, transported to certain others, it becomes a mere facade behind which the traditions of personal power or even organizations of clans and factions continue to flourish. Some peoples are incapable of realizing the idea of the public enterprise.[7]

Among peoples who are most sensitive to the action of ideas, the institution of the state is the model for a vast social organization that permits numerous human groups to abandon themselves to the passage of time in confidence that changes in their social condition will be sufficiently slow and uniform. Especially in the great modern states with developed administrative regimes, the populations are solidly framed in by a strong administrative hierarchy. Within the framework of civil life, education, military service, public elections,

5. On this theory of the incorporated institution that I have been building since 1906, see my article in the *Cahiers de la nouvelle journée* (1925) [translated above]. The present analysis clarifies the role played by the diverse elements of the form of the institution in its duration (*durée*).

6. ["There have been two successive human varieties, nomadic man and sedentary man, *homo vagus* and *homo manens.* Civilization and history begin with sedentary man, and so do most of the institutions that are familiar to us; for example, from the political point of view, the state regime, from the social point of view, private property in land and individualistic juridical commerce." Hauriou, "L'ordre social, la justice et le droit," 23 *Cahiers de la nouvelle journée,* p. 51.]

7. [*La chose publique.* G.]

taxes, and the innumerable public services in which he may be involved, the citizen is nothing more than a number—registered and interchangeable, and above all, obligated to follow the movement of the cadre. And yet the framework of the administrative state did not seem to be sufficient: the citizens added to it, a half-century ago, the framework of professional associations, which in time will probably be amalgamated with the administrative organization.

Of course, the slow and uniform movement of this framework does not proceed without modifications. It is not only the human matter that passes away and is renewed, but also the framework itself: new parts are added, like the professional associations; others are destroyed, like religious congregations; still others are transformed, as was higher education, for example, by the creation of universities, and as certain public services will be, by industrialization. But these modifications come about slowly and cautiously; they affect only a small number of forms. They call to mind those railroad repairs that do not interrupt the traffic. Social life is rarely bothered by them. Moreover, one of the great responsibilities of government is to keep careful watch over modifications in forms and institutions. From this point of view, there is a government of institutions rather than a government of men,[8] because institutions are more important than men to the duration of the social order.

All in all, the social order, in its ordered movement with its system of institutions and its government, traverses the unknown regions of time in the same way that an army in column advances into an enemy country.[9] States are civil armies on the move which, like the *agmen*,[10] must carefully keep to their marching order. This presents some evident advantages.

1. Order in the troop on the march provides against the dangers of the route; it avoids surprises, ambushes, accidents, catastrophes. A people with a sense of evolving order avoids the risks of revolutions, the precipitous plunges into the unknown that they inspire, the reactions that almost inevitably follow upon them; such a people teaches itself to march systematically in order to travel safely.

2. Order in the march enables the troop to go further and to march longer. Peoples, just like individuals, have only a certain dose of

8. [Cf. the "government of laws, not of men," of the Massachusetts constitution of 1780.]

9. [Although this passage, with its emphasis on time and duration, recalls Bergson (who was so influential in French thought of the twenties), it actually goes back, in almost this precise form, to Hauriou's early writings. See *Principes de droit public,* 1st ed. (Paris, 1910), pp. 7–9; 2nd ed. (Paris, 1916), pp. 15–17.]

10. [I.e., the Roman marching column.]

energy, of love of innovation, and of will to realize this innovation; if this allotment of energy is not used with economy, after a period of rapid—too rapid—progress, a need for rest at any price settles in and a period of torpor is to be feared.

3. Order in the march of a troop prevents the desertions of stragglers, the dislocations that give rise to ardor and impatience in some, torpor and resistance in others; it makes possible the organization of functions.

4. Order in the march enables the troop to choose a direction, to glean information, to reflect, not to wander completely at random.

5. Finally, order in the march is not just any random order; it obeys certain necessities. First of all, it must have a chief[11] to maintain the cohesion of the troop, to provide for its functions, and to determine its direction. The necessity of a chief does not appear evident in an immobile state of things; but it is imperative where there is march and movement: every caravan has its guide, every ship its pilot.

Then there are rules. For the march of armies ages of experience have worked out a whole strategy. There is also a strategy in the movement of social transformations; now they march and now they rest, they set up camp for a more or less extensive time, then they set out again.

This order in the social troop on the march is what we call stability. We are certainly not overexacting as to the stability of our institutions. We are no longer under the illusion that this stability is a kind of immobility; we are better informed and more realistic. We know that nothing is immobile, that everything changes. It suffices for us that the transformations are slow and uniform. This slowness and this uniformity allow us to enjoy the present moment without any great shocks and even to make those relatively short-term calculations that characterize life. In other words, this sort of stability is closely related to liberty as we understand it, a liberty of enterprise; this stability is not divorced from action, nor from an action that needs to develop in order to attain a certain result; for an enterprise can neither attain its end nor develop if the milieu is too unstable—all foresight becomes impossible, and even all initiative[12] is stifled. It is a fact of experience that unstable political regimes discourage enterprises and make liberties virtually useless.

Practical liberty is won between two extremes: it must have order

11. [Cf. the expression "chief of state."]
12. [Élan. See Henri Bergson, L'évolution créatrice (Paris, 1907; 18th ed., Paris, 1966), pp. 254–258.]

and stability, and it must not have too much; it must have a slow and uniform movement.

II. *Transition to the study of the state.* This trip through time[13] is a perspective we should not abandon when we study the state. The state is not only order in space[14] (although there may be great emphasis on this phase of its organization); it is also order in time. It is the perfect organization of this slow, regular, uniform movement of the ensemble of social situations and relations, which gives us the impression of stability.

And because the state must be considered from the aspect of duration, it can only be understood under the figure of an incorporated institution. The bond of the state is an institutional bond; it is this customary consent spontaneously given by subjects to institutions just as they give it to juridical rules. The foundation and life of the state are juridical for the same reason that the foundation and life of every incorporated institution are juridical.

But the state far excels similar institutions, not only because of its perfect formal structure, but because it puts to advantage the individualist order that it contains.

13. [*Durée.* For Bergson's notion of "durée," see *L'évolution créatrice*, pp. 1–11: "The more we plumb the depths of the nature of time (*temps*) the more we understand that duration (*durée*) signifies invention, creation of forms, continuous elaboration of the absolutely new" (at p, 11). See also Bergson, *Durée et simultanéité à propos de la théorie d'Einstein* (Paris, 1922; 7th ed., 1968).]

14. [For the emphasis on social space, Hauriou goes back to Auguste Comte, *Synthèse subjective* (Paris, 1856). See Hauriou, *La science sociale traditionnelle* (Paris, 1896), pp. 261–293.]

Maurice Hauriou   by Marcel Waline

If you wanted to make a very general comparison of Léon Duguit's work[1] and Hauriou's, you might portray Duguit's by a straight line, for it is the work of a *logician* who proceeds by *rational deductions,* borrowing a syllogistic form to move, by way of a simple and apparently rigorous system, from premises to *determined* conclusions that, given the premises, are forseeable in advance. In the same way, knowing the source of a river and the contours of the land through which it flows, you might trace its course without a map. The schema of Hauriou's work would be entirely different and would appear under the form of a sprawling vine, which makes a synthetic exposition of it a much more difficult task.

Hauriou is dominated by a real aversion to monism and to simple or simplistic systems that are inspired by a single directing idea. His fundamental postulate seems to be quite the contrary, that the data of the social sciences are complex and consist in the conflicts of numerous antagonistic forces, among which provisional balances are established at every turn. Positive law, at a given moment, is the ratification of these balances; but the jurist must not be under any illusion; the balances are the result of compromise and not the application of a preconceived and a priori plan. Law, then, is imperfect, because it is the product of a transaction. It is like an armistice, a provisional peace in which diverse, conflicting social forces consent to suspend hostilities on the basis of a "cease fire agreement" that each will maintain the positions conquered. So, law will not satisfy

---

ED. NOTE: Translated from Marcel Waline, "Les idées maîtresses de deux grands publicistes français: Léon Duguit et Maurice Hauriou," Part II: "Maurice Hauriou," *L'année politique française et étrangère,* no. 17 (June 1930), pp. 39–63. Professor Waline, of the Faculté de Droit of Paris, is dean of French writers on administrative law. His authoritative *Droit administratif,* 9th ed., was published by Sirey in 1963. One of his earliest studies was a two-part article written on the occasion of the deaths of Léon Duguit and Maurice Hauriou. In the opinion of many leading French jurists this section on Hauriou remains the outstanding general critique of his work.

1. [The part of Waline's study devoted to Duguit appeared in *L'année politique,* no. 16 (December 1929).]

the mind like a beautiful, harmonious system; but it has the immense advantage of realizing, for a time, peace and balance. Logic and syllogisms are not good counselors for the legal theorist, but history and the social sciences are.

Far more than a logician, Hauriou is an observer of social facts and, especially, a historian. For example, in two characteristically pithy phrases he writes: "Logically, the self-limitation of the state appears as an absurdity. Historically, it is the constitutional truth."[2] History thus contradicts logic, and it is history we must follow if we do not want to lose contact with reality; unless it rests upon historical bases, the most beautiful logical reasoning is nothing more than mental gymnastics.

Rejection of monism; distrust of logic; recognition of the capital importance of observing social facts by historical methods, an observation that reveals the very marked complexity of these facts and that reveals law as the result of a play of forces, of a social dynamism: these seem to me to sum up Hauriou's fundamental conception. Moreover, the question of monism and pluralism clearly appears to be of primordial importance in the major problem of philosophy, that of knowledge. It is not surprising, then, that the position taken upon such an essential point has dominated the entire work of a jurist so imbued as Hauriou with the importance of philosophy.

After citing a few texts that establish our author's position with regard to monism, I shall point out the principal consequences of his pluralism, first for his criticism of the normativist doctrines of Duguit and Kelsen, then as to his own doctrines upon general public law and administrative law. But it is rather delicate to establish a line of demarcation in Hauriou's work between the critical part and the constructive part, for even his criticism of the normativists is essentially constructive. Ordinarily a critic begins with a negative effort, attacking what seems to have been established; then he tries—or perhaps he does not try—to substitute a new system for the one he denounces. Nothing of the sort with Hauriou; his criticism is not a demolition, for it consists in reproaching the normativists for having seen only one aspect of reality and for having neglected the others. He indicates the indispensable complement at the very same time that he points out the lacunae. For this reason, the critical part of his work is intimately tied in with the positive part; nevertheless, I shall distinguish them insofar as possible for the sake of clarity in studying them. I shall close by a few remarks on Hauriou's expository procedures and his method.

2. Hauriou, *Précis de droit constitutionnel,* 2nd ed. (Paris, 1929) p. 101.

HAURIOU AGAINST MONISM

Philosophical monism is now in full decline; it has been for more than twenty years. The labors of Antoine-Augustin Cournot, of Henri Poincaré, and chiefly of Henri Bergson have dealt it blows that seem to have been decisive.[3] Just recently Vialleton's book on *L'origine des êtres vivants*[4] has completed the criticism from a biological point of view. Hauriou, who has always kept in the current of the philosophical movement and who seems to have been particularly influenced by Bergson, was very quickly won over to pluralistic ideas. As early as 1898, in his *Leçons sur le mouvement social*, he writes: "The doctrine of evolution is preoccupied with reducing to unity all the entities of the world. We have no such preoccupation. On the contrary, we proclaim the distinct qualitative reality of social facts" (p. 5). He reproaches Herbert Spencer for his monism (p. 117). This attitude remains with him throughout the diverse epochs of his life: in 1902, in an article in the *Revue du droit public* on the first important work of Duguit, he rises up against monism, which he defines in the following proposition: "All things must proceed from one another in the unfolding of a single series, and up to a certain point, they must be mingled with one another." He sees an error here "because, in reality, we have to make a place for the fact of conflicts, which reveals an irreducible fundament of differences in things." He believes in the complexity of phenomena, and especially of social phenomena. Each social phenomenon is the result of a combination of many factors of very diverse origins, of a synthesis in which the conflicts of antagonistic forces are resolved: "Society is a form of life wherein the differences and contradictions of men are actually reconciled; it is a peace that is progressively realized in the midst of perpetual conflicts; it is a synthesis; it is established upon combinations of opinions and ideas, just as life is dependent upon chemical combinations . . . There is a double constant current."[5]

He returns to this idea in 1911[6] and especially criticizes the form of monism he calls "philosophical belief (in) unilinear determinism, that is . . . belief in an interrelation of all natural phenomena in a single series." What does he denounce in this unilinear determinism? Notably this: "It aims at finding the explanation of a fact in a single antecedent, while in reality several antecedent facts almost always

3. See Georges Sorel, *De l'utilité du pragmatisme* (Paris, 1928).
4. [Louis Vialleton, *L'origine des êtres vivants, l'illusion transformiste* (Paris, 1929).]
5. Review (in collaboration with Achille Mestre) in *L'état, le droit objectif et la loi positive*, in *Revue du droit public*, vol. 17, pp. 346ff, esp. pp. 357 and 358.
6. Hauriou, *Les idées de M. Duguit* (Toulouse, 1911), pp. 15ff. This article is absolutely fundamental.

combine to cause a consequent fact." In 1928 again, a few months before his death, he reproaches Kelsen for "the supreme prejudice, the prejudice of monism."[7]

CRITICISM OF NORMATIVISM FROM THE PLURALISTIC POINT OF VIEW

With this attitude toward monism, Duguit's system, which is simply a "unilinear series," would be bound to provoke Hauriou's criticism. Not that Hauriou is any less concerned than Duguit with limiting the arbitrariness of rulers by a subordination of the state to law.[8] But he refuses to look for the solution of this problem, or any problem, in a single direction, that is, for the question at hand, in the direction of the juridical rule. This attitude would be too monistic. He criticizes in Duguit "that solidarity which, in evolving, produces the juridical rule, which produces positive law."[9] He thinks that, if all social phenomena have multiple causes, it would be quite extraordinary if, unlike all the others, law had a single origin (the consciousness of social solidarity), and a single process of formation (that of the juridical rule). So he tries to find out first if law does not have other modes of development; second, he asks if law is only a system of norms, or if, alongside norms, we must not leave a large place, a *larger* place, for institutions and even, more simply still, for the spontaneous power of action of individuals; he wants to know if these elements are not also moderators of power, which the normativist doctrines had neglected. And because Hauriou mistrusts monism, he naturally arrives at the conclusion that, in Geny's phrase, "all law is not encrusted in legality";[10] that, consequently, the problem of law is not, as Duguit had thought, simply that of the juridical rule. Duguit is without doubt "well-intentioned" in trying to subordinate the positive legislator to the juridical rule, this new Minerva that had risen entirely armed from the mass of individual consciences, Hauriou says, but this subordination is both dangerous and insufficient: dangerous, because the juridical rule is, so to speak, a

7. *Droit constitutionnel,* 2nd ed., p. xi.
8. He says, concerning the question of the self-limitation of the state and of the realization of juridical state (*L'état de droit*), "that in a certain sense it is the only question in public law." Hauriou, *Principes de droit public,* 1st ed. (Paris, 1910), p. 106.
9. Review of Duguit in *Revue du droit public,* p. 353.
10. Hauriou, "Police juridique et fond du droit," *Revue trimestrielle* (1926), reprinted in 23 *Cahiers de la nouvelle journée* (1933), pp. 152ff.

two-edged sword, and if one deifies it, it can cover any abuse; insufficient, because before putting the juridical rule in the forefront under its apparently habitual form of legislation, prudence urges us at least to find out if there are not other sources of law that may afford a better counterweight to legislative arbitrariness.

THE DANGERS TO POLITICAL LIBERTIES IN DUGUIT'S
DEFINITION OF THE JURIDICAL RULE

On the first point, Hauriou states that in Duguit's system undoubtedly everything the rulers[11] attempt against the juridical rule will be condemned—and this on condition that one admits his demonstration of the inferiority of the state to law,[12] which is subject to reservations, as we have seen—but conversely, everything the rulers do in conformity with this rule will be perfect, correct. This rule is recognized in practice, as I have indicated in my study on Duguit, when the mass of individual consciences regard it as favorable to the development of social solidarity and as conforming with justice. Then what will be decided if the mass of individuals is not unanimous on this point? This question is important, for we all know too well that in reality there is no rule that does not produce dissenters, nonconformists. In this case, it will be necessary either to confess that for want of unanimity there is no law, or to content oneself with a simple majority. The practical criterion of the juridical rule in Duguit's system will then ultimately be—whatever he might have said or thought it to be—the will of the majority; so that the subordination of the rulers to law is simply their submission to the will of the majority. Duguit thus turns out to be a theorist of democracy, just like Rousseau; but he does not succeed in offering any practically efficacious solution to the problem of the limitation of governmental or legislative arbitrariness, as he would have liked. Actually, he checks this arbitrariness only when it is contrary to the will of the mass, that is, when it is really no longer dangerous in our democratic age, when nothing can be done against public opinion. But he rather strengthens it, by affirming its conformity with law, when it is in complicity with an oppressive majority. Minorities are thus totally sacrificed in his system.

11. [In striking at the traditional notions of "state" and "public power," Duguit stressed that there were simply individuals who ruled (*les gouvernants*), and others who were ruled (*les gouvernés*). See Léon Duguit, *Manuel de droit constitutionnel*, 2nd ed. (Paris, 1911), pp. 29–30, 126ff.]

12. ["Law" for Duguit is *droit objectif*. See G.]

SOURCES OF LAW OTHER THAN LEGISLATION

The second point (Does legality exhaust all of law?) is the object of Hauriou's researches upon the directive and the standard, and upon police justice as opposed to the substance of law. These researches constitute a study of the *customary formation of law*.

Directives and standards. According to Hauriou, jurisprudential or even administrative directives contribute to the formation of law, and counterbalance the influence of the legislator properly so-called, thus realizing an effective limitation of his power, if we are to believe Montesquieu's celebrated dictum: "power checks power."

To grasp what Hauriou means by "directive," we must first understand his definition of *"standard": every argument, every consideration by which a judge or an administrator habitually resolves to settle cases in a certain way,* that is, to make a certain type of decision. *The directive is an application of the standard* and *the solution-type* to which the standard has led the judge or the administrator. Notable among directives are jurisprudential principles[13] and administrative practices.

We can see from these definitions that if a certain directive is used a certain number of times, it tends to become a true rule of customary law, competing with the written law; all praetorian law (and not only that of Roman law but also that of French administrative law) has no other origin. Consequently, this directive will be a means of balancing the legislative power and correcting its abuses, a means of achieving the result Duguit was looking for (limitation of the arbitrariness of the government); at the same time it will "moralize" law. For when an administrator "makes it a rule" always to resolve a certain type of case in a certain way (and "to make it a rule" is the very essence of the directive), he has limited his own power, his *arbitrium;* in this way he enables those subject to his power to benefit by the classical advantages attributed to the generality of the written law (*loi*). Incontestably, the directive is a check upon the excesses of the powerful, a check that is purely moral and spontaneous at the outset, but which tends to become juridical (*du droit*). In Hauriou's thought, it seems, a good many juridical rules originally derive from a spontaneous submission by those who had a discretionary power to a rule of moral origin. This submission is the rehabilitation (from a certain point of view) of regulatory decisions: a

13. [A court decision that purports (or seems) to establish a jurisprudential principle of significance is referred to by French jurists as a *décision de principe*. Cf. a "leading case" in the common law.]

sovereign authority decides to replace the reign of its own fancy and good pleasure by a rule of conduct (therefore, a moral rule) that it imposes upon itself out of benevolence; from then on, this moral rule is launched upon its way to become, more or less rapidly, a juridical rule. In this fashion the law is being constantly renewed—and independently of any legislative intervention—by the contributions of moral elements.[14]

Of course, doubt may be easily cast upon the efficacy of this limitation of power by likening it to the celebrated self-limitation of Jellinek. Duguit, in particular, writes that "a voluntary limitation is not a limitation," that "a voluntary subordination is not a subordination,"[15] and consequently denies that there is any interest at all in the study of the directive and the standard. I think that Duguit, who tries to observe facts, to be "realistic," sins this time by a want of observation. We know very well that subordination to law (*loi*) is *in practice* voluntary; that fear of the policeman plays no great role in it; that the mass of citizens need only revolt against the laws or against any one law, and the whole marshalcy of France will be incapable of having their authority respected, as every revolution proves besides.

Then would you claim that the habitual subordination of citizens to the law has no value because it is voluntary? Certainly the directive has a value here as a moderator of arbitrariness, a value all the greater because it is only the expression of the force of limitation of arbitrariness that is natural to the institution.

The institution. Hauriou reproaches the objectivists for not admitting any self-limitation of power.[16] He admits there is none "under the form of a resolution taken *in petto*," but insists there is one "under the form of the creation of institutions." In other words, to those who claim that the directive has no value at all as a limitation of power, under the pretext that one can always change one's directives without having to account to anyone for it, Hauriou replies with the following reasoning. In order to have authority, the one who claims to command must do so in the name of an institution. Conse-

14. See on all these points, Hauriou, "Police juridique et fond du droit." One should note well that directive and standard (1) are not rules of law (p. 11), and (2) are nevertheless juridical (*de droit*) (p. 12). There is no clearer way of saying that the juridical rule does not exhaust the whole of law. See also Hauriou, "De la répétition des précédents judiciaries à la règle de droit coutumière," 15 *Cahiers de la nouvelle journée* (1929), pp. 109–115.

15. Duguit, *Traité de droit constitutionnel*, 3rd ed. (Paris, 1927), I, 105, 645.

16. "Le pouvoir, l'ordre, la liberté et les erreurs des systemes objectivistes," *Revue de metaphysique et de morale* (1929), p. 197; *Droit constitutionnel*, 2nd ed., p. 5.

quently, he must adopt, not purely arbitrary directives, but on the contrary, directives that are in the spirit of the institution upon which his authority depends; for "they are not arbitrary orders of a power if they are produced as acts that are accepted by the people. The power itself is not accepted, but the political institution in the name of which the power commands."[17] The one who commands is then obeyed only insofar as he acts in the name of an institution, and this is a limit to his arbitrariness; if he has recourse to the institution to found his authority, at the same time "it is in order the better to tie his own hands."

Here we have, besides the directive and the standard, a second way of limiting the arbitrariness of the rulers, a second juridical notion that the normativists failed to see or else neglected. What is the institution then? What place does Hauriou give it in his system, and how do his institutional theories oppose normativism, especially Kelsen's?

Hauriou's efforts to penetrate the notion of institution were unceasing and brought about a succession of retouches. The last stage of his thought on this point is expressed in an article published in 1925: "An institution is an *idea of a work or enterprise* that is realized and that endures juridically in a social milieu; for the realization of this idea a power is organized that equips it with organs; on the other hand, among the members of the social group interested in the realization of the idea, manifestations of communion occur that are directed by these organs of the power and regulated by procedures."[18] According to this definition, an institution is created as soon as several persons who have decided to pursue a certain end organize themselves to this effect in a durable way. The institution asserts itself, first of all, as a distinct entity. It has its own individuality in social life, and this in two ways: it proves to be *distinct from its members* (a public office, for example, exists independently of the personality of its successive occupants), and it proves to be *distinct from neighboring institutions,* with which it engages in a life of balanced and normal relationships; it has relationships with its neighbors, but by this very fact asserts its autonomy for the accomplishment of its special function (e.g., relationships of a ministerial department with the other ministries, relationships of a public ministry with the jurisdiction for which it is instituted, etc.). In the second place, the institution creates or receives an internal organi-

17. "Le pouvoir, l'ordre," p. 146; *Droit constitutionnel,* 2nd ed., p. 4.
18. "La théorie de l'institution et de la foundation," 4 *Cahiers de la nouvelle journée* (1925), p. 10 [translated above].

zation; a dominant force is moderated in it by resistant forces (e.g., a deliberative assembly, with its majority moderated by the minority and by the permanent secretariat; Parliament, with the dominant force of the Chamber [of Deputies] and the resistant force of the Senate, etc.). This organization is realized with a minimum of hierarchy (officials, deliberative council, administrative commission, etc.) and an internal juridical rule (regulations of an assembly; statutes of an association; testament of the founder, for foundations, etc.). The state itself appears as the most remarkable of institutions, in which all these characteristics are found. The juridical rule is no more than an element of the institution, and even a product of it. The law of the state is both an element and a product of the state, but nothing more.

HAURIOU'S INSTITUTIONAL THEORIES AS OPPOSED TO KELSEN'S NORMATIVISM

You can see from this notion of institution that the chasm separating Hauriou from Kelsen is profound. Between the school of the institution and the school of the norm we might hear a dialogue something like this:

K.—The state, says the Kelsenian, is a system of norms and nothing esle.[19]

H.—No, answers the disciple of Hauriou; the state is not law, it is the milieu in which law is born and develops.

K.—At the very least, let us say that *from the juridical point of view* the state is a system of norms. Whatever you understand under the name of state other than norms is no longer a juridical notion. Refuse to identify the state with law if you like; but then you must specify clearly that the notion of state to which you allude is a sociological or political notion, not a juridical one.

19. See Hans Kelsen, "Théorie générale de l'état," *Revue du droit public* (1926), esp. pp. 576–577, where he sets forth his "pantheist" conception of the state and the law [*droit*], which coincide in the same way as God and Nature coincide for a pantheist. [See Kelsen, *General Theory of Law and State* (Cambridge, 1945), p. 182: "The State as a legal community is not something apart from its legal order, any more than the corporation is distinct from its constitutive order . . . Since we have no reason to assume that there exist two different normative orders, the order of the State and its legal order, we must admit that the community we call "State" is 'its' legal order." Cf. Kelsen's criticism of metaphysical dualism (*General Theory of Law and State*, p. 433): "We cannot here survey the various forms of transition which lead from one system to another. One might single out the pantheistic system, which places God in the world, because it is the one which plays a great role in the history of natural-law theory."]

H.—Why should I? Is there nothing in law but norms? How about the notions of person, of property? Are they not prime elements of juridical science by the very same claim as the notion of norm? Why eliminate the former a priori while retaining the latter? This exclusivism is unjustifiable. The postulate according to which norms alone furnish the prime elements of the science of law is an indemonstrable postulate.

K.—Quite the contrary: in order to call a notion juridical, one must establish a certain affinity between this notion and law, that is, objective law, therefore a system of norms. Before the state creates norms, before these norms exist, one of the necessary terms of the affinity that must be established in order to call the state a juridical notion is lacking. Consequently, without objective law, without a system of norms with which to establish some sort of affinity, the state does not exist juridically.

Hauriou, it seems, foresaw the objection. From the very first edition of his *Principes de droit public* [1910] he underscored the difference that exists between the social group that does not yet have juridical rules (the institution in the process of formation) and the one that has one or more juridical rules giving it access to the level of juridical notions (the institution definitively formed). This is Hauriou's classical distinction between the *nation* and the *state:* "the state is the juridical personification of a nation that has been arranged into an ordered and balanced regime."[20] Beneath the state lies the nation, which is, if not a juridical notion, at least a sociological notion—a notion Hauriou expresses by contrasting "the objective individuality" of the nation to the juridical personality of the state. These two words, nation and state, designate the same social group; the nation is this group envisaged *before* it has worked out a juridical system, and even afterward when this same group is envisaged from a political rather than a juridical point of view. Of course, the two concepts of state and system of norms are closely connected; but the thing designated by the concept of state was pre-existent. The state existed before it had a law;[21] only it did not exist as state, but simply as nation. We can say then that *as long as the nation has no law, it lacks an element that is prerequisite to its being called a state; that law is an essential element of the state. But we cannot say that law is the state!*

We may generalize these conclusions; the state alone is too narrow a viewpoint, so we shall expand our horizon to include every social

20. *Principes du droit public*, 1st ed. (Paris, 1910), p. 72.
21. [*Un droit*, that is, a system of law.]

group tending to organize itself into an institution. We shall say: norms are created by institutions. For example, for there to be statutes of an association, there must certainly first be a social group that draws them up and accepts them; for there to be any regulation of a municipal council, there must certainly first be a municipal council; but the institution, it is true, will exist *as such* only from the moment it creates such a norm, which is one of its essential elements. From the juridical point of view, the concepts of institution and state appear simultaneously with the concepts of institutional norm and the law of the state. But, from the social point of view, the institution, the nation, precede in time the corporate or state law.

To sum up, in Kelsen's theory the concepts of the state and of the objective law of this state coincide exactly. In Hauriou's institutional theory, they are distinguished, and between them the following relationships are established. (a) The institution is an absolutely necessary *cause* of norms; in other words, there is no juridical rule unless there is first of all a social group that can serve as its field of application. (b) But norms are not a cause of the institution; they are only *one of the conditions* of its complete development, entitling it to the name of juridical institution, but without their appearance creating any "transubstantiation"; the social group is one and the same, before and after; norms simply give it the right to a new designation. Clearly then, the norm is dependent upon the institution: *without the institution, there would be no norm at all, whereas without objective law, the institution would not lose its objective existence, but only its juridical qualification.* As Hauriou puts it: "Here is the whole problem: we must know where in society the creative power lies; whether juridical rules create institutions, or institutions produce juridical rules, owing to the power of government they contain."[22]

To take up the pantheistic comparisons so dear to Kelsen, it is not true that God is identified with nature, the Creator with the world created. If God had not created the world, obviously he would have no right to the title of Creator, but he would be no less God; the creature is, then, in no way necessary to the objective existence of God, but only to his designation, to his title of Creator; whereas without his Creator, the creature would not exist at all. The same thing applies, *si parva licet componere magnis*, to law in relation to the state, to the institution. It seems then that Kelsen commits the same error as the pantheists who assimilate creation to God, and that Hauriou is certainly right: the fundamental juridical conception

22. *La théorie de l'institution*, p. 7.

is the institution, because it is through the institution that law binds itself to social facts and takes its support in them. To claim the contrary is to isolate law from its neighboring sciences, to suspend it between heaven and earth, in the clouds. This precise criticism we have seen Duguit direct to Kelsen when "he reproaches him chiefly for placing the juridical order outside of living reality and sense experience."[23] And this concurrence between Duguit and what one can deduce from Hauriou's theories confirms what I said previously: with regard to Kelsen, Duguit and Hauriou are on the same side.

CONCLUSION ON THE THEORY OF THE INSTITUTION

The theory of the institution seems to me one of the most fertile that has been proposed in a long time in the works of jurists. By considering the state as only one of the institutions that create law, we come to take entirely new views upon corporate law, disciplinary law,[24] penal law, etc. To take just two examples, we understand, in the light of the idea of institution, what sort of law is born of the Covenant of the League of Nations: an international corporate law, since there is no super-state. And on the other hand, we understand that there is no essential difference, but a profound similarity, despite the many natural differences of regime, between disciplinary law and penal law, which is simply the disciplinary law of the state. These examples could be developed; but this is not the place; they could also be multiplied.

THE TWO LEVELS OF LAW

The normativists who make all law consist in a system of norms have then neglected directives and institutions. But this is not all. Hauriou also criticizes their monism, which flatly insists upon reducing law to the juridical rule alone,[25] for having neglected still

23. *Traité de droit constitutionnel*, 3rd ed., p. 64.
24. [*Droit disciplinaire*. G. See Alfred Légal and Jean Brèthe de la Grassaye, *Le pouvoir disciplinaire dans les institutions privés* (Paris, 1938).]
25. This unbridled monism is carried to an improbable extreme by the Austrians, who would like to prove that all rules derive from general norms, by progressive adaptation to concrete cases, and perhaps even, for any given branch of law, from one sole norm of which they would be the corollary. See on this point Roger Bonnard, "La théorie de la formation du droit par degrés dans l'oeuvre d'Adolf Markl," *Revue du droit public* (1928), p. 668. If Merkl's attempt were to succeed, not only would all law be reduced to the juridical rule alone, as we said in the text, but even to a single juridical rule. This would be the apotheosis of monism, the triumph of pure logic, the definitive isolation of law outside social reality.

another element of the diversity of law: "You assert the logical unity of the juridical system: are you sure of this unity? What tells you that there are not several juridical systems and, indeed, that one kind of law cannot contest against another kind of law?"[26] If such should be the case, the normativists would be wrong again, both for clinging exclusively to the juridical rule and for neglecting a new element of limitation of power by this competition of two laws. But, in his brochure on *Les idées de M. Duguit,* Hauriou establishes the fact that an observation of past and present juridical systems shows us a very frequent coexistence of two juridical systems, one ordained to establish order on the spot by imposing provisional but immediate solutions of an approximate justice; the other ordained, once the danger of disorder is thus avoided, to give solutions that are definitive and, this time, as just as possible. The opposition of these two systems is the opposition of the superficial level or stratum of law, which Hauriou calls "police justice," and the substance of law.

This police justice is found, in Roman law, in the interdicts of the praetor; in modern law, it is found in police measures, in questions of possession, in provisional remedies, in the appeal for *excès de pouvoir,* etc. The possessory solutions often differ from those of the courts deciding title;[27] the solutions of the judges on provisional remedies from those of the judges on the merits; an appeal for *excès de pouvoir* is often the prelude to an action for damages; the police administration gives orders that are sometimes contestable although generally useful, and which deserve to be temporarily enforced. Can you affirm, against this background, that law is a system? The provisional solutions of police justice will be corrected by those on the merits of the substantive law; is this not a division of powers and, therefore, a limitation of arbitrariness, power checking power?[28]

THE INDIVIDUAL'S POWER OF ACTION

Finally, Hauriou's last criticism of the normativists: there is still another essential element in the formation of law—the power of action of the individual. For Hauriou, there is no need to say, with Duguit: "In the beginning is the juridical rule, and from this rule proceed all the effects of juridical acts, all juridical situations." One should say, on the contrary: "In the beginning is man, with his creative activity; he has produced social institutions, and social institu-

26. Hauriou, *Les idées de M. Duguit,* p. 20.
27. [*Petitoire.* G.]
28. Ideas developed at length in "Le pouvoir, l'ordre," pp. 194ff. Cf. *Droit constitutionnel,* 2nd ed., p. 3.

tions produce juridical rules." Juridical rules then come last, and not first. For Duguit, juridical situations are the effects of legislation; juridical acts of individual initiative only condition them. For Hauriou, on the contrary, rights[29] are the direct effects of human initiatives; the role of legislation is simply to oppose its veto to them if the case requires it; if not, the absence of a prohibition of itself constitutes an authorization. Rights are simply the exercise of the natural and spontaneous power of action of man upon his milieu, limited by the vetoes of legislation. In the first rank, then, will be man, considered from the juridical point of view, man as a person; or to put it another way, man as the subject of all juridical activity, the subject of rights. In this sense, one can say that Hauriou is a *subjectivist*. And after all, he is simply restoring the *principle of the autonomy of the will,* which has been too neglected by Duguit and the objectivists: "We can say that the juridical force of acts rests upon the disciplined autonomy of the will."[30]

Hauriou did not content himself with showing the lacunae of the normativist systems. He made a much more personal and constructive contribution by applying his pluralistic tendencies to the study of public law and administrative law.

DUALISM IN HAURIOU'S SOCIOLOGICAL STUDIES

We have already had occasion to verify, in passing, Hauriou's tendency to show the constant opposition of the forces at play in social life: legislation as opposed to directives; norms and institutions as opposed to individual power; police justice as opposed to the substance of law.

This concern for pointing out on all sides the effects of universal pluralism, which is perhaps a consequence or simply an expression of the "dualism of form and matter, irreducible for four thousand years of philosophy,"[31] guides Hauriou in his social studies. He sees everywhere two possible points of view upon things: in his *Leçons sur le mouvement social,* he distinguishes the social movement itself and man's concept of it, which correspond respectively to the organic point of view and to the conceptual point of view. The antagonistic forces that appear everywhere in society inevitably clash with one

29. [*Les droits.* This is used in the same sense as "juridical situations" in the previous sentence.]
30. [Hauriou, *Les idées de M. Duquit,* pp. 30.]
31. *Droit constitutionnel,* 2nd ed., preface, at end.

another and, after some critical times, an organic compromise is established between them: every social relationship thus ends by becoming reciprocal.[32] The public lawyer must then double as an historian, for he cannot understand anything of the contemporary social and juridical situation if he knows nothing of the play of forces of which it is the resultant. In his sociological studies, Hauriou is supported by an impressive background in history (at the beginning of his teaching career in the law schools he taught history, and before that he was already known and esteemed for several studies in Roman law, especially upon correality). This knowledge of history as well as his pluralism lead him to give the juridical facts he studies a *dynamic,* evolutionary view. For him, law is like a beautiful river that has existence, reality, only through movement, that cannot be imagined at a standstill, congealed, and that would cease being itself if new water springing from its source did not incessantly push toward the sea the water that preceded it. For him, it is of first importance to apply to law the celebrated maxim: *Panta rei.*[33]

This concern for explaining institutions and law as the result of a play of social forces was pushed so far by Hauriou that one of his earliest works, the *Leçons sur le mouvement social,* is simply a long parallel between social science and thermodynamics—a parallel that is ingenious but too forced.

SOCIAL BALANCES

This preoccupation with the dynamic point of view makes Hauriou a tireless describer of movement. But what is movement if not a perpetual displacement of balances? To describe social movement will be then to show that it consists in a constant renewal of balances. To describe juridical movement will be chiefly to point out the equilibrium of institutions as it is achieved and shattered unceasingly: "politics should be defined as both the science and the art of balances of power."[34] At the beginning of his *Principes de droit public* he posits as fundamental "the point of view of balance" and of the order that results from it. Balance among powers; which powers? First of all, those that exist before the state and clear the way for it: families, *gentes,* tribes, cities, provinces, etc. Then, in the state itself, secular and religious power; civil and military power; political and economic power, the former using the political institution, the latter, juridical

32. Hauriou, *Leçons sur le mouvement social* (Paris, 1899), p. 19.
33. [All is in flux.]
34. *Droit constitutionnel,* 1st ed. (Paris, 1923), p. 20.

transactions on the basis of contractual relationships; power of individuals and of rulers and, consequently, equilibrium between a minority of aristocratic power of government and a majority or democratic power of control; hence also, equilibrium among a deliberative power, an executive power, and a power of suffrage; central power and local or specialized powers; power of government and administrative power.[35] Clearly, to describe the institutions of a country is to show how they realize these continuous separations of powers among themselves from age to age in order to reach that fleeting and temporary state of equilibrium that is called the present. Hauriou's view of this separation of powers is indeed broad, as one can see; it transcends, even far transcends, Montesquieu's, which seems almost narrow in comparison.

THE STATE REGIME

When he has described all these balances, Hauriou discovers that he has composed a magnificent fresco of the state as history has formed it. He has recomposed, according to history, the picture of what he calls the "state regime." To characterize what he means by this term, I can find no better expression than this: what a communist would call the bourgeois state. Hauriou is the apologist of the bourgeois state; by this I mean the state that is *balanced, stable, organized in view of political conceptions as well as the economic needs of citizens, set up so that laws assure order,* as opposed to the state that is *unbalanced* in favor of a single class that plays the role of dictator, *unstable* because imperialistic, *organized exclusively in view of economic needs,* set up so that there is *no legal order*—a regime that the adversaries of the bourgeois state oppose to it under the name of the soviet regime. And for this reason alone Hauriou deserves to be ranked, in the history of ideas, in as important a place as is Marx, for example. The state regime is the organization of the nation upon the basis of the balances I have enumerated.

ADMINISTRATIVE LAW

Again, it is owing to his aversion to monism that Hauriou was able to play a great role in the formation of French administrative law. A monist is shocked to see different juridical rules being applied

---

35. Cf. the ideas of Henri Chardon developed in *L'organisation d'une démocratie; les deux forces: le nombre, l'élite* (Paris, 1921).

to public agents and to private persons. Duguit revolted against the idea of an autonomous administrative law: as if all juridical relationships did not have to be appreciated in one and the same spirit— the spirit of justice—whether it is a question of the Administration or not! But Hauriou's pluralism allowed him to find it quite natural that there should be a law proper to the Administration and founded upon its privilege. And so he was able to make a very great contribution to the erection of administrative law into an autonomous branch of law. To appreciate the full value of his contribution to the general theory of administrative law, we must remember the chaotic state in which he found it. Before him, all the works that dealt with the subject could be reduced to two types rather well characterized by Gabriel Dufour's *Traité général de droit administratif appliqué*[36] and by Anselme Batbie's *Précis du cours de droit public et administratif*.[37] In the first, after a few chapters on the powers of the diverse administrative authorities, we are surprised to see that the subjects are classified according to *alphabetical* order! Such a procedure was current among nineteenth century authors; they did not compose systematic treatises, they compiled encyclopedias without any view of the whole. There was no attempt to interrelate the particular solutions; the presumption was that there was no unity, no directing principle to give individuality to administrative law. In the works of the second type, the paradox of alphabetical order seems to have been renounced. But in reality there was no great progress; instead of the encyclopedia, a long enumeration of the diverse officials and their powers appeared, followed by a study of the organization of the state, the *départements*, the communes, etc. Finally came diverse questions that the author could not integrate into his summary and that he stuck in haphazardly at the end of the volume. Conflicts of jurisdictions, which today seem to us among the dominating questions of administrative law, were relegated to the very last paragraph. In a word, administrative law, in this sort of work, still remained purely descriptive; it was utterly spineless.

There was one exception in this heap of books devoid of scientific value: Théophile Ducrocq's *Cours de droit administratif*.[38] This book was the only attempt at a systematization of administrative law

36. [Paris, 1843–1847, 4 vols.; 2nd ed. Paris, 1854–1857, 7 vols.; 3rd ed. Paris, 1869–1901, 12 vols.]

37. [Apparently Batbie's *Précis du cours de droit public et administratif professé à la Faculté de Droit de Paris*, 2nd ed. (Paris, 1864).]

38. [Paris, 1862; 6th ed., Paris, 1881.]

before Hauriou. But how primitive it seems to us today! The first edition appeared in 1859; the last was finished in 1907. Unfortunately, 1859 is the date that "marks" the work, that "dates" it. In a half-century the author did not learn how "to put off the old man."

In this almost total void of scientific literature[39] Édouard Laferriére's *La juridiction administrative* appeared in 1888 and, right on its heels, Hauriou's *Précis de droit administratif* in 1892.[40] These two books established the autonomy of administrative law in relation to the other branches of law and showed the solid bond that united the seemingly disconnected decisions of the Conseil d'État. Laferrière and Hauriou and, we should add, the Conseil d'État president, Romieu,[41] are the great minds to whom we are indebted for the first administrative law in the world, the one that other countries adopt or copy more and more.

To Dean Hauriou we are indebted for the theories of the administrative regime, of the privilege of the Administration, of the executory decision, of administrative responsibility; to his efforts we owe more than one modification of the jurisprudence of the Conseil d'État (especially on the acceptability of the appeal for *excès de pouvoir* and on the appropriate jurisdiction in connection with responsibility of administrative persons).[42] Perhaps we are also indebted to him for having avoided other unfortunate or hasty evolutions of jurisprudence toward which the Conseil d'État seemed to be headed, the perils of which he pointed out; for example, in the matter of responsibility for risks.[43]

Finally (and this is perhaps more important than one might think), Hauriou gave us a good plan for the study of administrative law,

39. [*La doctrine.* G.]

40. [Hauriou's second edition followed almost immediately, in 1893.]

41. Jean Romieu, a distinguished Commissaire du Gouvernement and President of the Conseil d'État in the first two decades of the twentieth century. " 'Conclusions Romieu; note Hauriou': Such was the mark of the great decisions of this era." Jacques Fournier, "Maurice Hauriou, Arrêtiste," Conseil d'État, *Études et Documents* (Paris, 1957), p. 157.

42. [I.e., when suit should be brought in the ordinary common (civil) law courts, and when before the tribunals of *droit administratif.*]

43. [Among Hauriou's "Notes" that seem to have restrained the Conseil d'État from rejecting the criterion of fault for risk as a basis of liability are: *Tomaso Greco and Auxerre,* S. 1905.3.113, *Notes d'arrêts,* I, p. 529ff, *Regnault-Desroziers,* S. 1918–19. 3.25, *Notes d'arrêts,* I, p. 686, and *Couitéas,* S. 1923. 3.57, *Notes d'arrêts,* I, p. 698, Hauriou's own earlier view had leaned toward the concept of risk as the prime criterion for public liability. See his note to *Cames,* S. 1897.3.33, *Notes d'arrêts,* I, p. 676; and *Précis de droit administratif,* 3rd ed. (Paris, 1897), pp. 174ff. But see 11th ed. (Paris, 1928), pp. 331ff.]

fixing our attention upon its real substance. While the school of Duguit tried to confine this law to the study of the public services, Hauriou opportunely recalled that beside these public services, administrative law included two other domains—police power and the administration of affairs of general interest. In a few vigorous pages of the preface to the 11th edition of his *Précis de droit administratif* he established that the notion of public service, however important it may be, cannot explain the whole of administrative law and that it must be combined with the traditional notion of public power.

HAURIOU'S EXPOSITORY PROCEDURES

Hauriou's zest for life asserts itself in his expository procedures and even in his style. He excels at "dramatizing" the most abstract questions—I mean at putting life into them—precisely because he sees these problems as an interaction of forces. For example, watch him study the respective roles of the appeal of *pleine juridiction* and of the appeal for *excès de pouvoir* in administrative litigation.[44] Here Hauriou stages a conflict of institutions. To give life to his presentation he in some way lends these institutions ambitions and energy; he even shows us the appeal of *pleine juridiction* defying its rival in the words of Tartufe: "The house is mine, it's for you to get out." And he speaks of "provinces annexed" by one institution at the expense of another. This flair for drama and imagery is what makes his works, especially his notes on the jurisprudence, so lively and intelligible. This is why they speak to the mind in such a striking way.

Must we then join in the complaints sometimes registered against Hauriou for having abused metaphors? I do not think so, and for two reasons. First of all, we must put these "dramatizations" of juridical phenomena in their proper place in Hauriou's thought: for him, they are ingenious expository procedures, but nothing more. We must not think that he is taken in by his own game or that he contents himself with images when he cannot find reasons. He uses these images to make himself better understood; but he has reasons in reserve that justify the proposed solution. One needs only read his article on "The Theory of the Institution" to realize that one is in a world of ideas and that the images are there only for exterior

44. [*Recours de pleine juridiction, recours pour excès de pouvoir.* G.]

decoration. They are like those architectural ornaments that help the mind of the spectator to understand the structure of a building by accentuating its lines, but which support nothing themselves; to accuse the architect of having built a flimsy building under the pretext that these ornaments are not able to support it, is to refuse to see the columns or walls that they decorate. Well, this is the reproof aimed at Hauriou when complaining of his abuse of images; a rather crude criticism, as one can see.

And here is the second reason why the reservations certain jurists have for Hauriou's procedures are not well founded: his taste for images and for "dramatization" is not "anthropomorphism," as many protest. I mean that it is false to say that Hauriou usually presents juridical institutions under a human form, to personify them. If this were true, the objection would indeed be serious; for it is not worthy of a scholar who claims to carry out a scientific work to indulge in such crude procedures even for the purpose of making himself better understood. But, as anyone can easily see, this is not Hauriou's attitude at all. To take just one example, consider his comparison of the moral person and the human person. If Hauriou were an "anthropomorphist," if he were someone who capriciously transformed everything into living personages, what would be his inclination here? Obviously, to show the analogy between the moral and the physical person *by making the attributes of the moral person like those of the physical person;* just as the organicists did when they described the organs of the moral person as analogous to the limbs, mouth, eyes, etc., of man; as the sociologist-biologists still do; and finally, as certain jurists like Bluntschli do by attributing a sex to moral persons! All this is obviously rather childish; and Hauriou does nothing of the sort, despite the all too frequent complaints. You need only open his article on "The Theory of the Institution" to realize that he does the exact opposite: he tries to describe the human person as analogous to institutions, as presenting the essential elements of institutions. To say that this is "anthropomorphism" is, then, a direct contradiction.

In short, we find in Hauriou a tendency to animate his juridico-sociological studies by "dramatizing" them, but under the reservation that this is only a procedure to explicate the results of his researches, and not the method of these researches; that he does not dispense himself from basing propositions upon arguments in a logical order; and that this very legitimate "dramatization" is not an "anthropomorphism" of fantasy.

METHOD

If this "dramatization" is not Hauriou's working method, what is his method? It can be summed up in two phrases: to see things from a lofty point of view, and to see them as they are.

Hauriou's is a very synthetic mind; when he studies a question, he wants to embrace all its elements in a glance, leaving analysis until later. Hence his taste for formulas: he wants to gather his whole thought on a subject in one phrase; the phrase is often long, and obscure on first reading; but later developments clarify it. If after having read them, one goes back to the initial formula, one is surprised to find it much more simple and intelligible than it first seemed (see, for example, his definition of the institution in the article cited above). His article in the *Revue trimestrielle de droit civil* on "The Social Order, Justice, and Law"[45] is a synthesis in less than thirty pages of the whole movement that leads men to law in proportion as they become civilized; a synthesis that leaves the reader with an impression of the "definitive," of satisfaction of mind.

Hauriou possesses to the highest degree the art of "elevating the debate" even in his brief notes on the *jurisprudence*. "Even the smallest party wall dispute involves metaphysics," is a saying of his, and the saying is profoundly true. For example, consider a modest question of administrative law: which court is competent to judge an action brought against a syndical association of proprietors by its creditors?—a question that nine out of ten readers of the case would consider dull. The note Hauriou devotes to it at the end of two pages poses a serious political and constitutional question, that of the role of the collective interest and of the Administration's exercise of control over its enterprises, which "is the substance of the collectivist doctrine"; and under this aspect Hauriou tackles the whole problem of socialism![46] Reading him is like suddenly discovering a view of a vast countryside when we thought we were in a dense forest with no hope of escape.

These examples could easily be multiplied. I just want to give two others here. A taxpayer contests the total of his assessment because his commune has been involved in illegal expenditures. From this modest tax case Hauriou extracts a philosophy of the commune and describes it as superimposing a political group upon an economic market, and he shows that this is the substance of the problem raised

45. "L'ordre social, la justice et droit," *Revue trimestrielle de droit civil* (1927).
46. Note to *Sirey.* 1900.3.49; *Notes d'arrêts*, I, 413.

by the case![47] In a question of educational procedure (when can the departmental council and the minister authorize the creation of a mixed school in a commune?) he first studies the problem in the light of the texts of the laws and regulations; but at the end of a few pages he leaves aside these trivial considerations and poses the real problems—the respect due to children, the dangers in their education, etc.[48]

But is this perpetual "elevation of the debate" really prudent? When one takes too lofty a view of things, is one not apt to miss seeing things as they are? Hauriou, most of the time at least, knew how to avoid this pitfall. A reading of his notes gives one quite the contrary impression: that he knew how to see the profound reality of things, while not letting himself be distracted by the accidental. Between his view of things and that of a less "elevated" observer lies the gulf that separates those crude old-fashioned maps that were drawn from ground level and disfigured the topography from maps established with the aid of air photography, which gives a much more accurate picture of the configuration of a country precisely because it is seen from above.

Not to disfigure the aspect of problems as they appear and yet to see them in a very synthetic way—this is the secret of Hauriou's method. He applied it so well and, especially in his notes on the *jurisprudence,* he showed such an evident concern for and grasp of the necessities of practice, and of the Administration in particular, that we can say he created a "science of administration," which is for administrative law what political science is for constitutional law.

CONCLUSION

At the close of this study, which I have tried to make both objective and critical, I just want to add a few words to point out how the fundamental problems of law are dominated by two or three philosophical problems that man inevitably meets on his path as soon as he reflects upon the anguishing mystery of his destiny and of the universe that surrounds him: the problem of liberty or determinism, which we have seen dominates the search for the higher juridical rule and governs the choice between natural law and juridical positivism; and the problem of monism or pluralism. In law, too, the frightening, haunting warning of Pascal holds true: "You must wager: this is not purely voluntary, you are already committed."

47. Note to *Sirey.* 1900.e.65; *Notes d'arrêts,* II, 213; see esp. #2, pp. 220ff.
48. Note to *Sirey.* 1928.3.49; *Notes d'arrêts,* II, 772.

PART II   GEORGES RENARD AND

            JOSEPH T. DELOS

GEORGES RENARD   The Degrees of Institutional

Existence: The General Characteristics of the

Institution

Kant's conception of law was individualistic. Law, he said, is "the complex of conditions under which the liberty of each man can coexist with the liberty of others according to a general law of liberty."[1] Contrary to Kant, our conception of law is institutional.[2]

ED. NOTE: Georges Renard became an avowed disciple of Hauriou soon after being named Professor of Public Law at the University of Nancy in 1920. However, the first of his full-length works on the theory of the institution was not published until 1930, shortly after Hauriou's death. Entitled *La théorie de l'institution* (Paris, 1930), it was planned as the first of a two-volume work, of which it was the juridical portion. The second volume, offering the philosophical analysis, did not appear until 1939, under the title *La philosophie de l'institution* (Paris, 1939).

Many French jurists had been disaffected by Renard's sponsorship of thomist legal and social doctrine, which he had made clear in three volumes loosely grouped under the series title *L'introduction philosophique à l'étude du droit* (*Le droit, la justice et la volonté*, Paris, 1924; *Le droit, la logique et le bon sens*, Paris, 1925; and *Le droit, l'ordre et la raison*, Paris, 1927, as well as in his *La valeur de la loi* (Paris, 1929). Renard frankly avowed in his preface to *La théorie de l'institution* (p. xvi) that he had gone beyond "Hauriou's formulas" but, he insisted, "not beyond his thought." The volume, presented as a series of lectures, is divided into three sections: an introduction, "Toward the Theory of the Institution," which is a sort of intellectual itinerary; Part One, "The Institutional Phenomenon," concerning private law (including the family and marriage) and public law (including international law); and Part Two, "The Juridical Theory of the Institution." The two selections translated here come from Part Two, chs. v (pp. 221–281) and vi, (pp. 285–353).

1. [Kant, *The Metaphysics of Morals* (1797), tr. John Ladd (Indianapolis, 1965), p. 34. Ladd translates the celebrated passage thus: "Justice (*recht*) is therefore the aggregate of those conditions under which the will of one person can be conjoined with the will of another in accordance with a universal law of freedom."]

2. [Renard here cites Giorgio del Vecchio as rejecting Hans Kelsen's identification of "law" and "state," agrees with him, and then elaborates the point as follows:] To say that every institution produces a rule of law, is not to say that every rule of law is institutional. We have admitted the existence of individualistic juridical rules (i.e. "rules proceeding from individual juridical acts," *La théorie de l'institution* p. 105, n. 1); this correction must be carried over to the institutional conception of law. We

163

There are as many juridical systems as there are institutions . . .[3] In each institution law is the principle of a rational adaptation of the parts to the whole, of the whole to the parts, and of the parts to each other in view of the whole.[4] Such is the importance of the institutional concept for juridical science.

The institution is a flexible concept. I have shown you something of the variety of its applications; today I should like to have you understand its suppleness. Do not expect to find, under the rubric of the theory of the institution, some rigid structure, fashioned by rule and compass. These instruments are not admissible in the social sciences; and in proportion as juridical science resorts to them, it withdraws from reality. But the theory of the institution justly prides itself on reducing juridical speculation to reality.

First of all, institutions come in all sizes: I mean in the sense that they participate unequally in the quality of juridical subject.[5] There are many mansions under the shelter of the institutional concept.

---

do not identify law and the institution as Kelsen identifies law and the state; the institution is only the framework of juridical rules of *genera!* import—the most important and most interesting, very obviously, for juridical science. Individuals and institutions can also enter into engagements *without general import* formulating among themselves a juridical rule for a particular case, but only insofar as these particular engagements respect the statutes of the institutions of which they are part; with this reservation, I will later make an application to international law (the impossibility for member states of the League of Nations to prohibit, by particular conventions, recourse to the procedures provided by the Covenant [of the League]. In this sense Jacques Chevalier maintains that the "science of the general" prevails over the "science of the individual."

3. [In the passage omitted here Renard describes a range of institutions, from "the family and the nation to humanity." He later repudiates this designation of humanity itself as an "institution." See *La philosophie de l'institution,* translated in part below.]

4. "Jus sive justum est aliquid opus adaequatum alteri . . . dicuntur enim vulgariter ea quae adaequantur justari." *Summa Theologiae,* II II, q.57, aa.1–2.

5. The institution-thing (See Renard, *La théorie de l'institution,* p.90, n.1) is only a framework, a machinery; it is impossible to recognize in it any juridical subjectivity at all. This does not mean that it does not have a power to enrich human activity by disciplining it. Taking the word in this wide sense Paul Archambault writes in a recent article: "An institution is a specific reality, having its causes, its properties, its relatively constant effects. There are institutions that guarantee fruitful parliamentary work by limiting useless interruptions, by regulating debates, by moderating the effects of the difficulties of open sessions: we could speak of a parliamentary technique. There are institutions that guarantee peace by procuring in case of conflict an immediate redress, a competent and impartial adjudiction, appropriate sanctions: we could speak of a technique of peace. There are institutions that guarantee a proper execution of public services by assuring unity of authority, complete information, prompt decisions: we could speak of an administrative technique." Archambault, "Qu'est-ce que la politique? Technique, art et mystique," *Politique,* 1929, p. 331. I have said that I prefer to reserve the name of institution for the corporative type. [See Hauriou, "The Theory of the Institution and the Foundation," above].

And then, between the "institutional" and the "noninstitutional," or to be more precise, between the "institutional" and the "contractual," there is no rigid frontier. Bit by bit the theory of the institution creeps into juridical matters governed by the contractual principle; the "contractual" tends to flow toward the "institutional," and sometimes the "institutional" ebbs back toward the "contractual."

The institution is not an abstract model like the Roman *stipulatio;*[6] it is more like a current that one moment sweeps off an entire department of juridical life and another moment, in some other department, inflects the logical unfolding of the consequences of the contractual principle. The old *stipulatio* was a ready-made garment; the institution is tailored to measure.

I admit that there is something elusive about the theory of the institution. Its tremendous plasticity bewilders our Latin or latinized minds;[7] every time we try to grasp it, it slips through our fingers like sand . . .

In this conference I shall propose a juridical theory of the institution—a difficult task, so please bear with me. In the first part, I shall consider the gradation of institutional existence; in the second, I shall begin investigating the general characteristics of the institution; a comparison of institution and contract will come later.

There are degrees of being. There is more being in living things than in brute matter; because the matter of a living thing is given form by an idea, not from without but from within. This interior and therefore intimate nature of the idea's ascendancy over matter is the mark of organization, in the biological sense of the word.[8]

And among living things, life is all the more abundant as the idea "informs" the matter more profoundly. The more the idea "informs" the elements of a living thing, the more these elements lose their autonomous individuality, and the more incapable they are of recovering it—and the more life there is in the organism. Plants have a minimal life, and a minimal subordination of organ to organism; a cutting planted in the earth grows new foliage. Invertebrates have

---

6. [G.]

7. A perfect example of the complexity of the institutional phenomenon and the intermingling of all kinds of institutions is the British Empire . . . Our neighbors on the other side of the Channel, who are much more concerned with positive reality than we are and rather less concerned with principles, are predestined by temperament to welcome into their feathery juridical technique, the category of the institution . . .

8. "Vitae nomen est impositum ad significandam substantiam cui convenit secundum suam naturam movere seipsam." Aquinas, *Summa Theologiae,* I, q.18, a.2.

a mediocre life; cut up an earthworm and its sections continue to live. As we climb up the hierarchy of beings, the integration becomes more intimate, and separated life more difficult or impossible. As the scale of being ascends, the subjugation of matter to form becomes more complete; as the scale of living things ascends, organic life develops and cellular life becomes more closely dependent upon it.[9]

To this progressive development of being and life, which is the ABC of biological philosophy, there corresponds in juridical philosophy a progressive development of institutional existence.

The institution is a juridical subject like the reasonable being; but they do not have the same sort of subjectivity. Moreover, there are institutions and institutions; there are even many more degrees among institutions than among human persons, which, properly speaking, are the only persons, for personality is an exclusive attribute of the reasonable being.

Personality belongs to every reasonable being[10] (I am leaving aside the slave whose condition is against nature, as the Romans said long ago).[11] Since every reasonable being is capable of becoming an owner, creditor, debtor, man is born with a potential patrimony, and this is his juridical personality.[12] And among men there are certainly degrees of personality: men have distinguished, according to the era, between persons *sui juris* and persons *alieni juris,* nobles, clerics, commoners, serfs, clients; today we distinguish between the legally competent, the legally incompetent, and the legally semicompetent. In short, the reckoning quickly takes the shape of categories.

9. . . . I have already pointed out in the Foreword that for the subtitle Maurice Hauriou gave to "The Theory of the Institution and the Foundation"—"A Study in Social Vitalism"—I have substituted the rubric "A Study in Juridical Ontology." The expression *social vitalism* [G.] seems to me to incur the same reproach as the expression *juridical personality.* The latter has entered into our vocabulary; I have resigned myself to it, while taking the necessary precautions against the mirage it conjures up; but *social vitalism* has not yet acquired citizen's rights, and I believe it would be better not to let it acquire them. I want to make it clear that, despite this difference in terminology, my doctrine remains that of my master: Maurice Hauriou did not ascribe a true "life" to institutions any more than I do. [At *La théorie de l'institution,* p. 260, n.1, Renard adds: " . . . 'Vitalism' belongs to the scientific vocabulary and almost inevitably implies a reference to organicist doctrine."]

10. Duguit, taking the standpoint of a positivist, considered only the fact of personality, that is, reason in *act.* Duguit, I say, did not recognize any juridical subjectivity or juridical personality (it makes no difference what you call it) in the *infans.* Speaking as a metaphysician, I take the viewpoint of being, not of phenomena, and consequently I consider not only act but *potency* [G.]; therefore, I hold that the *infans* is a person, a juridical subject.

11. Dig., 1, 5, *De statu hominum,* 4,§1, Florentinus.

12. Without forgetting that ensemble of attributes which private lawyers readily call, in a rather special sense, the "rights of personality": right to one's name, to honor, etc. (See François Geny, *Des droits sur les lettres missives* (Paris, 1911), I, 88, where there is an ample bibliography on this subject.)

Turning to the institution, the categories are innumerable; they form a continuous ascent from nonbeing to the fullness of being. First of all there is an infra-juridical manner of being, and even this compartment is of interest to law in the sense that it constitutes the point of departure of a gradual ascent toward the lower limit of juridical existence: it is the nursery of juridical subjects[13]. . .

I would never finish if I tried to establish a nomenclature for all the categories of institutions. Some play their role in the vast theater of international law, others appear on smaller yet important scenes, and others only come onto the humblest stages. There are elementary institutions and institutions composed of other institutions: the unitary state is an elementary institution, the federal state is an institution of institutions. There are institutions of the order of sovereignty and institutions of the order of property, institutions of the governmental order, of the administrative order, of the commercial order. But these classifications do not touch on the problem that concerns us at the moment. We are looking for the degree of "being" that institutions are capable of attaining, and for the diverse measures of their participation in the quality of "juridical being."

Keep in mind the general rule I mentioned at the outset—a rule common to law and to the biological sciences—that there is more being in a whole in proportion as the idea (or form) that constitutes it is more perfectly integrated within its parts; there is more being in an institution, or in any organism, in proportion as its members are more perfectly subjected to it.

There is more being in the nation than in the state, more being in the state than in the particular constitutional regime under which it currently acts; the proof is that the state survives changes of government, and the nation survives every annexation, every dismemberment, every exodus. But why? Why do we say *subjects* of the state, or at most *citizens* of the state, when we say *children* of the nation? Do we not understand that the nation has a different sort of "hold" over her children than the state (much less the constitu-

13. . . . Certain *institution-corporations* begin by a prejuridical stage that explains certain particular characteristics they have after entering into the orbit of law. See on this subject the very fine theory of the nation presented by Joseph T. Delos in *La société internationale et les principes du droit public* (Paris, 1929). Like the nation, the family is a juridical unity, but it is more than a juridical unity, and juridical analysis nowhere near exhausts the relationships and obligations that follow upon it . . . "Society," in the common understanding of the word, is an institution, but it is not a juridical institution; however in the measure that it takes concrete form it becomes a "class," and bit by bit classes achieve juridical existence; they can even become the basis of the political regime. The same movement takes place in the opposite direction: institutions go up and down the ladder of juridical being. We could easily multiply examples, e.g., the nation again, minorities in international law.

tional regime) has over its subjects? The nation "possesses" its "children" in an *intimacy*—remember this word—that is quasifamilial; they are hers. The state administers to them, the republic governs them; this is not the same thing at all! We can get rid of the constitutional regime by a parliamentary vote, or by a shove of the shoulder; we can drop our citizenship in the state by initiating naturalization proceedings in another state: it only takes a few years. And this is why the masters of international law say that nationality is voluntary—some have even made the mistake of calling it contractual. But they only mean citizenship in a state: true nationality is belonging to a nation, and this quality is almost indelible; it is a tunic of Nessus. I repeat: it "holds" you, *ossibus adhaeret,* it follows you and identifies you wherever you go. To get rid of it or to change it takes a slow process of assimilation; the span of a lifetime usually does not suffice, the effort of generations does not always succeed.[14]

There is indeed, then, a certain symmetry between institutional gradation and biological gradation. The difference is that in institutions it is a question of a purely psychological integration. Yet in the case of familial institutions and of certain national institutions this psychological integration is supported by bonds of blood. There is no break in continuity here. "Social life is continuous," Hauriou used to say. This is distressing for a certain pigeon-holing spirit. I would like to appease it—not to satisfy it, I give up on that!—by two distinctions: the first fixes the maximum limit of the institutional gamut, the second deals with the nature and number of its steps.

The most vigorous institutions are usually given the name of moral or civil or juridical persons. The word is dangerous. For no matter what perfection of being an institution may attain, it will never rise, in potency of being, to the level of personality in the true sense of the word. Yet I recognize the convenience of the fiction. I find it charming, like the little girl who shows her doll the countryside out of a train window, I appreciate the poetry of it, and I shall tell you presently that I am resigned to the expression. But I do not intend to be duped by it.

Between the person and the institution there is this enormous difference: juridical personality has its principle in the human rea-

---

14. Sometimes positive law imitates the natural classifications furnished by psychological observation by artificial classifications that depend solely on technique. For example, in French law the "social idea" is much more independent of the "person" of the associates in the *association* [G.] than in the *société* [G.]; the *association* is more "institutional." The juridical personality of the *société* is only a tunnel that temporarily hides the individual rights of the members; in the *association* these rights are abolished and replaced by a simple title to participation in the benefits of the group.

son; the institution is simply suspended from an *idea*; and between the two there is an abyss. The human *reason* is a spring overflowing with ideas, and its productivity is indefinite and undetermined. The *idea* produced by reason is "instituted" in an organic system where it develops and which it causes to grow just as leaven raises dough or seeds invigorate the earth. And yet this is a closed system. Like a doll, it will not grow up with its little mother; closed like the potentialities of plant life or animal instinct. Only man can vary seeds and breeds, vary his physical or intellectual activity, vary his ideas. The institution is riveted to *its idea*.

Of course, there is a dynamic element in *the idea*—I am not taking anything back from what I said on this. But this dynamism is assigned to a *concrete* end; *reason* acts as it will, simultaneously or successively, in any direction it chooses; it is an *abstract* power.

Reason is a *living* faculty, the *idea* is only a theme to be *developed*: here is the whole difference between the person and the institution; and this is why I do not admit, any more than Duguit, the terms social consciousness and social will, or institutional consciousness and institutional will; this is why, later on, I shall reject the vitalist explanation of the institutional phenomenon. In the institution, outside of the human beings who cooperate in it *individually*, there is only an *idea*; but this idea is *common* to them.

It would hardly be flattery to tell someone he is a *man of one idea*; this would suggest that his horizon is narrowly limited, that his reason is weak, that he has a streak of mania. It would be the same thing as telling him: you behave not like a man but like an institution. For an institution is precisely a *being of one idea*. Some logician may be called a walking syllogism, and this does not prove that he is a great mind; the institution is an idea on the march.

The juridical interpretation of this inferiority of the institution in relation to human personality is the *principle of specialty*. This principle is founded in reason—a true principle of *natural law:* the security given a founder, by natural law, that his intention, his *idea*, will be respected, the guarantee given him against the caprice of his successors, the *non licet* in which he necessarily places his trust.[15]

The commune, the *département*, the public establishment[16] or public utility,[17] are juridical subjects restricted to certain special tasks; their juridical subjectivity is *relative;* functions of general interest are distributed among them according to a set order; each

15. New application of the theory of Emmanuel Levy: law is founded upon "necessary trust." Cf. my conferences, *Le droit, l'ordre et la raison* (Paris, 1927).
16. [*Établissement public.* G.]
17. [*Établissement d'utilité public.* G.]

one has its *competence* fixed by law or by its act of foundation; and outside the orbit of their function and their competence, they are no longer juridical subjects.[18] Man, the person, is an *absolute* juridical subject.

And the same thing applies to associations, labor unions, mutual companies; their capacity to acquire and assume obligations is circumscribed by their service of an idea. And the same for business companies. It is true that the state is an exception; but this exception, to the degree to which it is justified, is the consequence of the state's special mission among other institutions. It is the perfect society, say the theologians; it is sovereign, say the jurists. Beyond this degree, which I shall specify later,[19] it manifests a pathological hypertrophy that political science must put an end to by fixing its special task, for it too has limitations.[20]

It seems to me that we have just taken an important step. There are two juridical subjects, man and the institution, but the latter is in no sense an imitation of the former. This is the illusion created by the term moral or juridical or civil personality, and the reason why this term has brought so much ridicule from its adversaries. Its partisans have certainly asked for it: did they not even get the idea, one day, to discuss the sex of moral persons?

The two juridical subjects are neither equal nor similar; they are neither of the same size nor of the same nature; they are as far apart as an *idea* is from that *fountain of ideas* which is *reason*. The institution is a juridical subject of secondary rank.

This is my first pronouncement, and already you can see that I am getting into an investigation of the affinities between the human person and the juridical institution; I shall pursue this later on.

Here is the second pronouncement. Institutions can never reach the fullness of juridical being, but they can ascend toward this limit.

18. Léon Michoud has clearly shown that the principle of speciality is fundamental to moral personality (let us say institution) and has given it a very different physiognomy from that of human personality. Michoud, *La théorie de la personnalité morale* (Paris, 1916), I, 243ff. Cf. Hauriou, *Droit public,* 2nd ed., pp. 73ff; *Droit administratif,* 11th ed., pp. 928ff.

19. [*La théorie de l'institution,* pp. 536–585, not translated here.]

20. This is what explains the difference between individual property and the property of public administrations. The latter is a property affected to a special purpose; the former is a free property. In this connection Léon Michoud suggests that we substitute the distinction between individual right and institutional right for individual right and public right as the *divisio summa* of juridical science, namely, that there is in the property of every moral (institutional) person an element of affectation which distinguishes it from private property and restricts it like public property. [A lengthy quotation in this note from Léon Michoud, *La théorie de la personalité morale,* I, 243, is omitted.]

We propose to count the steps of this ascent. To make you feel the psychological realism of my doctrine once more, I am going to open up the debate with examples.

I am employed as a clerk in the city hall. I belong to the birth registration bureau, or to the marriage registration bureau, or to the death registration bureau—the three sections of the municipal register. In my bureau the work is divided. One clerk receives the registrants, another takes care of drawing up the documents, a third prepares the demographic statistics. But this distribution of tasks is *interior* to the bureau; the public does not have to know about it. And just as the three bureaus make up the division of the municipal register, so various divisions make up the department of City Hall, and various departments make up the city administration: there is the office of the mayor, the mayor's secretariat, the department of highways, the police, fire, and tax departments, education, fine arts, relief, health. All this compartmenting belongs to the *interior* order; each department, each division, each bureau has its individuality, its discipline, its head, and its personnel, just as it has its special task and the responsibility of its mission—not before the public—but before the mayor; each one is an institution[21] within the office of the mayor. But in the eyes of the public only the mayor and the city count, and the mayor as representing the city. All the divisions and departments form a bloc; to put it more juridically, they are mingled in one institution, which alone possesses juridical being for the *exterior*. And the same thing goes for a laboratory within a medical school, and for a clinic within a hospital.

The same phenomenon occurs in commercial life. Each store of a company with many branches has its own accounts, and each branch manager has his own responsibility with respect to the central office; but in the eyes of the public there is only one company and one responsibility; the total assets of the company guarantee its total debts. The autonomy of the branches is a purely *interior* affair: the branch is a juridical subject within the company, but with regard to outsiders it is not. And there are even smaller accountable individualities: the department of a big store,[22] whose whole accountability is simply an individualization in the accounts of different parts of an enterprise.

Public accountability, in turn, offers a veritable wealth of individ-

21. ["Institution" is used here in a secondary sense connoting only a certain *interior* autonomy, not an *exterior* juridical life.]

22. . . . The administration of the P. T. T. [*Poste-Télégraphe-Téléphone* sets up its bureaus in the same way: embryos of institutional individuality.

ualities of all dimensions. First come the administrative units with financial autonomy even with respect to outsiders: the circumscriptions[23] and the decentralized public services.[24] Below these, among purely accountable units, some have a budgetary individuality: they possess a special budget, called an annex-budget, which is simply attached to the state's budget by the entry of a difference. Still further down the scale, among the public services that have no special budget, some have credits voted separately by the Chambers. In France, the budget of state expenditures is voted according to ministries and by chapters; hence the prohibition of transferring appropriations from chapter to chapter and a fortiori from ministry to ministry; the service designated by each appropriation is thus individualized by a sum guaranteed each year by the finance law. Finally, the chapters are divided into articles, and each branch of service is designated by an article: this is still an accountable individuality, but it is weaker, since a simple ministerial decision suffices to reduce its credit in favor of another branch of the same service. Even more clearly than commercial accountability, administrative accountability reveals to us the distinction between the two degrees of individualization, the one that appears on the profound level of patrimony and external responsibility, the other that is just an internal affair of banking and accounts . . .[25]

Now we are in a position to distinguish two degrees of being in the institution. The maximum power of being that the institution can attain belongs to those units whose individuality can stand in opposition to anything whatever; they exist *erga omnes* like human persons; I am prepared to say that their existence is absolute. Like human persons, and with them, they enter into the ordinary commerce of juridical life—and this is why they are commonly and, in general, indifferently called *moral* or *juridical persons*. The others have an existence that is only *minuto jure*, relative, interior in rela-

23. [*Circonscriptions*. G. A "decentralized circumscription" is a governmental subdivision that is not subject to the hierarchical control of the central government authority, such as the *département* or the commune. The central "government cannot send orders to the municipal council or mayor" of a commune. Waline, *Droit administratif*, 9th ed. (Paris, 1963), p. 302.]

24. [Renard here refers to a decentralized governmental or quasigovernmental unit that "exploits a property or an enterprise." Duguit and others (chiefly adherents of the so-called "School of *Service Public*" at Bordeaux) sought to confine the scope of *droit administratif* to a theory of "public service" considered as a function.]

25. Accountability and patrimony are two subjacent juridical planes. The first is only a policing measure; it answers the most urgent need; it is provisional; a restoration takes place later on the plane of patrimony. It is a case in point of the rule that the juridical order is established in two steps . . .

tion to a certain circle beyond which they disappear, absorbed in a more powerful individuality. They do not enter into the ordinary commerce of juridical life; they are so far beneath human persons that they are no longer called persons. The doll is carved to look like a child; institutions of the second degree are not even dolls.

With regard to the first degree, moral or juridical persons, I have expressed my reservations about using this name, and I hope they will counteract the peril it presents. I keep it chiefly out of deference to established usage, but only on condition that a distinction is maintained between *moral personality* and *juridical personality*— two expressions I provisionally held as equivalents—a distinction that is often unnoticed, although it was judiciously pointed out by Hauriou[26] and immediately confirmed by Geny,[27] and which is of tremendous importance to the theory of the institution.

The theory of the institution is a "study in juridical ontology"; its aim is to find out just what a juridical subject *is*, to analyze its *being*; it calls for a classification of institutions according to their *power of being*. This is where we are now: the theory of *moral* personality takes this latter point of view—the point of view of *being*, the *ontological* point of view.

The theory of *juridical* personality does not aim so high. It takes the point of view—some would say the distinctly juridical point of view—of the *capacity* of institutions; that is, it supposes that the problem of institutional existence is already resolved. To certain institutions it issues a "permit" that enables them to take part without protection, *under their own name,* in the acts of juridical life; the others will act, as they can, *under the name of another*—an individual person or a personalized institution that will cover them with its own capacity.

And in principle, this representation of an institution without juridical capacity is perfectly licit: an institution is not prohibited because it has not received the *dignus es intrare* on stage; the wings of juridical commerce are filled with institutions, and while some of them aspire to appear before the footlights, others adjust very well to their lot. Neither the family nor the nation has a *juridical personality;* yet they have every right to the highest place in the scale of institutions; there are none more necessary, none more real. We must not hesitate to recognize their *moral personality.*

Moral personality fits into the institutional theory: it designates,

26. Hauriou, *Droit administratif,* 11th ed., pp. 286ff.
27. Geny, *Science et technique,* IV, p. xviii. It is the *liberty of foundation* that is at stake.

not a degree of institutional capacity, but a degree of institutional *status*, the summit of institutional existence, the highest *power of being* the institution can reach: that degree at which it is able to oppose its being, not only to its organs, but to the world outside.

What is more, moral personality thus understood is not a rigid concept but a framework for the most diverse realities. In French law, for example, *départements* and communes do not have the same sort of personality as public establishments and public utilities, nor as private companies and associations; and the personality of associations is itself subdivided into great and small. And then, international personality is above all these and involves a whole new gradation in itself. Think of the unequal interdependence of states associated in a real union or a personal union or grouped in a confederation or incorporated in a federal state, not to forget the commonwealth. All these varieties have one characteristic in common: all the institutions of this first degree have an *exterior* juridical commerce.[28]

Those of the second degree have only an *interior* autonomy, they are just a part of some greater personalized institution. They are autonomous in relation to the other parts of the same moral person, but this moral person indivisibly represents all its parts in exterior relations. These secondary individualities are only organs in an organism, and they participate only in a commerce of organ to organ within this organism: bureaus and divisions with regard to the city, branches with regard to the business company, etc. Since they must have a label, I shall call them *objective individualities;* the most striking of these are the *accountable individualities.* And of course, like moral persons, these institutions of the second rank are subdivided into a host of categories.[29]

And then, this ladder of the institution is like Jacob's ladder. Institutions go up and down the degrees of being. The institution is, in every respect, the category of movement. Like every juridical system,

28. This diversification is complicated by the already established fact of institutional interpenetration: each institution is both an organism and the organ of a greater institution: the measure of its personality is then dependent both upon its own power of being and upon the power of being of the institution, and ultimately of the series of institutions, of which it is tributary . . .

29. The accountable individuality is already a rather high degree in the scale of objective individuality: to have accounts, to keep cash, to use capital, even when this is only *affectation* [G.] and not strict property—this is something more than being just an administration. This is the first rung.

the institutional system is a stylization of social life[30]—but a free-flowing, moving stylization: no hierarchical poses, just like modern art! It is an infinitely plastic stylization where life plays with ease, like light on the glasswork of our Lorraine artists. The theory of the institution holds nothing for those who ascribe to law the somber mission of establishing eternal repose in this world. Its sparkling facets and colors give them a headache, so they close their eyes. Would you believe it? There are still people who prefer magic lanterns to moving pictures. Will our grandchildren believe it? Our big stores still build stairs next to escalators for the clumsy people who stumble on them! There are jurists who stumble over the institution. It moves! But this is why the theory adapts itself to reality; reality is shifting! . . .

Let us see how the institution really moves. A certain administrative service—I am thinking of the French publicly-operated railroads and postal-telephone-telegraph service—rises from the level of budgetary inscription to budgetary autonomy and finally to personality.[31] Certain accountable individualities, like the special accounts of the Treasury, the extraordinary budget, the budget on recoverable resources, are reabsorbed into the anonymity of state finances.[32] A certain possession—I am thinking of Algeria—was long treated like a simple territorial prolongation of France, and then a legislative

30. ["The moral personality of instituted bodies is *a social and moral institution* while the juridical personality is only a *juridical institution.* Consequently, the moral personality of constituted bodies can have a reality about it as a social and moral institution, while juridical personality would be considered as a simple means of technique, designed to adapt the moral being of social institutions to the demands of law, just as it already serves to adapt the moral being of individual human beings to law. Juridical personality is only a mask (*persona*) placed over moral personality; its purpose is to fix the moral physiognomy of man in a certain attitude, for in reality this physiogomy is too mobile, too variable, and too diverse to serve as the subject of essentially stable subjective rights. Juridical personality is, if you like, a stylization of moral personality in which something artificial is introduced, as in every work of art. But every moral person has the right to be thus stylized as a juridical person, the social-institution-moral-person as well as the individual-human-moral-person. (Note: I insisted on the distinction of moral personality and juridical personality and on the stylization of the one by the other in an article in the *Revue générale de droit* of 1898 entitled "De la personnalité comme élément de la réalité sociale.)" Hauriou, *Droit constitutionnel,* 2nd ed., p. 405.]

31. Cf. Hauriou, *Droit administratif,* 11th ed., pp. 60ff. [Renard here adds illustrations of juridical personality conferred by French legislation on educational bodies.]

32. In his conclusions under *Conseil d'État,* 14 Dec. 1928, *Pilliard,* in the *Revue du droit public* (1919), p. 109, Auguste Rivet underscores the difference between the new municipal administrations (*décrets Poincaré*) endowed with a simple financial autonomy, and the "ancient model" services, which are true public establishments with full personality.

impulse gave it a turn toward financial autonomy and moral personality. In Alsace and Lorraine, since the de-annexation, the tide is going from a kind of particularism toward assimilation. A certain province rises to autonomy within a state—like northern Ireland—and another reaches international personality—southern Ireland. But in reverse, a certain protectorate turns into a colony—France and Madagascar; a confederation into a federal state—the United States, Switzerland, Germany; a personal union into an annexation—Belgium and the Congo. This alternation of rises, falls, and recoveries fills the annals of international law. But on the level of international law, as on that of national law, all this coming-and-going revolves around two pivots: *external personality* and *internal individuality;* there are institutions whose development remains entirely interior, there are others that reach out into the exterior.[33]

This distinction brings to mind an idea from Roman law. The *peculium* of the son of a family was a patrimonial individuality from the angle of family accounts; but on the level of personality, in relation to outsiders, it was absorbed into the patrimony of the *paterfamilias.* And it is still the same today: clothes, school books, and toys, the "allowance," pocket money, are the property of each one of the children in relation to his brothers and sisters, and this is the way they are initiated into the meaning of "mine" and "yours." But in relation to the public, all this belongs to the father; it is one mass. This kind of "mine" and "yours" does not depend upon the distinctions made by public courts; the disputes it provokes are entirely under family jurisdiction, which is administered with sanctions of dry bread and dark closets.

I hope that you are getting more and more of a grasp of what I called at the outset "the institutional conception of law." There are stages in the juridical order, and each stage has an order of its own. The coordination of these fragmentary orders is what forms the general order.[34]

So this very old thing, Roman law, leads us right back to the latest fashion in scientific philosophy. These juridical rules that exhaust their force within the atmosphere of one institution resemble those

33. Countless are the collective individualities that French law considers capable of participating to a certain extent in juridical commerce without the attribution of personality.

34. Cf. my *Droit de la profession pharmaceutique,* pp. 8ff; cf. Georges Davy, *Le droit, l'idéalisme et l'experience* (Paris, 1922), pp. 16ff, who in analyzing Hauriou's thought, distinguishes the plane of individuality and the plane of personality, the first being constituted by disciplinary and statutory law, the second by juridical commerce and contracts.

physical laws whose truth is related to just one previously established system of reference. Time does not exist in itself, but only
in relation to the interior constitution of our world, which may be
just a grain of sand in the immensity of the universe. And certainly
this disposition of things, this row of events we call chronology, is
tremendously important for us, just as the distribution of briefs to
the members of the court is very important for the attorney—beware
of a mistake!—or as the foreman's distribution of work assignments
is crucial for the factory worker. But all this hardly interests the
litigant or the client: for him this great importance vanishes; as does
chronology outside of our orbit. The theory of the institution and
the institutional conception of law are a profoundly traditional
juridical translation of the modern principle of relativity. Roman
law had discovered this; perhaps the homage I give it here will make
up for the rough treatment I have given it on other days.

Now we are in a position to attempt an enumeration of the general
characteristics of the institution. The first trait to record is—as one
would expect—the predominant role of the idea. The idea is, in the
institution, the converging point for the initial founding will and the
successive adhering wills that eventually will stick to it; the institution
is an idea that snowballs. There is something institutional in the
multilateral act that the Germans call *Vereinbarung*[35]—Duguit translates it "union"—and which they justly oppose to contract.

The institution is the integration of an idea; and note that the same
idea may be involved in a series of institutional integrations. It can
assume a succession of institutional existences and, by reason of this
fact, establish among them a continuity that the science of law must
take into account. For example, religious or diocesan associations
"institute" (less completely, it is true) on the level of the separation
of church and state[36] the same idea that the old public religious
establishments had "instituted" on the level of the regime of concordats, and that theology and canon law, and our administrative
case law as well, look upon as "instituted" in the Church, while
international law looks upon it as "instituted" in the papacy.

This is the institution. In contract there is no integration of an idea;
there is simply a meeting of two wills, each of which follows its own
idea; and this phenomenon produces a balance. This balance is the
whole contract; the contractual effects are entirely included and

35. [G.]
36. [I.e., under the law of July 1, 1901. See Appendix.]

definitively enclosed in this balance. I offered 100 francs, you asked for 200; little by little I raised my proposals, you lowered your demands. The moment came when we both said the same figure, the matter is settled forever. We are caught, imprisoned, as our baby face was one day, in a snapshot, where it defies the irreparable outrage of years.

Contract is, in the domain of juridical things, the equivalent of unorganized matter. Its idea, its "form"—the balance—is entirely exterior to it, like the balance scale in relation to the weights placed on its plates. This balance, once reached, holds the contracting parties in an obligatory bond, just as a vessel holds liquid or a clay mold fixes a statue's form in bronze. This is the lowest degree in the hierarchy of being.

In the institution, the idea is a theme for collaboration; it is willed in common; it is the goal of a shared aspiration—a far cry from the balance of contrary wills. Here, the founders and followers are united in the same idea. This idea forms an interior bond between them; it is their "common good"; they are wedded in a certain mental concept; they join forces in the service of a task. This innerness of the institutional "form" in the members of the institution makes it truly a "juridical being" distinct from these members, yet supported by their personalities.

The *organizing idea* is the first trait of the institution. Contract lacks this trait, and this is why it is immutable. Contract is only an agreement of wills on a given object; the contracting parties must strictly abide by what was promised. There is no development for contract; if any occurs, it is due to an institutional infiltration, a check to the contractual principle.[37] Development is possible only where there is some intensity of being; and contract is just the tête-à-tête of creditor and debtor, of seller and buyer. The institution is much more than this; it is the organization of an idea. And so it is capable of approaching—if not reaching—that higher degree of being which is life.

Well then, are institutions really living beings? This is the second point to investigate. Jurists currently talk not about the life of institutions—for up to now they hardly mention the institution—but about the life of moral persons. "Social, economic, and political

37. Cf. Hauriou, "La teoria del riesgo imprevisible y los contratos infruidos per instituciones sociales," in *Revista de derecho privado* (Madrid), Jan. 15, 1926. [In this article Hauriou presents the theory of *imprévision* as it emerges from the jurisprudence of the Conseil d'État, as the application of distributive justice to the interpretation of a *commutative contract*.]

organisms, persons of international law, states are born, develop, prosper, suffer, weaken, die," as Fauchille puts it . . .[38] Institutions can never acquire personality, except by the metaphor I resigned myself to with certain reservations. Can they acquire life? And if so, what power of life, what level of life?

Life begins where form is integrated in matter, and life is all the more abundant as this integration is more perfect, as the organs become more dependent upon the organism. Just the statement of this truth makes it obvious that institutional life is an illusion. The individuals who enter into the institution and comprise its organs keep the fullness of their individual life. What is more, if the institution lives or appears to live, it is only by a life that is borrowed from the men who collaborate in the task of thinking for it, willing for it, and acting for it. The institution is the chain that binds them together; but they are the ones who carry the chain.[39]

Institutional existence is then below the *level of personality,* below the *level of life.* And yet it is above the *level of brute existence;* it belongs to what I call, inspired by Newman, the *level of development.* This is less than life and more than the trigger of a mechanical spring. Here is the great mystery that philosophy must explain to us one day. Those of you who are familiar with the hylomorphic[40] doctrine will understand that I am not perplexed. Of all philosophies only this doctrine adequately explains the institutional *fact;* it is the philosophy of experienced reality.

The institution lives only by the life men lend to it. But among these men, there are one or several whose will enchains the will of others for the future and indefinitely, until this institution vanishes. The great mystery is that the will of the founder or founders prevails over the wills of the successive adherents—the will of the living is chained to the will of the dead. This is the great postulate of the institutional theory.

I realize that this is difficult for the speculative reason to concede, but I claim that it is the way things are, and that there is a universal *consensus* on this point. Let philosophy explain it as best it can! We shall go into that later on. For the moment I just want to consider the unanimous opinion voiced in the adage "one does not disavow

38. Paul Fauchille, *Traité de droit international public,* 8th ed. (Paris, 1926), I, 300.
39. Life is determined by the ensemble of an individual's psychical characteristics . . . There are no psychical characteristics in the institution—of itself it has neither reason, nor consciousness, nor will. One can speak of institutional life in the same metaphorical sense in which one is permitted to speak of sensitivity among vegetables. Rémy Collin, *Reflexions sur le psychisme* (Paris, 1929), pp. 21, 107.
40. [Hylomorphiste. G.]

the debts of one's father": an adage that well expresses an application of institutional truth.

Life itself is the mystery of an immobile principle that passes through successive states. A similar mystery gives institutions some sort of power of development that, by allegory, one may call a life. But this is only an allegory: a figurative way of expressing the continuity of institutional development. But let us not confuse the fable with its moral.

The direction fixed by the founder is immobile! And what difference does it make whether or not we know this founder or the date of the foundation. I cannot trace my genealogy back further than a few generations, but this does not free me from my ancestors; all I need know is that I have their blood in my veins![41] There is a direction immanent in every institution, and what matters is that we recognize it and that we follow it. Whether inscribed in charterlike form, such as a law, a last will, an act of incorporation, or revealed in the spontaneous reactions of men, like national spirit, this direction is the institution's principle of stability.

And this principle is what those who continue the institution assimilate. Institutional assimilation is something like knowledge: they say that man is half in his knowledge; knowledge is a kind of communion between the knower and the object known.[42] So it is

41. Every institution presupposes a foundation. Foundation is, in an allegorical manner of speaking, a generation: there is no spontaneous juridical generation. This is true of institution-things as well as of institution-corporations. This very point is missed by the historical school, which holds that law is an organic product of social life, the development of which escapes the grasp of the human will. This is an error. Georg Jellinek writes very justly: "No institution could be born in the absence of an activity that is conscious of the end it pursues. In their origin all institutions and all usages in force among these peoples [even the least civilized] pursue a conscious end." Georg Jellinek, L'état moderne et son droit, I, 77.

42. I am alluding to the aristotelian and thomistic theory of knowledge; the present work being principally intended for academic lawyers who are, for the most part, poorly informed on this philosophy, I shall try to summarize it in a few lines.

This philosophy—traditionally formulated in the definition [of knowledge, and truth as] adaequatio rei et intellectus—offers, in comparison with most of its rivals, this particular characteristic (which justifies the suggestion of kinship made in the text)—it situates the epistemological problem not on the spatial plane in which the subject and object remain necessarily impenetrable, but on the metaphysical plane where they are able to compenetrate while each one keeps its individuality. [Renard's lengthy example is here omitted.]

In each object of knowledge there is an "intelligible," an "idea," a concept, of which this object is one of innumerable concrete realisations. This object is an abstract "form" individualized in a "matter" and realized by this individualization. The intellect of the subject makes its own, not the object in its concrete reality, but the "intelligible," the "idea," the concept that is included in it, or rather the multitude of concepts that are included in it. The object becomes the intellect by means of the intelligible which is in it, all the time remaining itself in its inexhaustible power. There you have, certainly, the limit of rational knowledge: analogical knowledge through images.

between the institution and those who successively continue it: they receive something from it and they bring something to it; and what they bring they transmit with what they have received, and there is only one single thing transmitted, for the new contributions are integrated into the old and into the core of the initial contribution—the foundation. The continuity of the institution is assured by the successive contributions of the generations that transmit its heritage: to continue an institution is not to put it under a glass nor to treat it as a museum attendant treats his treasures. To continue an institution is to cooperate with its founders, to provide for the current interests of its operation, and consequently to adapt it, to maintain it, to develop it, to make it prosper and live. In this analogical sense, institutions live.

Little by little, the rank of the institution on the ontological ladder is coming into focus. The institution is below the human person, which is the only true person in this world, and below organic life, which is the only true life; but it is higher than brute matter. This intermediate degree is in turn divided into the two positions that we have named: moral personality on top, objective individuality below. This is where we are now. And this having been said, a third trait of the institutional phenomenon is going to reveal itself.

There is in the ideal or collective juridical subject—the one, at least, that acquires personality—not a life in the analogical sense that we have accepted, but a double life, and consequently, there must be a double rule to govern this double life.

The first or at least the most apparent by definition, the only one apparent from the outside, is the life of relationships of juridical

---

Knowledge of things in their concrete reality is beyond this limit; we can distinguish "vital" forces in our affective powers by which we may sense, feel, experience. This is the role of *intuition,* a subsidiary process that may not achieve knowledge, strictly so-called, of the individual and the concrete, but certainly is capable of approximating knowledge beyond the operating limits of the apprehension of reason. It is so with the more humble objects of knowledge, and with the more lofty ones too: through rational knowledge it is possible to be raised up to the "idea" of God; but the "being" of God is inaccessible to it. It is by the vital force of his whole being that man is capable, not of understanding God, but of approaching him.

To remain oneself while becoming another: such is the thomistic theory of knowledge. To remain oneself while becoming the organ of an institution: such is the modern theory of the institution. It is by the mediation of the "idea" that each of these partial interpenetrations is realised; by "communion" in an "idea" the subject "becomes" the object in knowledge, the subject remaining itself vis-à-vis the object. Similarly, the person "becomes" the organ of an institution, all the time retaining his personal identity vis-à-vis the institution. On the terrain of action the theory of the institution reflects the *fundamental* but *reconcilable dualism* that the [thomistic] theory of knowledge deals with on the plane of speculation: these are two corollaries of the same ontology.

subject to juridical subject: the *obligations* that are tied by contract or otherwise between individual and individual, or between individual and institution, or between institution and institution. This is the *exterior life.*

The most salient manifestation of this exterior life is responsibility. One can be responsible only in relation to another. This is why responsibility can only be incurred by the institutions that have an exterior life, that can oppose their existence to the existence of others. The institutions that are simply accountable are covered, in the eyes of the public, by the person upon whom they depend; and between them there is no *responsibility,* there can only be an *account* to be adjusted. I am knocked down in the street by a fire engine; but I demand an indemnity from the city, not from the fire company. In the course of a war a public forest is damaged by the army; will the courts receive a request for damages from the ministry of agriculture against the ministry of war? Never! The state would be pleading against the state; the credit of indemnity is canceled in advance because creditor and debtor are part of the same moral person; there will only be a juggling of the accounts, a debit to the account of the ministry of war, a credit to the account of the ministry of agriculture. And if these two ministries cannot agree, the cabinet will decide: it is just a matter of accountability.

And this discloses a second life,[43] which cannot be perceived from the outside: a life of relationships of organ to organ within the same juridical subject, a life that circulates through the structure, the *constitution,* of each juridical subject, its *interior life.* Here is a new difference between the two kinds of juridical subjects—the human person and the institution—and a new warning against the mirage of confusing them!

The constitution of the human person as a juridical subject does not concern us as jurists, and we are not qualified to understand

43. I am putting the interior life in the second place only for convenience of exposition. In his *Droit public,* 2nd ed., and under the rubric "La Question de la Personnalité," pp. 41ff, Hauriou has well shown the natural and logical order of the two problems. First of all the foundation should be laid for the juridical subject, which is a chapter of objective law. Here he deals with the institution and its vocation first to moral personality and then to juridical personality; this chapter is similar to that which the physiologist or the psychologist writes when he explains child-birth and the stages of development of the human person. Next comes the chapter on *subjective law.* It opens at the moment when the previously founded juridical subjects are *put in relationship* with each other. "Thus," says Hauriou, "we are taking a stand on the direction of the evolution of law. We claim that it goes from the objective to the subjective; this position is the exact opposite of Duguit's . . . that law goes from the subjective to the objective."

it, at least not as jurists. It is not up to the science of law to study
the interplay of the biological organs and mental faculties that make
up human personality; and no one appeals to the courts for a cure.
The institution, on the other hand, is made up of human persons
(or of component institutions) each of which is itself, individually,
a juridical subject as well as an institutional organ. The interior life
of the institution presents a problem of the relationship of juridical
subject to juridical subject, inasmuch as the individual independence
of these two juridical subjects is complicated by their common institutional affiliation; the interior life of the institution presents the
problem of coordinating this independence and this affiliation. This
is a problem of law; it is our affair, as jurists. It is, they would say
in philosophy, a relationship *ad alterum,* therefore a relationship
of justice, therefore a juridical relationship.

In the same analogical sense that we spoke of institutional personality and institutional life, we may or rather we must investigate
the movements of *institutional psychology.* Institutional psychology
belongs to the domain of law—it is true "constitutional law." Moreover, I have already had occasion to point out how useful philosophers might find a juridical analysis of this psychology as a term
of comparison for an analysis of human psychology.[44]

To possess an interior life of a juridical character, just as human
persons possess an interior life of a physiological and psychological
character—this is the third trait I announced to you a moment ago.
It is this trait I have in mind when I say that every institution is
the seat of a more or less autonomous juridical system, or when I
talk of the institutional conception of law. This trait marks the sharpest point of contrast between the "institutional" and the "contractual" or the "obligatory": for an interior life is a very different thing
from a bond between persons: *vinculum juris quo necessitate astrin-
gimur alicujus solvendae.*

This thought is so important that I must insist upon it. I shall
illustrate it with two concrete examples—one from private law and
the other from public law. A business company . . . establishes *with
outsiders* relationships of all kinds. It buys from its suppliers, sells
to its customers, negotiates with this contractor over the construction
of a building, with that truck driver about the delivery of its com-
modities: *exterior* life; *obligatory* relationships! But it also maintains

44. Cf. *Le droit, la justice et la volonté,* p. 11, n. 4. The idea is treated again by
Hauriou, "Le droit, la justice et l'ordre sociale," in the *Revue trimestrielle de droit civil*
(1927), pp. 795ff. The term "institutional psychology" incurs the same criticism as the
expression "social vitalism"; unfortunately, I cannot find a better word.

a kind of commerce *with its shareholders*. They have contributed their money to it; it pays them dividends; they take part in the company management. Is this still a matter of obligatory relationships between creditor and debtor? No! It is the bondholder who is creditor, and he is outside the company; the shareholder is in the company. Then, is this a title of ownership, is the shareholder a coproprietor? No! They are as far apart as a company is from joint-property. A company is a cooperation of activities in the direction of an idea. Joint-property is just a balance: a contractual balance in the cases and in the measure that the law permits this sort of agreement, or even a purely chance balance that collapses at the first flick of the finger—this is what you have read in article 815 of the *Code civil*.[45] In any case, there is no internal principle of attraction and cohesion, no incorporation of an idea.

The shareholder, then, is neither a creditor nor a coproprietor. Property, credit: these titles refer to the relationships of person to person; the shareholder is very simply an integral part of the company; the company is *a small part* of him, since it lives only by his life and acts only by his activity and the life and activity of his fellow shareholders: *interior* life; *organic* relationships!

I said *a small part*. Now you are getting a picture, are you not, of the difference between the juridical organism and the biological organism, between the personified institution and the human person: the providential signpost set up at every dangerous turn where we might risk falling into the dizziness of confusing them? The biological organism assimilates its organs *entirely*, or better, the more perfect the organism, the less autonomous is the life of the organ. The juridical organism, the institution, assimilates only *a small part*, because in potency or in perfection of being it is even lower than the most feeble and most imperfect of biological organisms.

In the company, each shareholder fully preserves his personality at the same time as he becomes an organ of the institution. He is then capable of having two sorts of juridical relationships with the company: organ of the institution and, if the case arises, creditor or debtor of the institution. A certain shareholder of the Eastern Railroad Company is also a passenger, a shipper; and the clerk at the ticket window treats him like any other passenger or shipper. Perhaps you have noticed that train conductors have a different degree of deference for each of the three classes of compartments; they have no special respect for the shareholder-passenger.

45. [See Appendix.]

The shareholder appears as such only insofar as he forms a body with his co-shareholders. Together they occupy diverse posts: ordinary shareholder, founder, administrator, deputy administrator, trustee—this is the organism! And while he is acting in this secondary capacity, the shareholder assumes an impressive dignity *within the company* and in the estimation of the personnel. Yet *in the eyes of outsiders* he disappears; and he disappears all the more as the company reaches a higher degree of being, I mean as it becomes more independent of its members. A case in point is the stock corporation;[46] the creditors of a stock corporation can never personally pursue its shareholders—any more than the creditors of a city can demand payment from the personal fortune of one of its inhabitants.

What name can I give the juridical rules that govern these relationships between company and shareholders? Think it over carefully: they form a chapter of constitutional law; this is *private constitutional law.*

I know I am laying myself open to the charge of heresy; but science —I am aiming only at the secular sciences—hardly progresses at all but by heresy. The heretics are those who have a passion for truth and who, to serve it, dare to disturb the status quo of traditional formulas and the tranquillity of the well situated. What is more, the heresy of today sometimes becomes the orthodoxy of tomorrow. And, as for the point that concerns us, from today I hurl back the reproach upon an individualism that repudiates the reality of a private constitutional law. The real heretic is our system of private law, which tries to restrict the interior life of business companies to an alignment of subjective relationships of person to person and to reduce the company itself to a network of contractual obligations. The company, like the nation, the state, and every other institution, is neither a sum nor a resultant of individual activities. It is a "form" that affects—but only *pro parte qua*—the human individualities that it unites in one common destiny.

By taking as my first example a case of commercial law, I realize that I am putting myself in a difficult position. For our system of administrative law gives quite a different picture of the institutional phenomenon. But if I had featured this at the outset, I would have raised the suspicion of having artificially generalized a particular conception of French public law. I am coming to it, or rather I am coming back to it. All roads, in France, lead to the Administration.

The Administration, under its diverse personifications, state, dé-

---

46. [*Société anonyme.* G.]

partements, communes, public establishments, also exercises the double activity that you are now aware of; but it does so quite openly. This duality is most strikingly expressed on the level of procedure by a division of actions that I have already alluded to and that we shall come back to in the next class. Right now I want to give you the proof that administrative litigation is the prism that decomposes the two rays of institutional life; then we shall find its replica in the procedure of our private law.

Well then, like the shareholder of a business company, the citizen assumes, with regard to the state or to the *département,* a dual role: he is a member of it and he can be involved with it in a multitude of obligatory relationships (contractual obligations, obligations born of tortious conduct or of unjust enrichment, perhaps simply of risk). He can then bring before the administrative jurisdiction two sorts of appeals. He may plead on his own behalf and *against the Administration*—for instance, when he demands the payment of a remuneration or the liquidation of an indemnity. Or he may plead, if not *for the Administration,* at least in its interest, by soliciting a decision of annulment that would induce it to adjust a disturbance caused in the economy of the public services by a decision it had taken contrary to law or administrative ethics. Litigation of plenary jurisdiction or subjective litigation—this is for the exterior life; litigation of annulment or objective litigation (appeal for *excès de pouvoir*)— this is for the interior life.

In the first kind of action, the citizen acts on behalf of his own private interests—for example, he obtains damages—and the decision stands as authoritative only for his personal benefit. In the second kind of action, the citizen acts for the Administration, that is, for the public interest of which it has charge. He does not obtain any judgment for his own benefit, he seeks only the rectification of a vicious situation; but the decision rendered at his request has an effect *erga omnes;* he takes the part of a public minister.[47]

And like the citizens, the agents[48] of the public services play a double role: they are organs of the Administration, and they are themselves. It follows . . . that they can incur by their questionable deeds two kinds of responsibilities: individual responsibility for faults that are not connected with the exercise of their function; administrative responsibility for faults that are related to the exercise of their function. We call this personal fault and fault of office.

47. Cf. my *Notions très foncières de droit public français* (Paris, 1920), p. 77ff.
48. [*Agents.* Renard also refers to *fonctionnaires,* which have here been translated "officials."]

But is it not true that with diverse modalities and under diverse names the same discrimination applies to all sorts of institutions? To come back to the stock corporation: does every questionable deed of its directors expose their personal responsibility before outsiders? Is there not a circle of activity within which the directors' responsibility is covered by the corporation's responsibility to pay judgments awarded the injured party? Can the corporation, in any event, seek to recover against its directors? To state the question is to resolve it. As long as the directors do not stray from a certain line of conduct, the corporation answers for them, without redress against them. This necessary solution is but the commercial adaptation of the distinction between personal fault and fault of office.[49]

The great difference lies in the fact that the commercial corporation,[50] since it is only imperfectly "instituted," must look to the courts of common law to make this distinction, whereas the Administration, which is perfectly "instituted"—allow me the expression—"washes its linens in private." And there are two ways of doing this: either the citizen-official is treated as an official until the Administration disavows him; or the citizen-official is treated as a simple citizen until the Administration takes up his cause and claims responsibility for the prejudicial act for which he is sued. The constitution of the year VIII[51] sanctioned the first method by a procedure called the *mise en jugement*: a private individual who wished to sue a government official had first to ask the authorization of the Administration, as represented by the Conseil d'État; if the authorization was granted, it constituted, on the part of the Administration, a denial of responsibility—the "deliverance to the secular arm." Since the decree of September 19, 1870, the second method has been in use: private individuals are able to sue officials just as they sue anyone else; but the prefect can intervene to shield an official under the protective shadow of his two-cornered hat; this is called taking a decision of conflict. This decision is immediately brought before a higher court that is called the Tribunal des Conflits. By validating the decision, this higher jurisdiction proclaims that the act under

49. [After a lengthy quotation from Léon Michoud, *La théorie de la personnalité*, II, 276, Renard comments, "Michoud well understood that the administrative theory of responsibility is only a particular case of a larger theory; with regard to responsibility, just as with regard to property, we must not establish an overly rigorous opposition between private law and public law; the fundamental opposition is really between individual law and institutional law." Cf. *La théorie de l'institution*, pp. 123ff and 162ff.]

50. [Renard is still referring to the stock corporation.]

51. [I.e., 1799.]

attack is part of the activity of the Administration and that the Administration bears full responsibility for it; by annulling the decision, it pronounces a denial of administrative responsibility and definitively delivers the official over to private suit and to the courts of common law. Do you not find that this alternative procedure of the *mise en jugement* and the *conflit* is very telling of an institutional development that has reached full maturity in the French administrative regime?

Moreover, with all due allowances, parliamentary life is very like administrative life. For Parliament and each of its two Chambers is an institutional organism: it has its economy of varied commissions, each one with a special competence; its written internal constitution in the form of its rules; its interior and disciplinary jurisdiction represented by its bureau; a certain endowment of public force at the disposal of its president. Parliament and the Chambers are not responsible, and this immunity extends to their members, in anything that pertains to their parliamentary activity. And since the senator or the deputy—like the administrative official—is also a private person, the same question comes up of determining: *substantially*, when an act is imputable to the senator or deputy, therefore covered by parliamentary immunity, and when it is imputable to the private person, therefore justiciable in common law; and *formally*, how to make the proper distinction. And the answer is tangibly the same: each of the Chambers gives umbrage to the conduct of its members up until disavowal—with the same two modalities: during sessions the senator or deputy can be sued or prosecuted only with the authorization of the Chamber to which he belongs; between sessions he can be sued or prosecuted just like any other citizen, but at the reopening of Parliament the Chamber can order his release and a suspension of proceedings.

I must conclude. The symmetry between the administrative regime and the regime of private companies would be perfect if the institutional phenomenon were not thwarted in private positive law and its rational development paralyzed by a desperate effort of jurists to save the individualist dogma: an effort that reminds us of the devices of the ancients to save the theory of circular movement from the contradictions that the course of the stars and experimental physics took the liberty of opposing to it.

The administrative regime and the regime of private companies both bear the same institutional seed. But in private companies this seed grows slowly in a soil hardened by prejudice; in the administrative regime it has found good earth. There is a constitutional law of the family and of the business company, as of the Administration and the political society, and as of the profession and the enterprise in proportion as they depart from anarchical competition to ascend to organization; but this constitutional law is sometimes only an embryo, sometimes a developed system.

Although much slower to appear than the private society or the business company, the association immediately abandoned the contractual type to orient itself toward the institutional regime. The draft bill of November 14, 1899, organized the association in the image of the business company, on the principle of contractual law; but this was entirely reversed in the course of the parliamentary debates, and the only remaining trace of the first conception is in the title of the law of July 1, 1901[52]—"law relative to the contract of association"—which is not part of the law anyway. I cannot follow the positive rules that fix the frankly institutional physiognomy of the legal regime of associations and oppose it to the *apparently* contractual legal regime of companies.[53] Here, at least, is one institutional characteristic that is pointed out in a leading case[54] of our Cour de Cassation.

Since it has its own interior rules, the institution normally possesses the power and means to have them observed, at least by its members, and to apply to these members, if necessary, its internally fixed penalties.[55] In a contractual company, the expulsion of a member would be an application of the tacit abrogating clause established by article 1184 of the *Code civil;*[56] and it would be up to the courts to pronounce it. In an association, on the other hand, expulsion is nothing other than that "excommunication" which is the legitimate prerogative of every "community," and which it has the legitimate power to pronounce itself, by its own organs—committee or assembly—without appealing to the public courts. And this is precisely what the Cour de Cassation decided.[57]

It seems possible that the institutional phenomenon will shake off its contractual shell in the law of companies as it has in the law

52. [See Appendix.]

53. On this subject, see Hauriou, *Droit constitutionnel,* 2nd ed., pp. 668ff.

54. [Renard does not cite here the case in question. See n. 57 below.]

55. In his thesis *De la répression disciplinaire* (Bordeaux, 1902), Roger Bonnard develops this idea that disciplinary law is the interior penal law of corporations that are distinct from the state; hence the tendency of modern legislation to confide the exercise of this law to organs of a judicial character. [See also Alfred Légal and Jean Brèthe de la Grassaye, *Le Pouvoir disciplinaire dans les institutions privées* (Paris, 1938).]

56. [See Appendix.]

57. Civ., Dec. 22, 1920, S. 1922.1.369, note R. Morel.

of associations. And I wonder if the vogue of actions by plural vote and the pending bills on this subject, inasmuch as they reveal a preoccupation for defending the *idea* and the founders' orientation against the power of accumulated *capital* in an enterprise, are not to be scored to the credit of the progress of the institutional concept in private law and, by this very same token, to be noted as a flash of spiritualism in the capitalistic economy of our industrial organization and our commercial law. This is not the least interesting aspect of *rationalization*.[58]

And since I am talking commercial law (philosophers are exempt from the prohibition against the blind speaking of colors), do we not see, under the sign and at the summons of the law that authorizes arbitration clauses, true interior jurisdictions being organized in commercial or professional societies, in economic unions, in labor organizations—jurisdictions that are destined to take the place of public courts in resolving, according to the rules of corporate ethics and scorning legal subtleties, the disputed claims of contracts that attribute jurisdiction to them? The law of December 31, 1925, someone has very justly written, will function in proportion as it establishes permanent organisms of arbitration within and among the professions. This new law certainly tends to "institute" the professions; and just the other day a friend and colleague made a conscientious survey of the legislative and jurisprudential documents that tend to organize "authority in the profession":[59] but to say authority, differentiation, organization, in matters of law, is to say institution.

The institution asserts itself by the force of things. It is one of those notions of natural law that comes in by the window when we chase it out the door. No legislation can do without it; it is only possible to camouflage it. There is a camouflage of contract, a camouflage of fiction. But these devices cannot withstand the usury of time, nor the necessities of practice, nor the impartial and conscientious investigations of the science of law. The theory of circular movement collapsed under the eccentrics and epicycles; the old individualist dogma crumbles before the evidence of institutional truth. But there is no merit in denouncing it since we no longer mark fallen idols for burning.

---

58. [See Renard, "L'organisation rationnelle de l'état," *La théorie de l'institution*, Appendix III, pp. 537ff.]

59. Joseph Danel, "L'autorité dans la profession," *Politique* (1927), pp. 512ff.

GEORGES RENARD   The Interior Life of the Institution:

Intimacy, Authority, Objectivity

We have not yet sounded the depths of this "interior life" that essentially distinguishes the institution from contract and raises it, with the human person though on a lower rung, to the dignity of a juridical subject. Actually, we have established the existence of this "interior life" rather than analyzed it; we have looked at it from the very discreet position of outside observers. We shall now try to probe its intimacy; we are going to leap the wall of private life.

This is a difficult task. Intimacy resists all inventory; it is not amenable to the laws of quantity. Not long ago someone judiciously wrote: "Mathematical regulators are not admissible in friendship."[1] Friendship, intimacy, is experienced from within; one must live it to understand it; it is something spiritual, and therefore it cannot be taken apart.

There is an institutional intimacy, just as there is a personal intimacy; and the former is no more closed to the investigations of the jurist than is the latter to the investigations of psychology. When it comes to institutions, intimacy is a subject for juridical research.

But the result of these investigations will not satisfy us fully: we must reconcile ourselves to this in advance. We shall not grasp everything and we shall not reach the end. This fatal lack of understanding is precisely what makes struggles inevitable in social life. To do away with them forever, it would be necessary for peoples to understand one another completely,—for the civil legislator to fathom the mentality of the different religious communities, for parties and classes of society to open their hearts to one another. And because this is impossible, even to loyalty and good will, we must resign ourselves to the risk of misunderstanding and the semi-security of compromise.

---

1. H. D. Noble, *L'amitié avec Dieu* (Lille-Paris-Bruges, 1927), p. 264.

But just because an end is unattainable, it does not follow that we should not try to approach it. The maxim "all or nothing" expresses the worst of political, social, and scientific errors. There is, in the center of every institution, an impregnable citadel; we cannot carry it by storm, but I hope we shall succeed in surrounding it.

I shall invite you first to meditate upon this notion of institutional intimacy; and because—as you know well—I have no taste for speculation for its own sake, I propose to test the juridical efficiency of this notion by two applications, which you will excuse me for developing rather fully: the question of the limits of law and of ethics, and the question of the limits of the professional secret. This will be the object of my first part.

The second part will aim at an evaluation of the special character of institutional intimacy: it is an *organized* intimacy, therefore a *differentiated* intimacy.[2] Among reasonable beings, differentiation is the effect of authority. Intimacy and authority are the first two characteristics of the internal life of institutions.

The development of these two characteristics will lead me to new insights into a third characteristic, which I have already discussed in the preceding conference. Because the institution is organized, the mutual relationships of its members, as such, are not simple relationships of person to person, analogous to the relationships that contract establishes between creditor and debtor; they are relationships of incorporation, of organ to organ, deriving from their common affiliation to the same organism. The distinctive characteristic of these relationships is objectivity. I shall stress this in a last part.

Let us consider first of all the notion of institutional intimacy.[3] Intimacy is an affective disposition, the most salient characteristic of which is clearly exclusiveness; it easily takes on a nuance of jealousy. To be intimate is to take pleasure in the company of a few people, in a certain isolation from the public. When an intimacy is jealous, it barricades itself within the mutual delights it affords the chosen few; when it is generous, it can do no more than distribute

2. [Renard contrasts "differentiation" with "equality." Cf. *La théorie de l'institution* p. 122: "The institution's interior life is made up of the relationships of its organs among themselves; it is 'organized,' and to say organism is to say differentiation; the institution is the *seat of an authority*. This marks the great difference between the 'institutional' and the 'contractual': the 'contractual' is egalitarian; equality is the great rule of contracts, and despite Rousseau's sophism you will never derive the principle of authority from contract."]

3. [Cf. Hauriou's notion of spiritual relationship (*Droit constitutionnel,* 1st ed., pp. 255ff) and spiritual community (*Droit constitutionnel,* 2nd ed., pp. 81ff).]

the crumbs of these delights. You cannot be an intimate friend of the whole human race.

The term institutional intimacy signifies that the institution is more than a "milieu"; it is a "home"; and the closer the intimacy, the warmer the home. There are very intime institutions that are mostly "home"; and there are very extensive ones that are more "milieu"; and between the two there is an endless series of nuances. What constitutes the strength of our Conseil d'État is a corporate intimacy that is maintained and developed by the rules that govern its recruitment; it is stronger than our judicial courts, even though their members are appointed for life. The Conseil d'État assimilates its magistrates in a different way than a Cour d'Appel or than the Cour de Cassation.

Human intimacy belongs to the domain of moral philosophy. Moral philosophy teaches us to order our intimacies in conformity with reason. Well-ordered charity condemns eccentricities; it directs us to love all men, but beginning with the nearest, our relatives, our friends, our work companions, our fellow citizens—and only then the unknown, foreigners, enemies. Institutional intimacy is a matter for juridical philosophy, and—with a reservation for some later additions—it seems to me that from this point of view of intimacy we can draw a double lesson for the benefit of the theory of the institution.

First of all, intimacy is a bond of trust, and the more trust you have, the fewer guarantees you demand. The great guarantee of juridical relationships is the rule. Positive law establishes rules to protect those subject to the courts and to the administration against the blunders of magistrates and administrative agents. When government officials demand fixed tenure, it is to protect themselves against the caprices of their hierarchical superiors: they lack trust.

In an earlier series of conferences, I recalled that in every juridical system—and each institution has its juridical economy—there is a place for concrete ad hoc evaluation.[4] To want nothing more than concrete evaluation is to rely on the judgment of another—a regime of trust; guarantees are unnecessary. This is only possible where there is a maximal intimacy. The less intimate an institution becomes, the more rules you will see appearing. There are obviously

---

4. [Renard, *La valeur de la loi* (Paris, 1928), pp. 36–49: "Law (*la loi ou la réglementation*) is only one of the two fundamental processes of juridical technique. There is a second: the *direct and concrete evaluation* of the elements of each particular situation insofar as they are manifest, without previously applicable legislation, inspired solely by the idea of Justice."]

many less rules in the government of a family than in the administration of a university library: a regime of regulations, indeed! What
is more, the rule changes character according to the intimacy of the
institution considered. And this leads me to bring the notions of
intimacy and institution closer together.

Every intimacy effects an ascendancy over personality. In friendship this is a *reciprocal ascendancy of one human personality over
another personality*: I ache in your heart. If the substantive "con-
dolence" had not become so hackneyed and so emptied of serious
meaning that we have to put it in the plural and add the epithet
"sincere" to give it the illusion of strength, it would express rather
exactly this friendly or *individual* intimacy.

In *institutional* intimacy the ascendancy is that of *the whole over
its parts.* And this ascendancy, with the consequent intrusion of
the institutional power upon the exterior personal activity of the
members of the institution (and even, with an important reservation
that I have made elsewhere,[5] upon their simple intentions)—this
ascendancy, this intrusion, is legitimate in proportion as it is reasonable, that is, in conformity with the requirements of the final end
of the institution: and the institutional final end is the common good.
The common good does not swallow up the particular good of each
individual; on the contrary, it is the necessary condition of the fulfillment of each individual's good from a certain point of view[6] or
within a certain sphere. This end, this common good, is what makes
the institution insofar as it takes root in a certain human milieu,
"informs" it, organizes it, differentiates it, elicits a power within it.

I do not want to grieve any of my colleagues, and still less to

5. Renard, *Contribution juridique aux rapports du droit positif et de la théologie
morale; La théorie des "leges mere poenales"* (Paris, 1929), pp. 5ff.

6. "Bonum proprium non potest esse sine [bono] communi [vel familiae vel civitates
aut regni] et bona dispositio partis est in respectu ad totum." Aquinas, *Summa
Theologiae,* II II, q. 47, a. 10, ad 2. The following passage also shows very well how
the good of each individual is included in that of the community, without either being
reducible to the other; and this is why there are two branches in the virtue of justice:
"Justitia ordinat hominem in comparatione ad alium. Quod quidem potest esse
dupliciter: uno modo ad alium singulariter consideratum; alio modo ad alium in
communi, secundum quod ille, qui servit alicui communitati, servit omnibus qui sub
communitate illa continentur; ad utrumque ergo potest haberi justitia secundum
propriam rationem," St. Thomas, *Summa Theologiae,* II II, q. 58, a.5. [In his introduction to *La théorie de l'institution,* Renard wrote: "The relationship between individual
goods and the 'common good' is neither a mathematical relationship—sum or difference—nor a dynamic relationship—mechanical balance; it is an ontological relationship: matter and form." But Renard postponed consideration of this philosophical
theme, promising that it would be central to his second volume, *La philosophie de
l'institution.*]

reproach the memory of a great jurisconsult whom I have always admired and respected.[7] But I must speak plainly. If the state is only an agglomeration or a federation or even a syndicate of public services; if, above the public services, each of which has its own end and internal hierarchy, there is no state end that coordinates the particular ends and hierarchies of the public services while assimilating them and subjecting them to itself; if the state is not, above all, a power exterior and superior to the public services, which, in the measure necessary to the pursuit of a dominant end, has the capacity to intrude upon the autonomy of the diverse public services and to lead them back to itself—then the state is only a label and there is no more state. Administrative syndicalism, thus understood, is not a theory of the state; it is a negation of the state.

This goes for the state, the Church, and all institutions. They do not subsist by the "matter" of which they are formed, but by the "form" that raises up this "matter." "We aspire to a betterment of stability and organization," wrote André Tardieu not long ago, "but we are not very concerned about analyzing the resources of this aspiration."[8] The resource, the soul, the "form," of human organizations is power.

The ascendancy of the power of the state over civil institutions is legitimized by the end of the state; the ascendancy of the power of the Church over what were formerly called the diverse "religions" is legitimized by the end of the Church; the ascendancy of every institutional power over the human personality is legitimized by the end of the institution. This ascendancy has its norm in the requirements and the character of the institutional end; this end is what determines the intensity of institutional intimacy: and the more intense the intimacy, the more right the power has to intrude. The institutional rule cannot but reflect the nuances of this intimacy and this power.

And, for example, the goal of the state is more exterior to its subjects than is the goal of the Church to its faithful. There is more intimacy in the religious community than in the political community. The power of the state is one thing, the power of the Church is something else. The laws of the Church are different from the laws of the state. It is clear that they both refer to the external forum; it is clear that as long as they don't infringe justice, the laws of the

---

7. [Reference is to Léon Duguit and his "School of *Service Public*."]

8. André Tardieu, Preface to Maurice Petsche and Jacques Donge, *A la recherche des temps nouveaux* (Paris, 1928).

state oblige in conscience as well as the laws of the Church. However, there is no question that the laws of the Church inspire in its members a different confidence than do the laws of the state in its subjects. Most notably the question of the right of resistance to laws contrary to the natural law does not impose itself in the same manner with ecclesiastical laws as with civil laws. When one loses confidence in the government of the Church to the point of imputing to it a violation of the natural law, one does not disobey the law, one leaves the Church. It is just a different sort of situation. I am not expressing myself now as a believer; I have not introduced any dogma bearing on the decision of ecclesiastical authority. I am speaking in psychological terms; there is no cult whose priests claim a higher prestige before the consciences of their religious followers than do civil magistrates before the people. That is why princes have also sought to be enrobed by some ecclesiastical investiture, when they are not made themselves head of the Church.

The frontier between legality and morality is very hazy from the viewpoint of this institutional conception of law.[9] Just look at the juridical rules that govern the interior life of every institution other than the state—churches, professional associations, families, etc.

Not only does a more perfect institutional intimacy call for a more spontaneous obedience to institutional laws, but it also legitimizes, on the part of these laws, more rigorous demands. The Administration, which is a particular intimacy within the state, exacts of its officials a different punishment than the *Code pénal* exacts of ordinary citizens, and a government official may expose himself to dismissal who would be acquitted before the courts of common law. A certain direction or prohibition that would seem an intolerable abuse of authority if given by the political power, becomes perfectly legitimate when decreed by a more intimate power. The more integration and therefore being are in the organism, the less the organs need guarantees. To put it bluntly, a closer intimacy legitimizes a certain despotism in the application of a more benign rule. The civil law is not the model for the juridical rule; it owes to citizens a guarantee in the measure of the intimacy of the political institution. There are as many degrees of intimacy and as many measures to

9. St. Augustine differentiates between morality and law in this way: Law, since its objective is the good of the community, must overlook a host of individual shortcomings, whereas morality, since its objective is to lead man to eternal happiness, does not overlook the slightest fault, not even a fault in thought. Otto Schilling, "Die Rechtsphilosophie bei den Kirchenvätern," in *Archiv fur Rechts und Wirtschaftsphilosophie,* vol. 26, no. 1, p. 110).

find as there are institutions; the "just" measure is the one adapted to the situation.[10]

Institutional intimacy suggests a second lesson. The first was chiefly to impress politicians and philosophers.[11] This one is more for jurists: it concerns the interpretation of a text! And here I have no scruples about laboring my point.

There is no intimacy without secrecy, and there is no worse fault against intimacy than to betray its secrets. The virtue you appreciate most, gentlemen, in your secretary, and you, ladies, in your maid, is discretion. They belong to the intimacy of your office and your home; they are of the *domus* in the old sense of the word. The secretary is part of your personal intimacy: she owes it to you to keep silence on the mystery of your scientific or literary activity. The maid is part of the intimacy of your family: she should not reveal what she has seen or heard while serving you. You expose your secrets to both of them; there are secrets that you do not, that you cannot, keep from them. The lawyer does not make a case of conscience out of confiding to his secretary *utriusque sexus* his correspondence with his clients; he reveals his secrets. But the secretary is bound to keep them; they are no longer the secrets of the lawyer, but the secrets of the office. And the same thing goes for the barrister, the notary—the secrets of the public official are shared with his clerks and become the secrets of the office; the secrets of the doctor become the secrets of the clinic, and the secrets of the pharmacist

---

10. "Justitiae proprium est inter alias virtutes ut ordinet hominem in his quae sunt ad alterum. Important enim aequalitatem quandam, ut ipsum nomen demonstrat: dicuntur enim ea quae adaequantur, justari." (Aquinas, *Summa Theologiae*, II II, q. 57, a.1). Cf. my observations in the form of a Preface to the book of Henri Welter, *Le contrôle juridictionnel de la moralité administrative* (Paris, 1929): "The control of morality is justified by *institutional intimacy*, an intimacy that unites its members so that they are no longer truly 'other' with respect to each other: they are, in a certain way, 'members' of each other in the structure of an organism; an intimacy, like charity, that goes beyond the kind of *security* that rests on a charter, and that rests entirely on *trust;* an intimacy that consists essentially in a moral bond. There you have the atmosphere for the control of morality. But there are many degrees of institutional intimacy, and it seems that the closer the bonds of this intimacy, the more the control of the institutional judge must be able to transcend the bounds of legality . . . Judicial control should not go beyond *legality* in the political community; it would reach to *morality* in the administrative body (that is, morality in the sense in which Welter takes the word in comparing the end pursued by the administrative agent *in concreto* with the abstract end of the function that is committed to him); it would even embrace expediency in the closest communities, such as the family . . ."

11. [Renard's notion impressed a sociologist, Georges Gurvitch, who was otherwise unsympathetic to his extension of Hauriou's institutional thought. See Gurvitch, "Les idées maîtresses de Maurice Hauriou," *Archives de philosophie du droit et de sociologie juridique* (1931), p. 159.]

the secrets of the laboratory. The secret, if I dare say it, becomes "institutionalized." Someone has recently spoken of the socialization of the professional secret.[12]

Of course, this idea does not fit in very well with Article 378 of the *Code pénal*,[13] which undeniably makes the professional secret an entirely individual obligation. But the authors of the *Code pénal* were not acquainted with secretaries nor with the theory of the institution. I cannot imagine what sort of sentiments secretaries would have stirred up in them; as for the institution, it would have horrified their individualism. This still leaves the maids, but the code draftsmen did not envisage the domestic secret, which is perhaps an error as to the juridical character of domesticity . . .

In reality, the interpretation of Article 378 raises considerable difficulties, over which torrents of ink have been spilt.[14] And if we cannot say that they have seriously increased for the judicial professions, it is a different story for government posts and the medical profession.

As for government posts, you can guess that the aggravation of difficulties is a consequence of the fiscal reform. The law had to intervene in order to authorize, among the officials of the different public administrations, an exchange of information that was necessary for the control of declarations of revenue. "The administrations of the state, of the *départements*, and of the communes," says Article 31 of the law of July 31, 1920, "cannot use the claim of professional secrecy against the agents of the finance administration who, in order to impose taxes instituted by existing laws, demand from them communication of documents of service that they withhold."

A derogation from the individual secret of the government official to the professional secret! But did this individual secret ever exist? Has not the clerk who receives the registration documents always shared his secrets with his fellow clerks? And here again, were not the secrets of the man always the secrets of the bureau?

12. Pierre Tiberghien, "Le secret medical chez le 'médecin de groupement,'" *Chronique sociale de France* (May 1927).

13. [See Appendix.]

14. See all the treatises of criminal law, the works on the legal profession or the medical profession, and the innumerable special studies, among which I point out the recent article of André Perraud-Charmantier, "La controverse du secret medical," *Revue critique de législation* (1928), pp. 211ff. I have touched on this question myself in *Le droit de la profession pharmaceutique* (Paris, 1924), pp. 154ff, where I already related the professional secret to the juridical notion of intimacy, but where I erred in considering intimacy solely as a right of personality.

Moreover, can this clerk use the claim of secrecy against his superiors in the department? How could they exercise any supervision over his activity if he could put them off by posting on his files the three magic figures: 378? Do you see the secrets of the bureau becoming the secrets of the department?

And finally, all the public administrations form one body. The administrative body has its secrets from the public, but it has none from its members. The combined secrets of all the members of the administrative body form a mass; they are the secret of the community—of the institution. Article 31 of the law of July 31, 1920, is but the re-establishment of the professional secret on its true base: the secret of the government official is the secret of the Administration; it is up to the Administration, by means of its network of organs, to guard it. The prohibition against revealing the professional secret belongs to the law that regulates the relationships of person to person, not to the one that deals with the relationships of organ to organ within an institution; it has nothing to do with constitutional law, in the exhaustive sense of the word: political constitution, administrative constitution, constitution of private moral persons. Article 378 treats only with the "system of reference" of relationships of subject to subject.

So far I have shown you exemplifications of the theory of the institution in private law, commercial law, civil procedure, constitutional law, administrative law, international law, even military law;[15] Article 378 illustrates it in both penal law and fiscal law. Now I want to show you an illustration in medical law.

Unlike the administrative secret, the medical secret first appears, not as an institutional secret, but as an individual secret. I confide in this government official because he holds such-and-such a position, and in this bank clerk because he is behind such-and-such a window. But I consult this doctor or this lawyer because he is Dr. So-and-so.

It is true that in every age doctors' servants and chauffeurs have been in a position to learn the patients' names; and it may very well be that doctors have always had the bad habit of entrusting their bookkeeping to their wives; but this concerns the domestic secret rather than the medical secret. It is also true that hospital doctors have always had to enter into a certain professional intimacy with

---

15. [These examples were elaborated in earlier chapters of La théorie de l'institution.]

hospital administrations, and that scientific interest has always legitimized the publication of medical or surgical observations in
professional journals, provided that suitable precautions are taken;
and this proves very simply that there has always been some necessity for "socializing" the medical secret. But all in all, one could still
comply with Article 378: it just took a little conniving.[16]

Yet since faraway times more troublesome cases have come up.
In a short but substantial study, to which I have already alluded,
Tiberghien—from whom I have borrowed the notion of the "socialization" of the professional secret—brings up the case of the military
doctor (he is readily granted the right to reveal certain necessary
things to his hierarchical superiors), the case of the public school
or boarding school doctor (is he not obligated to disclose certain
confidences to the principal in the hygienic interest of the school?),
the case of the doctor called by the head of a home to attend a
domestic (must he let the family be contaminated?). Finally, the same
question is repeated with increasing frequency as the new modality
of the medical profession develops that Tiberghien calls the "group
doctor": factory doctor, doctor of a mutual company, municipal
doctor, public health doctor, etc.

Certainly, this sort of doctor participates in several "intimacies,"
and he finds himself the confidant of as many secrets. He is the doctor
both of the sick person and of the factory, of the mutual company—
let us say right out: the institution. He comes to know both secrets
that belong to the sick person in his own private right and that are
consequently incommunicable, and secrets that belong to the sick
person as a member, with the doctor himself and with the director
of the factory or the committee of the mutual company, etc., of the
same institutional organism. Well, we have just seen that the law
on the professional secret does not concern the relationships of organ
to organ: as employee of the factory or of the mutual company, etc.,
the doctor is vis-à-vis the latter in a position like that of the registration bureau clerk vis-à-vis the state and the different public departments.

The line of demarcation remains to be established. Certainly this
is a matter of professional conscience, and it seems astonishing that
our medical faculties have not yet begun to teach professional ethics—

16. This is the place to recall, as I did in *Le droit, la logique et le bon sens* (Paris,
1925), pp. 263ff, that "connivings," derogations, exceptions, fictions, always reveal the
inexact adaptation of a rational system to reality and forecast the overthrow of the
system: the exceptions to the *individual secret* forecast the *institutional secret*.

nor professional law[17]—following the example of their younger sisters, the faculties of pharmacy.[18] But the professional conscience needs the support, not of a dissipating casuistry, but of a directing principle.

The theory of the institution is there for the asking. Have I not driven the point home that the institution is a limited system, that it is assigned to a special end, that it is the organization of an idea in which it unites the human beings who sustain it today with those who have transmitted it and with those to whom they will transmit it, and that outside of this system, this end, this idea, nothing remains but individuals, each one independent of the others, each one master of his activities in face of the others? You have made the transposition yourselves: the medical secret is, in principle, the secret of the sick person; it becomes the secret of the institution—or of the group—only insofar as the idea of the institution or the end of the group is seriously concerned in a communication, a confidential communication, of the secret to those in the group or institution who are entitled to receive it. Finally, any doubt must be resolved by a judgment of incommunicability.

In all these hypotheses, the professional secret is simply an aspect of institutional intimacy. A very general principle of justice tells us that no one has the right to shout in the streets what he has heard in the intimacy of a home. In morality this is called breach of faith. In positive law it is a penal offense only on the occasions specified by penal law. But beyond the criminal text there is a civil tort sanctioned by damages, and at the very least an ethical fault sanctioned by the institutional discipline, a lack of discretion condemned by one's own conscience and even by public opinion. So it is with the domestic secret—the commercial or industrial secret, even though their violation would slip through the knots of Article 378 or any other legislative text—the corporate secret, for honor forbids "selling oneself" among one's colleagues, and public contempt brands "informers" in politics as well as in college—and lastly the governmental secret, for there are secrets of state that are indispensable to public security and that must be respected by those in power, and even after they have descended from it.

17. Legal medicine has an entirely different object—the juridical use of medicine. I have pointed out elsewhere the possible and desirable extension of its program: legal medicine, a subject for the doctor to teach; medical law, a subject for the jurist to teach. See *Le droit, l'ordre et la raison* (Paris, 1927), pp. 223ff; cf. *La valeur de la loi*, pp. 285ff.)

18. [See Renard, *Le droit de la profession pharmaceutique*.]

Natural law is opposed to the violation of secrets, whether they be personal or institutional. It is equally opposed to the robbery of secrets. Violation comes from within; robbery from without.[19] In order to violate a secret, you must have received it in confidence; certain landladies, they say, snatch, on their own authority, the secrets of "their" tenants: robbery!

Robbery is not indiscriminately culpable, any more than is violation. And very justly in this regard the theory of the institution suggests distinctions analogous to those that practice was forced, by the nature of things, to introduce into the interpretation of the overly absolute text of Article 378. From every point of view the institutional doctrine appears as the revenge of juridical realism upon the ideologism of the old school; it is a practitioner's construction.

Well then, the human person belongs first of all to himself, clearly! But he also belongs to a whole gamut of institutions, and each one of them has an "advantage" over him proportionate to the requirements of the common good it bears[20] for the benefit of each of the members of the collectivity. Within this limit, it has a claim upon his intimacy, it has a right to his secrets. This is a new aspect of the "socialization" of the secret that Tiberghien has spoken about.

Some robberies of the secret are not juridically or morally culpable. After all, you would not reproach the father of a family for looking at his children's correspondence. This is not only his right but his duty, and this duty is contained in the hierarchical constitution of the family. As for the wife's correspondence, more discretion is in order, of course, and the *Code Napoléon* undoubtedly exaggerates the husband's powers—this individualistic code lacks tact. But all the same there is a certain want of taste in some excesses of the feminist movement: marital authority is of the natural law.

Above all, do not ask the jurist for a precise demarcation. I repeat, it is a matter of tact: the whole thing depends on the state of civilization and the general disposition of men at a given moment,[21] on the

19. ["Robbery" (*effraction*) here connotes a taking (of the secret) against the will of the owner, "violation" a disclosure of a secret willingly confided. As appears from the text, just as "violation" is not necessarily culpable, neither is "robbery."]

20. [Cf. Hauriou, "The Theory of the Institution and the Foundation," above.]

21. The intimate union of justice and security in the scientific postulates of the juridical economy (therefore preliminary to any technical fashioning) is stressed under a different aspect by Jean Dabin in his critical analysis of Georges Cornil's *Droit privé* in *Belgique judiciaire* (1924), pp. 522ff, and by Procurator-General Meyer in his address of October 1, 1924, at the Cour d'Appel of Liège on "La répression de la pornographie," when they show that the moral science to be expressed in the legal process is not the pure moral science "whose principles never change," but only an average morality,

social conditions of the family, on a host of concrete circumstances that escape all regulation and can be determined, in litigation, only by the "direct evaluation" of the judge. This is certainly the way our jurisprudence understands it in appraising alleged injuries in support of suits for divorce or separation.[22]

Similarly, if each institution belongs first of all to itself, it also belongs to one or more groups of institutions. Every "institution of institutions"[23] has an "advantage" over the institutions that are tributary to it; it has a claim upon their intimacy, rights to their secrets, within the limit of the requirements of the common good it pursues. This is the viewpoint we must take in considering the robbery of certain secrets by legal violence—you are thinking of tax law—or even of administrative law. How many letters are intercepted and opened in the censor's office in certain times of crisis! This does not tally with the principles of '89, but '89 indulged in individualist ideology; the modern science of law has gotten over this. We must take this same viewpoint in considering intervention in international law.[24] Here again, do not expect a sharp discrimination: it is impossible and it would be disastrous. All this is a matter of tact and of concrete estimation, a matter of common sense: if you do not have any, I cannot give it to you.

The institution is an intimacy. I have shown you the juridical significance of this intimacy. I continue: the institution is an *organized* intimacy; in this respect it differs from friendship.

You know the proverb: *amicitia pares invenit vel facit;*[25] it is not

a respect for which is demanded by public opinion in a given milieu and at a given moment . . . This public opinion is variable. Positive law rises and falls with it . . . peoples have the laws and the jurisprudence [G.] that they deserve, and you cannot raise the level of public law without raising the level of public morality. But all this does not mean, according to Dabin's just observation, that the legislator's tolerance should go so far as to constitute slavishness to this opinion; he should rather, "take note of its preferences, and try to prepare and speed on the coming of a better rule."

22. Renard, *La valeur de la loi,* pp. 37ff.

23. Cf. *La théorie de l'institution,* p. 231: "The unitary state is an elemental institution; the federal state is an institution of institutions."

24. I am not referring to the direct intervention of a state in the affairs of its neighbor, but to the intervention of the League of Nations, as legal representative of the international community, according to the role it assigns itself and in conformity with Article 17 of the Covenant.

25. But is this egalitarian variety true friendship? No, Pierre Rousselot replies from the thomistic point of view: "According to the principle of St. Thomas which is in perfectly logical coherence with the rest of his philosophy, the worst position to take from the standpoint of a metaphysics of love is to adopt the view of egalitarian friendship." For the prototype of true friendship is the relationship between God and

so with the institution. To say organization is to say differentiation; the juridical differentiation that transforms intimacy into institution is hierarchy. Think quite simply of the difference between mere cohabitation and marriage. Cohabitation is only an agreement; marriage is an institution. Similarly, it has been remarked that the constitutional regime cannot adapt itself to an equality of executive power and deliberative power, not even in parliamentary government; it is absolutely necessary for one of them to have some preponderance: this is the vital law that presides over the institutional organism as well as the biological organism.

The second trait of institutional interior life, then, is authority. "In any whole whatsoever," says St. Thomas, "there must be a formal and predominant part," and he adds that this predominance is what "makes the whole more than a collection, what forms it into a unity."[26]

Because the institution is not "any whole whatsoever," this "predominant part" is not an extrinsic principle. It is an interior, immanent principle, like the one that resides in the biological organism and gives it a living being. But because the institution is not a biological organism but purely juridical, this "predominant part" is nothing other than a juridical principle. This internal juridical principle that sustains the institutional organism by subjugating it to its end, its "idea," its "form" is what I call authority.[27] My conception of authority then, like my conception of law, is institutional. All authority is institutional, every institution contains an authority. This is what I want to explain now.

To create, to found a particular institution within the universal

---

man; and "the more disparate a friendship is, the closer it comes to the model of affection." Rousselot, "Pour l'histoire du problème de l'amour au Moyen age," Martin Grabmann, ed., *Beiträge zur Geschichte der Philosophie und Theologie des Mittelalters* (Münster, 1908), vol. VI, monograph 6, pp. 28f. A friendship is strong to the extent that it is "instituted," and it is "instituted" to the extent that it is differentiated: in this sense once again institutional doctrine rejoins thomistic philosophy. In the friendship that *pares invenit aut facit*—that which is envisaged in the text—I see a disastrous fragility. When St. Thomas refers to the marriage of friendship, it is differentiated and "instituted" friendship that he has in view—true friendship. He was thinking of the community in which *authority* is unburdened of all *constraint* (see note 27 below).

26. St. Thomas. *Summa Theologiae* II II, q. 49, a. 6, ad 1.

27. It seems to me that we should distinguish three elements in authority: (1) *differentiation*, which is a trait common to every organism; (2) *command*, which is the special trait of the juridical organism—the institution—and by which it is contrasted with the biological organism, just as the moral and juridical norm (imperative law) is contrasted with the physical or psychological norm (indicative law); (3) *constraint*, which prolongs and sanctions command.

institution of the human race is a two-step operation. The first step is to circumscribe the portion of the common good to which the institution tends, that is, to fix its end, its idea, its "form." The second is to dispose accordingly the means at hand, the "matter," that is, to arrange an authority capable of distributing tasks and coordinating them to this end, to this idea, to this "form," in pursuit of this portion of the common good.

The doctrine of authority holds the same intermediary position between individualism and sociologism as does the institution. Vainly individualism tries to give rise to order and to assure continuity, without which there is no order, by the play of liberty and of contract. Contract, because of the static immobility that characterizes it, is incapable of communicating to juridical situations the power of adaptation they must have in order to endure. And as for liberty, either you understand this to be a liberty without law, and this is anarchy,[28] or you subjugate it to some end where individual liberties are united with one another, and you have come back to the institution.

Vainly also, sociologism, following the vagaries of pantheism, tries to crush the human personality in a vast machinery and reduce it to the impersonal activity of an organ within an organism. The human person rebels against this servitude. He is an organ, certainly! but he is still and first of all himself. The social body has a hold upon him, but it does not possess him entirely. He admits that he is bound to the destiny of the social body, but he also has his individual destiny. He is a reasonable being and consequently responsible. He has a vocation to direct himself as well as to obey, and the obedience to which he consents is not that of a beast to its master nor that of an organ of the human body to the command of the will: it is a rational obedience. Even to God man owes no other.[29] The human person is not an *object* of *property,* he is only *subject* to an *authority;* and this word authority simply expresses the *fundamental dualism* that is at the heart of the theory of the institution: the irreducible autonomy of the human person and his integration in the institutional phenomenon.

---

28. "However far the mass of men may develop intellectually," writes Auguste Comte, "it is obvious that the social order will always remain necessarily incompatible with a liberty that permanently entitles every individual, without the preliminary fulfillment of any rational condition, to bring up each day in endless discussion the very basis of society." Comte, *Cours de philosophie positive,* 5th ed. (Paris, 1893), IV, 46ff.

29. *Rationabile obsequium,* Rom. 12:1.

Authority is intrinsic to the institution. I am not saying that it is an attribute, an endowment, an adjunct, of the institution; it is its very condition of existence, its manner of being, its "comportment." Sovereignty, for example, is not the crown inherited by the nation from the princes and dynasties who wore it in the past; it is the institutional manner of being of the nation. Authority is in the community, and from the community it rebounds, as to its exercise, upon the individuals who provide for, and in proportion as they provide for, the common good. They do not possess authority, they are ministers of it. To deny the existence of the institution is to deny the existence of authority, or to make it the privilege of certain persons who would have been invested with it from above, which is neither a very juridical opinion nor a very "catholic" doctrine.

"No man," taught Pope Leo XIII, "has in himself or of himself the power to bind in conscience the free will of his fellow men."[30] For want of the bond of conscience, all that remains is the bond of force; but force, even that of the majority, has nothing about it of a juridical principle: "A million thieves," said Alfred Fouillée, "have more force than a single one, but no more rights; numbers cannot produce metamorphoses here."[31]

Authority does not spring from numbers; it springs from "organization," that is, from the integration of an end, of an idea, of a "form" in a collectivity of persons that attains institutional existence by reason of this integration. And the more this end, this idea, this "form" is worth, the more the institution is worth, the more natural law authorizes its existence, the more juridical authority philosophy discovers in it . . .

Authority is contained in the institution. Men do not exercise their authority over the institution; it is the institution, by means of the men who serve it, that exercises its authority.

Authority does not come from men. Neither from below: the law of numbers. Nor from above: the divine law of the legists. Authority is not a special quality by which the will of this or that one appears superior to the will of this or that other: the will of the prince or of the majority superior to the will of the subjects or of the minority. Authority has its immediate foundation in the exigencies of social life, as they appear to the investigation of reason.

Of course, authority comes from God. But the human intellect, will,

30. Encyclical *Diuturnum* of June 29, 1881.

31. Alfred Fouillée, *La science sociale contemporaine* (Paris, 1880; 5th ed. Paris, 1910), p. 27.

and liberty also come from God; they are nonetheless inherent in our nature and capable of being recognized there by reason. Similarly authority is inherent in the institution.

Most of the commentary on St. Paul's *Non est potestas nisi a Deo*[32] is concerned only with political authority; and besides, no authorized commentator takes this the way the legists do. "Political authority," writes Gillet, "is of natural law, not divine law."[33] Actually, the problem comes up for every authority, and consequently for every institution.

There is no authority that does not descend from God; but this principle has different modalities in its application. By grouping under the same commandment the obligation of obedience to all legitimate authority, the Decalogue does not necessarily invest with the same degree of divine power the authority of the head of the family and that of the head of the state, the command of the civil legislator and that of the ecclesiastical legislator, the judgment of the magistrate and the order of the corporal in charge of a barracks. It is still true, however, that no authority can be legitimately exercised unless it is directed to the good of the community; all authority comes from God, but no authority is justified unless it serves the ends of the community. Even from the standpoint of the divine origin of power, all authority is institutional . . .[34]

We said the other day that there is all the more being in a whole as the idea—the form—is more perfectly integrated into its parts. When it is a question of human groups, this integration is manifested by the fullness of the authority that is exercised in them. Just as a reasonable being is all the more a man as his reason and will have more control over his lower faculties, so there is all the more juridical being in an institution as the authority exercised in it has more sway.

It follows that the hierarchy of institutions is not the same from the point of view of juridical ontology as it is from the point of view of their social importance. As for social importance, or "respectability" if you wish, the state is below the family; ontologically, it is above; it has more being because it has more of the fullness of authority. This is why the theologians hold that it is, like the Church, a *perfect society*.[35] "In the family," writes St. Thomas, "the authority

32. Rom. 13:1.
33. Martin Gillet, *Semaine Sociale de Lyon,* (Paris, 1925), p. 214.
34. [Omitted here is a passage on the institutional elements in some contracts, e.g., "contracts designed . . . to create a permanent situation affecting the status of persons, characterized by the dependence of one of the parties with respect to the other." La théorie de l'institution, p. 322.]
35. Aquinas, *Summa Theologiae,* II II, q. 50, a. 3, ad 3.

of the father has a resemblance to that of a king . . . but he does not have that full power of government that characterizes royalty." And a little further on Aquinas clarifies his thought by developments that can be translated quite exactly, I believe, into modern juridical parlance in this way: a *perfect society,* the state, is invested with a *penal jurisdiction;* an *imperfect society,* the family, is invested only with a *disciplinary jurisdiction.*[36] In the main, this is the same idea that jurists express by the distinction between public and private law: public law is the discipline of perfect societies and the rule of their relationships with one another and with their members.

Authority is the salient feature of the institution: a feature that becomes more pronounced as the institution gathers strength. In every institution there is an embryo of authority, and this embryo will develop and be differentiated in proportion as the organism progresses. For example, the differentiation of executive and deliberative powers marks the attainment of a great perfection on the part of the state regime;[37] their collaboration is still more of a perfection in what is called, in political law,[38] parliamentary government. Other institutions simply have a vocation, as they progress, to differentiate their organs, either according to the example of the powers of the state,[39] or according to any other model that is adapted to their special end.[40] A regression of authority is the infallible sign of decadence in institutions. An institution that loses its structure of authority soon wastes away; before long its being disintegrates and it fades into the anonymity of the "common law"; and a "juridical system" disappears.

Institutional intimacy, because it is organized, implies differentiation, inequality, authority. Authority is the head of the institutional

36. *Summa Theologiae,* II II, q. 65, a. 2, ad 2. St. Thomas makes the "perfection" of societies a question of degree. He clearly says that the state is a perfect community: "civitas est communitas perfecta" *Summa Theologiae,* I II, q. 90, a. 3, ad 3); but he adds that a society is all the more perfect as it is more sufficient unto itself: "tanto perfectior . . . quanto magis per se sufficiens" (*De regimine principis,* I, 1); and he adds: "Communitatum cum diversi sint gradus et ordines ultima est communitas civitatis ordinata ad per se sufficientia vitae humanae. Unde inter omnes communitates humanas ipsa est perfectissima . . . ad quam omnes communitates humanae referuntur" (*Politics,* I, 1, lect. 1).

37. [*Régime d'état.* G. The terminology originated with Hauriou.]

38. [*En droit politique.*]

39. This seems to be the case with organizations in the professions and with international organizations.

40. For example, in the *Administration* [G.], the separation of administrators and judges; in public accountability, the separation of managers, accountants and judges, etc.

organism: the relationships of head to members are juridical relationships. What is their character? A distinction is imperative here, which leads us to a third and last trait of institutional relationships: objectivity.

To understand this, we must return once more to our "fundamental dualism." The organs incorporated in every institution are reasonable beings. Along with being organs, they are persons. Outside of the juridical status that they derive from their affiliation to this or that institution, and before it, they possess a juridical status that they derive exclusively from their individual personality and that they are permitted to oppose to the diverse institutions of which they form a part. Man is not "caught" in the institution the way cells are in the organism; he is both inside the institution and outside it: inside the institution for a certain sphere of activity, and outside it for everything else. He has not sold it his being, and he does not have the power to do so; he simply lends it his intellect, his will, and his activity in pursuit of a certain end.

The relationships of organ to organ are objective relationships; the organ has no rights against its organism; it simply obeys the organism's vital law; and there are no other relationships in the biological organism. Matters are different in the institutional organism; each of its members is a living being, more living than the organism itself—what am I saying?—this organism borrows life from its members: a far cry from sustaining them with its own!—these members are reasonable beings whose power of being infinitely transcends that of the organism. On the ontological ladder the biological organism is above its organs, the institutional organism below.

This observation is expressed, in the technique of our profession, by a dual classification of individual juridical situations,[41] an examination of which is not without profit for the institutional theory. There are two kinds of individual juridical situations: the active and passive rights that derive from our personality, which I call *subjective rights;* the advantages and obligations that derive from our affiliation to this or that institution and are simply the reflection of

---

41. The phobia of *droit subjectif* has led certain authors to restrict the import of this term. They consider that the individual can find himself either in a general juridical situation whose contours are fixed by the law (*loi*) without regard to the persons involved and whose individual application is made by means of an act-condition (e.g., marriage), or he can find himself in a juridical situation that is specially formed in view of a particular case. And they reserve the term individual juridical situation (e.g., contract) for this second type. I use the term much more generally and mean by individual juridical situation every juridical situation in which the individual finds himself.

it upon its members, which I call objective situations or *statuses*.[42]
I have a standing in my family, in the French state, I am inscribed
on the list of voters, on the list of taxpayers: these are *statuses*.
Furthermore, I carry on a commerce of *subjective rights* with my
landlord, my tradesmen, my editor; but I can also be in a relationship
of subjective rights with my family in an inheritance settlement, with
the state as bondholder, with the administration as creditor of my
salary in proportion as I have done my job.

You see, do you not, that these two labels correspond to a distinction that is confused perhaps, but real. It is very disagreeable to see
your tax assessment grow; yet it is nowhere near the same thing as
seeing your investments crash: this is called bankruptcy; the tax
increase is not even a surprise. It is very disagreeable to learn of
the marriage of an old cousin whose money you were hoping to
inherit: his new wife imposes an alliance upon you that annoys you,
and you are free to regret the place she takes in his affection and
the place she will take in his will; yet you have nothing to say; the
quality of heir presumptive is only a family status.

Thus, the respective natures of subjective right and status come
into focus. The status participates in the mobility of the institution;
the subjective right is rigid. A subjective right, once constituted,
defies events; a status follows the fate of the institution; it adapts
itself day by day to the institution's vicissitudes. A subjective right
belongs to me; it is mine: *hanc rem meam esse aio;* a status is the
consequence of a disposition of things of which I am not the master;
it is a post that I occupy: the judge his bench, the professor his chair,
and the governmental minister his portfolio—a symbol of institutional instability! A subjective right is a ray of my personality; a
status is a reflection of the institution.

Situations of status, like subjective rights, are active and passive
goods, and between these two kinds of goods there are equiva-
lences . . . "Situations" are goods in proportion as they are guaran-

---

42. Status is an intermediate condition between right (*droit*) and no-right (*non-droit*).
As René Demogue judiciously observed, these two extreme situations "have less
importance as to the number of acts that relate to them directly than the intermediate
situation." Demogue, *Notions fondamentales du droit privé* (Paris, 1911), p. 9. Status
is the exemplar-type of these intermediate situations: because it is not a right, it is
deprived of subjective sanction, it is not protected against new laws and new regulations; but because it is more than a "no-right," it is sufficiently acceptable to support
an objective recourse . . . Furthermore, the gamut extends below the status situation
protected by the objective recourse: there are degrees between status and juridical
nothingness just as there are between subjective right and status. On this last point,
see *La valeur de la loi,* p. 165, n. 1, and *La théorie de l'institution,* pp. 229ff.

teed; and Hauriou aptly remarked that administrative law "gives rise to a whole new category of goods that are functions, professions, and occupations."[43] As a matter of fact, every institution engenders goods that are not rights, but states: it is a good to be the son of a great man, to occupy such-and-such a post in such-and-such an enterprise, to flaunt this title or that ribbon. To underestimate these goods would be evidence of a poor psychology. And these goods occasion a commerce that is similar—but on the objective level—to the commerce of subjective rights: the commerce of the order of sovereignty in international relations, the commerce of the governmental order in the collaboration of "powers" or in the relations between the electoral body and Parliament, *possession d'état* and theory of de facto government officials with regard to *possession des choses.*[44]

Bona ex eo dicuntur quod beant, hoc est beatos faciunt; but as there are many kinds of happiness, there are at least two kinds of goods. The distinction between subjective right and status appears as a *summa divisio* of goods. Now I want to detail the practical interests of this division.

Rights are part of one's patrimony; therefore they are transmitted. Statuses are untransmissible. A right is transferable: the holder of a right can renounce it, sell it, give it away. A status is untransferable, inalienable; it does not admit of renunciation. Notably, we cannot modify by special agreements the individual situations that we have because we belong in certain institutional frames: the status of nationality or of family, the status of government official, the status of member of the League of Nations, etc. Only the frames themselves can be modified, and this is not a matter of contract but of foundation: every agreement that goes against the institutional frame is nullified by natural law (this is the "public order" sought by art. 6, *Code civil*):[45] *the institutional prevails over the contractual.*

Rights are included in the general pledge of a creditor; they are distrainable; the actions that sanction them can, without exception, be exercised by creditors. Not so for statuses.

Rights can be exercised by representation. Situations of status do not admit of representation; we exercise the attributes of our status

43. Hauriou, *Droit administratif,* 11th ed., p. 38. Hauriou even envisaged the analogy of status and real rights: status is a claim to the application for and conservation of the post; as in a real right, there is a direct relationship between the man and the thing. *Droit public,* 2nd ed., p. 171.

44. [*Possession d'état; possessions des choses.* G.]

45. [See Appendix.]

personally or we do not exercise them at all; the power and the exercise of it are inseparable.[46]

The principle of the nonretroactivity of laws and regulations ought to be interpreted in the light of this distinction between right and status.[47] The law has ordained a certain state of things (it has forbidden the investigation of paternity, proclaimed the indissolubility of marriage or authorized divorce, established or suppressed universal suffrage, created or abolished such-and-such an administrative service); if the law is abrogated, the individual situations that exist only because of it, that is, the statuses it creates, fall with it. They are constantly adapting themselves to the law. They conform to its variations day by day. A father could be investigated by a child conceived at a time when investigation was forbidden, a divorce could be granted to a couple who were married under the law of indissolubility, and a marriage that took place under the law of divorce could become indissoluble. It is not the same with subjective rights. Thanks to the law that was in effect when the subjective right was constituted, this right has acquired a stability that shelters it from the assaults of the law to come. The law of the future respects the subjective right established in the past; or if it does not respect this right, it commits an abuse of authority; or if public necessity requires this dispossession, the holder of the right must at least be indemnified.

Corresponding to this distinction of goods into subjective rights and status situations is a classification of juridical acts. Among individual acts, some engender subjective rights—transfer of property, sale, loan—and others simply launch a legal and regulatory situation, a "state," a status—recognition of a natural child, nomination of a government official, conferring of a university degree: act-conditions, according to the current terminology. You notice that this classification deals only with the substance, and not with the form: thus the contractual form generates obligations in sale, rent, etc.; on the contrary, in marriage it effects a foundation: marriage is a contract-condition.

46. Contra, Hauriou, Droit administratif, 11th ed., pp. 441ff, and Droit constitutionnel, 2nd ed., pp. 570ff. The right to power, says Jacques Leclercq, cannot be separated from its exercise, or at least from the capacity of exercising it. Leclercq, Leçons de droit naturel, vol. 2, L'état ou la politique (Namur, 1929), p. 25.

47. So you could support the position that the theory of the institution is virtually included in Article 2 of the Code civil [See Appendix] (cf. "l'ordre public" of Article 6). Of course, nobody would have thought of it in 1804. But it is in the nature of things: the redactors of the code of individualism spoke institutional language, just as Monsieur Jourdain spoke prose. [See Molière, Le bourgeois gentilhomme.]

Among regulatory provisions, and chiefly those of legislation, some are simply *regulators* of pre-existing subjective rights: such as the law that regulates the arrangements made between the creditors of an insolvent debtor; but a host of other legal or regulatory provisions are themselves creators of the situations of status that they organize: I am taxable, mobilizable, only in virtue of the fiscal law or the military law. And here again the substance alone is at stake, since both kinds of provisions are decreed according to the same forms.

Finally, corresponding to the distinction between right and status and to the correlative classification of juridical acts is a classification of appeals in administrative litigation, whose philosophical import I have already pointed out to you.[48] A right is sanctioned by actions that tend to vindicate it; a status does not give rise to any action in justice; it simply constitutes, if the case should require it, a sufficient interest to permit a defense of legality[49] or institutional morality,[50] and an appeal tending to procure a re-establishment of the institution's balance: an annulment, a redress, a censure; for example, in private law *actions d'état*,[51] in penal law the *action publique*,[52] in administrative law the appeal for *excès de pouvoir*.[53]

To conclude, the distinction between subjective right and status is simply a new aspect of that *fundamental dualism* upon which I rest the whole science of law and which has repercussions in every department of the juridical economy: the human person and the institution. It thus concurs with the demonstration of the one truth I have had the ambition of convincing you of this year.

48. [Renard, *La théorie de l'institution* pp. 272ff.]

49. [One ground for granting a *recours pour excès de pouvoir* is *la violation de la loi*. See Georges Vedel, *Droit administratif*, 3rd ed. (Paris, 1964), pp. 437ff; Charles Eisenmann, "Le droit administratif et le principe de légalité" in Conseil d'État, *Etudes et Documents* (Paris, 1957), pp. 25–40.]

50. [Hauriou advanced the theory that one of the four *ouvertures* by which the Administration was subject to control by the administrative judge—the *détournement de pouvoir*—submitted it to control of "morality", i.e., to enforcement of "good" administration. Renard shared this view. It is most extensively discussed in Welter, *Le contrôle juridictionnel de la moralité administratif* (Paris, 1929), a work that was prepared as a thesis under Renard's direction at the Faculté de droit of the University of Nancy. In the introduction he supplied to the work, Renard concluded that in the sense intended here, "'morality' amounts to 'rationality.'"]

51. [*Action d'état.* G.]

52. [*Action publique.* G.]

53. [G.]

A Critical Meditation on Georges Renard's *La Théorie*

de L'Institution   by François Geny

I should like to reflect upon a profound study in the philosophy of law that has recently been presented to us and that merits our careful attention. This is Georges Renard's *La théorie de l'institution,* the first volume of which, designated as the juridical part, appeared in 1930. A second volume, promised soon, will be more strictly philosophical, and will determine the significance of the work and undoubtedly reveal its deepest meaning. But right now—the author invites us to the task by stimulating our observations[1]—we must meditate upon this powerful effort to fathom the notion of law, an effort that goes beyond the sphere of research to listen to the very heartbeat of juridical realities and to draw from them a general directing principle capable of renewing both science and technique.[2]

What I want to do is to gather together, in a spirit of sympathetic criticism, the profound and complex impressions an attentive and

ED. NOTE: François Geny and Léon Duguit are perhaps the best-known French jurists of the twentieth century in common law countries. Geny was the author cited most often by Cardozo in *The Nature of the Judicial Process* (New Haven, 1921). He is the French master of legal method, whose terms *donné, construit, science,* and *technique* (G.) have remained familiar in continental juristic literature. Neither of his two major works, *Méthode d'interprétation et sources en droit privé positif* (Paris, 1899; 2nd ed., 1919) or *Science et technique en droit privé positif* (Paris, 1914–1924), has yet been fully translated into English, although excerpts have appeared. See Wortley, "François Geny," in Ivor Jennings, ed., *Modern Theories of Law* (London, 1933), pp. 139–159.

The translation here is of the third and concluding section of Geny's article "La notion du droit en France," *Archives de philosophie du droit et de sociologie juridique* (1931), pp. 33–41. In Part I he had summarized the notion of "droit" as generally understood by contemporary French jurists; in Part II he had proposed aspects of the notion that needed further research and clarification.

1. Renard, *La théorie de l'institution* (Paris, 1930) p. xxiv.
2. [Geny himself popularized this dichotomy. See G. It remains influential. Horvath calls it "the *summa divisio* of French legal thought." See Horvath, "Social Value and Reality in Current French Legal Thought," American Journal of Comparative Law, I (1950), 243, 244.]

repeated reading of this work has left upon me. This rich and force-
ful volume attracts the jurist by the multiplicity, ingenuity, and
fecundity of its views, yet it baffles him by the elusiveness of its
developments and the indecisiveness of its conclusions.

I do not intend to investigate here whether or not Georges Renard's
theory of the institution is identical with that of his master, Maurice
Hauriou. Certainly it was suggested by Hauriou's. But today it stands
on its own, sufficiently vigorous and complete to merit consideration
for itself as presented by its author. In taking it this way, I should
like in the following pages to attest to its timeliness and fecundity,
to admire its fine structure, to point out the hesitations and difficulties suggested to me, and finally to suggest the possibility of recti-
fying it a bit, or at least of completing it, putting it in order, even
calming it down, so that it will be more acceptable and fruitful.

Without doubt the essential ideas expressed in *La théorie de l'institution* have been "in the air" for several years, longed for and
anticipated by new generations of jurists. Announced and highly
promoted by Hauriou, already extensively used by several authors,
notably Cuche[3] and Bonnecasse,[4] even inferentially introduced into
certain manuals of public or private law, the notion of a specific
element that would complement free will, or perhaps even check
it, in marriage, corporations, labor unions, and associations of all
kinds, collective agreements and other modes of labor organization,
seemed necessary in order to satisfy certain needs of the time and
to enable juridical thought to cope with the realities it was facing.
I remember in particular in 1929 having seen the *institutional idea*
reappear again and again, somewhat like a leitmotiv expressing a
common aspiration, in the lectures at the *concours d'agrégation*[5] in
private law, at which the subjects designated to the candidates lent
themselves, more or less, to the introduction of this concept.

Renard's *La théorie de l'institution* impresses us most by the beneficial and lively light it sheds, animating and vivifying the most
varied juridical matters, notably: marriage and the family; property;

3. See esp. Paul Cuche, "La législation du travail et les transformations du droit,"
in *La cité moderne et les transformations du droit,* 4 *Cahiers de la nouvelle journée,*
(1925), 166–193; also his lectures at the Semaine Sociale of Grenoble in 1923, *Proceedings,* pp. 289–296, and of Lyon in 1925, "Manifestations nouvelles d'authorité dans
la vie sociale par le développement de l'institution," *Proceedings,* pp. 349–368.
4. See esp. Julien Bonnecase, "Où en est le droit civil?" in *La cité moderne,*
pp. 70–82, 84; also his *Supplement au traité de droit civil de Baudry-Lacantinerie et
autres,* I (1924), nos. 380–386; II (1928), nos. 120–128, 160, 352–371.
5. [The *concours d'agrégation* is the postdoctoral competitive examination from
which faculty members are selected for French universities.]

corporations, associations, and labor unions; the international community and peace treaties; the modern wage-earning class; situations of status;[6] the foundation and the liberty it postulates; the limits of the professional secret; the political regime; the administrative regime. I have not only experienced this impression in a profound way myself; I have noticed echos of it reverberating from the audience of Renard's public lectures, where he presented the principal themes of his theory in a most lively form, and from his students who heard this doctrine in the freer and more familiar atmosphere of the classroom. What is more, I have seen this theory flood with light one young mind, who thought—rightly or wrongly, I am not discussing this point—that this light alone could clarify a subject taken from the most technical parts of administrative law.[7]

All these observations—which are sheer fact—give us a sort of experimental proof that Renard's theory of the institution has come at the right time and is likely to rejuvenate and develop the juridical disciplines in a useful, fruitful way. This is more than enough to testify to its value.

Having perceived the birth and genesis of the theory of the institution,[8] we see its mighty structure rise under the ingenious and agile pen of its author.[9] We cannot fail to admire the vigor and richness of this doctrine, whether we are looking at the general characteristics of the institution, or counting its numerous degrees, or penetrating its interior life to observe the causes of its special power: intimacy, authority, objectivity. Corresponding to the most salient needs of a social life organized in view of its end, the institution appears as the powerful ferment of a wisely balanced and highly promising juridical development. An extensive comparison with contract highlights its merits even more.[10] And we see the most timely and pressing problems of law fit into this theory without difficulty, to draw on its rich and fruitful sap.[11]

6. [*Les situations statuaires*. G.]

7. Bernard Geny, *De la collaboration des particuliers avec l'Administration*, with Preface by Georges Renard (Paris, 1930).

8. Renard, *La théorie de l'institution*, pp. 3–105.

9. Renard, *La théorie de l'institution*, pp. 221–353.

10. Renard, *La théorie de l'institution*, pp. 357–472.

11. See the four Appendices, Renard, *La théorie de l'institution*, pp. 475–610. Geny notes two other studies of Renard "La pensée chrétienne sur la propriété privée," in Renard and Louis Trotabas, *La fonction sociale de la propriété privée* (Paris, 1934), pp. 3–34, and "La doctrine de la souveraineté et la condition internationale du Saint-Siège" (apropos of Le Fur, *Le Saint-Siège et le droit des gens*), *Bulletin thomiste* (1930–1931), pp. 212–225.

Yet why do so many men, even those who are all for progress, feel uneasy about this doctrine and refrain from giving it their un- reserved adherence? The answer, I believe, lies in its very richness and in the difficulties one experiences in determining its contours and establishing its limits, difficulties that are inherent in every scientific *theory* worthy of the name.

But it is quite true that in his presentation of the institution Renard multiplies his points of view at will and pushes complexity to the extreme. He does not want to let any aspect of the things and situa- tions he considers escape him. He turns them around again and again in all directions, for fear of neglecting or misjudging some facet. He scrutinizes them and examines them thoroughly, trying to find their secrets. He accumulates and repeats analyses, suspecting every syn- thesis, and sometimes attempting one only to abandon it.

I know well that Renard has the best of reasons for this. He rightly bases his research upon reality. Well, reality is multiple, undulating, and complicated;[12] it is constantly moving and changing, as though in continuous flux. Ideas rise up in it, develop, get entangled and confused to such a point that they defy stability and precise deter- mination. Juridical reality must be considered as it is, with its infinite variations, flexibilities, deformations; it cannot be enclosed in a definite, fixed mold without being denatured.

This was also Hauriou's[13] scientific procedure, which was not without analogy to Saleilles'.[14] And these two names might seem to provide it with an adequate guarantee. Yet I am not sure that we ought to rely on so simplistic an argument from authority. It is not certain, first of all, that the methodological conception of these masters constituted the most solid part of their work. And many among us will think that they have largely surpassed this method, and that they proved to be truly superior in their works of detail and application, where they remained more faithful to traditional logic and gave their concepts a well-defined aspect. But the main thing is that the example of these eminent masters, however con- clusive for them, cannot be taken as a model for everyone. Their

12. Renard, *La théorie de l'institution,* pp. 40–43, 273–325 [translated here in part as "The Interior Life of the Institution"].

13. See François Geny, *Science et technique en droit privé positif,* II (Paris, 1914– 1924), nos. 88–91; and Marcel Waline, "Les idées maîtresses de deux grands publicistes français: Léon Duguit et Maurice Hauriou," *L'Année politique française et etrangère* (Dec. 1929–March 1930), pp. 26–50 [translated here in part].

14. See Raymond Saleilles, *L'oeuvre juridique de Raymond Saleilles* (Paris, 1914), passim.

incontestable merit comes from their personal qualities of perspicacity, tact, and judgment, which could assure them of finding the right direction in the midst of the most inextricable network of facts and ideas.[15] We cannot expect such perspicacity or perfection of the general run of men, who risk—if directing instruments are not put in their hands—losing their way in the undulating and deceptive complexities of juridical life. For this general run—whom you must take into consideration if you want appreciable results—the method recommended by Renard runs the risk of ending in that "disorganizing empiricism" whose illusions and evils he has so brilliantly exposed and condemned.[16]

To assure to the theory of the institution the success it deserves among jurists, and to make it a popular and fruitful instrument of juridical elaboration, two steps seem essential: first, to renounce the excess of abstractions and the magic of metaphors in order to return to a simpler consideration of things; and second, to complete the theory, or rather to correct the multiplicity, variety, and elusiveness of the analyses with which its partisans have been satisfied up to now. We should seek a synthesis that could adapt these analyses to the ordinary needs of the mind, unite the splash of solutions around fixed centers, and thus enable us to penetrate juridical realities, while keeping them well in hand to apply to all the needs of life.

I do not feel qualified to attempt such a synthesis here. I just want to sum up the fundamental ideas that Renard's *La théorie de l'institution* has suggested to me, to point out the questions it raises in my mind, and to express the desires it leaves me with.

The fundamental juridical problem of the modern world has for about fifty years been generally presented as a conflict between the individual and society represented by the state; a struggle of socialism (Renard prefers sociologism) against individualism, of social rights against individual rights. The eighteenth century, intoxicated by the idea of liberty, affirmed the primacy of the rights of the human individual. Progress, as we conceive it, has consisted, especially since the second third of the nineteenth century, in a determined, continuous reaction in favor of the rights of the democratic society. This

15. Cf. François Geny, "La conception générale du droit, de ses sources, de sa méthode dans l'oeuvre de Raymond Saleilles," in *L'oeuvre juridique de Raymond Saleilles*, pp. 60–63.

16. Renard, *La théorie de l'institution*, pp. 539–543, 230, 233 [translated here as "The Degrees of Institutional Existence"].

is the sense in which a popular formula describes the distinctive characteristic of the contemporary juridical movement as the unceasing *socialization of law*. And all our professional works, from the most scientific books to school manuals, are penetrated with this conviction, which is even more rampant in legislative discussions, regulatory or administrative decisions, and judicial writings.

Without directly attacking such a popularized thought, Renard proposes to modify its terms. In his eyes, the fundamental opposition is not between individual and state, individualism and socialism (or sociologism), but between the human being (individual, if you wish), the only being endowed with a real personality, and the institution; consequently, between individual rights and institutional rights.

But what is the institution? Among the different expressions, images, metaphors, comparisons, or contrasts by means of which Renard tries to lay siege to it, because he either cannot or does not want to penetrate it directly, the one that strikes me most is the notion of an organic arrangement of a society of men in view of a good common to all of them. This arrangement follows from the rules established by God to assure the order of the world. It includes individuals themselves, and it is organized, in part at least, by the activity of their wills, which are capable of founding institutions (whence the liberty of foundation). But it dominates these same wills, which do not have the power to contradict it. Under this restriction, entities will rise up in it that are more or less like the human person; these entities will be institutions themselves and could be tiered in a continuous series.

Thus, the institution (in itself) pre-exists the state, which is itself an institution among others, and it dominates the state. The institution really stands in contrast only to the individual human being, who, while being from a certain point of view subordinate to it, enjoys in opposition to it his own proper rights.

The institution, thus understood, takes on more definite shape when the notions it contains are confronted with their contraries. Thus, it implies: order as opposed to anarchy; the organism as opposed to the cell; the objective as opposed to the subjective; idealism as opposed to voluntarism; the collectivity as opposed to the individual; public order as opposed to the autonomous will; distributive or social justice as opposed to commutative justice; moral personality as opposed to physical personality; the great as opposed to the small. And among its inferior degrees, it also opposes foundation to the subjective juridical act or to contract; institutional rights to contractual rights; institutional responsibility to individual responsibility; "rationalization" to nonorganized competition.[17]

Actually, most of these contrasts were already known. But, in order to make them useful and to deduce consequences from them, they were considered in isolation and for themselves. The theory of the institution aims to examine them together in order to explain them by one another, or rather, to illuminate them all together by means of the common idea that presides over and animates them.

The result is sometimes disconcerting. For example, it may seem strange to try to explain by the same notion juridical matters as different from one another as marriage, the professional secret, and the administrative regime. And so the task remains to discover and to justify, in a more rigorous way than has so far been done, the quality inherent in the notion of institution that would enable us—with respect to the well-defined notion of individual human being—to connect to a clearly distinct entity (which Renard characterizes, somewhat obscurely perhaps, as a juridical subject) all the rules by which order is maintained in society, so as to harmonize Ulpian's *jus suum cuique tribuere* with Cicero's *utilitate communi servata, suam cuique tribuere dignitatem.*

To arrive at this result, three steps are necessary: (1) identify the social realities that are at the basis of this somewhat mysterious entity, specify them and underscore all the elements, all the qualities, that contrast them to the individual; (2) reduce these realities to a concept that is both determined and comprehensive enough to grip the mind while enabling it to embrace in one glance the whole complex of situations that are subjected to a common regime; (3) compose or choose the term that best expresses this concept with respect to the realities so envisaged.

Renard began by the word. And the one he adopted, borrowing it from everyday language, "the institution," was so vague that it was difficult to give it a specific meaning. Be that as it may, the term has been adopted. And this *fait accompli* justifies retaining it, from a practical point of view, far more than the debatable reasons Renard has used to defend its value.

Once the term had been accepted as a rallying sign, it had to be filled with the realities it was supposed to express. And these realities

17. [Page references by Geny to the items enumerated in this paragraph have been omitted. The notion of "rationalization" was treated by Renard in an appendix to *La théorie de l'institution* ("L'organisation rationnelle de l'état"), pp. 537–585, and also by Hauriou in "Police juridique et fond du droit," *Revue trimestrielle de droit civil* (1926), reprinted in Hauriou, *Aux Sources du Droit* (Paris, 1933), pp. 147–191.]

proved to be so copious, so rich, and so fruitful that the term could hardly contain them.

It seems that what we need here is a concept that, owing to its logical demands, can sift realities through the sieve of ideas, dissociate contraries, unite similarities, make indispensable eliminations, in order to assign limits to the institution and make it an apt instrument by which to realize the progress of law.

We think then that an effort of *construction* leading, by means of necessary sacrifices, to the discovery of a *unifying concept* would assure the theory of the institution of the assent of minds and the concord of wills it must have to bear full fruit. Such an effort is not beyond the means of its partisans. The theory of the institution brings more than a hope: it is a superb and impressive testimony in favor of the future of the philosophy of law in France.

JOSEPH T. DELOS   The Theory of the Institution:

The Realist Solution of the Problem of Moral

Personality and Law with an Objective Foundation

The theory of the institution has won a place in the philosophy of
law. We can discuss its value, but we can no longer ignore its existence. Too many great names are connected with it. It has also made
a very marked impression on others who, without building it into
a system, are in intellectual sympathy with it and are influenced by
it.

And yet the institution still remains an elusive Proteus. Read, for
example, the alert and suggestive volumes published one after the
other since 1924 by Renard.[1] The institution, which appeared only
sporadically in his earlier books, occupies a growing place as his
work progresses, until it becomes predominant. Where is there not—
if we are to believe Renard—"an institution under rock"? The family
and marriage, churches and the League of Nations, are institutions;
and so are a regimental mess, the *Café du Commerce,* or a railroad
station. There are institutions in private law and public law, in in-

ED. NOTE: Translated from "La théorie de l'institution," *Archives de philosophie du
droit et de sociologie juridique* (1931), pp. 97–153. First a law graduate, then a theolo-
gian, then a doctor of laws at the Faculté de Droit of Paris, then a professor of
sociology and of law, and finally a professor of social theology and a diplomat, Joseph
T. Delos has long been a disciple of Hauriou. His *Société internationale et les principes
du droit public* (Paris, 1929; 2nd ed., 1950) is a thoroughgoing application of Hauriou's
institutional theory to the field of international law. In the article translated here,
Delos (1) summarizes the essential tenets of the theory of the institution as presented
by Hauriou and Renard; (2) argues, with Hauriou and against Renard, that this theory
must affirm the reality of moral personality; (3) argues, against Renard, on the institutional nature of contract and suggests that the theory of the institution should be
expanded into a general theory of the juridical act and of law; and (4) evaluates the
contributions of Hauriou and Renard to the return to an objective conception of
law—the return to reality.

1. [See Bibliography.]

ternal law and international law.[2] So many diverse aspects trouble, even discourage, the least biased minds. They want to seize this "monster" with the fleeting countenance and have a good look at its characteristics.

Perhaps a definitive theory of the institution was taking shape in Hauriou's thought; it would have crowned his scholarly career. But that powerful mind, that indefatigable worker, died before he was able to exploit his most fundamental discoveries. Renard modestly calls himself the disciple of the "Toulousian master," to whose memory he has given moving testimonials.[3] In reality he is the heir to a larger doctrinal tradition, which he continues and renews with the mastery and originality of thought for which he is known. He owed it to himself even more than to the one he calls his master to fill in the lacunae and to formulate the "theory of the institution" that his earlier works called for. He conceived a plan of magnificent amplitude;[4] he has commenced the realization of it. Because of him, today we possess a coherent exposition with synthetic aims; the phase of elaboration of the doctrine has advanced far enough for us to subject it to a critical examination.

In beginning this examination, I want to say that my ambitions are limited. Is the theory of the institution, as it appears today, an *exhaustive interpretation of the facts upon which it is based?* What can explain the imprecision in which it floundered for so long and the multiform aspects it still has, other than the fact that the *sociological data*[5] upon which the system rests are more general than one might believe at first? Consequently, should not the theory of the institution be given certain complements—complements that its very principles call for? Is it not committed, in the name of these same principles, to enlarge its basis, to develop from its present position as a distinct part of the philosophy of law into a *general theory of law?* In a word, shall we not be led to rally to an institutional theory of law rather than to a theory of the institution constructed on its present bases? These are the questions I should like to try to answer. Perhaps in doing so I shall also succeed in showing what a great

2. [Renard, *La théorie de L'institution* (Paris, 1930), pp. 92, 151–152.]

3. See in particular the pages entitled "To the Memory of Maurice Hauriou," which form the magnificent and moving introduction to Renard's *La théorie de l'institution.*

4. [Renard recites this plan in *La théorie de l'institution,* pp. 108–110, and Delos comments on it here: "This grandiose but not foolhardy plan would justify by itself what I shall soon say about the true nature of the theory of the institution: it should consider *every fact* of societal life, upon whatever plane that life develops."]

5. [*Données here, not* Geny's *donnés.*]

place the powerful intellectual effort of Hauriou and Renard occupies in the return to an *objectivist conception of law.*

It is only fair to ask Renard for the main lines of the institutional
doctrine. His recent and very suggestive work[6] certainly represents
the most considerable effort yet attempted to give it a rational explanation.

1. Faithful to the method of observation to which he persistently
adheres, and which is the only basis for giving precedence in the
philosophy of law to realities over constructed notions,[7] Renard
begins by describing the institution, or rather the institutional phenomenon. He points out the existence of juridical activities that
cannot be reduced to manifestations of individual rights, to contract,
or to the law of the state.[8] The only juridical realities recognized
by an individualist science of law, says Renard, are the individual
and contracts that manifest agreements of individual wills, on one
side, and the state and its manifestations of sovereign will, on the
other. But such a legal science overlooks a whole category of facts,
juridical activities, and even juridical subjects that an alert observer
of social and juridical life has no right to ignore. For institutional
phenomena, foundations—in a word, "institutions"—also have a
place "on the scene of juridical commerce."[9]

If we are to believe Renard—and I intend to return to this point
later on—the institution properly so-called would be one of the three
manifestations of juridical activity, the first being *legislation,* the
second *contract.* The institution would appear only where communion in an idea or in an end groups individuals and gives birth
to a body, a foundation, that takes its place in positive law between
the individual and the state.

From this description, it is clear that the institutional fact appears
in private law as well as in public law. Besides, Renard has never
believed in a radical and absolute separation of these two branches
of law.[10] There is a "common fund" of ideas, of principles, of notions,
that reappear in private law as in public law. The institution is one

6. [Renard, *La théorie de l'institution*]
7. [See *construit,* G. In Geny's terminology, *construit* contrasts with *donné, technique* with *science.*]
8. Renard, *La théorie de l'institution,* p. 108.
9. [*Commerce juridique.* G.]
10. Renard, *La théorie de l'institution,* p. 123.

of these. Some examples of the institution are, in private law, the family and marriage; in public law, the state and, "at the heart of the state, the nation," at its "periphery, the political regime," over and above the political regime, the administrative regime,[11] and finally the "international society,"[12] to whose institutional character Renard has devoted some of his most brilliant studies. We could easily add numerous examples to this summary list. The institution is a social reality common to all the domains of law, a sociological "datum" that transcends the confines of "lay law"[13] and that we meet again in canon law and in the mixed disciplines.

2. But what is the institution? The substance of Hauriou's solid writings has passed into Renard's doctrine, and agreement is reached on a general definition of the institution. . . . [14] Hauriou's definition, which has chiefly juridical designs, remains accurate when transposed to the sociological terrain. Renard has clarified it, refined it, plumbed its depths.

The institution, says Renard, results from the communion of men in an idea. It is the body, the reality, the *being* that is born of this communion. An idea to be realized, an end, "creates a solidarity among those who pursue it simultaneously or successively"; it establishes a communion between men and between generations. The institution, Renard continues, is an *idea* endowed with appropriate *ways and means* that enable it to be established, realized, and perpetuated by giving it a body and an objective existence. "Rousseau . . . spoke of 'one who dares to institute a people.' Aristide Briand . . . in the famous discourse of the *Salon de l'Horloge* . . . spoke of 'the institution of peace.' To institute peace is to provide an idea with the ways and means of being realized. To institute a people is to provide a people with the means to maintain itself and to develop";[15] to give it an internal charter and organs that will enable it to act externally; that is, to constitute it as a social body endowed with an internal life and an external activity.

3. Although all institutions correspond to the same general definition, they are all very far from being of the same type. There is no uniformity among them. This diversity is of the greatest importance

---

11. Renard, *La théorie de l'institution,* pp. 163ff.

12. Renard, *Le droit international, la société des nations et les traités de paix* (Paris, 1930).

13. [*Droit laic,* in contrast with church law, *droit canonique.*]

14. [Delos here quotes in full Hauriou's classic definition of "the institution" from his *La théorie de l'institution,* pp. 10ff, translated above.]

15. Renard, *La théorie de l'institution,* pp. 95–97.

for the jurist; because the law of institutions, the kind of juridical situations they produce and enjoy, varies according to their character. All institutions do not have the same consistency, the same density. Renard is a philosopher; he does not shrink from a philosophical vocabulary; besides, nothing less can adequately express his thought. There are, he says, *degrees of institutional existence. . .*[16]

The progressive development of being and of life, that is, the ever more perfect integration of the idea, or the form, in the matter, is "the abc of biological philosophy."

Similarly, "the progressive development of institutional existence"[17] is the abc of juridical philosophy. Renard does not add "and of sociology," but he would hardly object if I ventured this addition. Just as there are *degrees* in *the being* of physical beings, so there are *degrees* in *the being* of social bodies. Institutions are graded, like living things in biology, on the diverse steps of an ascending hierarchy. This hierarchy, says Renard, is "a continuous ascent up to the fullness of being."[18] Some institutions are not distinct enough to be of interest to the jurist; they cannot yet be considered juridical subjects, that is, precise, definite beings, whose nature and prerogatives stand irreducibly in opposition to those of others. As I understand it, although Renard does not explicitly say so, such institutions remain provisionally or definitively in the sphere of the sociologist, without entering that of the jurist; for the jurist confines himself to protecting certain more apparent, more readily grasped, and more necessary manifestations of social activity. Other institutions reach a greater fullness of being and development. They attain an autonomous life; they become juridical subjects. And if the sociologist studies the manifestations of their natural activity, the jurist defines their rights, sanctions their obligations, regulates their juridical activities, and surrounds them with procedures. Thus among institutions a gamut is created that follows a progression of infinite nuances, just as in biology there are infinite nuances in the gamut of beings that goes by successive degrees from the invertebrate to the thinking and willing man.

What explains this intrinsic difference—this difference of being— among institutions? It results from the more or less perfect integration of the idea in the mass of men of whom it makes a body. It depends upon the more or less profound ascendancy that the idea

16. [Delos here quotes a passage from chap. v of Renard, *La théorie l'institution,* pp. 225-226, translated above.]
    17. [Renard, *La théorie de l'institution,* p. 229.]
    18. [Renard, *La théorie de l'institution,* p. 230.]

has over those whom it unites, whom it binds together into a distinct whole. . .[19]

Renard applies the principles of his general philosophy to social realities. The ascendancy of the idea is what marks the degree of internal cohesion of the institution. This gives a presentiment of the conclusions that could be drawn from this doctrine to explain the moral personality of social bodies. The degree of consciousness elicited by the directing idea, the mother-idea of the institution, is what determines whether it is a "person," that is, a being conscious of itself and of its natural ends, and capable of realizing these ends knowingly. But I am going to explore this phase later on, so let me finish my exposition of the theory.

4. After the description and definition of the institution comes the study of its *interior life*. Hauriou had pointed out and studied on several occasions the *movement of communion* that is manifested among the members of the group. These members, he said, commune either "in the idea of the work to be realized or in the idea of the means to realize it." Owing to this phenomenon of communion, "the directing idea of the work passes momentarily into the subjective state". . . [20]

Renard replaces the idea of communion by another idea—more moral than philosophical—that of *intimacy*. The consequences he draws from this idea are much more precise and clear than such a vague word would lead one to suspect at first. The institution is a milieu, a home, for its members. A bond of confidence—*fides*—is established among them, which varies according to the nature of the particular institution, but which even a fledgling psychology finds everywhere. This intimacy results from the ascendancy that the idea of the institution exercises over its members. The idea—or the end, the common good that it represents—is "what makes an institution insofar as it takes root in a certain human milieu, 'informs' it, organizes it, differentiates it, and elicits a power within it." Institutional intimacy manifests itself by the appearance of an *authority;* for authority is simply the result of "the ascendancy of the whole over its parts . . . with the ensuing expansion of the institutional power

19. Renard, *La théorie de l'institution,* p. 231: "Keep in mind the general rule I mentioned at the outset—a rule common to law and to the biological sciences—that there is more being in a whole in proportion as the idea (or form) that constitutes it is more perfectly integrated into its parts; there is more being in an institution, or any organism, in proportion as its members are more perfectly subjected to it." [This quotation appears in Delos' text.]

20. Hauriou, *La théorie de l'institution,* p. 20. Delos then quotes further from this passage; see Hauriou, "The Theory of the Institution," above.

over the external personal activity of the members of the institution" . . .[21] For, continues Renard, "every institution is *the seat of
a juridical system;* there is at least a potential juridical system within
it."[22]

These are the characteristics of the institution as depicted by
Renard. I shall not digress to praise the soundness of the principles
upon which his doctrine rests. I shall also forego showing what new
paths it opens, what immense tasks it assigns to law and to the
philosophy of law. Although not all institutions are juridical subjects
in the proper sense of the word, all do create juridical situations,
either among their members, or from the fact of their coexistence
with other institutions: they must be distinguished, guaranteed, and
their power characters safeguarded. Each institution is the seat of
a power: we must recognize its juridical value, its aptitude for creating law. Finally, institutions are ordered among themselves within
the state and within the international community: their relations with
each must be distinguished. A whole world opens up here to the
reflections of the philosopher, to the work of the jurist and the legislator.

But we cannot let ourselves be distracted from our plan, and lose
sight of the basic question: Does the theory of the institution as it
is presented today take sufficient account of reality? Does it not call
for a natural and necessary extension that Renard—for the moment
at least—seems to hesitate to ascribe to it? And with its help should
one not resolve the problem of moral personality? This is the first
of the two questions that must be examined.

THE THEORY OF THE INSTITUTION AND THE REALIST
SOLUTION OF THE PROBLEM OF MORAL PERSONALITY

5. Since institutions admit of more or less, or to use the philosophical and more exact language of Renard, since they have more
or less being, what are the extreme degrees of their ascending scale?

21. Renard, *La théorie de l'institution,* pp. 288ff, 311ff.
22. Renard, *La théorie de l'institution,* p. 324. [Renard's passages, *La théorie de
l'institution,* pp. 122, 325–327, are here quoted in the text by Delos: "The institution's
ˑinterior life is made up of the relationships of its organs among themselves; it is
'organized,' and to say organism is to say differentiation: it is the *seat of an authority*
. . . In every institution there is an embryo of authority, and this embryo will develop
and be differentiated in proportion as the organism progresses . . . A regression of
authority is the infallible sign of decadence in institutions. An institution that loses
its structure of authority soon wastes away; its being quickly disintegrates, and then
it fades away into the anonymity of the 'common law,' and a 'juridical system' disappears."]

Actually, the jurist has no great interest in determining the starting point of the lower echelon. But the sociologist has: it is up to him to discover embryonic institutional forms wherever certain solidarities begin to take form from social masses, to assume the contours of social groups in the process of formation. I myself have used the expression "*de facto* institutional groups" to designate these purely sociological forms of "institutions" and of groups.[23] Every good of civilization, I said, can give rise to bonds of human solidarity; it is an objective center of interests around which a mass of interested parties gravitates, "a pole whose attraction can elicit a movement within an amorphous mass." Each one of these goods of civilization can instigate a phenomenon of grouping, of an institutional order: that is, ruled by an objective end that sparks individuals into motion by its power of attraction.

These embryonic institutional movements always interest the sociologist, but not necessarily the jurist. For in practice the jurist has to devote his attention to protecting the rights of institutions and bodies that have already been constituted. The imperfection of the technical means he has at his disposal limits his activity too much for him to be able to attempt to guarantee certain social activities, certain too tenuous solidarities. He must not ignore them, but he cannot get entangled in them; subject as he is to the "law of success," he turns to more urgent things.

On the other hand, it is of fundamental importance to the jurist to know how far the differentiation of institutions can go, to know the *maximum degree of being they can reach*. Under the apparent obscurity of these metaphysical terms, the *problem of the natural moral personality of institutions and social groups* appears—and on its true ground.

Everyone readily admits that the highest form of existence a being can reach is personality. The person is universally held to be this superior being who thinks, who wills, who physically and morally moves himself, determines himself, and directs himself. Among physical beings, the human individual obviously has these characteristics. And because he represents the highest form of being— intelligent, capable of willing, free—he has an eminent dignity, he is by nature, in the social order, the only native juridical subject.

But are there *social bodies* that also merit—by nature and not by metaphor or fiction[24]—the title "person"? The law is accustomed to

23. Delos, *La société internationale et les principes du droit public* (Paris, 1929), pp. 96ff.

24. [Hauriou maintained that the fiction theory of the corporate group had been generally rejected in France (see "The Theory of the Institution," above). Renard, on

seeing on the scene of juridical commerce bodies and institutions that act in the capacity of a juridical subject and with the characteristics of personality. By what right do they do this? Is their nature such that only the title "person" can adequately express their real, intrinsic characteristics, so that the recognition of their personality by positive law has a declarative rather than an attributive value? And so that this recognition is imposed upon positive law which, by its theory of juridical personality, only sanctions and guarantees natural sociological situations?

6. It is on this precise point that the theory of the institution as Renard expounds it up to now seems to call for a complement—a complement that is but a direct extension of its own principles.

Civil personality, and analogously, it seems, moral personality, remain "fictions" in his eyes. But we must understand this word in the sense the author gives it. "Is there," asks Renard, "some reality behind the fiction of civil personality?" No, replies the jacobin doctrine: "There is nothing between the individual and the state; the state is all-powerful, it can produce juridical subjects at will. It is against this negation that I rebel and raise up the theory of the institution."[25]

Between the individual and the state there is a multitude of institutions. The "collective"—groups of every kind—fill the space left open between the two entities that have seemed absolute for so long—the individual and the state. And these groups also have their rights, which they do not get from the state or from the will of their members, but from their own nature and their particular end.

The institution then is also a juridical subject.[26] This is why, thinks Renard, "the most vigorous institutions have been given the name of moral or civil or juridical persons." The term is used to designate a "degree" of *status* of an institution, a degree of being from the ontological point of view, the highest rank an institution can reach: "the degree at which it is able to act as a being not only with respect to its organs, but as to the world outside." By reason of "their maximum power of being," the "individuality of these institutions can stand in opposition to anything whatsoever. They exist *erga omnes*, like human persons. I am prepared to say that their existence is

---

the other hand, in his first institutional volume retained the terminology of fiction (see Renard, "The Degrees of Institutional Existence," above); but he moved away from it later (see below).]

25. Renard, *La théorie de l'institution*, pp. 38–39.
26. Renard, *La théorie de l'institution*, p. 239.

absolute; like human persons, and with them, they enter into the ordinary commerce of juridical life." This is why they are commonly and indifferently called moral or juridical persons.

But "the word is dangerous," adds Renard. "In fact, no matter what perfection of being an institution may attain, it will never reach the level of personality in the true sense of the word; I recognize the convenience of the fiction . . . I appreciate the poetry of it . . . I am resigned to the expression; but I do not intend to be duped by it. I keep it chiefly out of deference for established usage."[27]

One can, then, without any distortion, sum up Renard's thought in these few words. The "collective," or better, the diverse institutions, have their own reality independent of the state that recognizes them. Society is no longer created by a mind that merges the diversity of individuals into a single pattern. Institutions have an objective reality. Their being is tiered in different, ascending levels that bring them closer and closer to true personality, to the point of giving them the appearance of it, but without ever enabling them to attain it. True personality is reserved to man. It marks a limit toward which institutions tend but never reach—a sort of mathematical limit—and the application of the word personality to anything other than the human individual always implies a fiction: "I cannot admit the *reality* of the juridical personality of the state."[28]

Between Renard's concept and what I believe to be called for by the philosophical interpretation of sociological and juridical realities, there is only the thickness of a misunderstanding, I am quite sure. Far from combatting Renard's position, I wish to strengthen it. Far from opposing his doctrine, I think that I am faithful to it—he will pardon this temerity—to the end. I should like, by dispelling one last bit of fog, to contribute to a definitive elucidation of the notion of moral personality and to substitute the word "reality" for "fiction," which I would banish forever. The study of sociological realities, which contributes its whole value to the institutional doctrine, cannot fail to overcome on this point the last intellectual resistance of the advocates of the institution.

7. It is then in the light of sociological observation that I wish to try to give the theory of the institution the extension it calls for; for the theory of moral personality is only an interpretation, a metaphysical transcription, of certain sociological data.

The point of departure on which I easily agree with all the parti-

27. Renard, *La théorie de l'institution*, pp. 233, 243.
28. [Renard, *La théorie de l'institution*, p. 188, n.1.]

sans of the institutional doctrine is the affirmation of the objective and real existence of the social factor, the affirmation of the reality of social bodies or groups. This truth is so common that I would not bother to defend it if it did not sometimes happen that we agree on words without agreeing on their meanings, and if it were not that this affirmation is not so familiar in law as in sociology.

I have noted elsewhere that the difficulty experienced by common sense in admitting the "reality" of social beings comes from the very nature of social relationships. The senses, the imagination, and the intellect readily admit the objective existence of substantial or accidental realities or values that can be grasped and expressed in a definite sharply defined concept, a concept that is perfectly one: a substance, an idea, a quality, a sentiment. But the mind is very ill at ease when it tries to grasp a *relationship*. A relationship requires the presence of definite, substantial individual beings, for there must be someone or something that enters into relations, that serves as the support or term of mutual references. In the language of traditional philosophy,[29] a relationship can only be an accident, that is, it presupposes objects of which it is a "manner of being."[30] It is accidental to one individual to be related to certain others; it is accidental to a mind to assimilate a particular truth, that is, to have a relationship with a particular object of knowledge. A relationship then acts upon a subject and orders it to another, it establishes a connection between them: it is in this ordering and this orientation that it consists.

Many have a secret difficulty, it seems, in admitting the objective reality of social relationships. They have a real existence, these people feel, only in the mind of the one who thinks, or who observes society. Not that they do not have a foundation in exterior reality, but just as the conventional time of our clocks is a measure that the mind applies to the continuum of movement and duration, society would contain no other objective reality than its individuals, the only "real existents," with their interests, their needs, their opinions. The bond that envelops them and permits us to speak of their plurality as though it were a whole and a body would be just a mental image, authorizing a certain manner of speaking: still a fiction, but giving this word fiction a profound sense that eliminates any idea of arbitrariness.

I shall not discuss here this conception, which seems to me to

29. [I.e., in Delos' sense, the philosophy of Aristotle and Aquinas.]
30. [I.e., an existential mode, in the sense of Aristotle's predicaments.]

conceal both a metaphysical and a sociological error. I shall merely recall the point of departure of our conception of the natural moral personality of social groups. I readily concede that it would be unintelligible to anyone who would refuse to admit the distinctive reality and objective existence of social bodies, but I think that once these premises are admitted, it is impossible to escape their natural consequences.

Renard has found excellent terms to describe the special nature of social bodies. They are, he says, units that are "ideal but not purely verbal, invisible but in no sense unreal, imperceptible but perfectly intelligible."[31] Not only are relationships, for him and for me, a form of reality, but social relationships—with which we are chiefly concerned here—constitute an *objective* reality, exterior to the individuals who are the support and the terms of these relationships, and they are irreducible to psychological or interpsychological realities. Since I have recently[32] tried to explain how the objective, external nature of social relationships is to be understood, you will excuse me from developing the same ideas here although I shall have recourse to the same terms. Not every relationship, I said, *has the objectivity of the societal relationship:* a relationship among individuals does not *become objective* itself, at least not in the same sense. In order for it to do so, a new factor must intervene, a factor that is exterior to the individuals concerned and independent of them—objective in this sense. This element, which is the cause of the relationship established between individuals, can be a material element; it can also be a purely spiritual element, like an idea. Because of its objectivity, the idea is a factor of societal aggregation. But whether it is material or ideal, the object always lies between the individuals involved, and this is what gives the social relationship its exterior, objective character. The societal relationship goes from an individual to an object that establishes the bond with other individuals, and this is why the social relationship takes on an "objectivity," an externality. This characteristic objectivity is what distinguishes it from interindividual relationships, which may be adequately explained by subjective individual psychology.

And so, social groups engendered by the development of social relationships have a distinctive reality; they are distinct from the sum of members who compose them. They are beings, in the exact

31. Renard, *La théorie de l'institution*, p. 93.

32. Delos, "L'objet de la sociologie," *Vie intellectuelle* (March 1930) [translated below]; *La société internationale*, pp. 153ff.

sense of the word and without metaphor. Not substantial beings, like human individuals, but bodies whose members are united by mutual relations. They are beings of a special kind, certainly—*constituted by the network of relationships established between substantial subjects and the objects that unite them;* beings that are therefore irreducible to the physical realities our senses apprehend. But all the elements that integrate a social body—substantial subjects, common ideas, mutual relations—are *realities,* and thus a social body constitutes a reality that is objective and one. To say that it is endowed with a moral unity rather than a physical unity is not to diminish in the least its objectivity, its reality, its unity, but only to identify its intrinsic nature: it is made up of relations that create among its members a bond that is moral and not physical.

8. Equipped with these premises, one can tackle the problem of moral personality. There can be persons only where there are real beings who possess the qualities designated by the word personality. For a person to exist, there must first be "a someone." This is why I have taken care to establish the reality of social groups. The question is whether or not such a being—a real being, certainly, but a moral being—is capable of becoming a person in the precise sense of the word. Does the personality attributed to certain groups or certain institutions retain something of the metaphorical? Does it imply an aspect of fiction? Or is it the exact expression of some reality, of an objective quality of certain social groups?

If one supposes this first question to be resolved in the affirmative, a second question appears. Are there not groups or institutions that are by nature moral persons, that is to say, groups or institutions to which this quality intrinsically belongs, so that, although the formation of such groups could perhaps be prevented,[33] it would be contradictory to permit their existence and deny them moral personality? I have no doubt that these two questions must be answered in the affirmative.

Hauriou distinguished two types of institutions: those that are personified, which he calls institution-persons, and those that are not personified: institution-things.[34] The explanations he joins to his distinction remain, I confess, very confused. But the distinction retains its value. There are de facto human groups in which the members are not conscious of the bonds that are established among them; or at least it does not matter very much to the formation of these

33. [E.g., for reasons of policy by the state.]
34. Hauriou, *La théorie de l'institution,* p. 10.

groups whether these bonds are conscious or not because they entirely escape the human will and human liberty. When an ethnographer draws a map of the diverse racial groups in a given territory, he geographically marks out human groups whose formation is independent of the will of the groups involved. An ethnic group, however diversified it may be in the eyes of somatic anthropology, is never a moral person; it is merely a de facto group. The bond—the community of blood—does not become an idea; it remains a pure fact. Neither the fact that produces the solidarity, nor this solidarity itself, becomes an idea or passes, as Hauriou would say, to the subjective state in the consciousness of individuals. It is not necessary to be a *person* to feel the impact of a fact; in this case, there is a creation of a *state of fact,* not a *state of consciousness.*

But inversely, and at the opposite extreme, there are groups in which the individual does manifest his quality as a person. In such social groups the members appear as beings conscious of the end that brings them together, capable of determining the ways and means of realizing the common ends. They act as responsible beings in social life, and the action of the social body rightly appears under the aspects of an action that is both conscious and free. The acts by which the group realizes it ends—whether by directing its own members or by dealing with outsiders—will be the acts of a person, of a being that knows where it is going, that directs itself in the choice of its acts, and that for this reason bears responsibility for them.

Do I mean by this that a group is a moral person because it is composed of individuals who are physical persons and because within a society they do not cease acting as free and willing persons? If I meant only this, an agreement could easily be reached with the adversaries of moral personality. But I would betray the conception of the *reality of natural moral personality.* I would leave in the shadows the fundamental affirmation of sociology: that social bodies are real, that they are specifically distinct from the sum of the individuals who compose them.

It is clear that a group can be a moral person only if it is composed of intelligent and free beings, but the person formed by the group is distinct from the persons of each one of its members. The social body has a personality of its own, distinct from the personalities of its members. It acts as a being conscious of its ends and free to choose the best means of realizing them. And if it is true that it can act in this way only because its component parts are physical persons, it is no less true that its action is specifically distinct from every other action—*and imputable to a subject other than the individuals composing the group,* so that the social body, not the individual, incurs moral responsibility. This responsibility certainly falls back, in the last analysis, on individuals, but it will weigh on each one only in virtue of his *function* in the life of the society. It will be measured by this same function. Nothing could be more indicative of the fact that it is a question of a responsibility of the group and not of individuals.

You will give me enough credit, I hope, not to accuse me of having been taken in by that famous collective conscience,[35] that group consciousness endowed with an independent existence outside the thinking subjects who compose the society. What I am saying is that the operation of the group is due to *individuals* as its *efficient cause,* in the sense that the human individual is the original source of all social activity. The group acts only by the efficient effort of its members. The point of origin of this act is the individual, but its term and *raison d'être* are the society, the common end. The social act is precisely the relationship that originates in the individual, its efficient support, and terminates in the social end. Its formal cause is the idea, which "informs" the individual, the official organ of the social body. Its final cause is the dimly seen common good, which stirs up individual action and then "informs" it. Individual as to its efficient origin, the act is social as to both its end and its form; it is then social by its *raison d'être* and by what specifies it. Its rule, like its end, is social and not individual. Can we further affirm that although the social act is a human act, it is nonetheless in its very essence distinct from acts of *individual* life?

When the waters of a single source separate as they rise out of the earth and descend the opposite slopes of a mountain, flowing into opposite seas, would you deny that there are two rivers on the pretext that there is only one source?

Man is an individual being—an absolute who lives for himself and is the direct term of his own operations. But at the same time he is a social being, a member who lives for the society of which he is only a part. We are well aware that man as an individuated substance is the unique source of all the energies that are manifested in his *social* life as well as in his *individual* life; but does this prevent his social life from being specifically distinct from his individual life?

The functional operations of individuals within the group are nothing other than the life of the group itself. Individuals forget themselves, they abstract from their individual interests. We ask the

---

35. [I.e., of Durkheim, not Duguit. See above.]

citizen, as citizen, to think only of his country, the official of the League of Nations to act as an "international person" and to forget his national interests; we make this a *moral duty* for them. *This moral duty is the expression of a sociological reality.* In fact, we do not understand how there could be a moral duty without this sociological reality. The social action of one of the members of the body is simply the act by which this body moves itself, organizes itself, administers itself, rules itself internally and regulates its relationships with others; it is the exercise of one of the *functions* of the social body. This act is in the strict sense attributed to the group, because the one who performs it acts only in the capacity of organ, member, or minister. Since an act performed by the individual for the ends of the society is only a *function,* it is in its very essence an act of the group. An act is not imputable to the society as its responsible author simply because it is simultaneously performed by a plurality of individuals. The numerical coefficient of acts is not what makes them social; it is a question of their nature. An act is social when it is performed in view of the ends of a society by one of its members. What difference does it make that the same individual can act today as a member of the social body and tomorrow for his own individual ends? Does this prove anything more than his double capacity of individual being and social being?

When a group then is so constituted that its members, in the realization of the social ends, in the accomplishment of the diverse functions comprising the life of the society, behave as conscious and free "persons," the social body itself is a person, distinct from all others. The manifestations of activity of such a group are reduced to a series of conscious and voluntary operations, and since the life of the social body is a totality specifically distinct from individuals lives, the social body is truly a person, a being conscious of its destiny and responsible for the realization of this destiny.

It is not enough, then, to say that a group is a person because it is composed of individual persons, if you do not add that these individuals, in the natural accomplishment of social *functions,* are expected to behave as conscious members, and that in this way the life of the group, constituted by the hierarchical ensemble of functions, is the organic life of a being conscious of its ends and master of its acts.[36] There is then no reason to look for a collective consciousness distinct from individual consciousnesses: all the acts of

36. [I.e., a certain capacity for effective choice that is indispensable to human liberty.]

the collective life are decomposed into functions served by the members of the group; but the ensemble of these functions constitutes the life of a real being, the group, and this life is in the proper sense the life of a person and not of a thing, the life of a being that acts knowingly, with full control of its acts, even though these acts are complex and are decomposed by analysis into a series of functions emanating from organs or from diverse ministers hierarchically ordered among themselves.

Moral person—I repeat this again to calm the anxieties raised by the affirmation of the reality of the moral personality of societies. The evidence is glaring. A group is a moral body; a moral body, when it is a person, can *only* be a moral person. How a being endowed with a physical unity differs from a moral body I need not explain again: the parts of the physical being are united by a bond that makes it a unique, concrete, and individual substance—whatever philosophical sense you attribute to the word substance. On the other hand, among the elements that compose the moral body there is only a *relationship*. The bond that joins the parts and makes a unity of the whole is then an *accidental* bond *established among substantial subjects;* namely, the individuals and the things that compose the society. Just as an individual consciousness is an idea in a single subject, a collective consciousness is an idea in several subjects. And as the individual idea brings about the substantial unity of the elements of the individual subject, so the social idea brings about the accidental unity, the unity of order, the moral unity of the social elements.

9. The difficulty that baffles many excellent minds in this matter seems to come from a confusion, an incorrect identification of the two terms *substantial being* and *personality.* Or rather, do they not unconsciously imagine that to admit the reality of moral personality, and to recognize that the quality of moral person is natural to certain societies, would be to put these societies on the same level as man, the only concrete subject, the only native juridical subject, who must conserve as an undivided privilege his absolute value and eminent dignity?[37]

The confusion is easily dispelled. The human individual is obviously the only being who thinks and acts as a subsisting subject, the only source of all intellectual and moral activity, the only substance. Endowed with intelligence and liberty, he is the first to merit the name person.

37. There seems to be an echo of this fear in Renard, *La théorie de l'institution,* pp. 92–93, 233, 243, 188, 189n, etc.

But does it follow that the same title does not belong to the new being that is formed by concrete men united by their societal relationships? For even though society is not an individual and physical substance, it is nonetheless real—as real as substantial beings and the relationships that unite them. And this social whole can have personality if it has all the qualities that are characteristic of this state: consciousness of its destiny and ends, control of its acts, responsibility. The difficulty I am trying to dispel comes from a confusion of personality, as a simple quality that denotes the status, the manner of being of certain beings, with these beings themselves, these substances endowed with personality. Personality belongs properly to physical, substantial beings, but also, morally, to the social body that they form among themselves. *Moral* personality, but moral is not a synonym for fictitious; the moral being, composed of relationships, is a real being, and moral personality expresses a real state of this being.

The fear is vain, then, of seeing the state, for example, as equal to man, of seeing man deprived of his privileged rank, his preeminent dignity, for the benefit of the state, a pure fact of political and juridical organization, a contingent formation due to human industry. What gives an absolute value to the human person is his nature as a spiritual *substance*. A society can never aspire to this eminent dignity because, made up of relationships, it is simply an aggregate of accidental elements. An examination of its internal structure shows that it is composed of substantial individuals united by their mutual relationships. The intrinsic metaphysical superiority of man over society comes from the fact that he is an autonomous, spiritual, immortal substance, whereas society is only an accidental being—in the philosophical sense of the term[38]—a network of relationships woven between subsistent individuals without whom it would have no support and could not exist.

Thus, the theory of the moral personality of societies seems to us to withstand victoriously all critical examination. If, relying on the data of sociology, you see in the institution—or more exactly, in the social bodies that appear on the juridical terrain—an ensemble of men grouped around an idea to be realized, you must certainly admit that the ascending scale of institutions leads us to moral persons. To recognize a personality in some of them, *without any fiction*, is

---

38. [Delos defines "substances" as "beings that are individuated by themselves, which do not, like accidents, have need to borrow from [another] subject their existence". *La théorie de l'institution*, p. 137, n.1.]

simply to attest that they have a quality, a mode of being, that is intrinsic to them, just as to recognize a personality in the human individual is to acknowledge his natural aptitude to act knowingly and responsibly. The recognition of the "reality" of the moral person, without fiction or metaphor, is a consequence of the recognition of the "reality" of social bodies; for personality is only a manner of being that is proper to certain of these bodies and verified in them.[39]

10. This brings me to the second problem that I said I should solve by the institutional doctrine: are there groups that by nature are moral persons?

This new problem is of direct interest to the jurist. For has he not the task of assigning to every individual or group the juridical situations required by its nature and function in a given state of civilization? Natural moral personality implies the recognition of certain rights and calls for the juridical protection of certain liberties; it creates for those groups who possess it a right to juridical personality and claims for them an appropriate juridical status.

When I say that there are natural moral persons, I mean that the social end—the one that provides the mother-idea, the generating idea of the society—is one of those ends that the members must pursue freely and consciously if they wish to obey nature itself and its injunctions. The responsibility of attaining the social ends weighs upon them and creates a duty for each one of them, at least in proportion to the social function incumbent on him. The members of such a society have a natural vocation to act as conscious, free, responsible persons in the accomplishment of their social functions. Of necessity they must act as men and as persons.

We can say, then, that a group is naturally endowed with a moral personality when it is in itself of such a nature that the social activities necessary to obtain its ends must be determined and executed by members who are conscious of the ends of the society. Societal life then in the proper sense is the natural exercise of a conscious and responsible activity.

The problem will take on its full interest if in pursuing these investigations we ask which societies among the groups that are natural to man present these characteristics and necessarily assume the nature of moral person.

39. . . . In the eyes of a rather clumsy positivism that confuses reality with what can be perceived by the senses, society as such is dissolved into its component individuals; they are the only sensible, material beings—but not the only real beings. There is more objective reality in the world than the positivist's senses and observation perceive of it . . . [In the lengthy footnote from which the previous sentence is excerpted, Delos criticizes Léon Duguit for failing "to admit the 'reality' of social bodies."]

11. In the first rank among these groups must be placed the state. To what end does it respond? From what generating idea does it proceed if not, in the broadest sense, from the desire of assuring an integral protectorate of individual life and of putting each individual in a position to realize fully his human destiny? What necessity imposes the state upon us if not the very duty of living as man? This is why the old traditional formula assigns it the object "of assuring the complete good of human life," which puts in a phrase the basis of all the duties of the citizen and all the rights of the state. This desire of expanding to the full our physical, intellectual, and moral faculties is what constrains us to live in society, in a group politically and juridically organized. And this natural desire is accompanied by a duty: we have the obligation of living in a state regime because such a regime is necessary for the realization of our human destiny.

But along with this duty, our condition as free and responsible citizens is asserted. Who is the citizen if not the man conscious of the destiny he must realize by his own effort, by the exercise of his liberty under the control of his responsibility. The civic rights of man are founded upon his moral duties, which may be summed up in just one duty: to realize, in the only manner consonant with his dignity as a person, by a conscious, voluntary, and responsible effort, his social destiny, the necessary condition of his individual life. Therefore, man must realize his civic destiny in the state and through the state, under the same conditions of responsibility and liberty that preside over his individual life. He enters into the state with a natural vocation to fulfill as man, under the ordinary conditions of liberty and conscience implied by this word, the civic functions necessary to the life of the state.

Yet the nature of the political society would not be changed by shortcomings on the part of certain members of the social body or of one class of citizens. Such shortcomings would modify the distribution of functions, but not the nature of the state. Even should the population behave as an inert mass, it would suffice for the existence of the state that the organs make their own the idea of the common good and public order and, acting as ministers for all, apply themselves to achieving this idea while coordinating individual activities. Even if the entire social consciousness and will were concentrated in a single organ, only the form and interior organization of the state would be modified. When the popular mass—a dead weight today— remains passive and fulfills only a negligible civic function, the state is nonetheless a moral person, conscious of its end and acting to realize this end. When a considerable number of citizens do not serve the functions to which they are called as men and as citizens, the lacuna requires an effort of political education, which may be a prelude to constitutional reorganization. But these problems do not touch the nature of the state. The state is a natural moral person in the full force of the term: it is first of all a natural society; but this society is by nature a moral person, because political life is, by its very nature, based upon consciousness and responsibility.

12. We cannot say the same of that other natural society—the family. This may surprise those who are accustomed to placing, with good reason, the family in the first rank of those necessary societies for whom a respect is indispensable to the moral health of individuals and peoples. The family is truly the cell society, the crucible in which the individual is formed and educated. And when it seems to be threatened by encroaching action of the state as well as by changing customs, there is more need than ever to proclaim its rights. Perhaps it is because they are very much imbued with this necessity and justly convinced of the primacy of the family that some see in it, even more than in the state, a natural moral person.[40] But this confusion is of benefit neither to the family nor to the defense of its rights. . .[41]

That we deny the family the quality of natural moral person in no way prevents it from being a natural society of primary importance. Nor does it prejudice its inviolable rights. These rights are attached to its quality as a natural society, they are derived from its educative and generative function, which is of primary importance for the perpetuation and moral progress of humanity. If we evaluate institutions by their moral and social value, we must give first place to the family. Renard, in his study of the institution, very successfully brings out the fact that a respect for institutions imposes itself upon the state and upon positive law all the more as these institutions have a greater human value and fulfill a higher function. The state is the servant of all these values, the guarantor and protector of the accomplishment of these functions. This is why the protection of the rights of the family imposes itself upon the state as the gravest of its obligations.

40. Cf. Renard, *La théorie de l'institution*, p. 245. On this point even more than any other, the divergences between Renard and me are differences of expression far more than differences of doctrine.

41. [In the textual passage omitted here Delos argues that the end of the family is "the generation and education of the child, who does not take his place in the familial society with the conditions of autonomy and responsibility that characterize man." In fact, "the family loses its *raison d'être* as the child reaches manhood and becomes a 'person.' "]

But these rights exist whether or not the family has a natural moral personality. This personality is a character that belongs to societies, or does not, according to their *internal structure,* according to the nature of the bonds they create among their members and the nature of the relationships they establish between these members and the end to be attained. If a group is a natural moral person, it should have a juridical status to this effect; if it is not, its juridical status should nonetheless protect its rights—but under other forms.

13. I do not hesitate to acknowledge that unlike the family, the organized international society is in the order of natural moral persons. It has an incontestable natural foundation. As long as the modern state lasts, we must admit that it is naturally social; that is, to serve the function that marks its end and destiny, it must lead a societal life with other national groups. For the state enters into this international society with the essential characteristics of a natural moral person. Each state is a being *sui juris,* responsible for its acts, and each member of the League of Nations entered into it with the vocation to liberty and moral responsibility that distinguishes moral persons.

Without doubt, international society is not to be identified with a society of states. The League of Nations, created by the Covenant of 1919, is already breaking out of this narrow frame: all the more reason that the de facto international society must include many other elements. The rights that must be protected by a positive charter, the juridical situations that must be guaranteed, are not only those of states, but also those of organs, of groups, or of political, cultural, economic institutions not belonging to a state. But it is no less true that the state, whatever may be its future forms, is not expected to disappear, for it serves a natural and necessary human function. In the international political order, because of its quality as a natural moral person and because of its own nature, the state appears as the juridical subject par excellence. I can use an analogical argument here that is rather enlightening: the state is not made up merely of citizens; between individuals and the state lies the whole range of the "collective," the ensemble of more or less vigorously differentiated groups. There are many other situations to be protected than those of the citizen. Nevertheless, the citizen is the juridical subject par excellence within the state. The state, we can say, plays the role within the international society that the citizen plays within the state itself.[42]

42. [See Delos, *La société internationale.*]

What I have just said of international society brings out the fact that political life is the most likely terrain for natural moral persons to appear. This is not surprising; it is a consequence of the very nature of civic and political life. For inasmuch as civic and political life is founded in the nature of man, it is based upon liberty, consciousness, and responsibility. The natural groups to which it gives birth are then naturally based upon liberty and responsibility; they have a natural vocation to moral personality.

14. The examples of natural moral personality just studied are all taken from natural societies. Although from a certain point of view these may be the most important, they are not the only ones, nor even perhaps the most numerous: many groups are due to the free agreement of interested parties!

Once these free societies are created, I do not see any reason not to apply to them our definition of natural moral personality. These societies cannot be "natural" in the sense that they respond to a direct and immediate demand of man's nature, which would impose them upon him with necessity. But *moral personality* can be *natural* to them in the sense that it is derived from their very structure. From a sociological point of view this personality presupposes only the conditions of consciousness that have already been spoken of.

Some might object that with such a definition many groups that are really too unimportant to merit the title of moral person could claim it anyway. Suppose that several students form an athletic society, which they provide with a charter, and suppose that this society, equipped with all its organs, administers itself responsibly— would this be a new moral person appearing on the scene of social life? The difficulty, which is only apparent, comes once more from a confusion. Such a society is in fact very tenuous, very fragile. Born at the beginning of the season, it will vanish at vacation time. But what are we to conclude from this? That the relations that bind the members to the group's end and to one another are fragile, accidental to their life and to their fundamental interests, and that consequently the social body has only an insecure existence, a precarious cohesion, a meager consistency? Granted, it is a feeble body because its constituent relations are transitory. But how does this feebleness, foretelling an ephemeral existence, change the sociological nature of the group? Does it prevent it from having, as long as it lasts, the structure and characteristics of a moral person?

The point of view of the jurist and that of the sociologist differ here. The very feebleness of such a group dispenses the jurist from guaranteeing its rights. Its adventitious character removes it from the field of vision of the jurist, who is preoccupied with human rights and the real needs of human life. Such groups will therefore be kept apart from juridical life: mere whims do not generate rights. But although such groups have no access to the scene of juridical commerce, from the sociological point of view they have all the requirements for personality. This is so true that in the event that the first obstacle should disappear, in the event that such societies should cease being the ephemeral manifestation of a mere whim and render real service to physical and moral education, if they should give proof of their stability and acquire a patrimony, the law would hasten to take them into consideration. And at this stage, by virtue of their sociological structure, they could claim juridical personality.

These are the general lines of a theory of moral personality based upon sociology. A theory of the institution that is not rounded out by a doctrine of personality seems to me to be mutilitated, amputated of the consequences contained in its premises.

Would you say that the doctrine as I have expounded it is more sociological than juridical? I readily admit it. But as Hauriou and Renard present the theory of the institution, is it not itself, in its essence, more sociological than juridical? Or rather, have not these two eminent scholars brought to light and baptized with the name "institution" what is simply a *sociological reality rediscovered under a juridical reality?* This would enable us to understand why the institution seems to seep through everywhere from under positive law, as water seeps through from innumerable springs under the grass of the valley; and it would explain the multitude of groups that lie between the individual and the state, ranging from simple de facto institutional groups to moral persons; and it would justify the revolution brought about by this doctrine that revives the law of groups.

But if this is all true, the work that remains to be done would consist not so much in determining the contours of "a theory of the institution" as in enlarging our field of vision; there would be less need for us today to welcome the creation of a theory that would be simply a new wing in the edifice of the philosophy of law than to verify the appearance, under an inadequate name perhaps, of a general conception of law based upon a better understanding of social realities. Is not the theory of the institution a general theory of law unaware of itself? Although it purports to explain only a particular form of juridical activity, does it not really appear as a general theory of the juridical act, illustrating the connection between sociology and the philosophy of law?

THEORY OF THE INSTITUTION AND GENERAL THEORY OF LAW:
RETURN TO LAW WITH AN OBJECTIVE FOUNDATION OWING TO
SOCIOLOGY AND REALISM

15. The creators of the theory of the institution have been criticized for hoisting a flag whose symbolism is obscure. Why this term
institution, the critics ask, whose meaning is not immediately apparent? And if nothing more expressive can be found, are we to blame
the poverty of the language or the imprecision of a doctrine that is
trying to find itself but has not yet succeeded in defining itself?

I confess that while prizing the theory of the institution very
highly myself, I have been sensitive to this reproach. Upon consideration it seemed that the objection contained a part of the truth:
it is necessary, I think, to expand the limits of the theory; the facts
are uncomfortable and too tightly packed in it.

Hauriou and Renard—to whom one must always return in studying
this theory—reserve the name of institution to certain special phenomena of juridical life: to instances of grouping or foundation. This
is why Hauriou, in order to express his thought, has to join together
the two terms institution and foundation. Renard is very explicit.
For him, institutions only appear in one of the compartments of
juridical life. "Among juridical acts," he says in his *Valeur de la loi*,
"authors have devised diverse classifications: Taking the psychological point of view . . . of the will, earlier authors have tried to place
all juridical matter in two compartments . . . *legislation* and *contract*,
which would be the two great sources of juridical life . . . Certain
acts, like foundation, that resist classification in the contractual frame
could be realized only by virtue of a decision of the authoritative
will of the rulers: foundation will require an *act in the form of a
law*." Renard very justly adds, "This psychological classification—
legislation and contract—is not so much an error as an incomplete
truth; there are three fundamental juridical acts, of which all others
are merely satellites: *legislation, contract, foundation*. My whole
theory of the juridical act is based upon this classification."[43]

According to Renard, the theory of the institution would have for
its field of application only one of these three compartments into
which juridical acts are divided—that of foundations. In his last
work, Renard, defending the term institution against prospective
detractors, says: "The word *society*, which has long designated a
status, is today commonly used in the sense of a contract. Let us
leave it aside. The term *community* is taken to mean an undivided

43. Renard, *La valeur de la loi* (Paris 1928), pp. 81–82, 84.

coproperty. This will not do either. The term *institution,* on the other hand, has the advantage of not yet having acquired a precise meaning in juridical language." The term then is taken as a replacement for society and community. It embraces not only foundations in the juridical sense of the word, but in a larger sense, everything that answers to the general idea of social body, everything that answers to the description, as exact as it is picturesque, that Renard gives when he speaks of "this new being that appears upon the scene of juridical life, this being that lives, acts, perpetuates itself, and develops according to its own interior law; this being equipped with organs . . ."[44]

Faithful to his tripartite definition[45] of juridical acts—legislation, contract, and foundations or institutions—Renard makes a further refinement: there are two great manifestations of juridical life—rules and institutions. The first include both *laws* and *contracts.* Rules are in fact divided into *general juridical rules* that emanate from an authority and *particular rules* that proceed from individual juridical acts.

But, he adds, a manifestation of will can do more than establish rules: it can become an "act of creation." "This second role of the idea in juridical life is what I call institution," concludes Renard. Institutions then are these new juridical subjects, these "more or less vigorous" special beings that form, in the broad sense, the category of social bodies or foundations.

16. The field of application of the theory is then clearly circumscribed. But is this delimitation justified? Far be it from me to quibble over words. I have no prejudice against the special use of a term that has been so carefully defined. However, if this word, as Renard notes, is new in the vocabulary of juridical technique, it is not new in sociology or in history, and still less so in common speech. Of course, the fact of having a traditional meaning is no obstacle to giving the term a special sense in juridical technique; but the "ordinary sense" attached to words is often rich in a philosophy of common sense that it is wise to take into account.

From this point of view, what are the institutions of a society or

44. Renard, *La théorie de l'institution,* pp. 96, 102.

45. [I.e., in Renard, *La théorie de l'institution.* Delos quotes here from that work, p. 103: "Law and custom, the administrative act and the judicial decision, and lastly the doctrinal formulation are all rules . . . Private individuals, like public authorities, express their ideas in rules that are more limited in scope but of the very same character: my will, our contract, establish rules concerning the inheritance of my estate or the direction of our reciprocal activity."]

a differentiated group if not the totality of organized social bonds: social laws, traditions, customs, moral rules, that constitute the framework of this society and of the inferior groups of which it is composed? To go a step further: do not these institutions formally constitute the society? For example, are there not familial, economic, political, religious, cultural, and moral institutions that constitute society in its being as society, that give it existence and enable it to last and to live? The habitual, stabilized, fixed behavior of the primitives of a Central African tribe in exchanging a product of their making for another object of pleasure or utility constitutes one of the social institutions of their tribe or their cultural cycle. And what are the institutions of our modern states if not the complex of rules and juridical bonds that not only constitute the state's organs properly so-called, but that in a more all-embracing way define the private or public relationships of the individuals and groups within the state? So that in this word we reunite the whole gamut of politico-juridical realities that form the state, that make a politically and juridically organized society from a de facto society. In this sense, for example, the contract defined by articles 1101 ff. of the *Code civil*[46] is one of the institutions of our modern society.

If we refer then to common meaning, which Renard very properly holds in high esteem, we can say that institutions are the ensemble of organizing forms that constitute a society. They are, in the precise sense of the word, the actual *form* of a given society; for a society is only a fact of organization established among its constitutive elements, an order realized among them; institutions are the expression of this order, and indeed, this order itself.

Consequently, would it not be logical to call the theory of the institution in the philosophy of law simply a theory that studies all juridical institutions? The term institution is as broad as the term "social form"; in the philosophy of law it embraces all the juridical forms that constitute juridical society. For this reason I am inclined to think that the "theory of the institution" as it is presented today is an unintended truncation of a general theory of the nature of juridical realities, of a general theory of the juridical act and of positive law.

I am confirmed in this thought by an examination of the very principles upon which the authors rest their doctrine. The facts upon which they build are more general than they might first seem; they authorize larger doctrinal constructions. They call for an expansion,

---

46. [See Appendix.]

a breaking of the frame in which the theory of the institution is enclosed at the present time. To situate this theory on its true ground, to show it in its true light, we need only return to the verifications and principles that give the juridical philosophy of Hauriou and Renard its profound value. Here again, far from departing from them and repudiating their doctrine, I have the hope of remaining faithful to their authentic thought, and of giving testimony to its worth by developing it to the full.

17. Leaving aside the compartment of "general juridical rules," which can be designated by the general name of laws and which forms the object of a special study, Renard vigorously, almost violently, contrasts the *contractual* and the *institutional,* that is, the two other categories of juridical acts. The category of contract would be irreducible to that of institution. All juridical acts proceeding from private activity are divided between these two classes, which mark the "two poles of juridical activity": institutional foundation and contract. These are the two means we can use to attain the ends we pursue; we can choose the way of contract or the way of foundation—the liberty of founding is as essential as the liberty of contracting. But these two procedures are contrasted as two divergent and irreducible juridical activities.[47]

In what does this essential difference consist? In contract there is no "integration of an idea; there is simply a meeting of two wills, each of which follows its own idea; and this phenomenon produces a balance. This balance is the whole contract; the effects of a contract are entirely included and definitively enclosed within this balance . . . Contract is, in the domain of juridical things, the equivalent of unorganized matter: its idea, its form—the balance—is entirely exterior to it." Contract has no organizing-idea: "Contract is only the tête-à-tête of creditor and debtor, of seller and buyer."[48]

The institution, on the contrary, "is the organization of an idea"; it is "an idea detached, emancipated from the person or persons who have conceived it and integrated into an arrangement of ways and means capable of continuing its realization and eventually perpetuating its development."[49]

It would be hard to find clearer terms to contrast the contractual and the institutional, or to find better terms to pose the object of the debate I should like to open.

47. Renard, *La théorie de l'institution,* pp. 257, 260, 360, 363ff.
48. Renard, *La théorie de l'institution,* pp. 259ff.
49. Renard, *La théorie de l'institution,* p. 107.

Is not contract also the "organization of an idea"? If "to institute," to create any institution whatsoever, is, as Renard rightly says, "to provide an idea with the ways and means of being realized," do not contracting parties really "institute an idea"? They do so in a different manner than the legislator when he provides the idea of a law with the ways and means of being realized, or than the founders and their associates who launch an organization or a new work. A contract cannot be reduced to a law or a foundation; but even though these three juridical acts, contract, foundation, legislation, are specifically distinct, do they not have the same substantial nature, the *same internal structure?* And does not a contract, in binding the contracting parties and sealing their union, create a true "institution"?

If I can show that these questions must be answered in the affirmative, if I can establish that a contract, like a law or a foundation, has an institutional structure, I shall have brought to light the *internal structure of every juridical act* and shown that the "theory of the institution" is in reality a *general conception of law*—the true origin and basis of which we must still seek.

18. I shall recur to Renard's own analyses to prove the institutional nature of contract and to level the antithesis raised up[50] between the contractual and the institutional.

To see this barrier disappear, we must examine the nature of the juridical act. Renard has devoted to this some of the most penetrating and solid pages of his work. He distinguishes two phases, or rather two elements, in every juridical act. One, the idea, depends upon the intelligence; the other depends upon the will. The idea has a priority over the will that is both psychological and metaphysical. "Every act of the will," he says, "depends upon a certain *mental conception* that we have called the *idea*." In the juridical act the idea plays the primordial role: "it is a living principle at the heart of the juridical act."[51]

What is *a law* but an idea provided with its ways and means: an idea that the legislator chooses because of its conformity to the general welfare and to justice, that he provides with an organization of means that adhere to it, that "realize" it, and transform it from an ideal end into a positive law, into an objective juridical reality? Renard has expounded his conception of a law so clearly and forcefully in *La valeur de la loi* that there is no need to linger over it

50. [I.e., by Renard, *La théorie de l'institution*, pp. 357–430.]
51. Renard, *La valeur de la loi*, pp. 108, 111.

here; I merely refer you to these pages, the doctrine of which I make my own.

A *foundation,* in its turn, is an idea incorporated in an organization that gives it objective reality and transforms it into a concrete and special entity—into a body. The idea of the founder is the end he pursues in founding, the object that the foundation will realize when it has taken on an existence independent of the person of its founder. A foundation, in its objective and permanent reality, is the idea of the founder incorporated into the means that he has provided to assure for it this independent existence.

And a *contract?* It is comparable, says Renard, to a law and to a foundation, because "the scheme of procedure of every juridical act" is the same: for legislative act as for foundation, for foundation as for contract.[52] In the procedure of contract, as in the others, we find the union of the two elements, idea and will, with the same predominance of the idea. "The juridical act," concludes Renard, "is not a pure act of *will* but an act of intelligence" supported by a *decision* of the *will* that follows the judgment of the intellect:

"An act of intelligence, that is, a conception, a *mental image* of the consequences that will take place if the act is accomplished, an anticipated image of the state of things that will result from it, of the change that will occur in the currently existing state of things." Then "an *adherence* of the will, which receives as an order and takes as a duty the judgment of the *intellect* . . . finally, the *decision* of this same *will* which goes on to execution."

Such is the uniform cross-section of the juridical act: the contract, the legislative act, or the act of foundation and of institution—an idea ratified and realized by a manifestation of will, these two elements being, of course, indissolubly united, and the priority of the one taking nothing away from the essential character of the other.

It would be a pleasure to highlight the psychological preciseness of Renard's analysis, and the consequences his conception of the juridical act yields upon the terrain of law. It not only explains the internal structure of the juridical act, but also the "relativism," the "variability," the "perfectibility," to use Renard's terms, attached to it. Is not the juridical act in fact an "ensemble of ways and means" established in view of an end, of an idea to be realized? Therefore the contract, the legislative act, and the foundation admit of a certain flexibility, since the ways and means may prove to be poorly adapted to the end of the act. There is a "life" of the legislative act, of the

52. Renard, *La valeur de la loi,* 99.

foundation, and even of the contract, as we see in the classic examples of the theory of *imprévision*[53] in private law and the theory of the clause *rebus sic stantibus* in international law. And in "evaluating the *validity* of an act," in determining its *interpretation,* in making a judgment as to its *abrogation,* in considering its *revision* (I would add: in judging its *morality* and in assigning a basis for its *obligatory force*), we must always focus upon the *intellectual conceptions* that enable us to understand the end of the act, its true nature, as well as upon the *manifestation of will* that "realizes" it and gives it concrete existence.[54] The *juridical act is a complex whole in which the means are interpreted in terms of an end that is intrinsic to it:* We cannot exaggerate the importance of the practical consequences of such a conception, which restores to the juridical act its share of *internal dynamism.* But let us return to an examination of the theory itself.

19. I think, with Renard, that the basic scheme of every juridical act is the same; it can be recognized as substantially identical in the diverse acts to which it gives a similar internal structure. But this is why, temporarily parting company with Renard, I believe less in a "theory of the institution" in the restricted sense of the word, than in an *institutional conception of law,* if we are to retain this word institution. By this I mean a conception of juridical reality that, applied to foundations and groups, brings out the fundamental role of the directing idea; applied to the study of the legislative act, emphasizes its nature as an "incarnate idea"; and finally, applied to contract, explains its true nature, shows that it is not a simple balance between two wills but that it too is institutional in nature and gravitates around an organizing idea.

I shall dwell upon this last point because it is the only one in which the thought of the authors of institutional doctrine still shows some incertitude. Although Renard's thought, for example, has a magisterial assurance when dealing with legislation and foundation, it still seems to hesitate[55] before the problem of contract. In *La valeur de la loi* he appears to be seeking attenuation; and in *La théorie de l'institution* does he not stop short and thus deprive institutional doctrine of one of its most important extensions?

20. In what way does contract manifest the feature that is proper

53. [See Hauriou, "L'imprévision et les contrats dominés par des institutions sociales," *Revista de Derecho Privado,* January 15, 1928, reprinted in *Cahiers de la nouvelle journée,* XXIII (1933), 129–146.]

54. Renard, *La valeur de la loi,* pp. 100, 119, 120.

55. Renard, *La valeur de la loi,* pp. 100, 120, 364ff.

to every institution: an idea that has become the point of objective union of individuals, an idea that binds them, that commands and organizes their mutual relationships?

The theory of the *cause* of the contract enables us to resolve this problem.[56] In the pages Renard devotes to this he very nearly reaches a fully satisfying solution.

It is easy to distinguish, with Renard, between the *cause* of the contract and the personal *motives* of the contracting parties—the *cause* of the contract and the cause of entering into the contract. "The motives," says Renard, "are proper to each one of the parties; the motives are subjective . . . This landlord wants to rent his house because he has had some reverses of fortune, or because he intends to move out of town . . . which makes no difference to the prospective tenant. The prospective tenant wants to lease the house because he expects an appointment in this town . . . which makes no difference to the landlord. *Motives* are only at the periphery of the contract; they act individually upon each one of the contracting parties; they do not unite them. The judge of the contract does not have to delve into the very risky investigations of the *motives* of the juridical act; he studies the *cause*."[57]

What then is the *cause*? "The cause of the obligation of each one of the contracting parties," says Renard, "is the concept each has of the consideration promised by the other." If I rent an apartment, the cause of my obligation is the idea of the enjoyment of comfortable, well-furnished, pleasant rooms that attracts me: "This is the image I represent to myself, the end I wish to attain, the cause for which I bind myself." And inversely, the cause of the obligation of the landlord who rents me his apartment is the idea of the several thousands francs I shall pay him every year.

Does not this analysis of the cause reveal a first hesitation of thought that obscures the institutional character of contract? Thus understood, does not the cause remain a *subjective reality*, even if it is not confused with the personal motives from which Renard claims to distinguish it? If the cause of the contract were only the

56. [The relationship of the civil law doctrine of cause and the common law doctrine of consideration is discussed in Ernest Lorentzen, "Causa and Consideration in the Law of Contracts," 28 Yale L. J. 621 (1919), as revised in the Association of American Law Schools, *Selected Readings on the Law of Contracts* (New York, 1931), pp. 565–588; Amos Walton "Cause and Consideration in Contracts," 41 Law Q. Rev. 306 (1925); Lord Wright, "Ought the Doctrine of Consideration To Be Abolished from the Common Law," 49 Harvard L. Rev. 1225 (1936).]

57. Renard, *La théorie de l'institution*, pp. 92–93.

subjective concept each party has of the other party's fulfillment of his promises, there would actually be two causes—the idea each party has of the other's payment. And we would remain enclosed in subjectivity and, fundamentally, in motives.

Is this Renard's thought? He alone can say. Although certain developments and the definition he gives of contract might make one fear as much, I do not believe that this is his fundamental thought. A *subjective concept* of the cause must certainly exist; without it there would be no contracting parties. The cause *as considered* by a contracting party is what *arouses* in him the personal motives that will induce him to want to contract. The *subjective thought of the cause* awakens the desire to contract.

But the cause is something more than subjective concepts. It has its own reality, its *objective existence,* distinct from the subjective concepts that the contracting parties have of it. It is in its objective reality that it is the cause of the contract and that it is incorporated into the contract; and it is by reason of this quality that it transforms the contract itself into a social and juridical reality endowed with a proper existence, extra-individual and objective in relation to the two contracting parties—just as a law exists outside of the social authority that passes it and the citizens who fulfill it—and just as a social fact exists outside of individuals without whom, however, it would not be. The *intellects* of the contracting parties gravitate around the objective cause; concepts they form of it should be substantially in accord with its objective reality, under pain of an error that would vitiate the contract. The *wills* of the contracting parties gravitate around the objective cause; it imposes its conditions upon these wills, and this is what constitutes the law of their mutual undertakings. These undertakings escape the caprice of the wills involved because they are commanded and ruled by the cause. The cause gives an objective foundation to the contract; it provides the relationships established between the contracting parties with a principle and a rule—an organizing idea.

We must go further. It is within the cause that the justice of a contract, that is, the balance of its obligations, is realized. The justice of a contract is established objectively: it results from a balance that is realized in the cause, and not from a balance of subjective wills. Let us take an example. What is the cause of the contract by which I lease an apartment? Under its subjective form, the cause is each party's concept of what he will get from the other. But in its *objective reality* it is the *exchange,* that is, the simultaneous surrender of two values, the one being a sum of money, the other the use of an apart-

ment. This is the exchange, we say, in its objective reality of a reciprocal counterpayment of two real values.

This exchange forms a *whole,* a *system* in itself; and as such it
constitutes the cause of the contract. The will of the contracting
parties gravitates around this objective *system.* Each of the parties
sees it from his own point of view, finding profit or pleasure in it.
These subjective sentiments are not very important: the contract has
for its intrinsic cause and substance the exchange itself.

Now you understand why I just said that the cause bears within
itself the reason of its justice or injustice, and that the justice of the
cause makes the justice of the contract. This justice is nothing other
than the justness of the balance realized in the cause itself by the
equivalence of the two values exchanged. Today a given apartment
has a certain value—and this means that in the circumstances in
which it takes place, the exchange of the use of this apartment must
be made against such-and-such a price, if the two payments of the
contract are to be balanced. There is a just price for the apartment,
and the justice of the contract consists in the balance of the commitments exchanged.

This is an objective balance, and I mean by this that although the
conditions of the balance clearly vary according to certain causes—
social for the most part—which we do not have to study here, although the just price obeys certain fluctuations for complex reasons,
it is nonetheless true that the balance is realized between *objects*
(goods or services exchanged) outside and independent of the subjective concepts and wills of the contracting parties. Further still,
this balance is imposed upon them, and they must submit to it: one
who sells at too high a price destroys the balance as much as one
who does not pay a just price. Both perform an unjust act despite
the agreement of wills; for the balance of wills does not establish
the justice of the contract but, I repeat, the balance of the objects
exchanged, the exact equilibrium of which constitutes the just cause
of the contract. The balance is not established between the two wills
of the contracting parties; it is established between the things exchanged, and the wills of the contracting parties simply adhere to
this system of balanced exchange. In doing so, they too become just.
And because a contract balances objective values outside of the
subjects who contract, we can speak of the objectivity of the cause
of the contract, and of the objectivity of the balance realized by it.

21. And so we must abandon once and for all the concept of
contract that depicts it as a *balance between two wills* and nothing
more. It is not the wills of the contracting parties that establish a

true balance, but the exchanged commitments; they form together a closely-knit combination, a sort of organic whole like the scales of a balance that oscillate around a center which unifies them. This whole, once again, forms a system that is complete in itself. It is then incorrect to say that a contract puts at bay two wills that are seeking a subjective agreement. There is something more in a contract than the imaginary meeting point of two subjective wills, as it often seems to be understood: "I offered 100 francs, you asked for 200; little by little I raised my proposals, you lowered your demands. The moment came when we both said the same number; sold!" Such a contract would be only a meeting of two subjectivities, an agreement of two wills *each of which would be following its own idea*. The meeting is only a moment, an instant; two paths cross, but the point of crossing is no more of a reality than is a mathematical point. A precise analysis of such a contract will never reveal anything more than subjective, individual thoughts and acts of the will, and a "point" of crossing, a "moment" of balance between them. This does not get us out of a purely *subjective and interindividual* conception of contract.

If such were the reality you would be right to see contract as the "tête-à-tête" of creditor and debtor, each pursuing his own personal interest, materialized in the other's commitment, and to say that the conclusion of the contract marks the moment when each one of the parties "freezes" his will and forbids himself future variations, on condition that the other party imposes the same restrictions upon himself.

But in reality a contract is not the pure and simple "tête-à-tête" of two contracting parties because between them lies *an object* which is also complex: a system constituted by the objective values that maintain a balance and equalize one another. This object is the essential element of the contract, and we can agree with Renard that the cause in "incorporated" in the contract: the contract forms a complex and organic whole. At the center is the cause; around it gravitate the contracting parties who rally to it, adopt it, and henceforth submit to its law, carry out the transaction, and accept its conditions.

Thus, the cause furnishes the contract with its "organizing idea." It is an objective as the "idea" of a law, which lies between social authority and citizens and assures the liaison between this authority and the subjects who assent to obedience. It is as objective as the "idea" of a foundation, which lies between the cofounders and establishes the law among them. It plays in contract a role of organizer and regulator that is in every respect like the role the "idea" fulfills in a law or a foundation.

Just as the "idea" offers an end to the founders or to the legislator, the cause arouses in the parties a desire to contract. Just as the social authority has a power of initiative and is free to pass a law or not, and just as founders are free to found or not, contracting parties are free to contract or refuse to do so. But once any of these has decided to perform the act, he falls under the power of the object, he has submitted to it. The "idea" of a law imposes itself upon the legislator and upon the author of an administrative act; the "idea" of a foundation is the rule of all those who participate in the creation or life of a social body. And in the same way, contracting parties have no option to create or modify the internal balance that is realized within the cause between the objective values of the goods or services exchanged. The justice of a contract is realized within its object, just as the justice of a law and the legitimacy of a foundation are determined by their respective objects. Furthermore, the obligatory force of a law flows from its object or "idea" as from its source; the object is the basis of the authority exercised in every foundation. And in the same way, the object makes the law between two contracting parties because it imposes itself upon them and furnishes their mutual relations with their rule. The object is the principle of their "intimacy," to use Renard's terminology, that is, the mortar that binds them together.

22. Then what place shall we give to liberty in contract, which is taken for its impregnable sanctuary? The role of liberty appears very clearly in the determination of the *motives* of a contract, in the choice by which the contracting parties decide whether to make the contract or not. As the owner of a house, I am free to rent it or not, if the "just price" that I could ask for it does not seem to me to compensate for the disadvantages of renting it. Marriage is a contract the object of which is distinctly determined: although I am not free to modify it, I am free to remain celibate, provided at least that I have good personal reasons for doing so. Whether or not to make a contract, whether or not to submit to the obligations of an object, is left up to individual liberty: it is a personal act for which each man must answer before his own conscience. Each person decides this freely and determines his yes or no according to the reasons that convince him of the preferability of one or the other solution.

But is there not also room for subjectivity, a greater use of liberty, in the assessment of the object? We must understand this clearly.

The cause of contract, we have said, is objective, and the justice of a contract is realized in the object. Let us repeat, for example, that in a given state of the national economy there is an objectively just price of things necessary to life. But although the worth of economic goods has an objective basis, although this is something other than the point at which two rival wills are frozen, although it imposes itself upon the wills of future contracting parties, and although it puts in balance real values that are measured according to economic conditions—the reasonable standard of life in a given period of civilization, etc.—it remains no less true that this objectively just price can be determined only by the judgment of men. It can be established only by a series of inquiries, gropings, approximations, and discussions. Here liberty of contract is simply the contracting parties' use of liberty in a search for the objectively just price that will be the cause of the contract, so that the discussions of seller and buyer—their hagglings—do not present the spectacle of two wills feeling each other out before reaching the point where each one thinks the other will not budge. This liberty of contract is a collaboration in quest of an objective truth, a real balance between the thing sold, the work done, the service rendered—and the counterpayment.

Even contract, then, is truly of an institutional nature, and our conception of it is directly opposed to the view that bases it upon the autonomy of the will. Analysis shows that there are no autonomous wills, but only wills in submission to an *object:* the common good in the case of a law, the idea of the foundation in the creation or the life of groups, the object or cause of the contract in this last case . . . Thus we find in the foreground the object that reason strives to discover, and that the free will adopts at the moment of the conclusion of the contract.

23. A juridical act is then never a pure manifestation of will. A law is not the expression of the will of the rulers, nor is a foundation the meeting point of the wills of the group members (the effect of a social contract à la Rousseau), nor does a contract mark the conjunction of two liberties that fix their point of balance. In law there is no will that does not bow down before an object, *adhere* to it, and submit to its law. Thus, an analysis of the realities themselves, a study of the internal structure of the juridical act, definitively casts subjectivism and voluntarism outside the domain of the philosophy of law.

Clearly then, just as a law or an administrative act is not a pure direct relationship of governor to governed but interposes between them a purpose that partially embodies the social good of man and which is sought by the governor and is necessary to the governed; and just as a society, a group, or a foundation is not a tangle of interindividual relationships but a network of relationships organized around an idea or an end; so too a contract has an objective principle of the relationships of the parties involved, a pole of attraction that wins them over and brings them into agreement, that offers to their liberty an *object of adherence* in which their wills unite and which commands them from the moment they decide to enter the contract. The submission is voluntary, but once willed, it bows us down before an object, and not before our own will or that of another: individual liberty is objectively dominated in a contract as in an act of foundation or a legislative act.

And so a notion of the juridical act emerges, and with it a general conception of law. There are advantages to calling this an *institutional conception.* Law, contract, foundation are all institutional because they have the same cross-section, the same internal structure, that shows us diverse elements gravitating around an object. The "system" they form in this way takes on an external, stable, objective character that raises them to the level of institutions and distinguishes them from individual subjective activities.

But we could also call this a *conception of law with an objective basis,* and perhaps this term brings out more clearly the importance of the essential role of the "idea," of the object, in juridical relationships. Every juridical act is a relationship that is formed around an object; the object is the source of the obligations, the basis of the juridical liaisons that the act establishes between persons. A law, an administrative or regulatory decision, binds governor and governed; but the bond is formed around the idea of the law, around a concept of the common good. Within a foundation all the internal juridical liaisons gravitate around the end that the foundation aims to realize. In a contract minds and wills gravitate around a cause, and this cause forms a system complete in itself.

If, as we have said, every juridical relationship forms a system that turns around an object that is incorporated in the relationship, it follows that within this relationship the *object* commands *subjects.* These subjects enter into relationships through the medium of the object, their personal attitude is ruled by it: the object is truly the *basis* of every juridical *relationship,* although this relationship binds *persons, subjects.*

24. What finally results from this study—after the condemnation of juridical voluntarism—is the intimate solidarity between *sociology*

and the *philosophy of law*. Perhaps the sole psychological origin of the theory of the institution is a "rediscovery" of the sociological realities underlying juridical realities. Thus it marks a return of the philosophy of law to its true bases. For juridical realities are super-imposed upon sociological facts: the latter are the substratum, the internal substance of juridical facts and activities. This is the funda-mental truth that has been brought to light by the labors that have produced the theory of the institution.

What is the "juridical" if not something of the "social" that has received a "form" by the intervention of social authority? And by this word "form" we mean first, in the philosophical sense, that determination of a matter that gives it a new manner of being. Cer-tain social relationships take on a new expression owing to the inter-vention of organized society, which makes them its own, gives them a formula, and guarantees them: they enter into the domain of posi-tive law. But by this word "form" we also mean—legitimately, for this second sense is bound to the first—the technical "form," that "exterior and sensible element," as Geny says,[58] that envelops "cir-cumstances that are themselves immaterial, such as the acts of will or the facts of social life from which juridical situations proceed." Then he adds: "This exterior and sensible element is artificial in the precision of its structure and therefore it is a technical element." The "technical element," by which the "social" becomes the "juridi-cal," is essentially due to the intervention of an organized social body, that is, to an authority. Hence its "artificial" character: it is due to the skillful intervention of men, it is a work of art.[59] But this does not hinder the "juridical" from being fundamentally, in its internal substance, something of the "social," and this is why we may verify, by analysis, that the social fact and the juridical act have the same cross-section, the same internal structure. Jurists, in pro-portion as they philosophize upon the object of their investigations, seem astonished to find the "institutional" wave rising all about

58. François Geny, *Science et technique en droit privé positif,* III, 98, 101.
59. If one pressed this text of Geny's unduly, one might think that the author opposes *acts of will* to *social facts* when he speaks of the substratum destined to receive juridical "form." *In reality, the acts of will that constitute matter for positive law are themselves "social facts"* and not subjective facts; analysis discovers in them this *object*, because of which they become societal relationships. Without this object which exteriorizes them, they would remain among the *de internis* that escape the jurisdiction of positive law, because it cannot grasp them. If contract merely mani-fested the moment of balance of two subjective wills, it too would escape the regula-tion of positive law; it would not offer positive law anything to hold onto because, as I have said, it would be reduced to the coexistence of individual undertakings. A juxtaposition or a balance of the "individual" will never produce the "social."

them. It could not be otherwise, and this progressive invasion of the juridical field must continue till the whole field of law is won, that is, in less sibylline terms, until the true structure of every juridical reality is recognized as identical to that of social reality.

For there certainly is an identity between social reality and the substratum of juridical reality. But the jurist considers the latter first under its formal aspect. He takes hold of it by its form, and only if he assumes the philosopher's task of investigating the internal substance of positive law will he discover the societal relationship underlying the juridical act and verify their fundamental identity. The sociologist for his part is primarily interested in these societal relationships. But he perceives that they are "juridical" and prepositive when he looks at them from a certain angle, when he wonders what is their "reasonable" mode and what they should be to conform to the requirements of the nature of men and the nature of things. Under this aspect the *due* appears. Right and duty manifest themselves when reason fulfills its proper office and, considering the beings in question, *judges* what their reciprocal relationships should be in order to conform to their nature. Reason then discerns *an order of natural balance,* that is, an order of justice that is founded not on arbitrary subjective evaluations but on the objective value of beings. Law is born when reason is no longer content with simply verifying the nature of beings but draws normative consequences from them. The jurist is a sociologist who adds to his preoccupations a concern for order. And in the determination of this order the jurist remains in contact with the sociologist because he intends to find the principle of order in the very nature of the beings before him and in the ends that their nature and acts reveal.

25. In affirming the close connection of sociology and positive law—the one furnishing the other with its substratum—we remain faithful to the traditional doctrine that designates *justice* as the matter of positive law. *The connection of law and sociology is inscribed in the heart of the very notion of justice.* Have we not too often neglected an aspect of this notion—namely, that the relationship of justice is, in its internal structure, a societal or sociological relationship (taking sociological in the proper sense of the word)? Let us not fear to say that if this were not so, justice could not be the proper matter of positive law. But on the contrary, since this is truly its nature, we must recognize that relationships of justice form the essential matter of positive law, and that the indefinite progress of law will continue as long as justice is not entirely guaranteed.

What is justice, as the moralists teach it and as people universally interpret it, if not the virtue, the act of will by which each man renders to another *what* is due to him? It implies a relationship with another—according to the old terminology, it is *ad alterum*—but this relation is not interindividual. We mean that between two persons related in justice an *object* always intervenes—a thing, a service, or an act, it does not matter—that measures the obligation of the one and the right of the other, that commands both individuals and furnishes the *rule* of their subjective conduct. Do I owe a sum of money, a commodity? They strictly measure my duty in justice. Whether I pay them willingly, or they are taken from my patrimony by force, or my creditor appropriates their value by some open or secret compensation, justice is satisfied. Do I owe some service? The promised and due act also measures my whole obligation and the whole right of the other party. Here again, the cause of juridical liaisons and the measure of obligations are objective.

Why have the moralists who have so clearly discerned the nature of justice not been led by this fact to reflect on the true nature of society and the social relationship? Why is the notion of object so blurred? Why is the field so wide-open to the development of juridical voluntarism, the interindividual or subjectivist conception of the social relationship? But the philosophy that Christian moralists have unanimously professed has always affirmed that justice has a *medium rei,* and we would not be wrong in understanding this to mean that justice introduces between *persons,* between *wills* that are the subjects of the virtue of justice, an intermediate *object.* We could even sum up our sociological doctrine by literally translating the texts of one of the truest representatives of this philosophy.[60] The matter of justice, he says, are the exterior acts and things that put men in mutual communication: *exteriores actiones et exteriores res, quibus sibi invicem homines communicare possunt.* It is through the medium of these objective acts, of these things, that an order, a social state, is established between individuals *PER . . .* (eas) *attenditur ORDINATIO unius hominis ad alterum.* Two subjects enter into an agreement through an object, and this object measures their relationships; it provides these relationships with their principle of order, their "organizing idea." Justice will reign, then, when balance and proportion are established between persons, but in reference to an object, *res exteriores.* We know of no better way of showing that

60. Aquinas, *Summa Theologiae,* II II, q. 58, aa. 8 and 10.

justice is a societal relationship with an objective basis, as sociological analysis defines it.

It follows that the realization of the reign of justice is equivalent
to the *creation of an objective social order.* Justice will reign the
day when the men who communicate among themselves in and
through "objects"—things or acts—model their subjective attitudes
upon the requirements of these objects, the day when their mutual
relationships fulfill the requirements of the object that is the medium
of these relationships, the day when the debtor hands over the thing
or renders the service, the day when the creditor claims the sum
due him and nothing more.

Such an order is essentially an order of *social* relationships; that
is, *exterior, extra-individual, objective* relationships. Such an order
is both *immanent to individuals,* since they have to regulate their
personal conduct, sentiments, and attitudes—and *exterior, objective*
in itself, *extra-subjective* since a relationship goes from the human
individual to an object and "performs" an exterior act or realizes
an exchange. When all the objects that put men in relationships with
one another elicit from them proportioned and fitting attitudes, then
justice reigns, but then also a just *social state* is realized: each thing,
each exterior act is what it should be and elicits the psychological
attitudes it should elicit.

Positive law is the expression of this social order of justice and
balance. It is a sort of abstract tracing of this order for a given group.
It is also the normative expression of this order, the mold to which
individuals should conform; it points out the place of each thing and
the nature of each act, and these things and acts are the measure
and the cause of the individual conduct of each person.

The order of justice is then truly a societal order, and every act
of justice performed by an individual whatsoever realizes an "element" of the social order. Here again we must break free from a
certain conception of justice, which we shall call psychological or
notional. This conception regards justice as commanding us to conform our interior attitude to the right of another, or more exactly,
to our notion of the right of another, to the interior concept we have
of the right of another; and, passing in silence over the role of the
object, it forgets that it is upon this extra-subjective reality that the
relationships of those having rights and their debtors are regulated.
The notion of justice must take advantage of the *return to objectivism,* the *return to realism,* that is the salient feature of juridical
thought at the present time, and the reason of the new successes won

by the philosophy of law. This is the conclusion that evolves from the study of the juridical act to which the theory of the institution has led us. This theory itself is a manifestation of the new *realism,* of the return to the object.

26. An important change has actually taken place in the study of the juridical rule. This is no longer studied independently of its social *matter* as if the juridical *form* were the whole of the juridical rule and its very essence. The juridical rule is no longer regarded as a purely formal reality; liaison has been re-established between the juridical form and the social reality that is its internal substratum. The juridical rule has become again in jurists' eyes what it is in fact: a social form, a social manner of behavior that for certain reasons and according to a certain process takes on a positive juridical form. If the juridical form is a creation due to art and for this reason "artificial," the social substratum that constitutes its internal substance gives it "reality" and concreteness. For this substratum is the stuff of human life; in it are expressed human activities, whose objects are, if one can so speak, warm with ideas, passions, and human interests. The reality here is society, that sum total of relationships by which living persons unite their activities in order to live, and to live better.

This return to reality has most certainly been effected under the influence of the development of sociological studies, which have refocused men's attention upon the social fact considered in its proper reality and adopted as a subject of study. An outcome of this has been a profound *change of method.* Instead of taking a certain *notion* as a point of departure—the notion of the state, or of the individual, or of the moral person, or of the rights of man, or of a legislative text that provides the jurist with the "first principles" of his exegesis and constructions—we have come back to an *observation* of juridical and social realities. Instead of believing that the fundamental principles of law are essentially *notions* that reside in the *mind* of *thinking subjects,* and the logically possible developments of which must be brought out by reason, we have come to realize that social and juridical life is a fact that responds to the essential inclinations of human nature, that these inclinations manifest the fundamental needs of human life, and consequently that the rule of behavior must be sought in a study of these inclinations themselves, which, by enabling us to identify the object of societal activities, gives us the principle of their normative regulation.

This *return to reality* extends to the study of *natural law* and justifies the revival of favor it now rightly enjoys, although it has not entirely recovered from the discredit into which it was plunged by an abstract and notional conception. Natural law rests upon a consideration of human nature, and we are finally convinced, it seems, that human nature *is not first of all a notion or a concept* but a *reality*. It resides in each individual; it is what is most real and most living in each one, the principle of all the instincts, vital forces, intellectual, moral or physical needs, that give birth to the life of society and provide it with its ends.

The return to reality has then compelled us to go from juridical form to the study of its sociological content, from positive and formal law to natural law, the expression of the requirements of our living and concrete nature. It has forced us to distinguish in social and juridical relationships the role of *objects,* of *ends,* which are the concrete *raison d'être* of these relationships. It explains in a general way the *return to objectivist conceptions of law,* to *teleological* conceptions.

This is why we are witnessing today in law a great revival of the *real* over the *notional,* of the *object* (man, his needs, his ends) over the *thinking subject enclosed within his objects of knowledge* and his conceptual notions. This revival has multiple manifestations: the adoption of the method of observation, the recourse to sociology, and what is called (without giving an exact account of the phenomenon) the revival of natural law. The discovery of the institution is also an effect of this return to reality: and this explains its quasi-universal and somewhat disordered flowering. One of the scholars who has contributed the most in bringing it to light has written a phrase that we might make the motto of our study: "The institutional doctrine is not a system, it is a most supple interpretation of reality."[61] We could not find a better way to express its merit and the reason why it opens almost boundless perspectives to the progress of the philosophy of law and juridical sociology.

61. [Renard, *La théorie de l'institution,* pp. 110–111.]

JOSEPH T. DELOS   The Object of Sociology:

For the Redress of Contemporary Sociology

Sociology seems to be nothing but incertitude. Even its name is a kind of monster which begins in Latin and ends in Greek, as has been humorously noted. Its birth is uncertain. Auguste Comte created the hybrid word—is he also the father of the new science it designates? Some assure us that he is. As the daughter of Comte's genius, sociology would have been born about 1830, and would now be just a century old. But others protest against this superficial judgment. Once again, they say, enthusiastic disciples distort the truth by attributing the paternity of a science to a single master. Ever since men have reflected and philosophized, they have been concerned with comparing and explaining social facts. Plato and Aristotle are sociologists, the one in his *Laws,* the other in his *Politics.*

René Maunier, in his recent *Introduction à la sociologie,* happily reconciles the two theses by saying that if sociology's "preparation" is ancient, its "foundation" is recent. Sociology is just one more discipline to illustrate the law that presides over the development of every science: it was established by "formation and progression," rather than by "revelation" and "creation."[1] The sciences go through

ED. NOTE: Translated from "L'objet de la sociologie," *Vie intellectuelle,* VII (May 10, 1930), pp. 264–287. With Hauriou, Delos insists that social facts must be objective. His analysis reveals that they contain an essential element distinct from the individuals who enter into social relationships: this element is the "object," which alone explains the formation, duration, and life of social groups and institutions. The objective character of social relationships is what makes them the proper matter of a special science, distinct from psychology. Sociology is also distinct from moral science, argues Delos, in currently familiar terms, in that it is the science of social facts, and moral science is the science of values. More rigorous perhaps than Hauriou in limiting the role of sociology, Delos aligns himself with the "measuring sociologists": "We must not ask a science of facts to teach us what ought to be."

1. René Maunier, professor at the University of Paris, *Introduction à la sociologie* (Paris, 1929), p. 67.

much retouching before they reach the classical age that marks their maturity and the moment when they are in possession of their method, their principles, and their object.

Despite its brilliant progress, sociology has not reached this stage. This would be reason enough to oppose its introduction in primary scholastic programs, and even in those of higher levels of education. As yet it is hardly ready to leave the universities and the institutes of research. The diversity of the works that claim its name is not so much a mark of its perfection as a symptom of a crisis of growth, from which it suffers profoundly. It does not feel sure of its method, and it has not sharply defined its object.

For reasons that will appear more clearly in the course of this essay, French sociology has had more difficulty than others in resisting the illicit intrusion of moral science[2] and metaphysical preoccupations. This is the source of its greatest difficulties and its most regrettable reverses. Some sociologists understood very well that sociology had an objective matter to study, that its domain of investigation was fact, and fact alone; but after having established this truth, they could not deduce from it the methodological consequences implied. They let themselves be led astray by metaphysical or political (in the scientific sense of the word) concerns that were foreign to their science. Auguste Comte, the first among them, let himself be carried away by an impatient desire to reorganize society. The reformer in him supplanted the sociologist, and the man of action smothered the man of science. "What a regression compared to the 18th century!" says Maunier, in talking of his work. "Auguste Comte was very fine on synthesis and construction; but sociology did not find a worker in him."[3]

Émile Durkheim too "was and remains in some sense a philosopher"—we might perhaps add, an apostle—as much as and more than a sociologist.[4] The need for a metaphysics is what led him to sociology; he came to it "in order to find there and to found there a moral science," and this concern, however noble it may be in itself,

2. [*La morale.* G.]

3. "How much broader was the vision of a Montesquieu, a Ferguson, an Adam Smith! How much more truly anxious to learn they were, and how much more erudite (than Auguste Comte)! It is astonishing to see that in Comte's time the historians themselves scorned comparative studies. Savigny disapproved of the study of the history of comparative law; he thought it useless to attempt to extend comparisons beyond the terrain of Roman and barbarian laws. This whole period marks a great step backward." Maunier, *Introduction,* pp. 95–96.

4. Maunier, *Introduction,* pp. 98–99.

vitiated his sociological work. It led him to anticipate his conclusions; it diverted him from the scientific rigor that sociological work requires. His error lies in his attempt to use sociology for ends that it cannot attain.

At any rate Comte left to his disciples a useful heritage—after him we understand better that societies constitute the objective matter of a distinct science, and that social facts have distinctive causes that can be recognized and formulated. Durkheim himself understood the value and importance of the patient method of comparison and observation that sociology requires, even if he did not practice it. From a scientific and methodological point of view these steps forward can be scored to their credit.

Other sociologists, on the contrary, thought for a long time they were devoting themselves to sociology when they were actually working on social morality, social politics, or social philosophy. They were slow to recognize that social facts furnished the objective matter of a scientific discipline based on observation. Their trouble was that they were led to sociology by the political or moral sciences they had been working in, and sociology naturally appeared to them as an annex or chapter of their former field of study. How many, for example, have identified sociology with the solution of social questions and have confused it with *social politics,* with the science of government applied to the arrangement of social institutions![5]

How many others have studied social facts as if they were in exclusive subordination to moral science, and by an application of its method! Social facts, they say, are really human facts, the life of *societies* is simply the life of *individuals* in society; on analysis it reveals only a multitude of interwoven and entangled individual actions. Sociological law seems to them merely the moral law that presides over the social life of individuals and groups. We just saw sociology as absorbed by political science; here it is threatened with absorption by social morality and natural philosophy. Either way its proper object vanishes, it loses its independence and is nothing but a chapter of another science.

In opposition to each of these schools of thought—or rather, if my plan is not too ambitious, for the benefit of each of them—I would like, in this brief essay, to determine the proper object of sociology and to clarify its limits.

5. "Everything that they say and write on political and moral science they call sociology; under this term they mingle *science* and *art,* verification and appreciation. They judge and censure in the name of sociology. Every ideologist and every reformer and every prophet calls himself a 'sociologist.' " Maunier, *Introduction,* p. 8.

THE PROPER OBJECT OF SOCIOLOGY

All readily agree that sociology is "the science of social facts" or "the study of human societies." But this aphorism does not resolve the problem. It does not say what a social fact *is*, and only by defining it can we determine the object of sociological science. To the French school[6] the nature of the social fact seemed so special as to warrant classification in a kingdom all its own. The adversaries against whom the French school reacted (with a vigor that perhaps explains some of its excesses) had reduced the "social" to the "psychological" and ultimately to the "individual." The controversy can only be resolved by an analysis of the social fact.

Such an analysis permits us to reject from the outset a conception of societies that has—allow me to say it—cluttered up the field of social philosophy for centuries. This conception, arm in arm with the individualism and voluntarism that were given new life by the Renaissance, enervated the resistance that Christian thought should have given to individualism and to juridical and social liberalism.

Neglecting an essential aspect of the social relationship, this conception sees no more in it than a connection established between individual and individual, between subject and subject. Men are incited or constrained to enter into relationships by motives of physical necessity, interest, sympathy, moral duty, or any other reason; but whatever may be the subjective motive that gives birth to social relationships, in their essence they are constituted by a tie that links individuals to one another directly. A social fact, whatever may be the influences that condition it, remains in the last analysis a bond that unites individuals to individuals without mediation or intermediary: a social relationship is only a relationship between individuals.

What would society be on this hypothesis but an aggregate of interindividual, or in Célestin Bouglé's term, interpsychological relationships? It follows that the cause of social facts is essentially psychological. Since the social relationship presupposes only *two* elements on the scene—the *two individuals* who confront one another and between whom the social relationship is established—the cause of this relationship will be found in the individual and in him alone. The cause is thus confused with the subjective, psychological motives that prompt men to enter into relations. Of course, these psychological decisions themselves are influenced by innumerable circumstances that act upon men and exert pressures upon

6. [The sociological school of Émile Durkheim.]

them. The types of association that men adopt, for example, depend greatly upon historical data, upon circumstances, upon the physical or moral milieu in which they live—in short, upon everything that influences the psychology of man in society and bears upon his choices. It would take a careful study of these influences to explain the particular modes of a given epoch's social life and the character of the social institutions it produces. But however much light may be shed on social forms by a study of the external conditions of their development, this theory still leaves the social fact as an interindividual relationship, whose existence and modalities are explained by the psychological reactions of two subjects. And so sociology shrinks into a chapter of psychology—*the psychology of "ad alterum" relationships.*

It seems to me that this conception excludes sociology from the ranks of autonomous disciplines. Its proper object, its matter, vanishes the moment the social fact loses its *objective* existence; it remains nothing more than the study of the psychological motives that man obeys in his societal life. Even if such a study were accompanied by an analysis of the circumstances that condition man's choices, would this suffice to constitute a distinct scientific discipline? Of course one can claim to find in this interindividual relationship the two characteristics of externality and objectivity that are generally held to be requisites of the social fact. But this would be utterly unjustifiable. Undoubtedly every relationship is in itself something extra-individual: it "binds" two subjects; it makes the bond, so to speak, and throws the bridge between them. The span of a bridge is neither on one bank nor on the other; it is exterior to both. But this is not enough to give the societal relation the objectivity and externality it must have to become a distinct object of science. The old doctrine of traditional metaphysics is simply translating a truth of common sense when it says that every relationship is defined by its terms. The *subjective* psychology of the two authors of a social relationship suffices to account for it and to define it: an interindividual relationship *does not become objective,* properly speaking. For this a third factor must intervene, a factor *foreign to the individuals concerned,* independent of them—objective in this sense. This third term is contained in the societal relationship; owing to it, the societal relationship will become truly objective. Because of it, psychology no longer suffices to explain all the constituent elements of the social fact, and because of it the social fact ceases to be purely psychological or interpsychological.

What is this new element that plays such a decisive role in sociology and gives it the character of an autonomous science? Analysis will reveal it to us. Let us take a very simple example. Imagine some people who live on a vast tract of land, so far apart they do not know one another. At the center of their territory suppose there is a spring that provides all of them with the water they need. You can guess what I am coming to—the spring constitutes their common treasure, the good of all: it is the cause of the societal relations that will be established among the users of this collective good.

I am not suggesting that the people just happen to meet at the spring when they go there to drink or to water their flocks. In this event the watering place would just be the occasion of their entering into relations; and such an occasion is not a cause, in the scientific sense of the word. But suppose that someone, while drawing out the water he needs, pollutes the well: he causes trouble for all the unknown people he injures, and they will not rest until they have discovered him, punished him, and seen to it that he will not be able to repeat the performance. Or suppose, on the other hand, that someone else, for any motive whatsoever, even personal interest, puts the spring in order, makes it more accessible, digs a basin where the water is settled and purified. Will not the beneficiaries of his initiative be grateful? And will they not express their gratitude to him?

In a word—and this conclusion is what my analysis of an imaginary event has been leading to—the spring is, in the strict sense, the cause of these societal relations; it explains their birth and their nature: gratitude or hate, honor given or punishment inflicted. It is their measure; it provides them with a scientific explanation in the eyes of the sociologist who seeks to determine the causes of social facts.

Thus, every social relationship contains an *objective* element that is essential to it. This can be a material element, as in my example; it can be a purely spiritual element, such as an idea, a system of thought, a doctrine. The idea, the scientific or moral truth, are *objective*. Once found, they have an existence independent of the finder. He disappears, and the idea makes its own way, it propagates itself in time and space; it produces effects he neither foresaw nor desired. There is a history of ideas and doctrines. Because of its objectivity, the idea is a factor of social grouping: let two persons agree on an idea, and a societal relationship is thereby established between them, caused and measured by the idea, that is, by an object. The desire to sound the depths of this idea, or to propagate it, or to unfold its consequences, is what engenders this societal relation: the cult of science or the service of the common idea is the cause of the association that is formed for this purpose. What is more, the idea, by reason of its objectivity, is universal: let a third, then a fourth, and a fifth person come to join in the idea; the societal relationship will extend to these newcomers, and the society will grow in numbers and importance. But the object will always remain the cause of this relationship: the object is what one must discover to explain the social fact; the object is what one must find to understand the formation of societies and their behavior.

Now you see what I mean in speaking of the objective character of the social fact. The societal relationship does not go directly from one individual to another, but from one individual to another by means of an object and because of this object. The object gives the relationship its form and measure. The example cited above makes it clear that the social relationship goes from men to men, but because of the spring, in the measure required by this object of common utility, and in the manner and under the form that it imposes. If any material or spiritual element has a sociological value, it is by reason of its capacity to cause social relationships, which have as their center and pivot this objective and extra-individual factor. This factor is integrated in the social fact; it enters into its definition as an essential element.

Durkheim and the French sociological school attached great importance to the objective character of the social relationship. They were right. If the social fact were not objective, there would be no sociology, for want of distinctive subject matter; psychology would exhaust the study of phenomena of influence and relationship. But if an essential element intervenes between the individuals who enter into relationships, an element that cannot be explained by psychology because it is objective and not psychological, sociology must certainly be something other than a simple psychology of *ad alterum* relationsips.

A social relationship thus understood—even if it involves only two people—is already a rudimentary society. The nature of a society is not changed in the least by fluctuations in the number of individuals who are united in its idea or object. The family exists before children are born; it exists the moment there is an association in the idea of the procreation and education of children. My analysis of the social fact manifests the primary and essential role of the object and end in every society and in every social institution. The factor that explains the formation, duration, and life of groups is the object, that is, the end that brings together the interested parties and constitutes the *raison d'être* of their society. Psychologically, this end represents the common good that assures the cohesion of the group by its power of attraction. It furnishes the society and its members with their social ideal; it is the fundamental principle of the law of the group and of the discipline the group imposes upon its members; it is the basis and justification for the authority that the group exercises over them.

Every society thus forms an ensemble whose keystone is the end. But this end is *objective*, extra-individual, which is why the social relationship itself takes on a "reality" that is exterior to its individual members. It is differentiated from their interindividual relations because an external element enters into its definition. Externality, objectivity, transcendence with reference to the facts of individual or interpsychological life—these are the essential traits of the social fact; the role played by the object gives them a meaning and an explanation, and it is these natural characteristics that make society an object of science distinct from psychological realities.

Under this aspect, sociology rejoins the sciences of observation, the sciences of reality. It "takes as its purpose the contemplation of what is and the contemplation of what was; but not the conjecture of what could be or what ought to be."[7] "The object and matter of a true science of societies is the real, present and past, not the ideal and the possible." By reason of their objectivity, social facts take their place among the things "that are of nature"; and the study of societies is conceived as "analogous in its course to the study of the beings of the animate or inanimate world." "Just as the end of every science of observation is first to describe things, then to compare or classify them, finally to explain them—so the science of man in society is concerned with describing, comparing, and explaining the facts of life in common." In concluding these remarks, Maunier defines sociology as "the descriptive, comparative and explicative study of human societies." This definition of Maunier's might also satisfy us if the meaning of the term "explicative" were clear. But it is not at all certain that our way of understanding the "explanation" of societies concurs with Maunier's.

Between sociology and the sciences of the animate or inanimate world there is, as Maunier notes, an analogy—but nothing more. These sciences resemble one another in the way they differ from the practical moral sciences—they are sciences of what is and not sciences of what ought to be. But we must not conclude from this that the causes of social facts are identical with the causes of physical

7. This quotation and those following are from Maunier, *Introduction*, p. 2.

or biological phenomena. The members of societies are men, that is, free and intelligent beings. The end that draws them together by its power of attraction does not act upon them after the fashion of a physical and determining cause; it acts upon them as a moral and objective cause that solicits the choice of a free will. The associates can be more or less explicitly conscious of the end; but, clear or confused, it is the "idea" of this end that moves them, and Hauriou was quite right to explain the genesis of groups and institutions by the role of the "mother-idea" or the generating idea.

Whether or not the end is adopted by a will that is fully conscious and free, it is nonetheless an integral part and an essential factor of the social relationship. When the sociologist has observed and compared social behavior, and sifted it from all the influences that condition it and stamp their particular modalities upon it, he must then always look for its proper cause, the element that explains the social fact. He will find it in the object, which is the *final cause* of social behavior. The object provides the human motive, of interest, passion, religion, etc., that gave the initial impulse to the members of the group and made these beings, who when all is said and done, are free, decide to commit themselves to a particular course and to precise forms. The sociologist will then have no scientific knowledge of social facts until he has sifted out the society's mother-idea, which plays for the members the role of final cause. And so, while the end is immanent to social behavior, the sociologist does not come upon it a priori. He does not impose it upon future societies by reforming existing institutions: by his special methods of observation, analysis, and comparison, he discovers it, as it is in fact revealed by an examination of the life of societies. In other words, the end does not impose itself upon the sociologist before he has begun his study, and he does not try to interpret it into the facts, nor implant it in institutions. It appears to him only at the termination of his work; it gives an answer to the ultimate why asked by his science, which is the science of what is, and not the art of realizing what ought to be.

SOCIOLOGY AND MORAL SCIENCE: THE REDRESS OF CONTEMPORARY SOCIOLOGY

But is it not clear that the scientific work of the sociologist, when it has reached this terminal point, permits a value judgment? One can even say that it calls for such a judgment, although sociology does not have the authority to pronounce it. Is it not clear, in other words, that sociology, an autonomous and distinct science, goes hand in hand with moral science and social philosophy?[8]

Sociology sifts out, I have said, the causes of social facts, and chief among them, this object, which is at the same time the final cause of the activity of those associated with it. At this point sociology has finished its work—but it has prepared the field for moral science. It makes possible the value judgment that moral science passes upon societies and social behavior; for because of its findings one can compare fact with right, the conduct of men with the moral rule that forbids them certain ends and prescribes others, the ends actually attained in social life with the ideal ends that morality assigns to human societies.

But obviously no one can make this value judgment until he has established a table of human values; until he has given himself a moral code and found the principles and bases of it. This is not the work of sociology; it is clearly quite outside its limits. Here we must appeal to rational philosophy.

And so we clearly see, on the one hand, the distinction between sociology and moral science, and on the other, their interconnection, their coordination. The confusion of the domains of sociology and social moral science has compromised the development of both of

8. What then is social philosophy? A chapter of moral philosophy. "Moral philosophy," says Marie-Benôit Schwalm very accurately in *Leçons de philosophie sociale* (Paris, 1910–1911), I, 168, 169, 170, 173, "has two distinct parts, each one of which constitutes a distinct science: individual morality and social morality." "But again," he adds, "in moral science we must distinguish two distinct sciences that are complimentary to one another." For there are "two orders of societies that are essentially distinct by reason of their object: the economic order, which has for its proper and immediate end the conservation of the individual and the species; the political order, which has for its proper and immediate end the general good of families and other groups of the economic order . . . Social philosophy is then this two-fold part of moral philosophy that has for its object the actions of private groups (economic order) and those of public groups (political order) in their relation with human nature. Social philosophy, according to St. Thomas, is the first of the sciences in the practical order . . . Just as metaphysics, which considers the general properties of being, furnishes, by means of this consideration, the first and universal principles of all speculative science, so social philosophy, which studies the most divine of human goods, the *common good of societies* . . . is the most beneficient and desirable of the practical sciences for the utility of the present life." Cf. Aquinas, *Ethics*, I.1, lect. 1 and 2; *Politics*, I.1, lect. 1.

General sociology goes hand in hand with sociology and social philosophy. It establishes the connection between them. It refers all social actions to their ultimate principle: human nature. It reveals in the needs of human nature the last cause, the ultimate end of all the manifestations of social life. It examines societies and social activities in their relations with human nature. It refers the multiplicity of social facts to their most universal cause; it makes a "philosophy" of them.

these sciences; it is by distinguishing their domains and pointing out the precise point of their interconnection that the redress of contemporary sociology will be achieved.

The confusion was brought about by two approaches that are diametrically opposed, and that work, so to speak, in contrary directions. (1) I recalled at the outset the "individualist" error, which sees in the social relationship only an interindividual or interpsychological bond. This conception dissolves the object of sociology; it does away with it by reducing the social to the individual. What will become of sociology? The individualists will use the name as a decoration for the study of the human relations of individual to individual. But because they will reduce sociology to the psychology of interindividual relationships, they cannot avoid, I think, turning it into a real moral science. The course seems inevitable.

Two human persons can indeed enter into relations only as subjects having rights; this capacity is inherent in personality; in fact, it is synonymous with it. The relationships between such subjects, who are of an absolute and equal value, can only be relationships of justice, based upon a respect for individual rights—unless they are altruistic relationships of friendship and charity. Justice and charity—these are the two chapter headings of moral science *ad alterum*. It would then follow that if societal relationships were only direct interpersonal relationships (conditioned, to be sure, by exterior circumstances; but this does affect the essence of the social relationship), the law of social relationships could only be the law of human actions with respect to one's neighbor. The study of what is would inevitably evoke the idea of what ought to be, because the individuals between whom the relationships are established would necessarily appear as subjects with rights. Their relationships would then be first of all relationships of justice and love—and so the sociologist would slip into the role of the moralist—or they would be juridical relationships—and then he would be tempted to plunge into the political and juridical sciences.

(2) In contrast to those who absorb sociology into the moral sciences or into the old cameral sciences,[9] the French sociological

9. [See Louise Sommer, "Cameralism," in *Encyclopedia of the Social Sciences* (New York, 1930), III, 158–161: "The term 'cameralism' is applied to the assorted political ideas gathered about the centralizing practices and tendencies in administration, finance and economic policies which characterized the absolute monarchy in Germany and Austria around the middle of the eighteenth century. The term also designates the system of political sciences of the same period which placed itself at the service of the absolute monarchy and attempted to work out a systematic account of the functioning of the various administrative services as a basis for the training of public officials. Cameralism is properly the German and Austrian variety of mercantilism."]

school asks sociology itself to furnish a foundation for moral science. Moral sentiments and imperative rules are, in the view of this school, only a creation of social life. "The moral sentiments, the moral practices of a given society are, for the savant, *necessarily* bound to its religious beliefs, to its economic and political state, to its intellectual accomplishments, to its climatic and geographical conditions, and consequently also to its past; and as they have evolved up to the present according to the variations of these factors, they are destined to evolve the same way in the future." Every society has its "own morality, dependent on its condition of existence"; it is "precisely what these conditions require it to be."[10]

On this hypothesis sociology will indeed be the science that will reveal to us the origin of moral principles, their genesis, and their foundation. And Lévy-Brühl sees it today as presaging "in the societies that are most advanced from an intellectual point of view," a "third period" in which religious and teleological postulates will disappear from moral science and be supplied by sociology, a period in which "social reality" will be "objectively and methodically studied by an army of scholars spurred on by the same spirit as those who have long been searching into inorganic and living nature." Sociology will first familiarize us "with the idea of the plurality of moralities, which correspond, in each given epoch, to the complex of conditions that exist in each society considered." After "the constitution of the particular sociological sciences[11] as well as general sociology, we would be prepared to investigate the religious, economic, etc., causes that act upon them" [the moral sciences].[12] "Later, in a future that we are barely allowed to foresee, these sciences (the particular sociologies and general sociology) will be far enough advanced to make applications of them possible."[13]

This is not the place to criticize the conception of moral science professed by Lévy-Brühl, nor to attack the notion of the "science of manners."[14] But, placing myself at the scientific point of view,

10. Henri Lévy-Brühl, *La morale et la science des moeurs* (Paris, 1927), pp. 198–199.

11. [A prominent current representative of the Durkheim tradition in French sociology contrasts with "general sociology" the following particular sociological sciences: social morphology (including sociogeography and demography), economic sociology, juridical and moral sociology, domestic sociology, and political sociology (state, nation, civilization). Armand Cuvillier, *Manuel de Sociologie* (Paris, 1958), 2 vols.]

12. [Bracketed phrase inserted by Delos.]

13. Lévy-Brühl, *La morale*, pp. 289–290.

14. [*Moeurs*. François Geny lists under "a generic name of *moeurs* (*mores, die Sitten*) the ensemble of customs, manners of being, attitudes, usages and practices, that being gradually sanctioned under the consolidating influence of a common opinion or of collective ways of acting come to direct the physical, moral or social life of a group

I ask that the proper object of sociology be at last recognized, that sociology be restored to its place as a science of observation, that there be an end to imposing demands upon it that it cannot satisfy. We just saw the necessity of taking care not to turn sociology into a moral science; it is equally necessary to avoid asking it for what only a metaphysics can accomplish: to *found* a morality, to furnish principles for value judgments, when it can only furnish a *matter* to which we shall apply our scale of values.

Bouglé, in one of his last works, gives a striking example, if not of this confusion between moral science and sociology, at any rate of this inversion of their connections, or reversal of the natural order that presides over their relations. Value judgments were the subject matter of Bouglé's *"Leçons de sociologie sur l'évolution des valeurs."* [15] From the point of view I am developing here, the theme is particularly interesting. We certainly cannot reproach Bouglé, nor the French sociological school, for willfully ignoring the role played by ideas, by concepts, or by value judgments in social life. Every man, remarks Bouglé, is guided by a certain number of "value judgments" about things or actions; and what has been said of ideas can also be said of "values"; they lead men—and societies.

The recognition of the role played by values in the life of societies might create an area of agreement between Bouglé and myself, or rather, might furnish a common point of departure that is not to be overlooked. This is why I have spoken of a redress of sociology, rather than a radical opposition between the two conceptions. But the differences are very apparent, and they are profound.

"Values" have in Bouglé's eyes an essential characteristic: objectivity. Value judgments are not like those tastes and opinions that everyone agrees are not to be discussed. They are independent of our subjective dispositions; they withstand our variations. When we say, for example, that a worker is conscientious, or that gold is more precious than iron, we clearly intend to affirm a truth that is independent of ourselves and others. In our value judgments, says Bouglé, we "assign to an ideal or material object—it does not matter which for now—a rating that is independent of our impressions of the

---

in a certain way, following a general idea of suitability or utility (customs of hygiene or of decency, forms of politeness or of decorum, common practices, fashion, prejudices, etc.) under the diverse pressures of opinion which expresses itself either in an approval leading to public esteem or in a disapproval that may go as far as disqualification". Geny, "La notion de droit en France," *Archives de philosophie du droit et de sociologie juridique*, I-II (1931), pp. 16–17.

15. Célestin Bouglé, *Leçons de sociologie sur l'evolution des valeurs* (Paris, 1922).

moment, a rating that is capable of withstanding our spontaneity, of dominating our own preferences and thus of assuming in our eyes a sort of reality." Values, he insists again, "are not just putty in men's hands. Would this not be because they are, in a sense, realities? . . . Value judgments, far from expressing my personal preferences, express realities of a sort that impose themselves upon the society in which I live."[16]

But where do these "realities" come from? What is their origin? What gives them this objective character, the force with which they impose themselves upon us? Why, in a word, are they imperative? That sociologists do not evade the problem of the foundation of moral obligation is entirely to their honor; but to believe that the solution of this problem will be found through sociology is to nourish a vain illusion.

We know how Bouglé resolved the problem. "If values rear up before us as realities independent of our momentary impressions and our changing desires, the principal reason is, without doubt, that in one way or another they tend to impose themselves upon us . . . The reality of the value, remarked Simmel, consists in an insistence: it demands recognition. This is the characteristic that Durkheim vigorously insists upon. Value judgments, in his eyes, are objective because they are imperative. But if they are imperative, is it not because they are collective? Where do they get the commanding prestige that they seem to assume in diverse degrees, if not from that special force that emanates from a meeting of minds?[17] . . . Here we recognize, we meet again, the dominant thought of the sociological work of Émile Durkheim. His last writings are full of this idea: society is, in essence, the creator of ideals. In its attributes, in the special forces that are let loose from a gathering of men, lies the explanation of the characteristics of these great magnets we call values: neither the attributes of things nor the faculties of individuals suffice to account for them. And, in short, values will be *objective* because they are *imperative,* and imperative because they are *collective.*"

Bouglé strongly insists upon the "function that is, according to Durkheim, the highest function, the characteristic function of societies: to create an ideal." Let us reread the now celebrated conclusion of the *Formes élémentaires de la vie religieuse:*[18] here we shall again meet the idea that "superior values cannot spring solely from the

16. Bouglé, Leçons, pp. 15–18.
17. Bouglé, Leçons, p. 27.
18. [Durkheim, Les formes élémentaires de la vie religieuse, le système totémique en Australie (Paris, 1912).]

attributes of things, nor solely from the faculties of the individual."
The ideal, moral or religious, is an "emanation of collective life."[19]
If each individual feels dominated by this ideal, it is because no one
in particular creates it entirely; it is the work of the collectivity.

But we must still see how this creation comes about, we must catch
it in the act, for sociology is a science of observation. Here Bouglé
resorts to a pitiful attempt at explanation, an attempt that is arbitrary
and imaginative—the theory of the projection of values. It irresistibly
calls to mind—with all due apologies!—the scientific explanations
of Molière's doctors. Values, imperative ideals, are only "projections,"
the result of an objectivation of what lives in us. "What lives in us
is projected outside of us." Values thus take on an exterior existence;
they become "the magnets that attract and deserve to attract our
convergent efforts,"[20] and how Bouglé can say they henceforth
"*deserve*" to attract our efforts I cannot see.

"When a common life is organized . . . new forces are let loose,"
forces that are of a spiritual nature, "that are beyond the capacity
of individual souls." Values are original products of the community,
"products of a sort of synthesis of consciences." They issue "from
the activity of that ardent center that is constituted by a drawing
together of consciences". If the ideal is superior and transcendent,
it is because it is not a creation of the individual: it emanates from
"the synthesis productive of new properties that is formed by (the)
association" of individual consciences.

It would be easy game, if we could indulge in such amusements,
to make sport of these explanations that crumble under analysis.
What is this "synthesis of individual consciences," endowed with
a productive force whose distinctive activity is to "create the ideal"?
What is this "ardent center," and what are these "new forces" that
are let loose from it? It is simply astonishing that such an alchemy
can be proposed to us as a scientific explanation.

Bouglé's theory of values implies, in the exposition he himself
gives, a flagrant contradiction. Ideals are a creation of society, a fruit
of community life. "A society," says Durkheim in his *Formes élémentaires de la vie religieuse,* "can neither be created nor recreated
without at the same time creating an ideal." Bouglé, who cites Durkheim here, is in complete agreement, and yet he recognizes in these
ideals—rightly this time—the cause itself, or the necessary condition,
of the existence of societies: "It is to be noted that without these

19. Bouglé, Leçons, p. 32.
20. Bouglé, Leçons, p. 37.

rallying points—without these stars—society, the synthesis of consciences, would lack an ordering principle. The existence of superior
values that demand universal reverence is a condition of its distinctive life."[21] I heartily agree, and this is precisely where I have a point
of contact with Bouglé's sociology. Are not these "stars," these rallying points, the *ends* that furnish the *mother-idea* of social institutions? If this is so, my sociological conception fits in with Bouglé's.
But then, how can these values and ends be, as Bouglé would have
it, *products* of society? You cannot have it both ways: either society
creates imperative values and ideals that then oblige our individual
consciences, and in this event society is anterior and superior to
them; or else it is the force of attraction of these rallying points that
gathers individuals into groups in order to realize a common idea.
But we must choose between the two, and not expect the causes of
social grouping to be at the same time products of it.

Bouglé has an inkling—occasionally even a clear notion—of the
role played by the idea and by values in the formation, duration,
and transformation of societies and institutions. The shortcomings
and contradictions into which he falls are a consequence of the error
that condemns the French sociological school to failure; it asks sociology to furnish what sociology cannot give: a foundation for moral
science.

Sociology has its own special method, a method of observation;
it is incapable of revealing anything other than what is or what was;
it cannot dictate what ought to be, nor prescribe what "deserves"
to attract our divergent efforts. The study of the sense of moral
obligation and of its *imperium* calls for a philosophical criticism of
the moral conscience. To wish to accomplish, by the observation and
comparison of social facts, the task that belongs to the critical faculty
of practical reason and moral conscience, is to have a very strange
idea of the critical problem and to denature the psychological sense
of moral obligation. This is what Duguit has done in his investigation
of the foundation of law;[22] this is what Fauconnet has done in his
study of responsibility.[23] The claim to resolve the problem of the
foundation of moral science by sociology has doomed to failure forty
years of effort in French sociology. The scientific effort of so many

---

21. Bouglé, *Leçons*, p. 35.
22. [See Léon Duguit, *L'état, le droit objectif et la loi positive* (Paris, 1901), *Le droit
social, le droit individuel et la transformation de l'état* (Paris, 1908), *Manuel de droit
constitutionnel*, 2nd ed. (Paris, 1923), and *Traité de droit constitutionnel*, 3rd ed. (Paris,
1927).]
23. [See Paul Fauconnet, *La responsabilité: Étude de sociologie* (Paris, 1920).]

ingenious minds has miscarried, not strictly speaking because of a confusion of moral science and sociology, but because of an inversion of their mutual relations. We must not ask a science of *facts* to teach us what *ought to be;* we must not attempt to lay the foundation for moral science and its normative rules upon a science of observation.

If these scholars had let each of the sciences pursue its proper object, they would have discovered that sociology, a science of observation, after attaining its proper end, becomes the useful auxiliary of the political sciences and moral science. By determining the often obscure and hidden ends of social activity, sociology enables social morality to pass its judgments, with knowledge of the facts, upon the value of social institutions. Owing to sociology, political science can act guided by experience; and law, which is the instrument of social politics, can play its part with justice and efficacy. Durkheim recognized the objectivity of the social fact, without understanding its nature; Bouglé had an intimation of the role of "values" in the life of societies; but sociology as they conceive it needs a drastic purification to be restored to itself, to the bareness of its object and its method. It is on this condition that sociology will be able to develop, and to render to the moral and political sciences the services they rightly expect from it.

GEORGES RENARD   The Philosophy of the Institution

1. Bringing Our Subject into Focus

As the subtitle of my earlier volume has already indicated, the theory of the institution raises a problem of juridical ontology. But up to now we have only considered the institution from the outside, in its conceptual aspect. Is the institution just another concept to be added to the roster of those used by the science of law to grasp reality? Is it a simple concept like contract or obligation? . . . Or is it not a reality, and if so, what sort of reality? A "being," but what type of "being"?

To use Geny's terminology, does the institution depend on a "datum," or on a "construct," on "science," or on "technique"?[1] If the question were to be resolved in this last sense—that of technique—we should end right here.

Let us suppose that it is resolved in the first sense—that of a datum. Then it amounts to a re-examination of the case of moral personality: *crux juris peritorum!* This in turn calls for a deeper study of the general notion of personality—yet still from the jurist's point of view, a point of view I shall not forsake.

There is a profusion of opinions about and explanations of moral personality. Some have even proposed to distinguish it from juridical personality. Hauriou thought that juridical personality had a merely conceptual value. Geny classified it as a construct, yet he considered moral personality a reality, a datum.[2] In the preceding volume I

ED. NOTE: What had in 1930 been planned by Renard as a second, philosophical part of *La théorie de l'institution: un essai en ontologie juridique* (Paris, 1930) finally emerged in 1939 as a philosophical development of considerably enlarged institutional premises. *La philosophie de l'institution* (Paris, 1939) is a work apart, distinct in itself. Four chapters (1, 2, 5, 7), somewhat abridged, are translated here.

1. [See *donné, construit, science,* and *technique* in G.]
2. [François Geny, *Science et technique en droit privé positif* (Paris, 1914–1922), vol. IV, p. xviii.]

suggested that moral personality be understood as one of the degrees of institutional existence, that degree in which the institution achieves a patrimonial capacity, the *jus commercii* of the Roman law. This is its usual meaning. Le Fur[3] has given us a delightful new suggestion—he has not published it, but I should like to render unto Caesar. If you determined the various stages of moral personality, he said, would you not have the economy of the institution? Perhaps! Then we would simply be faced with a question of vocabulary. Would it be easier for juridical classicism to digest the moral personality of the state ministries, of the branches of banks and other establishments with foreign agencies, of the departments of large stores, of the frail individualities constituted under the simple regime of the police power—than to digest the theory of the institution? If so, let us forget the institution and head for moral personality! And yet—

Is it really a question of degrees, that is, of specific concepts that must be carved out within a generic concept of moral personality? The law of July 1, 1901,[4] invited such an operation by distinguishing large and small within the category of patrimonial capacity: because, for the practicing lawyer, moral personality is only a graphic way of portraying the juridical capacity of a collectivity. But in taking inventory of our positive law alone, you would find many more than two degrees of patrimonial capacity: mutual aid societies, professional associations, business companies, public establishments, communes, *départements*, and communal or departmental *syndicats*,[5] all have different patrimonial capacities. On the conceptual level this picture—I almost said this jumble—calls for a classification. I did not inquire further in the "juridical part" precisely because this was my stopping point. But now we are on the ontological level, and I have a suggestion: can we not analyze moral personality in terms of a new analogy? Is not moral personality the "reason" of an analogy with the indefinite variety of "modes" in which we find it incorporated in the groups just listed? Is not the theory of the institution simply a development of the same "reason of personality" and a

3. [Professor Louis Le Fur of the law faculty of the University of Paris. See Le Fur, "Le droit naturel et la théorie de l'institution, *Vie intellectuelle* (January 10, 1931), pp. 76–102.]

4. [This law legalized noncommercial associations. See Appendix.]

5. [See Georges Vedel, *Droit administratif*, 2nd ed. (Paris, 1964), pp. 532–533: "The *syndicats* of communes are an old institution. Traditionally, they amounted to a *public establishment* (*etablissement public*, G.) originating from the cooperation of various communes with a view to the management of services of common interest. New aspects have emerged by terms of an ordinance of January 5, 1959."]

recognition of this "reason of personality" in a host of other groups not associated with this terminology and in which no jurist has seen a moral personality up to now? If the answer is yes, the institution is equivalent to the "analogy of moral personality." Once more analogy encourages us, not to veil doctrinal contrasts, but to reabsorb them in the continuity of a development.

Whether we say "institution" or "analogy of moral personality," the ontological problem before us is only a particular instance of the classical question of the relations of the whole with its parts. Is the whole something more than the sum of its parts or the resultant of their equilibrium? This question applies to the relations of individual goods with the common good, of which the institution is simply the juridical arrangement. It applies to Hauriou's *universitates rerum* or "institution-things," as well as to his *universitates personarum* or "institution-persons." Hauriou resolved the question for both by referring to the hylomorphic doctrine: the whole "informs" the parts, the parts are the "matter" informed by the whole.

But there are many ways of understanding this doctrine. The "institution-person," or moral person, understood according to the analogical interpretation, is a whole composed of human persons, and the human person has rights against institutions that belong to him alone. Institutions are for man, not man for institutions, even though he cannot do without them for his own personal life, and even though he must sometimes sacrifice his life for them. I maintain that institutional ontology is only an instance of the relations between the whole and its parts; but this instance has many variations, and these variations do not constitute a "univocal" species. The Church is not instituted like the nation; the Church is the mystical body of Christ, the nation is instituted by a mysterious bond that St. Thomas compares to the bond of blood which institutes the family. Our country is defined by this bond of similarity more than by contrasts with foreigners; patriotism is founded upon it, and not upon xenophobia; and Christian patriotism is distinguished from pagan nationalism by this bond.[6] A professional association is not instituted like a private enterprise, nor a private enterprise like a governmental service. Each institution has its own mode of being instituted: analogy!

From institutional analogy the "reason" of moral personality plunges into the center of another classic debate: the relations of personality and society; for us, their fundamental duality and their

6. Aquinas, *Summa Theologiae*, II II, q. 101, a. 1.

fundamental harmony under the primacy of personality.[7] *Institutional ontology* is dependent upon *institutional sociology* . . .

Ontology and sociology: these are the two key pieces of the philosophy of the institution. We shall study them first, and then investigate the external influence of the theory of the institution. First upon the science of law, where it cannot possibly fit without in some way renewing the general physiognomy of this science—especially the features that we have inherited from Roman law and still more especially the traditions of the legists.[8] This is the "institutional conception"—or better, analogical conception—of law. Do not interpret this to mean that I am giving the institution a vocation to absorb the entire juridical order . . . I have already condemned this sort of institutional monism by my protest against the illusion of seeing an institution in humanity *ut sic.*[9]

In reality, the "social" or the "institutional" takes its place between the "human" conceived as a nature and the "interindividual" conceived not as a common affiliation but as a relation *ad alterum.* This fact leads to a fundamental distinction.

There are rights that man possesses precisely as man; these include the right to life, not only the right to a physical life, but also to a human life, a "personal" life, and furthermore, in my opinion, the right of property, which is only an expansion of personality, the right of the creditor to payment, the right of the victim of an injury or loss to reparation, etc. These rights may suffer restrictions for the benefit of the "common good" of this or that institution. According to Catholic doctrine, even property is ordered, as to its use, to the common interest. The right to life itself may be held in check by the security needs of the "perfect society." But this is not to deny that the source of these rights is outside of and above the national institution and a fortiori all other institutions; they may be opposed to the national institution; they are in a position of balance with the

---

7. Cf. Renard, *La théorie de l'institution,* pp. 29ff, 42ff, and 327ff.
8. [See Hauriou's discussion of the "legists" in *La théorie de l'institution,* above.]
9. [In *La théorie de l'institution,* pp. 346ff (cf. p. 390), Renard himself had this "illusion." In *La philosophie de l'institution,* p. 17, n. 2, he corrects it: "the greatest institution is not the human race considered in its specific unity, but under its two modes of being, one of which is universal, the Church, and the other differentiated, nations [. . .] The human race is not an institution; it has existence only in the 'modifications' in which it is incarnate in each man, and through the tiered institutional 'modifications,' among which the Church and nations—the two 'perfect societies'— occupy the highest place: a simple juridical adaptation of the analogical metaphysic of being." In scholastic terminology "perfect society" connotes "complete," "self-sufficient," in the sense of having all that is needed to achieve its goal.]

rights of the national institution and all other institutions, just as the rights of diverse institutions are in a position of balance with the rights of the others.

On the contrary, the juridical situations of the individual within an institution (or those of inferior institutions within superior institutions), his *titles of participation,* may not be opposed to the institution because they derive from it—just as, analogically, the creature has no rights that may be opposed to the Creator. The reasonable creature simply has a title to the condition in which the Creator has placed him in the universe. Thus, every title of membership in an institution has prerogatives—and obligations—accruing to the particular state that it qualifies: citizen, elector, or magistrate—these words designate not "rights" but "states" or "statuses."

The "institutional conception of law" has, then, none of the exclusiveness of the "individualist" conception. The two expressions are not symmetrical: the institutional conception is not imperialistic; it maintains the "fundamental dualism" that I stressed in *La théorie de l'institution* simply by underscoring the second term, which the individualist conception neglects.

Finally, the institution extends its influence beyond the juridical order—above and below it. Above, toward theology[10] . . . Below, it reaches into political art. In the Greek sense, politics is the art of building societies; it is "political science" on condition that this term is not understood as a pure positive science nor as mere observation . . .

Even party politics could gain from the institutional inspiration. The institution condemns the maxim some good men think they can apply to practical politics: "Business is business." This maxim is the plague of business as well as politics. Like business, politics is subject to the control of moral science. Perhaps the finest expression in modern times of this subordination is Sertillanges'[11] response to a request he received to sponsor a new unification proposal: "I am certainly a partisan of the union of all Frenchmen against communism, and in principle I would gladly sign this proclamation. But first I would ask on what terrain do you intend to take action, what procedures of combat do you contemplate? And I fear that this prejudicial question already gravely impairs unity. And so for the

10. [Cf. Renard's last chapter, entitled "Theological Affinities," not translated here.]
11. [A. D. Sertillanges, O. P., member of the Academy, a pioneer in the revival of thomistic philosophy in France, and author of *La philosophie des lois* (Paris, 1948). He made this remark in June 1937.]

present I can only stand aside, being one of those who prefer the victory of communism to an unjust action against communism."

Politics is a function of the "common good." It can be understood in many ways, even contradictory ones. Errors are not excluded from it, nor are emotions: *humanum est!* But a politics that deliberately turns its back on the "common good" and subordinates it to the private interests of persons or factions is not even a "bad politics": it is quite outside the rules of the game . . .

2. Analogy

The theory of the institution calls for a re-evaluation of the juridical mind and of the mission of the juridical order; it poses the whole problem of law.[1] It has, in my view, no ambition of eliminating the traditional mentality, rightly or wrongly called classic. To defend this mentality is useless, for it has not been attacked; what is under fire is its monopoly. The problem is simply to counterbalance it by an opposing mentality, to provide it with the healthy rivalry of a contrast—the contrast of a philosophy ordered to the *definitive ends* of law to a technician's philosophy of the positive *application* of law—roughly, the contrast of the *ideal* of the juridical order to its concrete *possibilities* of realization. The value of the philosophy of the institution lies in the new dynamism it unleashes. It will no more destroy conceptualism than social law[2] will abolish interindividual law, or than social justice will dispense with commutative justice. Its ambitions go no further.

THE ROLE OF ANALOGY IN JURIDICAL SCIENCE

In an important work, the Canadian, Lachance,[3] stresses the experimental truth that thought ordinarily progresses by an explicit elaboration of the implicit content of words (he calls them names).[4]

1. [In the opening passages of this chapter, omitted here, Renard reviews comments on the theory of the institution by contemporary French authors.]

2. [*Droit social*. Earlier in *La philosophie de l'institution* (p. 6), Renard had cited an article by Joseph T. Delos, "Le nouveau Droit social," *Vie intellectuelle* (May 25, 1938), pp. 59–70, and the newly undertaken periodical *Droit social*, published by the Librairie Technique et Economique of Paris. This periodical, Renard notes, was edited by a board including professors of law, economists, members of the Conseil d'État and of the bar, representatives of industry, agriculture, and labor unions. It designated as "*droit social*" certain documents including "texts of laws, regulations, arbitration opinions, collective bargaining agreements, parliamentary bills, proposals emanating from labor organizations."]

3. Louis Lachance, O. P., *Le concept de droit selon Aristote et Saint Thomas* (Paris, Montreal, 1933). See my review of this work, "Le conception analogique du droit," *Vie intellectuelle*, July 25, 1934, pp. 268ff.

4. "The name is empiricism under its simplest form. The name is a crystallized observation. The name is an accumulation of experiences. Since the word of man

The term "institution" is rich. It evokes the mode of being that is founded upon the juridical act[5] that we call, in the full sense of the word, a "constitution." Constitution, institution, these two terms are complementary: one expresses the generating act and the other the being that is engendered.

Every institution has its charter, which gives it being while determining its manner of being and consequently of behaving: this is its constitution, written on parchment or immanent, like customary law, in its structure, its internal development, and its external activity—it matters little! This institutional charter does not merely provide for a system of mutual obligations among its members; it effects a mutual integration.

It follows that constitutional law is not just a branch of public law and a fortiori, within public law itself the object of constitutional law is not limited to the organization, operation, and relationships of powers in the state.[6] Here again I am not innovating. Bourcart and Thaller, two masters of commercial law, have claimed the constitutional regime for stock corporations.[7] And the chapters of administrative law that deal with the juridical structure of communes, *départements,* public establishments, chambers of commerce, agricultural and professional organizations, etc., all lead back to constitutional law.

We have an analogy here, an *analogy of attribution,* as it is called. "Why," writes Faribault, "are these organizations called institutions?" A little semantics will help us. To institute seems to come from two Latin words: *in statuere,* to establish upon. *Statuere,* in turn, comes from *statos,* a derivative of the Greek verb *istemi* that evokes the fundamental idea of something final, stable, fixed, distinct, con-

---

is the interpreter of his thought and the exterior manifestation of the impression he receives from things, the name given to objects by successive generations is literally gorged with meaning. It bears witness to a continuous manner of understanding these objects. So we can see that the name is in a certain way *the threshhold of science.* In point of fact, if you do not have an object at hand, you need only pronounce its name and it will immediately arise before the thought of your audience. For the name was already in an obscure and confused state the idea that is to be made clear and distinct. Consequently, it is useful to squeeze it until it gives up its whole content." Lachance, *Le concept de droit,* p. 29.

5. [*Acte juridique.* G.]

6. Cf. My article "Qu'est-ce que le droit constitutionnel?" in *Mélanges Carré de Malberg* (Paris, 1933), pp. 483ff.

7. Edmond Thaller in a note under *Cass.,* May 30, 1892, D. 93.1 105; Gabriel Bourcart, *De l'organisation et des pouvoirs des assemblées générales dans les sociétés par actions* (Paris, 1905), no. 18. I referred to these on different occasions in *La théorie de l'institution.*

structed, definitively established. The English language has kept this same idea in the derivatives state, statute, status, etc. But the institutions enumerated above do not all have this definitive character, which the very meaning of the name given them seems to require, because here, by a common phenomenon of linguistic derivation, disparate things have been united under one name solely on the basis of diverse similarities. The philosophers call this *analogy*. Thus, in our case, we apply the term institution not only to the organisms that *realize the definition perfectly*, but also to things connected with these organisms: their causes, their means of action, their laws, their constitutions, and sometimes even the signs that manifest their activity. All these things merit the name institution only by their relation to the mother-institution from which they proceed or to which they are ordered. Their whole institutional being comes to them from the external connection that they have with an institution. This is a typical case of *analogy of attribution*.[8]

Faribault's book deals with the *fiducie*, or what the English call trust, and the author argues energetically that, for the province of Quebec, this institution was not developed under English influences, which in his country rival French influences. The fact remains that the contact and even the friction of the two influences cannot help but make the jurists on both sides mutually more "understanding." With us, the study of comparative law brings about this broadening of view; and few are the jurists who have the time to devote themselves to it. In Quebec it is a vital necessity. This situation explains the warm reception given to analogy and the institution, under the form of the *fiducie*, by jurists who are most sensitive about national autonomy, especially when the theory comes from France! In Canada an interaction between the two juridical mentalities is produced by the force of events; we have no equivalent for this on our side of the ocean.

And then, as Hauriou has shown with respect to the origins of our administrative law, the French and the Anglo-Saxon juridical systems did not go their separate ways until the time of the Renaissance, when the French system departed from its own traditions to follow the lead of the legists. This deviation was consolidated by the Revolution and the Empire. Analogy is not just an article for export; it comes to us from the Christian Middle Ages; in the philosophical schools that claim this heritage it has remained in honor.

8. Marcel Faribault, *Traité théorique et pratique de la fiducie ou trust de droit civil dans le province de Quebec* (Montreal, 1936), pp. 107ff.

Institution is just a new word to signify the reconsideration, and even the restoration to honor, of a host of juridical entities that were understood under equivalent names in the Middle Ages but that later law repressed into univocal concepts in order to oust from the juridical order all other realities not included in these concepts. Community became coproperty; society became a "contract by which two or more persons put something in common with the intention of sharing the benefits that could result from it," etc. An historian of law pointed out to me that if it were not for the Romanist shift of the sixteenth century and the limitations following from it, there would be no need for the institution; it is only a weapon for a war of revenge. I agree!

Le Fur, who is on the road leading to the analogy of the institution, classifies under four headings the objectives of the promoters of the institution: "The theory of the institution was a reaction against the voluntarist and subjectivist theories that base all law upon contract; a reaction against the theory of fictitious personality; a reaction against a too static conception of law; and an attempt to place certain conceptions of legal philosophy upon new bases."[9] "Reaction," three times "reaction"! But this rather negative way of representing the institution does not displease me at all, far from it! Genetically it is perfectly true that the theory of the institution, like so many scientific doctrines, theological syntheses, and even dogmatic definitions, was born of errors that had to be corrected—of "juridical heresies" that were and still are in the air . . . And Le Fur might have added that it is also a reaction against an exaggerated separation of private and public law.

But there is something better; everything positive contained in this restoration of certain fundamental conceptions of law is, in Le Fur's judgment, and I heartily agree, only the residue of the negations from which it proceeds. The metaphysicians speak of being in much the same way. They say it is only the residue of the negations of every mode of being. Someone recently explained to me that the notion of law is only the residue of the negation of every mode of law. Being exists only in beings, and therefore mingled with nonbeing, and all existing things are distinguished from it and from each other only by the privation of what they are not. In the same way, law exists only in laws, and therefore mingled with nonlaw, and existing laws are distinguished from it and from one another only by privations

9. Le Fur, Introduction to André Desqueyrat, *L'institution, le droit objectif et la technique positive* (Paris, 1933).

of law. "Law," writes Lachance, "like man, does not exist in the abstract; there are French laws, German laws, Italian laws, and others, but there is no sheer law."[10] And this, he says, is the doctrine of Aristotle and St. Thomas. In other words, like being, law is an *analogical reason: ratio entis, ratio juris.* The analogical reason is grasped in its modes by way of a purification of what limits it in each one of them—what keeps *this* being from being *the* being, *this* law from being *the* law, *this* institution from being *the* institution.

Unlike conceptual apprehension, analogical perception grasps its object from within—this is its advantage; but it is entirely negative—this is the price of its superiority. Conceptual apprehension is the method of the sciences; it lends precision to scientific explanations. Analogical perception is the method of metaphysics, and metaphysics is a simple look at realities, beyond explanations, half-way toward a mystique.

You can imagine what perspectives this epistemology opens on the problem of natural law and its relationship with positive laws. Natural law is neither their exemplary model, nor their counterweight, nor the fine point where their specific diversity is reunited in generic unity. Natural law is very simply the analogical reason of law, the *ratio juris,* and the diverse positive laws are so many "analogues" of the analogy that philosophers call the *analogy of proportionality,* but not without admitting that no scientific language, not even that of mathematics, is capable of giving adequate expression to this metaphysical notion. Natural law is the "sheer law" that Lachance correctly says no more exists apart from its positive modes than "man" exists apart from the men who are born, live, and die on this earth. And so, at this stage of the juridical order, the institution, like contract, is itself an analogical reason, a residue of the most varied juridical matters. Le Fur is on the way to the analogy of proportionality.

Cuche has come even closer to port. "We call by the name institution," he writes, "such diverse things as the French Academy, the criminal jury, the Semaines Sociales,[11] tipping, property, prescription, the cadastral plan, the police register, and everyone understands us. We say that the French Academy is one of the rare institutions that have survived the Revolution, that tipping is a most annoying institution . . ." And everyone understands! Cuche rejoins—or rather outdoes—Lachance in the procedure of elucidating ideas from the

10. Lachance, *Le concept de droit,* p. 17.
11. [G.]

starting point of words. He insists: "If everyone understands, it is because there is something common at the basis of all these phenomena."[12] This something common is the "reason" of an *analogy of proportionality.*

The "reason" of institution is the juridical organization of the "common good."[13] (By "institution" here I mean the "institution-person" of Hauriou and the [comparable] institution-organism of Paul Cuche, to which I have always confined my investigation of a theory of the institution.) Where there is no common good, but simply a conglomeration of particular goods,[14] there is no matter for institution. But wherever there is a "common good," there is an "institution under rock," as Hauriou would say, an institution in act or in potency.

The "common good" is what "names" an institution; the name signifies the thing; the name of a thing (or of a person) is what is most intimately attached to its "being." The name is a flag, and the flag the emblem in which we honor our country. And it is by pronouncing his holy name that we honor God—and that others blaspheme him. From the name we go right to what it signifies; and this is why we need only express the name to find the thing.

The "common good" is the distinguishing characteristic of a "milieu," and an institution is simply a juridically "organized milieu," whether its law organizes a pre-existing milieu or constitutes a new one.[15] The milieu determines for its participants "conditions," which, in proportion as the milieu is instituted, are differentiated into "statuses," "offices," and "grades," each having duly catalogued prerogatives and responsibilities. Every "common good" implies a "community," and every "community" has a vocation to be instituted. The "common good" is the soul of the "community," and the "community" the soul of the institution.

12. Paul Cuche, "Manifestations nouvelles de l'authorité dans la vie sociale par le development de l'institution," *Semaines Sociales de France* (Lyon, 1925), pp. 349ff.

13. On this point, see Suzanne Michel, *Le notion thomiste de bien commun* (Paris, 1931).

14. "Bonum civitatis et bonum singulare unius personae non differunt solum secundum multum et paucum, sed secundum formalem differentiam; alia enim est ratio boni communis et boni singularis, sicut alia est ratio totius et partis, Et ideo Philosophus [Aristotle] dicit quod non bene dicunt qui dicunt civitatem et domum et alia hujusmodi differre solum multitudine et paucitate, et non specie." Aquinas, *Summa Theologiae,* II II, q. 58, a. 7.

15. Consider, as an example of the first situation, the relations of the nation (milieu) with the state (institution), as an example of the second, the circumstances that the act of foundation of an enterprise (institution) gives rise to: the workers' groups that follow from it beget collective solidarities and mentalities (milieus) that will reverberate sooner or later by organizing themselves into labor unions (institutions).

But a community may have a vocation to be instituted in the form of several institutions. Such is the case of the universal community: its institution is divided into two "perfect societies,"[16] and the second of these, the state, is divided in turn into a multiplicity of national political organizations. It follows, as Faribault justly concludes, that institutions are ranked according to their relation to the "common good," that is, according to the ends to which they are ordered: "And since, in the natural order, the perfect end is human well-being—for this is the perfect good of nature in this world—the perfect society or institution is the one that seeks this human well-being, the state.[17] All other institutions fall in place down the scale according to whether their goal is more or less natural, more or less human, according to whether the ends they pursue are more or less universal. This again is a problem of analogy: *of the analogy of proportionality* . . ."[18]

The institution is one of those simple notions that, in themselves, are beyond definition. For notions are defined only by calling upon other more elementary notions, and one cannot go on to infinity or merely turn round in a circle. This is the case with all metaphysical notions. We understand them by meditating upon them, by contemplating them. We teach them by focusing the attention of our interlocutor upon them again and again, by making him familiar with them. This is an accomodation; we adjust to these notions by reflecting upon them. Dictionaries, learned academies, juridical technique, harness such notions to make them fruitful, just as engineers harness the energy of waterfalls; but necessarily they do violence to the notions . . .

At the center of every science, of every art, and of every thing there is a mystery. You are free to leave to another the honor of penetrating it; so Duguit thought without doubt, and it was in this sense that he called himself a positivist (as a jurist, he specified). He was free, yes, but by resigning himself to a sort of *capitis deminutio.*[19] For a jurist to think he can exhaust his task with an apparatus

---

16. See above, "Bringing Our Subject Into Focus," n. 9. [The balance of Renard's long note here is omitted.]

17. Hence, its specific mission, as I have tried to trace it in my article "L'organisation rationnelle de l'état," reprinted as an appendix to *La théorie de l'institution,* pp. 537ff.

18. Faribault, *Traité théorique,* p. 114.

19. [Rules concerning change of status in Roman law. Hauriou commented on the *capitis deminutiones* in his important study "De la personnalité comme élément de la realité sociale," *"Revue générale du droit, de la législation et de la jurisprudence en France et à l'étranger* (1899), pp. 5-23, 119-140. "The juridical personality of the individual was broken by his change of family (*minima capitis deminutio*) and by

of definitions, classifications, and theories of magisterial architecture is to stop short at the signs and shy away from the search for the reality that they signify. This is just too modest! There is a mystique behind every conception of law that we can formulate; reflect well upon it! There is a mystique of personality and liberty, of contract, of legislation and the state; there is even a mirage (I dare not say a mystique) of technique; and these are no less mysterious than the institutional mystique. In every thing, as in every man, there is a secret, what Lacordaire called in man "his word." The institution also has its secret. This secret is its "reason"; and the participation of dissimilar things in a common reason is what constitutes analogy.

ANALOGY, GENUS, AND SPECIES

It seems fitting to speak analogically of analogy. I have squeezed the name for all it is worth, the word "analogy." The time has come to establish a protocol.

Some would think that it would have been more normal to offer first a general explanation of analogy, then to adapt it to the juridical problem I proposed to treat by this method. The analogical method led me, on the contrary, to start with concrete applications and to let the notion of analogy and its two modes, *analogy of attribution* and *analogy of proportionality,* come to light by way of purification. Quite intentionally I have launched these words before defining them, trusting in their evocative value to stimulate reflection and provoke the reader to discover their meaning. And since I am speaking to jurists and not to philosophers, and speaking to them in an unfamiliar language in order to express a conception of law that is untranslatable in current legal parlance, I wanted first to let them "touch" analogy in the concrete reality of its applications upon their professional territory. Now I shall rise above these interpretations *ad usum delphini*[20] . . .

There are two ways of grasping ideas. One way is to envelop them in a concept in which they can be passed from hand to hand; the envelope is a casing that keeps us from "touching" them. This process

---

the loss of his citizenship (*media capitis deminutio*); it was then bound up with his familial status and his political status, that is, it rested as much upon his quality as a member of a familial or political group as upon his quality as an individual. It is not until modern times that we see juridical personality sustained by the quality of individual alone" (p. 18).]

20. [Literally, "for the use of the Dauphin." The expression originally referred to expurgated editions of the latin classics, prepared for the Dauphin, son of Louis XIV. It is now used for expurgated or doctored editions.]

is a kind of dissection that isolates ideas, the way a biologist isolates a piece of living tissue in order to examine it under a microscope; it is the dissection of genus and species and the methodical classification that follows from it.

I am not disparaging this method at all . . . I am merely asking if there is not another way of apprehending ideas, if all ideas admit of this sort of manipulation, if the idea of law in general and of institution in particular are not amenable to another sort of treatment.

An image: a man who clutches a sphere between his two hands is certainly holding it; but would he not have a much better grip if, from its center, he grasped all its radial parts? Are there not ideas that we can and must grasp in this way, by the heart, so to speak, in their internal dynamism? Is it a weakness that such ideas are not harnessed like workhorses, a misfortune that they do not pace about a cage like circus tigers? Is the institution really a river at flood tide running wild in the formal gardens of juridical science?

Conceptual perception, classification by genus and species, are for sensible things and, consequently, for the elementary ideas that derive from them. But the higher we go, the more thought is freed from matter, the closer it comes in its ascent to the supreme reality of "being": the poorest of realities, since it includes no mode of existence; the strongest, since it is the support of all existence. And simultaneously, the more clearly appear the deficiency of conceptual perception, the resistance of reality to enrollment in genus and species, and finally the necessity of another sort of perception, a more supple and penetrating sort: analogical perception; and this is the metaphysical method.[21] An analogical reason is as far from a generic or specific concept as the supple is from the rigid, the continuous from the discontinuous, the concrete[22] from the abstract, the principle of things and the root of their ideas from their external envelope, the intuitive and the experimental from the defined.

---

21. Juridical science offers the equivalent. Generic and specific classification is at its best in private law; it presents the greatest difficulties for administrative law; and the jurisprudence of the Conseil d'État is, by and large, very analogical. Just recall the formula that it gives for the responsibility of public administrations. "This responsibility is neither general nor absolute; it has special rules that vary according to the needs of each service and the necessity of reconciling the rights of the state with private rights": a perfect specimen of analogical literature . . .

22. The concrete is the real, the existent, whether the existence be material or immaterial. Common language errs when it extends an abstract term to realities that are not perceived by the senses; jurists do not fall into this error; they have never taken incorporeal goods (debts, literary property, author's rights) for abstractions; they are realities.

In juridical methodology, genus and species belong to the "constructs," analogy belongs to the "data": social life is continuous.

To put it still more simply: it is one thing to compare two, three, or a hundred concrete beings . . . to look for similarities among them, to sift out the "reason" that is common to them; it is quite another thing to try to stuff them all in the same drawer. All concrete beings lend themselves to the first operation, for they all have in common the "reason" of being, the *ratio entis*. But being is not a genus; it is above every genus; genera come next, then species, and finally individual units. Among these individual units some have a likeness to one another over and above their share in the universal *ratio entis*, a similarity that authorizes us to call them by a common name—a something in common that "everyone understands," as Cuche said in enumerating the manifestations of the institutional phenomenon— and yet that cannot put them in the same genus or species because their differences would burst the confines of such a classification.

Can you find a genus in which to classify the light of the sun, the light of reason, and the heroes of science and philosophy who were "lights of their age"? Yet they are not equivocal; there is a relationship among them, an analogy. Can you find a "common genus" in which to place the two "specific differences" that qualify the farmer and his reaping machine? Yet they are both called harvesters by an obvious analogical extension. Can you find a drawer to hold the cadastral plan and the Semaines Sociales? And yet "everyone under stands" when they are called institutions . . .

Clearly, there is an analogy—an analogical reason—between the individuals of a species and the species of a genus; but it is solidified, confined in a rigid envelope. And this solidification is what enables the mind to have that sort of perception which is knowledge by proximate genus and specific difference. This is an external perception; it grasps the envelope, but the envelope remains closed. It is the sound perception of the postman who delivers packages knowing nothing of their content but what the sender has written on the label. What is more, this perception does not reach the singular, the concrete, for the individual is by definition irreducible to genus and species. If the individual can be grasped, it must be from within, intuitively.

But, does every analogical reason admit of this sort of solidification? I have already answered in the negative with regard to the institutional reason, the juridically organized common good.[23] Later

23. I might also have said "juridically organized milieu," the milieu that revolves around the common good that is its reason.

on I shall say as much of the reason of law, the *ratio juris*, which is the source of the institutional or analogical conception of law. These two "reasons" can be grasped only in their modal realizations, by way of purification. This sort of perception is more delicate precisely because it is more penetrating, interior, and concrete. It does not take much culture to be a good postman![24]

This is the first difference between concepts and analogy, but not the most important. It is rooted in another difference, the essential one: a genus or species is closed—a drawer, I said; an analogical reason is unlimited.[25]

Genus or species is a frame; an analogical reason is an angle, whose two arms reach out without limit. A genus or species can be "defined" precisely because it is limited; an analogical reason is "indefinable" because it is limitless.

A genus can be defined because it remains identically the same, whatever specific differences may be *joined* to it. And this is also true of a species in regard to individual differences. My dog is joined to the canine species, and this species is joined to the animal genus. But an analogical reason is not joined to the endless series of its analogues nor to any one of them; it is itself *modified* in them: light in the sun or in this or that luminous source; then, by an analogical extension, in the human reason or in infused faith; and by a further extension, in the scientist or philosopher who is called the light of his age, and in the apostle whom the Gospel calls the light of the world.

The analogical reason cannot be defined apart from its modal realizations, because it only exists in them. Yet it is independent of each one of these realizations, for it exists just as truly in each of the others. Thus, the *fiducie* or trust only exists in a series of existential modes and the number is staggering. Thus, the institution only exists in the state, the corporation, the regiment, the charitable establishment, the business company. Thus, law exists only in each of its modes, national or international, English or French, civil or

24. Besides, I have no objection to recognizing the advantage of the generic method with regard to that proper end of the juridic order, security (Cf. *La théorie de l'institution,* pp. 48ff.); in this sphere Roman law has certainly revealed its superiority. Still there is no need to exaggerate this method, with Rudolf von Ihering and Giorgio La Pira, to the point of making a mathematics of it, and no need to denounce, with Emilio Albertario, as a source of decadence the Christian influences that used it in the interest of making equity more supple. On this subject, see my note in *Revue des sciences philosophiques et théologiques,* 1938, pp. 53ff.

25. This is why I have avoided from the start the frequently used expression *analogical concept:* the word *concept* suggests the idea of a limit; it is just a question of vocabulary . . .

administrative. The analogical reason is only a potency with limitless possibilities of actualization: such is the trust, the institution, and even law. The greater the variety of modal realizations that an analogical reason may aspire to, the greater its resistance to solidification.

Although, of itself, every analogical reason admits of unlimited possibilities of realization, this does not mean that analogical reasons do not admit of different degrees of determination. The "reason" of the trust is more determined than that of the institution, that of the institution more than the *ratio juris,* which is itself much more[26] determined than the *ratio entis.* And the more these "reasons" are determined, the less resistance they offer to generic reduction. This is why much more is asked of us concerning the institution than would ever be asked of the metaphysician concerning the *ratio entis.*

The only perfect analogical reason is the *ratio entis* itself, the reason of being, which includes the transcendentals of being: unity, truth, and goodness. But there are secondary analogical reasons, which less rigorously but no less invincibly, offer the same resistance to generic classification. They are restricted not from without (as are species or genus by their proximate species or genus) but from within, by their internal determination and the capacity for modification that follows from it. This is why—to reassure Archambault and Desqueyrat—the institution has no vocation to absorb the entire juridical order, much less all *res scibiles.* It is still the angle with its two arms stretched out to infinity, but there are angles of all degrees. Only one is open to 360 degrees: the "reason of being"; without any play on words, it alone has the full "reason" of analogical reason.

One might say that in all other analogical reasons there is a beginning of generic or specific solidification; they are open on one side and closed on others. The *fiducie* is closed on the side of substitution, testamentary execution, etc.; the institution, on the side of obligation, contract, etc.; law, on the side of the "other rules of social life."[27]

From an epistemological point of view it is certainly true that juridical science is closer to metaphysics than to the physical sciences.[28] The physical sciences are concerned with matter. Although

26. [The text reads *moins.*]

27. On this subject, see *Le Fur, Le Saint Siège et le droit des gens* (Paris, 1930) pp. 190ff; and "Droit, morale, moeurs," *Annuaire de l'institut international de philosophie du droit,* 2nd session, 1935–1936 (Paris, 1936).

28. It is a thoroughgoing error to attribute to the moral sciences an aptitude for the methods of the physical sciences; I have battled this sort of "monism" and scientific imperialism—in which I easily detect an odor of "scientism"—apropos the book of Jacques Rueff, *Des sciences physiques aux sciences morales,* in an article published

order and all juridical notions have a foundation and reverberation in matter—Del Vecchio's *homo juridicus*[29] is no more angel, nor beast, than the *homo sapiens* or *homo economicus*—they are essentially spiritual because they refer to man, and in human nature the spirit is king. The same object that the physicist considers in its material consistency, or the tradesman in its exchange value, is seen by the jurist under the aspect of its appropriation or use by man as the basis of an immaterial claim, such as ownership, usufruct, credit, or mortgage. More spiritually still, the artist sees this same object as the pillar of beauty; and the believer, as the work of the Creator, which sings of the glory of God, the "sacrament of nature."

The institution is an excellent illustration of this affinity between metaphysics and the science of law. To realize this, we need only give it its spare name: the analogy of moral personality. This name is simply another application of analogy. But analogy is so foreign to the totally conceptual mentality of most jurists[30] that our predecessors could not see any reality in moral personality and called it a fiction. We are recovering from this blindness today! In a later chapter[31] I shall look for the real similarity, the analogical reason, that authorizes us to call the human person (the "physical" person, as some law books rather poorly put it) and the moral person by the same name. But let us look now at the difference between them.

The personality of man is deeply immersed in matter. Matter is more than a dwelling-place for the human soul: it is not the human soul that is a person, but the whole man in his one nature composed of body and spirit. The institution or moral person is only an idea, a "common good," organized in a system of ways and means that are arranged for the pursuit of this idea. These ways and means are integrated in the idea in the sense that they organize it according to basic statutes, and this statutory organization is still to an extent immaterial; but the material ways and means are not an integral part of the institution as the human body is of the human personality. The material resources of the institution are only its endowment,

---

under the same title in *Nouvelle journée*, (1923), I, 14ff. See also the article entitled "L'économie politique est-elle un science statistique?" (again in response to an article of Jacques Rueff), *Le droit, l'ordre et la raison* (Paris, 1927).

29. "*L'homo juridicus* et l'insuffisance du droit comme règle de vie," in the second *Annuaire de l'Institut international de philosophie du droit*, pp. 1ff.

30. [I.e., French jurists. Renard states in *La philosophie de l'institution*, p. 40, n. 3: "We know only one work on the function of analogy in the scientific elaboration of law (*droit*), the thesis defended at Paris during the scholastic year 1910–1911 by Janko Spassoievitch, entitled "L'analogie et l'interpretation: Contribution à l'étude des methods en droit privé."]

31. [Ch. 4, pp. 133–154.]

its "finances." Even its succession of personnel are only servants or beneficiaries. The founder himself fades into the background. He may be dead; then a thought detached from his departed person continues to direct the institution. If he is still living, the institution gets away from him: it lives according to its own law; it nourishes itself and develops by assimilating things and men from outside to its entirely ideal, entirely spiritual being. No juridical notion rebels more against generic or specific crystallization than the institution. This primacy can hardly be challenged, except by the notion of law itself . . .

ANALOGY OF ATTRIBUTION AND ANALOGY OF PROPORTIONALITY

What analogy is at stake here? The expression analogical "reason" is taken from the language of mathematics; in mathematics they speak of the "reason," the *ratio,* of a proportion. The *analogy of attribution,* which the philosophers distinguish from the *analogy of proportionality,* is itself a proportion, and it is called indiscriminately *analogy of proportion or of attribution.*[32] What does all this mean?

No scientific language has an entirely appropriate vocabulary for metaphysical notions. But the language of mathematics is the most suitable. Metaphysics and mathematics are certainly the most closely related disciplines!

The terms proportion and proportionality call to mind the "reason" by which analogues are analogous, just as the ratio of an arithmetic or geometric proportion expresses that by which its terms are proportional. For example, the "reason" that solar light and electric light are both called light; that there are two "harvesters" on your farm; that the business company, the professional association, the charitable foundation, the police register, the cadastral plan, and tipping are all institutions; that French law and English law, private law and administrative law, *droit objectif* and *droit subjectif,* all justly bear the name law.

But notice the nuance: the analogical proportion is not established in the same way between the two lights and the two harvesters. Sun and electricity give light in the same sense of the term, that is, univocally. The two harvesters harvest, but in two senses that are simply analogous; one sense is active, the other is in consequence of the activity of the first, a purely instrumental efficiency. Similarly, the proportion is established in one way between the business company, the professional association, and the charitable foundation, and in

32. [The terminology is traditional but confusing. From this point the first analogy is designated as "proportionality," the lesser analogy as "attribution."]

another way between any one of these three institutions and the small business property known as *fonds de commerce*,[33] the cadastral plan, and tipping.[34] This second type of analogy is like that of the two harvesters; the first is like that of electric light and solar light. Finally, there is a different sort of similarity between French, English, private, and administrative laws [*droits*]—which are rules—than there is between any of these and the subjective right [also *droit*]— which is a faculty, a power, resting upon one or other of these rules.

There you have the two sorts of analogy. The *analogy of attribution* consists in attributing the same term to a series of things because of the connection they have with another thing that alone formally possesses, in perfect plentitude, the reality signified by this term. The secondary analogues hang on in tow behind the *first analogue*. An example of this is the analogy signified by the term body: *first analogue*, the biological body; *secondary analogues*, the social body, constituted bodies, a body of doctrine, a body of writing, a body of men. To this first analogy belongs the relation of *droit subjectif* to *droit objectif*, that of the police register and of the cadastral plan to the charitable society by the reason of institution, or the analogy of the two harvesters and of the verb to harvest.

The *analogy of proportionality* consists in attributing the same term to different things because they each possess intrinsically and integrally, though in diverse degrees, the reality signified by this term. Here there is no *first analogue*. All the analogues form a circle around the reason expressed by this term: thus the *ratio entis* is at the center of all beings, the *ratio juris* at the center of all particular systems of objective law, the reason of "common good" at the center of all sociological milieus, the reason of "organized milieu" at the center of all the groups that Hauriou calls "institution-persons"— which play, on the contrary, the role of first analogue in the analogy of simple attribution of Hauriou's "institution-things," and of Cuche's "institution-rules" and "institution-mechanisms."

These two sorts of analogy are linked together in analogical reasoning. The analogy of proportionality occupies the summit; but it begins and ends in the analogy of attribution.[35] Ascent and descent!

Let me explain. The theory of the institution will help, for its

---

33. [G.]

34. [The first group corresponds to Hauriou's "institution-persons"; the second to his "institution-things."]

35. But many analogies of attribution are incapable of developing into analogies of proportionality. In my opinion this is the case with Cuche's four varieties of institutions. Cuche believes, however, that he can reduce them to a common term which they each possess intrinsically and integrally. If so, there would then be an analogy of proportionality.

genesis marvelously illustrates the rhythm of this analogical procedure: this is the advantage of its youth, or at least of its renaissance,
of its unfinished state, in any case. It is a theory in the process of
finding itself, a theory that has not yet emerged from the laboratory,
that has not yet been industrialized, trade-marked, commercialized,
given over to the exploits of publicity. It is still in that heroic age
which is so hard to remember after the age of vulgarization has come,
and then the age of vulgarity!

The theory of the institution proceeds from a first analogue, the
French administrative regime, as Hauriou fashioned it on the
foundation of the jurisprudence of the Conseil d'État.[36] Then a similarity became apparent between this first analogue and a number
of other cases: for instance, the family, the stock corporation, the
labor union; more remotely, the patrimony, the dowry, the *fonds de
commerce;* more remotely still, custom, the cadastral plan, the police
register. These secondary analogues came to stick behind the first,
in a vague disorder—an entirely empirical analogy; an entirely impulsive attribution, but one that "everyone understands."

At this stage, the first analogue takes the place of an analogical
reason. Thus, how many times in social life do we march, not behind
a principle, but behind a man! Yet in the man we are vaguely aware
of the principle. This perception is obscure but gripping. At this
stage, then, the analogical reason, for what concerns us, the institution, gives the impression of a bazaar. The institution is the administrative regime and everything that resembles it, closely or distantly.
And some protest that the notion is not viable because it did not
reach its destination the very day it set off; others want to put it
in a hot-house to precipitate its growth—as if wisdom did not mature
in the open air. Time works with man and for him!

The analogical reason matures in this slow way. Bit by bit it is
purified until it breaks free of the first analogue. The notion of institution breaks free of the administrative regime; it frees itself of all
other modal realizations; it emerges from the mystery that enveloped
it in the series of its analogues. It is the residue of a succession of
purifications that, if carried to the extreme, would leave only the
reason of being—if halted in their course at the ceiling of the juridi-

36. [Cf. Renard, *La philosophie de l'institution,* p. 12: "For a long time now our
familiarity with the very supple jurisprudence of the Conseil d'État has inclined us
to this sort of juristic thought; we know that it was in following the decisional law
of our highest administrative tribunal step by step, and in striving to fashion an
architectual synthesis of it, that Hauriou saw the silhouette of the institution gradually
take shape, as the scholar discovers in his observations the hypothesis that explains
them."]

cal order, they yield the "organized common good"—if interrupted a little higher, at the ceiling of the social order, they render the reason of "milieu," or the "common good." Thus, these particular reasons are steps ascending toward the summit, the reason of being. A moment ago, institutional matter was centered on a first analogue; now it is centered on a *ratio*: this is the transition from empiricism to science, from the analogy of attribution to the analogy of proportionality.

The theory of the institution has made this crucial transition. A host of monographs has concentrated on an institutional interpretation of points of law as specialized as the perpetuity of property,[37] the dowry,[38] the interior juridical life of public administrations,[39] the disciplinary power in private institutions,[40] the institutional origin of real rights,[41] the institutional organization of the power of enterprise, of corporate power and political power,[42] the institutional character of the professional secret[43] and the stock corporation.[44] Even the most strictly technical of these monographs, such as the last, contribute to the growth of the institution at least as efficaciously as the essays of synthesis. Ideas grow like men—imperceptibly, and not without errors; but truth always prevails in the end, and its value is increased by the errors it corrects. Ideas advance like men, step by step, and advancement, as Sertillanges well says, is a series of recovered falls.

Now that the theory of the institution has reached the analogy of proportionality, we can substitute for the initial impulsive analogy of attribution a second, rational, scientific analogy of attribution that discriminates between the analogues that were first piled up pell-mell. This second analogy of attribution eliminates and relegates to the lower bracket of the "equivocal" the analogues that had been wrongly included in the first empirical grouping;[45] it orders to the

37. Marcel Chauffardet, *Le problème de la perpétuité de la propriété* (Paris, 1933).

38. Plaussard, Preface to Pierre Raynaud, *La nature juridique de la dot* (Paris, 1934).

39. Jean Rivero, *Les mesures d'ordre interieur administratives* (Paris, 1934).

40. Alfred Légal and Jean Brèthe de la Grassaye, *Le pouvoir disciplinaire dans les institutions privées: Étude de sociologie juridique* (Paris, 1938).

41. Louis Rigaud, *Le droit réel, histoire et théorie, son origine institutionnelle* (Paris, 1912).

42. Louis Boucraut, *État, corporation et entreprise* (Paris, 1938); cf. Pierre Loyer, *L'entreprise, fondements de la profession* (Paris, 1938).

43. Louis Clement, *Notariat et secret professionnel* (Lyon, 1938).

44. Jean Gaillard, *La société anonyme de demain: La théorie institutionnelle et le fonctionnement de la société anonyme* (Paris, 1932).

45. For example, rights of registration and custom duties as compared with the "reason" of *droit*. For the use of the word *droit* to signify a tax is purely equivocal (*La philosophie de l'institution*, p. 88, n. 1).

analogical reason and, in the same stroke, to one another, those unscathed by this revision; it recovers others that had escaped the first attribution and that this revision saves from oblivion; finally, it divides them all between the two regions: proportionality, which is the plenitude of analogy, and simple attribution, which is only an imperfect analogy. This is the analogical family and its "connections": the members of proportionality all possess the "reason" integrally, just as in a family, the old and the young, the close and the distant, all have the same right to the family name; the members of simple attribution participate in the "reason" only *pro parte qua,* each in his own manner.[46]

Such is the conjunction of the two analogies. In conclusion, I should note that the phases of this analogical procedure are not hermetically sealed off from one another. The spring continues to flow from the mountain, while civil law and private property cross the river to the public domain[47] and to administrative law at the point where the water is supposed to have become navigable, while the prefectoral administration crosses over to the maritime administration at a point supposedly determined by the separation of the river banks from their parallel course, by the salinity of the water, and by the kind of fish found in it. The spring is the first analogy, the empirical analogy, of attribution; the one that "everyone understands," but which philosophy has not yet led to the clarity of the analogy of proportionality.

This is why, in the legislative regime, we must keep a respectful regard not only for custom but also for this "direct evaluation" of concrete data[48] that, under all regimes, is and remains the natural adjunct of what Hauriou called "the administration of law" and which is simply the empiricism of the first analogy of attribution.

Besides, since every analogical reason, except the reason of being, is burdened with restrictions—the two arms of the angle, to continue the image—it is always possible to purify it in order to expand its

46. From the point of view of the institution, the public administration and each of the services of which it is composed are thus kept within the frame of the analogy of proportionality. The installation of a public official remains within the frame of the analogy of attribution: we call it the institution of an *agrégé.* At the time of the Concordat, an agreement by the Holy See to governmental presentations was called a canonical institution, etc. We could just as easily connect by the analogy of attribution the institution of heirship, the institution of contract, etc.

47. *Domaine public,* G. On Hauriou's contribution here, see Sfez, *Essai sur la contribution du Doyen Hauriou au droit administratif français* (Paris, 1966), pp. 156–165, 438–444.

48. *Données concrètes* (not Geny's *donnés*). Renard explains in a note that he adopted the expression in *La valeur de la loi* (Paris, 1928), pp. 37ff.

modal extension. This expansion is limited only by the *ratio entis,* the angle of 360 degrees. Below the *ratio entis,* every analogy of proportionality has a coefficient of relativity.

Here again, the case of the institution beautifully illustrates the movement from analogy of attribution to analogy of proportionality. The reason of "organized common good" has its modal extension restricted to what Hauriou called "institution-persons" and Cuche, "institution-organisms." At this degree of purification Hauriou's "institution-things" and Cuche's "institution-rules" and "institution-mechanisms" are secondary analogues of the "institution-person," according to the law of the analogy of attribution. But in a second phase, "institution-things" (the *fonds de commerce,* for example) can be grouped with "institution-persons" in an analogy of proportionality, under the reason of *universitas,* the "one out of many" . . .

In this entire chapter the institution has appeared only as an illustration of a philosophical method. In the same stroke I have placed it in its atmosphere. Now we can take up the problems it raises.[49]

49. In the following chapter, "Concept or Reality," omitted here, Renard concludes that "institution" is a reality.

3. Institutional Sociology

The central problem of sociology is to find the relationship between the "individual" and the "social," or to put it better, between "personality" and "society," taking this word in its wider generic sense. A priori, I can envisage three types of solutions.

One type would reabsorb society in the individual personality; another would reabsorb the individual personality in society. These two "monstrous" solutions are obviously the simplest and therefore the most alluring to the "geometric mind"[1] that is the bane of sociology. Nothing could be simpler than to reconcile two principles by abolishing one of them. But neither personality nor society can be abolished by an arbitrary negation; and this is the upshot of individualism and "sociologism"—two inadmissible doctrines from a scientific point of view. The first principle of positive science is the submission of the mind to duly verified facts; sociology, over which "sociologism" has no monopoly, prides itself on being a positive science. The facts upon which it rests are complex; it owes them the same docility as do history and the philosophy of history, to which it is closely related.

The third type of solution tries to discern a relationship between the individual and the social while considering both as elemental units: transaction or organization, equality or hierarchy, contract or institution. What is the principle of coordination underlying these pairs of terms? According to what law are the "parts"—which are human persons, that is, reasonable and responsible human beings— ordered on this principle to form a "whole"? And precisely what

ED. NOTE: The contrasting sociological approaches of the three Institutionalists are highlighted in this chapter. Delos stressed sociology's role in observing and grouping social facts. Hauriou accented the post-observation task of theory-making, somewhat in the spirit of Max Weber before him and Talcott Parsons today. Renard here turns his attention to what he calls "the central problem of sociology," the relationship between the individual and the society. If both the individualist position and the Durkheim-Duguit "sociologism" (primacy of the social) are rejected, as Renard feels they must be, the problem, he says, "slips over into the domain of ontology." He sees the institution as furnishing the only acceptable answer.

1. [The phrase is Pascal's.]

are we to understand by a "whole" formed of human persons? Here the sociological problem slips into the domain of ontology; there is no break in continuity between them. Contrary to the monist solutions, the sociological problem is resolved by the two-fold conclusion that the "whole" is crystallized without detriment to the irreducible personality of the "parts"; that, moreover, the "whole" is truly someone or something: not just the total of an addition, the difference of a subtraction, or the resultant of an equilibrium: neither an arithmetic resultant nor a mechanical resultant. And this is why it raises a problem of ontology.

Person and society: to try to find the way these two terms fit together is to raise the question of their respective origins, for ultimately they each derive their claims from their origins. Is society only a projection of human personality, or personality only a projection of the social order—but then only one or the other is "real"? Or must we envisage a vital interaction between them, and see in this interdependence the law, or at least one of the constitutive laws, of human nature? Is society only the product of a free decree of the human will? Or at the other extreme, is it a necessity imposed on man, either from without, by the pressure of the physical universe or of historical contingencies or by a combination of both pressures, or from within, by the impulsion of a blind instinct that puts on the mask of liberty before his psychological consciousness? Or must we even renounce knowing whether we are free, responsible, reasonable "persons," if the consciousness we have of our "self" is the accomplice of our environment in making sport of us? Does not the social fact rather derive from a collaboration of the human will, of the impulses of our nature—a spirituality immersed in flesh—and of the compulsions of the milieu? And on this hypothesis, is it possible to decipher the charter of this collaboration? Can we look for any light on this problem from the theory of the institution? Some have enough confidence in it to have expressed such a hope[2] . . .

THE FUNDAMENTAL HARMONY OF PERSONALITY AND SOCIETY

Society, thought Rousseau, is the *work of men*. Undoubtedly he did not at all believe in the social contract. For him it was only a poetic representation of the social fact:[3] "Man is born free, and he is everywhere in chains . . . How does this change come about? I

---

2. Paul Vignaux, "La théorie de l'institution," *Politique*, 1930, p. 989. [The next section, entitled "The Optimism of the Institutional Doctrine," is not translated.]

3. Cf. Giorgio Del Vecchio, "Des caractères fondamentaux de la philosophie politique de Rousseau," *Revue critique de législation et de jurisprudence*, 1914.

do not know. What can make it legitimate? I think I can resolve this question." The social contract was an explanation in the manner of the theories of rational science, in a sense similar to that of Henri Poincaré.[4] Not that it was a rational explanation! But where the expressive power of rational explanations fails, we have a right to recur to other methods: the sciences and philosophy, theology and even Sacred Scripture do not fail to make use of this right. Rousseau's error is not a monstrous historical error; it would be rather dense to attack him for that! His error is elsewhere.

First of all, it is in taking an *explanation* for a *justification*. The systems of rational science reduce to a synthesis facts *that have first been justified* by observation and experience, in order to derive general laws from them. This systematization and these laws are justified by the facts upon which they are based; they do not justify these facts, nor do they dispense us from justifying them.

Moreover, the explanation proposed by Rousseau explains nothing. For some sort of community must have existed among men *before* they could enter into contractual relations with one another; and in the same way—to underscore the inadequacy of the old conception of international law—a community of nations must exist *before* nations can bind themselves by reciprocal obligations. In a word, law must exist *before* the exchange of consents can produce juridical obligations. The obligatory force of contracts does not come from the contract; and there is no use in tossing about the words "indemonstrable postulate": the indemonstrable postulate is only a vicious circle. A *community of nature* must pre-exist and underlie all the *contractual communities* formed by men. And this is much more than a postulate; it is a demand of reason, therefore of human nature: man is a social animal.

For the positivist school,[5] the origin of society is independent of the will of men. Society is a *natural product*. So it is with human society as such, so also with the particular societies that are constituted in the midst of humanity. The formation of societies is governed by "laws of constancy and sequence like those of day and night, of heat and boiling," as a disciple of Auguste Comte expresses it.[6] And again: "Every society is constituted according to natural

---

4. [Henri Poincaré (1854–1912), noted French mathematician, who discovered the Fuchsian functions.]

5. [Here, as is true generally with the Institutionalists, "positivist school" signifies the sociological positivism deriving from Comte.]

6. Cf. Léon Duguit, *Traité de droit constitutionnel*, 3rd ed. (Paris, 1927), I, 16ff. [See discussion by Ernest Barker, *Principles of Social and Political Theory* (Oxford, 1961), pp. 112–117.]

necessities . . . in some way physical and mechanical."[7] There is no human action, and therefore no moral principle, in the structure of societies: conscious structure, yes! but free, oh no! or at least we know nothing about human liberty's having a role here, and it is impossible to know anything about it, and anyway it really does not matter.

This second social philosophy is shaded in different hues by the German historical school, by Durkheim's French school of sociology, and by Duguit's school of objective law. Whatever nuance it takes, it disregards or minimizes the fundamental difference between human societies and animal societies: reason, liberty, responsibility, in a word, personality; and for the believer, his immortal destiny.

Man is spirit, and the laws that govern him as such derive from his reason, insofar as this reason is a reflection of the divine reason. They do not admit of the absolute formulation that gives physical laws their implacable rigor. Their certitude, says St. Thomas, diminishes the more they are elaborated, first by way of conclusion, then by way of determination,[8] from the initial, and only truly universal, principle that man must do good, that is, he must act according to reason.

Man is also matter, but matter informed by a reasonable soul, forming with it one single being, one single nature: and therefore also subject, by reverberation, to the laws of reason. If man were just a reasonable soul housed in an animal body; if human nature were just a monstrous coupling of two opposed natures each of which would follow its own law . . . if there were nothing more than a contact between them, they could not have a common government. But such a hypothesis does not accord with reality, and if you reflect upon it, it is inconceivable. We do not house the spirit, precisely because it is spirit, but the spirit penetrates bodies and subjects them to itself and assimilates them. This is what makes a man.[9] And this is why our bodies are not only ruled by the laws that they have in common with animals, but also by the laws of the soul: laws that are imperative, but not constraining. The soul governs the body, not

7. Duguit, Traité, pp. 67ff.
8. Aquinas, Summa Theologiae, I II, q. 94, a. 4.
9. "People are often surprised to see that Spinoza brings the body into the definition of things that are in appearance most spiritual. St. Thomas does this quite as much as Spinoza, but no one seems to recognize it. In such instances, St Thomas says 'soul' but he means the soul that gives form, the living soul, the soul as soul and not as mind. His general doctrine holds that the soul thus understood includes the body in its definition and in its functioning, that it is the body itself in act." A. D. Sertillanges, Les grandes thèses de la philosophie thomiste (Paris, 1929) p. 190.

by physiological reflexes, but by the moral law, that is, by the magisterium of its reason and by the judgment of its conscience. In short, on the human level, there is a break in the hierarchy of beings and a reversal of values between the individual and the social. Beneath humanity, the good of the individual is ordered to the good of the species. In the human order, the society is ordered to the good of the person. Society—like the person called moral—is only a collective manner of acting and being[10] by the individuals who compose it. This fact does not prevent it from being a distinct juridical subject: distinct yet attached; distinguished by a process like that called decentralization in public law: *decentralization* is a *dispersion* from and around a "center" that remains; every *society* is a *convergence* from personalities that remain. The juridical subject born of this convergence does not separate from its creators as does the human being: its generation is continuous. It is simply "the associates as associated";[11] and the associates as associated is quite a different thing from the associates as separated by their individual personalities.

Maurras sees society as a *superimposition of the work of men on the product of nature.* In his doctrine, the social structure would be broken up into two periods: the *constitution* of a society—especially that of the city and the nation—would be a purely natural phenomenon: this is the meaning of the famous *Politics first!* In the second period human activity would intervene—and with it the moral

10. The social being is produced by social action. Cf. Renard, *La philosophie de l'institution,* pp. 144, 154.

11. With just a shade of a difference, the controversy that I had on this matter with Delos (see my article in *Bulletin thomiste,* 1929, pp. 563ff, on his fine book *La société internationale et les principes du droit public* (Paris, 1929); and my *La théorie de l'institution,* pp. 188, n. 1) is definitely closed by his very generous article (Delos, "The Theory of the Institution" [translated above]). "The social body is not a 'substance,'" writes Delos; "it consists in a 'relationship' between the subsisting subjects that it presupposes." With René Clemens, I have substituted "quality" for "relationship" (*La philosophie de l'institution,* pp. 146ff). It remains that this social reality is only a collective "manner of being," an "accident." [Renard agrees here with Delos' distinction, made in "The Object of Sociology, above, between the *interindividual* relationship of psychology—the relationship from Peter to Paul—and the exterior *societal relationship*—the relationship from Peter and Paul to a common object (real or ideal) and consequently from Peter to Paul. The second relationship is the only one that becomes objective, the only one that is a social reality. This reality, Delos continues, reaches personality, a real and true personality, when the convergence is not simply de facto (such as in an ethnic group) but conscious and free; then it possesses ipso facto personality from the sociological point of view and calls for a recognition of this personality from the juridical point of view, provided that it meets the proper requirements of juridical technique. On "stylization," cf. Hauriou and Renard, above.]

law—to elevate to the level of *civilization* the society previously constituted by a play of purely mechanical forces. This is simply a transposition of the Cartesian philosophy of the union of soul and body: the spiritual factor has no part in the construction of the boat, but once the boat is constructed, it takes over the helm.

This is an error! The soul does not dwell in a previously constituted body, nor civilization in a pre-existent society. Civilization is the development of a seed that is contained in social life, but that cannot grow without the work of the farmer. From the most primitive society to the most highly developed civilization there is no break:[12] there you have institutional sociology.[13] Society cannot be divided into two successive periods, the era of social physics and the era of moral law.

Nature and man collaborate in every stage of the development of societies, and this interaction has as much diversity as that of the body and soul in human activity. Or, to follow the analogy of the social and supernatural orders, this interaction is almost as mysterious and no less real and fruitful than that of grace and liberty.

There is no spiritual life for man, and no spiritual act, that is not rooted in his intellectual life and also connected in some way with his bodily dispositions and attitudes, and in exchange, which does not have the chance to reflect upon itself. With still more reason, no work is purely intellectual, or purely manual, and this is why manual work cannot be treated as a mere "thing."[14]

Man, then, is ever present at the origin of societies, and never is he alone. Man acts everywhere, and ever under the pressure of his social nature and his historical and cultural environment. It is an endless coming-and-going; or better, a single rhythm in two beats, like the rhythm of respiration or the heart. With man, liberty is everywhere, but with stimuli to put it into motion. For liberty does

---

12. Cf. Jacques Maritain, "Religion et culture," *Collection des "Questions disputées"* (Paris, 1930).

13. Hauriou was frank to say that the theory of the institution aligns itself with the thomistic conception of the relationship of soul and body. We may call this institutional theory thomistic if we mean, not a thomism that has been frozen in the formulas of the *Summa Theologiae*, but the progressive thomism of which Sertillanges writes that a great doctrine is not identical with its "transitory embodiments," and which he regrets has not reached the point of a crisis like the Galilean crisis, the Cartesian crisis, the Kantian crisis that have already occurred, like the Bergsonian crisis he is hoping for today, and like others he expects in the future. A. D. Sertillanges, "Saint Thomas d'Aquin," *Collection des grands coeurs* (Paris, 1931), pp. 207, 217.

14. Cf. my article "Le sens chrétien du travail intellectuel," *La vie spirituelle*, May 1, 1937, pp. 129ff.

not tear itself away from the torpor of indifference to put itself in
motion; it chooses among competing invitations. With liberty, reason
is everywhere: reason which is its code, reason which is the natural
energy of the human species, *diffusa in omnes, constans, sempi-
terna*,[15] just as gravity is the natural energy of bodies, and growth
the natural energy of living things. But reason does not operate in
a vacuum either. It is precisely because the reasonable activity of
man is involved in a natural order that multiplies its effects—as a
commutator circuit spreads light throughout an entire town—that
man has the power, not only to bind himself by contracts, but also
to bind future generations by means of his foundations. We have
called this a generation: juridical generation, like biological generation, is a work of the human will, whose effect surpasses the power
of the will, because in doing this work, the will harnesses the energies
of nature.

The analogy of generation is no more out of place here than in
epistemology and theology where it is currently in use. The classic
name for it is organization. The institution is nothing other than
Vitoria's "moral organism."[16] Generation or organization, these two
terms borrowed from biology are open to the same abuse—and why
not to the same jokes?—as the term moral personality in its extension
to collectivities. Much more, in fact, for the moral person has some
of the fundamental characteristics of personality—and this is what
justifies the designation—while the analogy of "moral organism" and
generation is scarcely more than a metaphor. This is why I have
preferred other labels: foundation, institution. Joined to personality,
the epithet "moral" is just an explanation; joined to organism, it is
really a correction. All in all, the value of the expression is chiefly
practical: it is hardly more than a manner of speaking to accentuate
the contrast between obligation and institution. The "moral organism" is the institution in image.

The institution is an organism, unlike obligation, which is only
a relation. But unlike the organism, the institution is not a subsistent
being; it is only, as Hauriou said, a "communion."[17]

Like the organism, the institution integrates its members into a
whole, but not so perfectly that their *self* does not remain intact and

15. Cicero, *De re publica*, III, 17, in Lactantius, *Institutes*, VI, 8.
16. The "moral organism" had been taken up by Suarez, but with a deformation,
according to Delos (review of Rommen, *Die Staatslehre des Fr. Suarez*, in *Bulletin
thomiste*, pp. 490ff). Vitoria's doctrine serves as a basis for the theory of the state
presented by Delos in his *La société internationale*.
17. See Hauriou, *La théorie de l'institution*, above.]

even gain from this integration. And this is why its members remain subjects whose relationships among themselves and with the institution are governed by justice: justice, the virtue that is practiced *ad alterum;* an integration mingled with otherness.

Like the organism, the institution is differentiated, and according to the degree of its integration, each one of its organs, animated by the institutional life, operates in behalf of the institution and under its responsibility. The institution is in each one of its organs and acts as a unit by means of each one of them, just as the human or animal organism sees by its two eyes, walks by its feet or paws, is nourished by the work of its digestive system.

But institutional life does not move itself; it is moved, and the institution is only an "apparatus" that groups many moving forces around a common center. The differentiation of its organs is not organic but hierarchical.

It would be easy to pursue this idea. The institution is as distant from the organism as the "juridical" is from the "biological," as one kingdom is from another. Organism, yes! but not biological, only "moral." Organism—I speak as best I can: the ambitions and power of apprehension of the human mind do not cease where concepts fail. Conceptual perception is the safe way—then comes analogy, more risky but still legitimate!—then allegory and imagery, more risky yet but still legitimate! The human mind makes use of all its resources to touch reality. This is its duty.

THE ANALOGICAL STRUCTURE OF THE JURIDICAL ORDER

The higher you go up the scale of the sciences, and the higher you go within each science, the more the reality you are pursuing escapes the grasp of concepts. Consequently, it becomes progressively more necessary to use other procedures (call them expedients if you wish) that can arouse an intuition of the indefinable: and so the more we call upon emotion to help the understanding, and the more knowledge becomes an art.[18] Hauriou liked to say that law is not a lump of dough rolled out flat on a board, it is a flaky pastry; in law there

18. Cf. "Où chercher le réel?" in *Cahiers de la nouvelle journée,* 5 (1926); compare my books *Le droit, la logique et le bon sens* (Paris, 1925), part iii, "Le casuisme," pp. 337ff, and *La valeur de la loi* (Paris, 1928), conference ii, "Le droit naturel à contenu progressif," pp. 36ff, and conference iii, "La notion soviétique du droit et la nôtre," pp. 51ff. Compare the theme of the "individual rule of law," Renard, *La théorie de l'institution,* p. 105, n. 1.

are strata superimposed upon one another;[19] the "juridical ordering" takes form "by degrees"; it is "plural" in the terminology of others.[20] And we can envisage several levels.

First that of the police power[21] and justice. Police justice is a "low grade" justice—taking this expression in a good sense—and we may include within police justice by analogy: in civil procedure and in Roman law, possession and the attribution of the *vindiciae*;[22] in administrative practice and administrative litigation, official execution at the risk of the administration;[23] and on the plane of public records, the written judgments given by the lower courts[24] (with the reservation of a re-examination on the plane of responsibility by

19. See, for example, Maurice Hauriou, "Police juridique et fond du droit," *Revue trimestrielle de droit civil,* 1926, pp. 265ff.

20. Roger Bonnard, "L'origine de l'ordonnancement juridique," in *Mélanges Maurice Hauriou* (Paris, 1929), pp. 31ff; Carré de Malberg, *Confrontation de la théorie de la formation du droit par degrés avec les idées et les institutions consacrées par le droit positif français relativement à sa formation* (Paris, 1933); Georges Gurvitch, *L'expérience juridique et la philosophie pluraliste du droit* (Paris, 1935). A *privilege,* at least when it is granted to a collectivity, is only a manner of introducing pluralism (or the institutional conception of law) by way of "correction" into the supposedly homogeneous or univocal regime of the juridical order; it is this regime that is the fabrication. Under the name of privilege, it is pluralism or the institutional conception of law that Thomas Philippe very happily justifies by the necessity of reconciling the two antithetical principles of equality and liberty. "Privilege is not a dispensation from the law, still less a tolerance. It is very properly a special law for particular cases of special significance. It is then commanded by the common good and social in character. Its end is to resolve the eternal antinomy between equality and liberty. Equality is essentially quantitative; liberty, on the other hand, is qualitative. Liberty is a true perfection, and by virtue of this, it has a calling, in a certain sense, to grow unceasingly (only the saints possess the liberty of the children of God). Equality, on the contrary, is essentially relative: it marks a stage, more exactly a point of departure, that should be surpassed." Philippe, "La predestination, mystère de dilection divine," *Études et documents,* in *La vie spirituelle,* Dec. 1, 1938, pp. 132ff.

21. [*La police.* G.]

22. [Phase of the *legis actio sacramenti* (the *sacramentum* was a deposit or pledge of money or property as security for the outcome of the litigation) in Roman law in which the praetor awards possession of the thing in dispute to one of the parties *pendente lite,* against his furnishing security for its restoration if he fails to establish his claim in the main suit. See R. W. Lee, *The Elements of Roman Law,* 4th ed. (London, 1956), p. 424.]

23. [In a limited set of situations the Administration may enforce an official's decision against a protesting citizen even though an appeal against that decision is pending at the Conseil d'État (*recours pour excès de pouvoir*). In such an event, however, the execution of the *décision executoire* is "at the risk of the Administration," and if the *recours* is granted, damages resulting from the enforcement will be awarded against the Administration. See Georges Vedel, *Droit administratif,* 3rd ed. (Paris, 1964), pp. 169-172; C. E. Zimmermann, S.1905.3.17 (note Hauriou).]

24. [*Les juridictions comptables,* e.g., the Cour des Comptes. See Hauriou's note to C. E. *Peytard,* S.1895.3.728, *Notes d'arrêts,* III, 728: "Accountability is only a species of [supervision of] records. The judge of accounts has only one mission: to see if the records are accurate."]

competent higher tribunals). Police power, administrative regulation, public accountability: here is the triumph of clear-cut order; but it is only the first measure of the juridical order; justice follows behind, *piano, sano.*

And then we come to the level of law that is parodied in the sally, "Depending on whether you are powerful or poor . . ." This reflection upon the integrity of the judge in distinguishing between law and nonlaw is a parody and an unjust insult. But everything is not finished when the judge has pronounced the sentence. It still has to be executed.[25] In fact, the ways of enforced execution under the Code of Procedure—the varieties of distraint—function well only between ordinary people. Our methods of execution are often useless against the great. In law, they are not available against public administrations.[26] In international relations, it is sheer pleasantry to talk about war as a sanction of law. And in the relations of the spiritual power and the temporal power, there is no proportion between the forces they each have at their disposal. And yet ordinary people contract and litigate with great lords, and great lords among themselves, and subjects with the administration, and administrations among themselves. And they deliberate at Geneva and argue at the Hague, and treaties are passed in all ages, and disappointments have not shaken the faith of diplomacy in concordats. The reason then is that the guarantee of an enforced execution is replaced by another guarantee: the faith and confidence of one party in a voluntary execution on the part of the other, out of concern for his own credit. People who live in high places can see further than those who live in the plains; they can more easily understand the wrong that one does oneself in betraying the trust of another.

It is at these higher stages that conceptual abstraction is least effective. We need only compare the jurisprudence of the Cour de Cassation with the "jurisprudential politics"[27] of the Conseil d'État, which is a triumph of analogical reasoning. Compare a treatise of international law with any treatise of civil or even administrative law, and count the number of pages each devotes to abstract dialectical argument and to an examination of the cases, not to mention the great role of fictions and of imagery in the international law book . . .

25. Cf. the preface [by Renard] to the thesis of Bernard Geny, *La collaboration des particuliers avec l'Administration* (Paris, 1930), pp. 19ff.
26. André Fayolle, *Peut-on contraindre l'Administration à executer les decisions de justice?* (Paris, 1926).
27. [The phrase is Hauriou's. See his note to C. E. *Chabot*, S.1904.3.1, *Notes d'arrêts*, I, 389.]

And lastly, there is a third level. At its lowest rung are the "obligatory" relations: contracts, *voisinage*,[28] reparation for damages, compensation for unjust enrichment. Of all the material of civil, administrative, and even international law, this is the easiest to handle; the choice field of conceptual elaboration; the point of most perfect crystallization. Above it lies the institution.

Would the ideal be for juridical science to stay on this first rung? I do not think so. The ideal of a science is not to mutilate its object; and to exclude everything from juridical science but obligations is to mutilate its object. Attempts have already been made. Did not someone, for example, try to analyze the partition of an inheritance into a series of exchanges by which each of the partitioners would cede to the others his undivided interest in the goods that would go to them, in return for their undivided interest in the goods that would come to him? Thus, the originality of the operation vanishes; partition is reabsorbed by sale. This theory is built *in abstracto* without regard for the distinct purpose of partition, and the article[29] that calls it a purely "declarative" act—and therefore not transferring anything—is considered to be an utilitarian expedient contrived to ward off certain awkward consequences of the theory. The theory has been rejected in favor of partition; I must certainly reject it in favor of the "institution."

The "institution" is, of all juridical notions, the one that most staunchly resists conceptual abstraction. From this point of view, it belongs on the highest rung of the juridical ladder. Instinctively, the ancients slashed it up into obligations, and the institution collapsed like an organism given over to vivisection. Its only chance of survival was the favor of the prince, the *deus ex machina* whose creative power brought beings and even persons out of nothingness. What a deplorable mentality that denies everything beyond the power of its customary means of knowledge! Such a narrow juridical outlook is like the astronomer who would do away with the stars that do not come into the field of his telescope or that upset his calculations. It is time that jurists adjust their glasses and their calculations to the institutional fact. The metaphor or remote analogy— as you wish—of moral organism has revived the institution; perhaps the institution will help revive moral personality.

28. [Literally, "neighborhood." See G.]
29. [*Code civil*, arts, 815, 819, and Law of Dec. 15, 1921. See Appendix.]

SOCIOLOGY, METAPHYSICS, AND POLITICAL ART

I could end this chapter on institutional sociology here. But juridical sociology and juridical philosophy are so closely connected that I think I should point out the reverberation of the former in the latter, even though a later chapter will be devoted to the institutional philosophy of law.

From the point of view of positive law, the institution is just one fragment of the juridical order. The theory of the institution aims at making a place for a slice of juridical reality that breaks out of the frame of obligation; better yet, it aims at recognizing this place[30]—the place of the "social," beyond the interindividual. This is also the point of view, equally positive, of juridical sociology. But with sociology the field of observation expands; it becomes apparent—as Delos has well remarked—that the new "part" reacts upon the "whole"; the institution casts its reflection upon obligation, and also upon the sources of obligation, contract and responsibility, upon property and inheritance, upon the juridical structure of marriage, the home, the family; for everything goes together. Thus, the institution has an influence on the whole juridical order; it changes its physiognomy; a new philosophy of law is "under rock."

If we disregard the varieties of juridical positivism (a self-contradictory term),[31] we can assert that there are in our time only *two essential juridical philosophies:* the old jacobin philosophy, which is also the unconscious philosophy of the jurists who do not philosophize, and institutional philosophy, which is not young, and in which is recognized a certain popular common sense that puts no more stock in juridical science than in philosophy, and whose self-confidence cannot be shaken by all the philosophical and juridical demonstrations in the world.

These two philosophies are based upon *two metaphysics of personality:* (1) the personality of man as it would be *if* it could exist outside of social interdependences and *if* these interdependences had

30. I have already said that the institution is more than a concept for recapturing a "given" that escapes the old-time conceptualism; it is the very reality that is enveloped by this concept.

31. Positivism is inevitably the negation of justice. For justice is a criterion for judging facts; it must therefore be outside and above them. A fact is as incapable of engendering justice as a contract is incapable of justifying the force of obligation of contract. It is the same vicious circle. Duguit has been told this twenty times; and his learned disciple, our colleague, René Reglade, has very openly accepted it, abandoning the thought of his master on this point. Reglade, "Perspectives qu'ouvrent les doctrines objectivistes de doyen Duguit pour un renouvellement de l'étude du droit international public," *Revue de droit international,* 1930, pp. 381ff.

no other origin than the juridical acts to which it seemed expedient to commit himself; and (2) the personality of man as it is. Man as man is just an abstraction that never existed and never can exist. This man is already a social being: the nonsocial man is no more a person than he is a man, no more than a man without a body is a man; it is non-sense. Every man that exists is then necessarily marked by concrete affiliations that are exclusive of other affiliations—by a social state—by a "moral personality," in the sense Pufendorf[32] gave to this term.

The two philosophies of law and the two metaphysics of personality coincide with *two political theories*. The first is really a mystique of the state: the Kelsenian assimilation of law and the state[33] and all the "totalitarianisms" that have appeared in recent times on the face of our old earth[34] are only a revival of a jacobinism that does not date from the Revolution but from the legists: its socialist or socializing phase is in direct continuity with its individualist and liberal phase. This arbitrary compression of the "social" into the "sovereign" is what institutional philosophy opposes. Institutional philosophy corresponds to the more positive, the more natural and spontaneous of the political theories. It liberates the "social"; it lets it relax and launch out according to its own energy, until it rejoins the "individual" and renews with it, in personality, the marriage of inclination that was so violently broken up by the arbitrary will of the philosophers. Once again, the institution is the minister, not of this reconciliation, but of this restoration—the restoration of the true and authentic "moral personality" as both the social qualification of the individual person and the juridical personification of the social being.

The juridical order is no longer a transaction between two contradictory principles. Law is no longer a network of restrictions upon natural liberties, necessary to their coexistence; it is a direction, an orientation. These two notions of law could be illustrated by two images: one, a game room where, two by two or four by four, men play cards without any concern for the other tables of players; the other, a dance floor where all the couples are carried away by the captivating (if not harmonious) rhythm of the same jazz. To put it

---

32. [Samuel Pufendorf (1632–1694), historian and jurist, was professor at Heidelberg and Lund, historiographer at Stockholm and Berlin. He was author of *De jure naturae et gentium* (1672), among many other works on jurisprudence and natural law.]

33. [Cf. Hans Kelsen, *General Theory of Law and State* (Cambridge, 1949), p. xvi.]

34. "Everything in the state; nothing outside the state; nothing against the state," is how Mussolini defines it. Cf. Le Fur, *Le Saint-Siège et le droit des gens* (Paris, 1930), p. 91, n. 1.

more seriously, the jacobin conception envisages only *external relationships* among men; the institutional conception sees an *interpenetration* of human activities in the harmony of the common good; on the one side, rights *in competition,* on the other, rights *in communion.*

This fundamental unification—I have not said confusion or identification—that has overridden the antagonism between the "individual" and the "social" is a victory of juridical pluralism, for this pluralism re-establishes the note of union. Thus institutional philosophy explains, first, the rupture of uniformity—in philosophical language, univocity—in positive law that I considered a few pages ago, a rupture that would be more aptly called a *decentralization of law:* for if it posits the multiplicity of juridical systems, it joins to this their coordination and their reconstitution into syntheses that ascend to the law of the two "perfect societies" and, from there, branch off into the high atmosphere of intersovereign law, of which international law is simply the largest piece. It explains, similarly, the conception of natural law that I have called progressive and that could be called the *decentralization of natural law* by reason of its determination in the diverse historical milieus and in the diverse regimes of positive law adapted to these milieus, and for which I claim the patronage of medieval philosophy: *diversificantur ea quae sunt de jure naturali secundum diversos status et conditiones hominum.*[35]

And to end—since I have pointed out the political affinities of the two juridical philosophies—the jacobin conception is nationalist: law is a piece of equipment of national defense. The institutional conception makes law a way of communication and exchanges among peoples: always unity in multiplicity. Here again is seen its Christian spirit.

35. Aquinas, *Summa Theologiae,* III, q. 41, a.1, ad 3.

4. The Institutional Conception of Law

The juridical order is differentiated. At the summit are two "perfect" juridical systems: the law of the religious society and the law of the political society; beneath are the unlimited variety of "imperfect"[1] juridical systems, constituted to rule the internal life of the institutions established on these two fundamental societies, either inside one or the other, or for the purpose of directing their external relations. This is an analogy of attribution: two "first analogues" that, alone, have the full "reason of law," in consequence of the full otherness—at least juridical—of the subjects whose relationships they rule: *justum secundum perfectam rationem justitiae,* says St. Thomas;[2] and a host of "secondary analogues," participating in this "reason" only *pro parte qua,* in which law and nonlaw are mixed in proportion as otherness and community are mixed within the institutions they govern. This is the institutional or analogical conception of law.

Not long ago some jurists had the gall to revive the preposterous double error that juridical science depends upon the discipline of the so-called exact sciences and that Roman law owes its perfection and immortality to the rigor with which it conformed to this discipline. And they added—in a publication of the Pontifical Institute *utriusque juris*—that Christian influences have weakened this juridical order. I have said elsewhere what I think of these bold statements: like the science of the legists in the *grand siècle,* they are part and parcel of the political system that has been given the name (newer than the thing) of "totalitarianism."[3]

If the science of law is a mathematical science and if Roman law is a "triumph" of mathematics, the conclusion is inescapable: they

---

1. ["Perfect" and "imperfect" are used here in the scholastic sense of "complete" or self-sufficient and "incomplete."]

2. Aquinas, *Summa Theologiae,* II II, q. 57, a. 4, ad 2 and 3.

3. [Renard criticized this view in his "Droit romain et pensée chrétienne," *Revue des sciences philosophiques et theologiques,* 1938, which he quotes here.]

are both diametrically opposed to Christian thought; they are even frankly inhuman . . . But another language is spoken at the Vatican: justice is incapable of organizing social life; the social order is founded upon collaboration; and collaboration can exist only on the basis of charity.[4]

Law is a moral science; and, as Aristotle well said, all things do not admit of the same degree of certitude; we must not look for more certitude in any science than its object allows.[5] As for Roman law, its entirely relative perfection was in its flexible adaptations in time and space to the demands of a governmental art that was marvelously served by its magistrates.

There is a Christian social order,[6] but Roman law did not invent it—any more than Aristotle invented Christian philosophy—for a very good reason! What remained to be seen was whether or not Roman law, like Greek philosophy, was capable of "conversion." The School of Bologna attempted such a conversion in the Middle Ages, at the same time that St. Thomas was boldly venturing upon his Christian purification of Aristotle's work. The Renaissance revived paganism on both terrains. Today we are witnessing a resurgence of thomism and the coming of "social law" and the institution . . .

The institution features three juridical truths that were denied by the Romanist interpretation of the Revolutionary doctrines of absolutism and jacobinism, and which, taken together, constitute "the institutional conception of law". First of all, as Le Fur saw very clearly, the institutional conception of law is a reaction against voluntarism . . . The second truth, complementary to the first, is that the juridical order is the basis of power: power is not a caprice that fashions and destroys, and submits or exempts itself, without having any account to render other than the declaration of its "good pleasure." Every power is ordered to an end; every social power is ordered to a common good of a social character; every social good implies a community that this power informs.

---

4. I must underscore the essential role that charity plays in *droit social*. This thesis is confirmed by Pius XI in his encyclical *Quadragesimo Anno*; but I shall show that, long before, it was the center of St. Thomas's thought (see *La philosophie de l'institution*, ch. viii, "Affinités theologiques"). Justice (*droit*) is not charity; but justice, even social justice, does not suffice. Justice is fully achieved only with the help of charity. The juridical order is neither opposed nor juxtaposed to charity; it is raised up in an atmosphere to charity, outside of which there is no peace to be hoped for.

5. "Certitudo non est similiter quaerenda in omnibus, sed in unaquaque materia secundum proprium modum" (in 1 *Ethic.*, ch. 3, circa princ. et ch. 7, circa fin.; cf. Aquinas, *Summa Theologiae*, II II, q. 47, a. 9, ad 2).

6. See appendix on "L'ordre social chrétien," *La philosophie de l'institution*, pp. 323–338.

There is more to law than rights; there are also powers. And if, from the metaphysical point of view, rights are pre-eminent because society is for the human person and not the human person for society, from the social point of view power stands out because society helps the person to develop and to attain his end only by the exercise of power.

In reality, law is a synthesis of rights and power. And the institutional conception marks a correction of the error committed by jacobin individualism in billeting them in separate camps, power in sovereignty and rights in the relations of private life.

For jacobin individualism, all power is in the state, or comes by delegation from the state, within whose hands it is absolute: *non est potestas nisi a Caesare*. The jacobins gave no .scandal in their day by teaching that paternal power is exercised in the name of the state! Aside from political power, they recognized only individual rights. The two were equally absolute, and their conflict with one another was the sole assurance of order under the regulation of the state. An insuperable wall was raised between rights and power: to this wall the equally water-tight separation of private law and public law obviously corresponded—public law being the poor relative who fits in as best he can. But is this truly law, this governmental and administrative machinery in which the abundance of regulations does not succeed in disguising the indigence of the rule and seems to serve only the purpose of offering excuses for whatever solutions political expediency may suggest? Is this truly law, when obscurity and instability join forces to legitimize the enterprises of power and the mutual revenges of political parties? When, rightly or wrongly, necessity makes the law or in any event prevails over the law, and when a preoccupation for the particular and concrete case prevails over the religion of principles and the rigor of deductions, and a practical sense of "prudence" over dialectical virtuosity? And when justice itself has no blindfold and holds a tilted scale? Is this really law? Where are the beautiful avenues of private law? Is this public law, the law of power? the most miserable of the "analogues" of private law—and so very distant from it! In a word, (objective) law is the harmonization of rights; power a paid servant—something like the policeman paid by taxpayers to wave his white stick.

There is a logic immanent in things. Extremes attract one another: the exaltation of individual rights in private law evoked an exaltation of political power and of the *raison d'état*. Conform to private law or renounce all pretention of constituting a true juridical system: this is the dilemma public law had to face. Laferrière[7] found an expedient after the fashion of King Solomon: he cut governmental and administrative activity into two sections: one for authority, the other for "management." This solution was a triumph of conceptual dichotomy. He was not aware that an organism cannot be cut like a piece of cloth; that organic activity consolidates all the organs that participate in it; that authority is attenuated in public management as an analogical reason in the series of its analogues; that the police power is encysted in the public services, as Hauriou said. Laferrière and his followers did not have a doctrine of the relations of "whole" and "parts." Their classification was entirely temporary, like the artificial classifications scholars tarry with while waiting for new lights.

The pendulum swings, then, between two absolutisms, between which there may be compromises, but never any organization: the divinization of the human person and his inalienable rights; the divinization of the state and its sovereign powers.

A radical error! There is no absolute right, no absolute power except in God; and this is why God is the keystone of the concord of human rights and human powers.

Under God, every power and every right is relative; and for this reason right and power always intersect. Power is a faculty whose exercise is ordered to a function of the social good; but it bestows a right upon the one in whom it is invested. For example, the public responsibilities attached to the "status" of government officials and the personal advantages that they draw from it. Reciprocally, there is an element of power in every right, which means that rights are not only burdened with social responsibilities but ordered, at least secondarily, to some portion of the "common good." St. Thomas boldly defines property as a *potestas*; the right of a creditor is held

7. *Édouard Louis Julien Laferrière*, (1841–1910), was the pioneer, immediately preceding Hauriou, in presenting *droit administratif* in an organized manner. The classical appraisal of Laferrière is that of Gaston Jèze: "Think of what French *droit administratif* was like before Laferrière wrote his *Traité de la jurisdiction administratif*, 1st ed. (Paris, 1886). Without any exaggeration, it was chaos, a more or less confused heap of incoherent, arbitrary, often unjustified and unjustifiable solutions. Finally Laferrière came [cf. Boileau's "Enfin Malherbe vint"], and he was the first in France to bring order and method to administrative law, to explain the solutions of practice. His immense merit was that he looked for the general ideas, the general principles that are behind all solutions. His serious fault was that he justified principles instead of presenting an impartial explanation of them." Gaston Jèze, *Les principes généraux du droit administratif* (Paris, 1904), pp. 383–384. By common consent, Hauriou was the "second" to Laferrière's "first," and one does not find the criticism of Jèze's final sentence leveled against Hauriou.

in check by the machinery of bankruptcy. Every juridical situation has indeed the double aspect of right and power. There are not two "genera" to be distinguished here; there is an "analogical" series in which the two terms simply have the value of a "reason"—as the philosophers say—abstracted from the concrete juridical titles in which it is "modified."

Since the second Romanist invasion, the domain of power had been more and more narrowly circumscribed. It was natural enough, then, that the theory of the institution first emerged from the public administration, in order next to spread to the regions of the juridical order that had been abandoned to the exclusivism of individual rights. There was no logical necessity in this; it was simply an incident in the history of the science of law. The institution consolidates, in the juridical order, the primacy of the point of view of power. In *La théorie de l'institution*[8] I established the correspondence between the notions of institution and authority.

The third truth included in the institutional conception of law is the differentiation of the juridical order. Some call it "pluralism." "Differentiation" or "institutional" or "analogical conception" are better because a simple plurality could be a disorder. Here is what I mean by that.

Jus sive justum, writes St. Thomas, *dicitur per commensurationem ad alterum:*[9] absolute or at least relative otherness is necessary to establish a juridical relationship. Therefore, only to the extent that institutional incorporation lets some otherness subsist among its members, will they be able to engage in a juridical relationship;[10] and this extent varies with institutions and with the positions held in each of them by the diverse members.

This condition is necessary, but not sufficient! Otherness looks toward justice. Justice is a moral virtue; this virtue is the foundation of law, but it is not law. We have considered the relationship of the juridical order with the social order; now we shall look at its relationship with the moral order. It plunges into both of them, but absorbs neither one . . .

---

8. Cf. Renard, *La théorie de l'institution,* pp. 310ff.

9. Aquinas, *Summa Theologiae,* II II, q. 57, a. 4.

10. Aquinas, *Summa Theologiae,* II II, q. 57, a. 4, ad 2: "Filius, in quantum filius, est aliquid patris, et similis servus, in quantum servus, est aliquid domini. Uterque tamen, prout consideratur ut quidam homo est aliquid secundum se subsistens ab aliis distinctum. Et ideo, in quantum uterque est homo aliquo modo, ad eos est justitia. Et proper hoc etiam aliquae leges dantur de his quae sunt patris ad filium et domini ad servum. Sed in quantum est aliquid alterius, secundum hoc deficit ibi perfecta ratio justi vel juris."

In the moral order, as in the social order, law holds a place comparable to that of a skeleton in an animal organism. But a comparison is never an adequate explanation. We must find out what the "reason of law" consists in and how its analogical modes behave.[11]

I use the terms law (*droit*) and juridical order interchangeably; this is because the word law first calls to mind the idea of order, and the end of order is to lead the diverse to unity without absorbing the diversity in the unity, to order the parts within a whole without destroying them. This is what St. Thomas meant by tracing the etymology of the word *jus* to the verb *justari*.[12] This is what the well-known adage tells us: *ubi societas, ibi jus; ubi ius, ibi societas.* And this is what establishes the essentially institutional character of law. Law is the "informing" principle of society: every society, therefore, must have its law. A society without law would be an unorganized society, which is nonsense. Order is the first characteristic of the "reason of law."

The juridical order—here is the second characteristic—is instituted among persons: personality must come out of this process intact. Such will be the case if the juridical rule has an imperative character and if its *imperium* is effectively ordered to the common good. The juridical rule has the precise objective of providing for this adjustment; in fact, it is juridical only insofar as it realizes this program, for the common good that is not shared by the members of the community is no longer a common good:[13] *omnis lex ordinatur ad hominum salutem, et in tantum obtinet vim et rationem legis; secundum vero quod ab hoc deficit, virtutem obligandi non habet.*[14] Neither the deficiencies inherent in every general rule, nor the blunders of the legislator, nor the rebellions of personality against its own law, prove anything against the nature of this law or against the nature of the juridical order. Perfection, they say, is not of this world, nor is perfect health, in the body, in manners, or in positive law. This is why the moralists, after declaring that an unjust law is not a law, narrowly limit the citizens' right to revolt, and after assigning to the legislators the noble task of raising the moral standards of their subjects, dissuade them from pursuing the best to the detriment

11. Again I am using fragments of my article "De la théorie de l'institution à la conception analogique du droit," *Archives de philosophie du droit*, 1935, pp. 81ff.

12. Aquinas, *Summa Theologiae*, II II, q. 57, a. 1.

13. Aquinas, *Commentary on Aristotle's Metaphysics*, book XII, 1. 12; cf. *Summa Theologiae* II II, q. 58, a. 5: "Qui servit alicui communitati, servit omnibus sub communitate illa continentur."

14. Aquinas, *Summa Theologiae*, I II, q. 96, a. 6; q. 96, a. 4; q. 92, a. 1.

of the good[15] . . . But this second characteristic, in which the juridical order departs from the physical order and joins the moral order, must be completed by a third.

Law has a special manner of providing for order, which is not that of moral science, and which limits its own jurisdiction accordingly. The branching off of the moral order into the juridical and social orders results from the fact that the human spirit is immersed in matter. Purely spiritual substances are free from the social regime and therefore from law. It is a consequence of the constitution of our nature itself—and not of its fall—that we need law in order to live, as we need conceptual procedure in order to know. Yet we may happen to transcend law and concepts: in our intellectual life, love has its lights that anticipate the steps of reason; it has marvelous "antennae" to inform us; in social life there is something far greater yet, a community virtue that leaves the social possibilities of justice way behind: charity.

It remains that we meet, we communicate, we agree or clash with one another only through the mediation of our corporal senses. Matter has a part in all the activities of our spirit: word and gesture in the communication of thought, rites in the communal manifestations of religion. Juridism is the moral regulation of social life in its sensible manifestations.

Let us not exaggerate: it is incorrect to say that law is not concerned with intentions; but it knows them only through the exterior signs that betray them or presume them. For example, an attempted crime that is interrupted by an event independent of the will of the offender offers a sufficiently grave presumption of his intention to complete the crime for the law to punish him "as for the crime itself."

The "reason of law" thus established resides in its fullness only in the "perfect societies." Moreover, it suffers two series of analogical developments: an analogy of proportionality in national laws (or the *jus politicum* of St. Thomas) and in canon law; an analogy of attribution, not only in secondary institutional laws, including the law of the intersovereign relations of states with each other and with the Church, but—more remotely—in the derived meanings of the word law:[16] legislation, right, science of law, administration of law,

15. Cf. my book, *L'église et la question sociale* (Paris, 1937), pp. 190ff, which follows Aquinas, *Summa Theologiae*, I II, q. 97, a. 2.

16. In the *Summa Theologiae*, II II, q. 57, a. 1, ad 1, St. Thomas names four: what is just; the art of discerning what is just; the place where this discernment is made (the tribunal); and the act by which it is administered (the judgment). There are many others.

case law. I shall not linger over these. I simply want to consider the juridical order in its institutional differentiation—a differentiation that corresponds to each of the three characteristic elements of the "reason of law."

Corresponding to the notion of order, there is the classic distinction of interindividual law and social law. Interindividual law regulates an order of relationships *a persona ad personam ut sic:* an order that respects otherness to the point that it does not give rise to any new unity or new being. There is no ontological phenomenon here. Social law regulates an order of integration: an order that touches the personality of its subjects with a common *quality* and that does produce a new unity, a collective being, a matter for ontological investigation. It takes an incredible misconception of medieval philosophy—as I have told Gurvitch very cordially but very frankly[17]—to attribute the discovery of social law to the Renaissance.

Because they are not simple relationships but true juridical subjects, the collective unities thus constituted—institutions—establish with each other or with individual persons bonds that, in turn, either remain at the level of a simple relationship or constitute new integrations. There are institutions of human persons and institutions of institutions. And on it goes, either in an ascent up to the two perfect societies or, for these two, in an expansion into international or intersovereign commerce and all the varieties of federalism.

The juridical order thus reveals, for each institution considered as a juridical milieu, a distinction between the internal law that organizes it and the external law that situates it in a higher institution: the internal law of the state is the external law of the communities formed within the state. This is the sense of the thomistic distinction between the *jus politicum* and the *jus paternum* or *domesticum;* Hauriou recognized it in the administrative jurisprudence.[18] Between the internal law and the external law there is only a difference of viewpoint: from the municipal or regional perspective, national legislation is a higher and exterior law; and so is federal legislation from the perspective of each one of the federated states; but if you put yourself at the center of the nation or the federation, it is an interior legislation.

From this angle—and this is the institutional conception of law exactly—it seems, at first sight, that positive law obliges only those

17. Renard, "Thomisme et droit social," *Revue des sciences philosophiques et théologiques,* 1934, pp. 40ff.

18. Cf. his note under *Conseil d'État,* February 22, 1918, Cochet d'Hattecourt, S. 1921.3.9.

who are under the jurisdiction of the institution to which it is directly or indirectly referred. This is true of secondary laws and institutions: the factory regulations of Le Creusot do not bind the personnel of the Marne steelworks in any way. This is equally true of one of the two perfect societies and of its law: St. Paul wrote this to the faithful of Corinth,[19] and canon law confirms it when it holds valid, even after their baptism, a marriage contracted outside the laws of the Church between nonbaptized persons, and when it forbids the baptism of the children of infidels without the consent of their parents.

As for national law, it finds itself in a special condition, not because the state is a perfect and sovereign society—the argument would hold as well for ecclesiastical legislation—but because of its territorial character: the Church has authority only over her faithful; the state has authority both over all its citizens wherever they may be and over all its territory whoever may be on it. This two-fold authority is the basis of the distinction of police laws, which even oblige foreigners who are within the national territory, and personal laws, which oblige citizens even when they are living abroad. Only these personal laws are, like ecclesiastical laws and the laws of secondary institutions, and in the same sense, internal laws . . .

The juridical order is imperative; this second notion leads us to a differentiation of the juridical order from the point of view of its value, its authority before conscience. This is the problem raised, but not resolved, by the casuists, who have invented the theory of *leges mere poenales*.[20] These so-called merely penal laws, although not branded unjust (for then they would no longer be laws), would not oblige their subjects to obey their injunctions, but only to submit, after infringement or transgression and judicial condemnation, to the penalty for disobeying them—this by interpretation of the will of the legislator. The objection to this theory is glaring. Does it suffice that the legislator declares he wishes to be obeyed in the precise terms in which he frames the law? But this is what must be presumed. Besides, there is no precept of any authority that would permit interpretations such as the casuists put on police laws and certain fiscal laws; and to avoid deception, an oath is required in support of declarations of income, value, or inheritance. Is this sort of maneuvering an abuse of legislative authority? If so, we must give up the criterion of the legislator's intention. But it is useless to criti-

19. Cf. I Cor. 5: 9ff.
20. I take the liberty of referring you to my study on this so-called thorny subject, "La théorie des leges mère poenales," in *Mélanges Hauriou*, (Paris 1929), pp. 625ff (printed separately).

cize the theory of *leges mere poenales* if we have nothing to put in its place. The problem remains: all laws do not have the same value.

The problem is to explain the universal opinion, the voice of which prevails over all demonstrations, that there is a gradation of prestige ranging from police or public service regulations, even college or military regulations, to the administrative law concerning obligatory military service or the civil law concerning respect for contracts or compensation for damages, and also to canon law for Christians or monastic constitutions for religious, and finally, piercing through the ceiling of juridism properly so-called, to liturgical statutes and sacramental solemnities.

This difference of prestige and "respectability" comes less from the content of these rules than from the plane on which they are situated—the grade in which they are classified in the hierarchy of the juridical order. When soldiers distinguish between lying and "faking," or college boys between stealing and "cribbing," they separate, rightly or wrongly, at least as to the consequences they deduce, the plane of interior discipline from the plane of common morality. In this they give evidence of an institutional sense that is sometimes lacking in the "prudent." And when the penal code decides that domestic theft is not punishable—although often morally more culpable—it is also because it sees the familial order on another plane than the general order: this trace of familial law has hardly been noticed in our individualistic regime.

This is the fact. If you reflect upon it, do you not see in this heterogenous mass of positive law, an ascending scale that goes from the notion of law as a barrier to channel human activities to the notion of law as the auxiliary, perhaps even the instigator or generator of these activities; a gamut from the law that curbs to the law that inspires; from the enveloping and constraining law, which may be salutary in the fashion of an orthopedic brace, to the assimilated, interiorized law, which is like the strong and supple bone structure of the human body—we have come back to the skeleton! This is a new aspect of the analogical conception of law.

At the starting point, law, as Hauriou said, is a "highway": people travel about on it, each on his own business, while respecting the white lines and the "one-way" signs; this sort of law is only a thoroughfare for public use; it has no moving force. At the destination, in the regions that are steeped in spirituality, in the codes allied to theology and cult, law changes character; it is charged with positive energy, like the electric cables from which we draw current, and the labor of our hands receives a fecundity from it that of them-selves they would not have been capable of . . . These are the two extremes: between them lies the analogical gamut.

Our reflections on the imperative character of the juridical order reveal a new feature of the mutual attraction of law and theology from their respective sides of the high wall that, despite everything, separates them *ratione materiae . . .*

Law has jurisdiction only over the external forum; and this is precisely why it furnishes matter for a technique and why its imple-mentation requires administrative and judiciary services.[21] In its aspect as rule, positive law is only a "modification" of natural law and does not constitute a distinct reality; but its technical formula-tion and administrative and judicial implementation do add some-thing to natural law, and therefore constitute a distinct reality.

The notion of external forum is a spiritual notion, rebellious, in itself, to a specific definition. The internal forum and the external forum are not two species cut out of a genus and sealed in an enve-lope; they are two terms of an analogical series. The internal forum is enclosed in the secret of the human personality, and this person-ality very truly is an impregnable fortress; yet, it is open in some way since by nature it is social. Again we come up against the ontological problem! The distinction of the two forums is simply a reflection of it, and so is the question of their relationship: it cannot be resolved by a blow of the sword.

To begin with, all institutions do not have the same ascendancy over personality. Personality, at its deepest core, always defies insti-tutional ascendancy, at least in law; it withdraws from every as-cendancy in an inviolable retreat. But the most intimate institutions make it withdraw the farthest: these are also the most gripping, the most enterprising: my "business" more than my corporation; my professional group more than my political party, if I am a member of a profession; my country more than the international community; my family more than the human race; the spiritual society, even from a purely juridical angle, more than the political society: precisely because this juridical angle is more open upon the beyond of the juridical system. The line of demarcation between the two forums follows the rhythm of this intimacy, and the juridical system of the

21. Actually, as I have said, there are three adjuncts that must be discerned: formu-lation, administrative and judiciary services, coercion: of the three extrinsic elements of the juridical order, coercion is the least solidly connected . . . and the most easily detached: formulation and juridical decision "express the law"; the administrative units organize obedience to the law, which is the norm; enforced compliance is only an auxiliary instrument of the juridical order; it is reserved for pathological cases.

more intimate institutions extends its jurisdiction far beyond the limits within which the juridical system of the more loosely knit institutions entrenches itself. The frontier between internal and external forums remains, but it shifts its position.

These variations are also explained by the inequality of the juridical guarantees offered to personality by the diverse institutional structures. In general, the more intimate the institution, the fewer the guarantees: for example, the separation of powers, which is a fundamental principle of political law, is unknown to canon law.

But they also vary according to another rule. As intimate institutions expand, their juridical systems become more and more strict. For example, the juridical elements in the early Christian communities were nothing compared to what they became later and compared to the place juridical stabilization and governmental centralization hold today in the Church. In every juridical system, it is logical and legitimate for the external forum and constitutional guarantees to progress, and to retrogress, arm in arm; the more solid the brake, the more boldly the machine can launch ahead. And what is true of constitutional guarantees is equally true, not only of all other juridical guarantees—judicial guarantees, for example—but of moral and social guarantees. There are men whose word is worth more than any guarantees and from whom it would be outrageous to demand any.[22]

22. [Omitted here is Renard's discussion of canon law, which he says (*La philosophie de l'institution*, p. 279) "offers a unique perspective on the institutional conception of law."

APPENDIX   BIBLIOGRAPHY   GLOSSARY   INDEX

APPENDIX   Code Provisions Cited in Text

CODE CIVIL

Section No.

2   La loi ne dispose que pour l'avenir: elle n'a point d'effet rétroactif.

6   On ne peut déroger, par des conventions particulières, aux lois qui intéressent l'ordre public et les bonnes moeurs.

539   Tous les biens vacants et sans maître, et ceux des personnes qui décèdent sans héritiers, ou dont les successions sont abandonnées, appartiennent au domaine public.

686   Il est permis aux propriétaires d'établir sur leurs propriétés, ou en faveur de leurs propriétés, telles servitudes que bon leur semble, pourvu néanmoins que les services établis ne soient imposés ni à la personne, ni en faveur de la personne, mais seulement à un fonds et pour un fonds, et pourvu que ces services n'aient d'ailleurs rien de contraire à l'ordre public. L'usage et l'étendue des servitudes ainsi établies se règlent par le titre qui les constitue; à défaut de titre, par les règles ci-après.

713   Les biens qui n'ont pas de maître appartiennent à l'État.

815   Nul ne peut être contraint à demeurer dans l'indivision, et le partage peut être toujours provoqué, nonobstant prohibitions et conventions contraires. On peut cependant convenir de suspendre le partage pendant un temps limité; cette convention ne peut être obligatoire au delà de cinq ans; mais elle peut être renouvelée.

819   Si tous les héritiers sont présents et majeurs, l'opposition de scellés sur les effets de la succession n'est pas nécessaire, et le partage peut être fait dans la forme et par tel acte que les parties intéressées jugent convenable.

822   [Law of Dec. 15, 1921] Si toutes les parties sont d'accord, le tribunal peut être saisi de la demande enpartage par une requête collective signée par leurs avoués. S'il y a lieu à lici-

tation, la requête contiendra une mise à prix qui servira d'estimation. Dans ce cas, le jugement est rendu en chambre du conseil et n'est pas susceptible d'appel si les conclusions de la requête sont admises par le tribunal sans modification.

1101   Le contrat est une convention par laquelle une ou plusieurs personnes s'obligent, envers une ou plusieurs autres, à donner à faire ou à ne pas faire quelque chose.

1102   Le contrat est *synallagmatique* ou bilateral lorsque les contractants s'obligent réciproquement les uns envers les autres.

1103   Il est *unilateral* lorsque une ou plusieurs personnes sont obligées envers une ou plusieurs autres, sans que de la part de ces dernières il y ait d'engagement.

1104   Il est *commutatif* lorsque chacune des parties s'engage à donner ou à faire une chose qui est regardée comme l'équivalent de ce qu'on lui donne, ou de ce qu'on fait pour elle.

Lorsque l'équivalent consiste dans la chance de gain ou de porte pour chacune des parties, d'apres un évènement incertain, le contrat est *aléatoire*.

1184   La condition résolutoire est toujours sous-entendue dans les contrats synallagmatiques, pour le cas où l'une des deux parties ne satisfera point à son engagement. Dans ce cas, le contrat n'est point résolu de plein droit. La partie envers laquelle l'engagement n'a point été exécuté, à le choix ou de forcer l'autre à l'execution de la convention lorsqu'elle est possible, ou d'en demander la résolution avec dommages et intérêts. La résolution doit être demandée en justice, et il peut être accordé au défendeur un delai selon les circonstances.

1382   Tout fait quelconque de l'homme, qui cause à autrui un dommage, oblige celui par la faute duquel il est arrivé à le réparer.

1780   On ne peut engager ses services qu'à temps, ou pour une entreprise determinée. [Cf. Art. 23, Law of July 19, 1928, relating to *Code de travail:* La louage de services fait sans détermination de durée peut toujours cesser par la volonté d'une des parties contractantes.]

1859   A défaut de stipulations spéciales sur le mode d'administration [de la Sociéte], l'on suit les règles suivantes:

(1) Les associés sont censés s'être donné réciproquement le pouvoir d'administrer l'un pour l'autre. Ce que chacun fait est valable, même pour la part de ses associés, sans qu'il ait pris leur consentement; sauf le droit qu'ont ces derniers, ou l'un d'eux, de s'opposer à l'opération avant qu'elle soit conclue;

(2) Chaque associé peut se servir des choses appartenant à la société, pourvu qu'il les emploie à leur destination fixée

par l'usage, et qu'il ne s'en serve pas contre l'intérêt de la société, ou de manière à empêcher ses associés d'en user selon leur droit;

(3) Chaque associé a le droit d'obliger ses associés à faire avec lui les dépenses qui sont nécessaires pour la conservation des choses de la société;

(4) L'un des associés ne peut faire d'innovations sur les immeubles dépendant de la société, même quand il les soutiendrait advantageuses à cette société, si les autres associés n'y consentent.

2092   Quiconque s'est obligé personnellement, est tenu de remplir son engagement sur tous ses biens mobiliers et immobiliers présents et à venir.

Law of July 1, 1901

This basic law of associations in France is lengthy and appears after Art. 1873 of the *Code civil* (Dalloz, Paris, 1964) together with the basic amending laws: Decree-Laws of April 12, 1939, and October 23, 1935, and Laws of May 30, 1941, and April 3, 1942.

CODE PÉNAL

378   [As amended by Law of February 21, 1944, and validated by Ordinance of June 28, 1945; the new material is italicized.] Les médecins, chirugiens et autre officiers de santé, ainsi que les pharmaciens, les sages-femmes et toutes autres personnes dépositaires, par état ou profession ou par fonctions temporaires ou permanentes, des secrets qu'on leur confie, qui, hors le cas où la loi les oblige, *ou les autorise,* à se porter dénonciateurs, auront révélé ces secrets, seront punis d'un imprisonnement d'un mois à six mois et d'une amende (Law of December 28, 1956, Art. 7) de 50,000 à 300,000 francs. [In the original article the fine was from "100 à 500 francs."]

BIBLIOGRAPHY

MAURICE HAURIOU

MAJOR BOOKS

La science sociale traditionnelle. Paris, 1896.
Étude sur le droit administratif français. Paris, 1897.
Leçons sur le mouvement social. Paris, 1899.
La gestion administrative. Paris, 1900.
La souveraineté nationale. Paris, 1912.
Notes d'arrêts sur decisions du Conseil d'État et du Tribunal des Conflits.
  3 vol. Paris, 1929.
Précis de droit administratif. 11 ed. Paris, 1892, 1893, 1897, 1901, 1903, 1907,
  1911, 1914, 1919, 1921, 1927.
Principes du droit public. 2 ed. Paris, 1910, 1916.
Précis de droit constitutionnel. 2 ed. Paris, 1923, 1929.
Précis élémentaire de droit constitutionnel. Paris, 1925.
Précis élémentaire de droit administratif. Paris, 1926.
Aux sources du droit. Cahiers de la nouvelle journée, vol. 23. Paris, 1933.
Teoria dell' istituzione e della fondazione. Milan, 1967.

ARTICLES

"Boni viri arbitrium et clausula doli," *Nouvelle revue historique,* 1881,
  pp. 99–114.
"Origine de la corréalité," *Nouvelle revue historique,* 1882, pp. 1–24.
"L'historie externe du droit," *Revue critique de législation et de jurispru-
  dence,* 1884, pp. 1–15.
"Note sur l'influence exercée par les institutes en matière de classification
  de droit," *Revue critique de législation et de jurisprudence,* 1887, pp. 1–24.
"Des services d'assistance," *Revue d'economie politique,* 1891, pp. 625f.
"Les facultés de droit et la sociologie," *Revue générale de droit,* 1893,
  pp. 1–8.
"Response à un docteur en droit sur la sociologie," *Revue internationale
  de sociologie,* 1894.
"Danger des monopoles de fait établis par occupation de la voie publique,"
  Revue du droit public, 1894, pp. 78–87.
"La crise de la science sociale," *Revue du droit public,* 1894, pp. 294–321.
"L'alternance des Moyen Ages et des Renaissance," *Revue de metaphysique
  et de morale,* 1895, pp. 1–22.
"Les actions en indemnité contre l'état pour prejudices causés dans l'admin-
  istration publique," *Revue du droit public,* 1896, pp. 51–65.
"De la personnalité comme élément de la réalité sociale," *Revue générale
  du droit,* 1898, pp. 1–23, 119–140.

"Philosophie du droit et science sociale," *Revue du droit public*, 1899, pp. 462f.

"Création de salles de travail à la faculté de droit de Toulouse," *Revue internationale de l'enseignement*, 1901, pp. 547–558.

"Duguit, l'état, le droit objectif et la loi positive" (with Achille Mestre), *Revue du droit public*, 1902, pp. 346–366.

"La force métrice des cours d'eau et le droit des riverains" (with Charles Ader), *Bulletin de la Société d'Études législatives*, 1903, pp. 507–531.

"Recherches de jurisprudence sur les dépenses obligatoires," *Revue de législation financière*; 1903, pp. 1–17.

"La declaration de volonté dans le droit administratif français," *Revue trimestrielle de droit civil*, 1903.

"Rapport au ministre de l'agriculture au nom de la commission estra-parlementaire chargés d'estudier un projet de loi sur les forces hydrauliques" (with Léon Michoud), *L'année administrative*, 1903.

"Les éléments du contentieux," *Recueil de législation de Toulouse*, 1905, pp. 1–98; 1908, pp. 149–191.

"L'institution et le droit statutaire," *Recueil de législation de Toulouse*, 1906, pp. 134–182.

"Du role de la prescription acquisitive en matière de propriété industrielle," *La defense de la propriété industrielle*, 1907, pp. 1–19.

"Le point de vue de l'ordre et de l'équilibre," *Recueil de législation de Toulouse*, 1909, pp. 1–86.

"Les idées de M. Duguit," *Recueil de législation de Toulouse*, 1911, pp. 1–40.

"Les deux realismes, *Recueil de législation de Toulouse*, 1912, pp. 1–10.

"L'arrêt Gaz de Bordeaux," *Revue politique et parlementaire*, 1916.

"An Interpretation of the Principles of Public Law," 31 *Harv. L. Rev.* 813 (1918).

"Le droit naturel et l'Allemagne," *Le Correspondant*, Sept. 25, 1918.

"La liberté politique et la personnalité morale de l'état," *Revue trimestielle de Derecho Privado*, 1926, pp. 1–23.

"La théorie de l'institution et de la fondation," *Cahiers de la nouvelle journée*, no. 4 (1925), pp. 2–45.

"L'imprévision et les contrats dominés par des institutions sociales," *Revista de Dereco Privado*, 1926, pp. 1–23.

"Police juridique et fond du droit," *Revue trimestrielle de droit civil*, January 15, 1926.

"L'ordre social, la justice et le droit," *Revue trimestrielle de droit civil*, 1927, pp. 795–825.

"Le pouvoir, l'ordre, la liberté et les erreurs des systèmes objectivistes," *Revue de metaphysique et de morale*, 1928, pp. 193–206.

"De la répétition des précédents judiciaires à la règle de droit coutumière," *Cahiers de la nouvelle journée*, no. 15 (1929), pp. 109–115.

OTHER WORKS

Quaterus verum sit venditorum non obligari ut rem faciat emptoris. Presentation at Agrégation of 1882. Paris, 1882.

De la conservation du privilège du vendeur d'immeubles. Presentation at Agrégation of 1882. Paris 1882.

Plan du cours de droit administratif, en ce qui concerne la théorie des patrimoines administratifs. Toulouse, 1888.

De la formation de droit positif français. Paris, Nancy, 1893.
Étude sur le droit administratif français. Paris, 1897.
L'année administrative. Paris, 1904. With Professors Gaston Jèze and Charles Rabany.
Principes de la loi de 1905 sur la separation des églises et de l'état. Paris, 1906.
Les conditions extérieures de développement du recours pour excès de pouvoir. St. Petersburg, 1913.
Notice sur les ceuvres de Léon Michoud. Grenoble, 1917.

UNPUBLISHED MANUSCRIPTS

"Du terme en droit romain et en droit français." Licentiate thesis, Bordeaux, 1876.
"Étude sur la condictio. Des contrats à titre onéreux entre époux." Doctoral thesis, Bordeaux, 1879.
"Introduction à l'étude du droit." In possession of Professor André Hauriou in preparation for publication.
"Letters to Jacques Chevalier." In possession of Professor André Hauriou.

GEORGES RENARD

BOOKS

Notre oeuvre social: le Sillon. 1st ed., Nancy, 1904; 2nd ed., Nancy, 1905.
Pour connaître le Sillon. Paris, 1906.
Sept conférences sur la democratie. 1st ed., Paris, 1906; 2nd ed., Paris, 1910.
Notions très sommaires de droit public français. Paris, 1920.
Sur quelques orientations modernes de la science du droit. Paris, 1922. *Cours élémentaire de droit public.* Paris, 1922.
Le droit de la profession pharmaceutique. Paris, 1924.
Le droit, la justice et la volonté. Paris, 1924.
Le droit, la logique et le bon sens. Paris, 1925.
Le droit, l'ordre et la raison. Paris, 1927.
La valeur de la loi. Paris, 1928.
La théorie de l'institution. Paris, 1930.
La fonction social de la propriété privée. With Louis Trotabas. Paris, 1930.
L'institution: fondement d'une rénovation de l'ordre social. Paris, 1933.
L'église et la question sociale. Paris, 1937.
La philosophie de l'institution. Paris, 1939.

ARTICLES

"De la nature juridique de l'indemnité de dommages de guerre," *Revue du droit public,* 1920, pp. 199f.
Preface to N. M. Boiron, *La prostitution dans l'histoire.* Paris, 1926.
"Où chercher le réel?" *Cahiers de la nouvelle journée,* no. 5, 1926.
"Propriété privée et propriété humaine," *L'aube nouvelle,* 1926. Republished as Appendix 2 in *La théorie de l'institution,* pp. 500–536.
"La théorie des 'leges mere poenales,' " in *Mélanges Maurice Hauriou.* Paris, 1929, pp. 623ff.
"Le droit international et la théorie de l'institution," *Vie intellectuelle,* vol. 5 (Oct.-Dec. 1929), pp. 390–404.

"Entre l'individualisme et la sociologisme: la théorie de l'institution," *L'aube nouvelle*, 1929, pp. 34ff.

Preface to Henri Welter, *La contrôle jurisdictionnel de la moralité administrative*. Paris, 1929.

"L'organisation rationnelle de l'état," in *Semaine Sociale de France*. Besançon, 1929. Republished as Appendix 3 in *La théorie de l'institution*, pp. 586–610.

"La société et l'état selon S. Thomas." Review of Delos, *La Société internationale et les principes du droit public*. *Bulletin thomiste*, Sept.–Nov. 1929, pp. 563–574.

"Qu'est-ce que le mariage? Institution ou contrat?" in *Mélanges Del Vecchio?* Paris, 1930.

Preface to Bernard Geny, *La collaboration des particuliers avec l'Administration*. Paris, 1930.

"Le droit international, la société des nations et les traités de paix," *Annales catholiques françaises*, Feb. 15, 1930. Republished Paris, 1930.

"La pensée Chrétienne sur le propriété et les inégalites sociales qui s'ensuivent," *Vie intellectuelle*, vol. 6 (July–Sept. 1930), pp. 242–270.

"Les bases philosophiques du droit international et la doctrine du "Bien commun," *Archives de philosophie du droit et de sociologie juridique*, 1931, pp. 465–480.

"La filosofia politica di Maurice Hauriou," in *Studi di diritto pubblico in onore Oreste Ranelletti*, vol. 2. Padua, 1931.

"La collaboration catholique à la S. D. N. [League of Nations]," *Vie intellectuelle*, vol. 10 (Jan. 10, 1931), pp. 29–34.

"La doctrine institutionnelle du mariage," *Vie intellectuelle*, vol. 12 (July–Sept. 1931), pp. 96–123.

"Une conception psychologique de la science du droit," *Revue de psychologie appliqué*, Dec. 1931.

"L'église et la souverainté," *Vie intellectuelle*, vol. 14, (Jan. 10, 1932), pp. 8–30.

"La pensée catholique dans le monde contemporain," *Vie intellectuelle*, vol. 15 (May 10, 1932), pp. 219–222.

"Romantisme et sociologie," *Vie intellectuelle*, vol. 26 (July–Aug. 1932), pp. 138–140.

Preface to Suzanne Michel, *La notion thomiste du bien commun*. Paris, 1932.

"Comment juger la sociologie contemporaine," *Vie intellectuelle*, vol. 17 (Oct. 10, 1932), pp. 85–89.

"La conception analogique du droit," *Vie intellectuelle*, vol. 26, (July 25, 1934), pp. 268–279.

"Qu'est-ce que le droit constitutionnel? Le droit constitutionnel et la théorie de l'Institution," in *Mélanges Carré de Malberg*. Paris, 1933, pp. 483f.

Review, *Bulletin thomiste*, IV, no. 7 (July–Sept. 1935), 530–534.

"Thomisme et droit social," *Revue des sciences philosophiques et théologiques* vol. 23 (1934), pp. 40–81.

"De l'institution à la conception analogique du droit," *Archives de philosophie du droit et de sociologie juridique*, vol. 5 (1935), pp. 80–145.

"La justice distributive et la théorie de l'institution," *Vie intellectuelle*, vol. 38 (Nov. 10, 1935), pp. 481–486.

Preface to F. I. Pereira dos Santos, *Un etat corporatif: la constitution sociale et politique portugaise*. Paris, 1935.

"Position du droit canonique," *Revue des sciences philosophiques et théologiques*, vol. 24 (1935), pp. 397–406.

"Contributo allo studio del rapporti tra diretto e teologia. La posizione del diretto canonice," in *Rivida internazionale di filosofia del diretto*, vol. 16, fasc. vi, Rome, 1936.

"De la propriété; rien ne sert de discuter," *Vie intellectuelle*, vol. 48 (Feb. 15, 1937).

"Les catholiques dans le cité," *Vie intellectuelle*, vol. 48 (March 25, 1937), pp. 362–368.

"Le sens chrétien du travail intellectuel," *Vie spirituelle*, vol. 51 (May 1, 1937), pp. 129–145.

"Droit romain et pensée chrétienne," *Revue des sciences philosophiques et théologiques*, vol. 27 (1938), pp. 53–62.

"La nature institutionnelle de l'entreprise," in *Anticipations Corporatives* (Paris, 1938).

"La contribution du droit canonique à la science du droit comparé," in *Recueil d'études en honneur d'Édouard Lambert*. Paris, 1938.

"Amitié et société," *Archives de philosophie du droit et de sociologie juridique*, vol. 9 (1939), pp. 196–215.

"De la conception revolutionnaire à la conception thomiste de l'état et du droit," *Revue des sciences philosophiques et théologiques* vol. 29 (1940), pp. 5–30.

JOSEPH T. DELOS

BOOKS

La société internationale et les principes du droit public. 1st ed., Paris, 1929; 2nd ed., Paris, 1950.

Le problème de civilisation: la nation. Montreal, 1944.

L'opinion, le gouvernement d'opinion, le gouvernement de foule. Quebec, 1947.

Essai sur l'ordre politique national et international. With Bruno de Solages. Paris, 1947.

ARTICLES

"La crise de l'autorité," in *Semaine Sociale de France*. Lyon 1925.

"La doctrine du droit international chez les théologiens," in *La Société internationale*. Paris, 1926.

"La société internationale et le droit naturel," *Revue des sciences philosophiques et théologiques*, vol. 15 (1926), pp. 145f.

"Le bien commun international: necessité d'organes pour en assure la gestion," in *Semaine Sociale de France*. Le Havre, 1926.

"Problème de l'autorité internationale d'après les principes du droit public chrétien et les publicistes espagnols du XVIieme siecle," *Revue générale de droit international public*, 1927, pp. 505f.

"La loi de charité dans les rapports internationaux," in *Semaine Sociale de France*. Paris, 1928.

"La sociologie: son introduction dans l'enseignement par les programmes du 18 août 1926," *Bulletin de la conférence Saint-Michel* (Paris), no. 7 (April 1928), pp. 250f.

"L'unité de l'Occident et l'association des universitaires catholiques alle-
mandes," *Vie intellectuelle*, vol. 3 (Oct. 1928), pp. 75–85.

"La doctrine de Monroe et les principes de droit public de Vitoria," *Vie
intellectuelle*, vol. 3 (Dec. 1928), pp. 461–475.

"Le point du rencontre du sociologie et du juriste," *Vie intellectuelle*, vol.
4 (Jan. 1929), pp. 136–153.

"Volk, Staat und Staaten gemeinschaft im Lichte der Christlichen Nachsten-
liebe," *Der Katholische Gedanke*, II (1929), 67–83.

"La paix du monde par l'organisation internationale," *Semaine catholique
internationale de Genève*, Sept. 1929. Summarized in *Documentation
Catholique*, Oct. 19, 1929.

"L'objet de la sociologie," *Vie intellectuelle*, vol. 7 (May 10, 1930), pp. 264–287.

"La théorie de l'institution," *Archives de philosophie du droit et de sociologie juridique*, 1931, pp. 87–153.

"Le désordre de l'economie internationale et la pensée Chrétienne," in
Semaine Sociale de France. Lille, 1932.

"Comment juger la sociologie contemporaine" (with Docy, Lemonnyer,
Trouard, Riolle, Troude, Znedek, and Ullrich), *Vie intellectuelle*, vol. 17
(1932).

"Le problème des rapports du droit et de la morale," *Archives de philosophie du droit et de sociologie juridique*, 1933, pp. 84–111.

Introduction to Lemonnyer-Tonneau-Troude, *Précis du sociologie*. Paris,
1934.

Notes and appendices to Martin Gillet, tr., *Saint Thomas d'Aquin, Somme
Théologique, La Justice*, Vol. 2 (II II, QQ. 57–62). Paris, 1934.

"Esquisse d'un plan de travail," *Vie intellectuelle*, vol. 34 (Feb. 25, 1935), pp.
44–47.

"L'idée autrichienne et le destin de l'Occident," *Vie intellectuelle*, vol. 35
(May 10, 1935), pp. 407–439.

"Ou en est la philosophie du droit," *Vie intellectuelle*, vol. 38 (Nov. 10, 1935),
pp. 464–475.

"La cooperation naturelle: ses fondements," in *Semaine Sociale de France*.
Versailles, 1936.

"Les idéologies regnantes en matière d'organisation corporative," in *Semaine Sociale de France*. Angers, 1936.

"Le bien commun," *Dictionnaire de sociologie* (Letouzey). Paris, 1936. vol.
III, col. 831–855.

"Société et personnalité morale," in *Semaine Sociale de France*. Clermont-
Ferrand, 1937.

"Heurts et courant d'idées dans le domaine du droit," *Vie intellectuelle*, vol.
50 (May–June 1937), pp. 209f.

"Culture et patriotisme autrichien," *Vie intellectuelle*, vol. 55 (Feb. 25, 1938),
pp. 109–112.

"Sur l'Autriche disparue, *Vie intellectuelle*, vol. 55 (March 25, 1938), pp.
368–379.

"Le nouveau droit social," *Vie intellectuelle*, vol. 57 (May 25, 1938), pp. 59–70.

"Retour aux sources de l'action internationale," *Vie intellectuelle*, vol. 62
(March 25, 1939), pp. 372–386.

"Le problème des universités catholiques," *Vie intellectuelle*, vol. 62 (March
10, 1939), pp. 252–271.

"La théorie thomiste de la paix mondiale," in *Semaine Religieuse de Quebec*.
Montreal, 1942.

"The Idea of Democracy," *Review of Politics,* vol. 5, no. 1 (1943), pp. 38–54.
"La sociologie de S. Thomas et le fondement du droit international," *Angelicum,* vol 22. Rome, 1945.
"The Dialectics of War and Peace," *The Thomist,* vol. 13 (July, Oct. 1950), pp. 305–324, 528–566.
"Sociologie de la guerre moderne et la théorie de la juste guerre," in *Semaine Sociale de France.* Pau, 1953.

SECONDARY SOURCES

BOOKS

Bonnecase, Julien. *Le conflit des conceptions juridiques en France de 1800 à l'heure actuelle.* Paris, 1928.
————. *La pensée juridique française de 1804 à l'heure présente.* Bordeaux, 1933.
Boucraut, Louis, *État, corporation et entreprise.* Paris, 1938.
Brèthe de la Gressaye, Jean, and Marcel Laborde-Lacoste. *Introduction générale à l'étude du droit.* Paris, 1948.
Brèthe de la Gressaye, Jean, and Alfred Légal. *Le pouvoir disciplinaire dans les institutions privées.* Paris, 1938.
Burdeau, Georges. *Traité de science politique,* Paris, 1949, II, 234–246.
Callies, Rolf-Peter. *Eigentum als Institution.* Munich, 1962.
Caron, Jeanne. *Le Sillon et la democratie chrétienne, 1894–1910.* Paris, 1966.
Chauffardet, Marcel. *Le problème de la perpetuité de la propriété.* Paris. 1933.
Haberle, Peter. *Die Wesensgehaltsgarantie des Art. 19 Abs. 2 Grundgesetz. Zugleich ein Betrag zum Institutionellen Verständnis der Grundrechte und zur Lehre vom Gesetzesvorbehalt.* Karlsruhe, 1962.
Clemens, Rene. *Personnalité morale et personnalité juridique.* Paris, 1935.
Clement, Louis. *Notariat et secret professionel.* Lyon, 1938.
Darricau, André. *Marc Sangnier.* Paris, 1958.
Davy, Georges. *Le droit, l'idéalisme et l'expérience.* Paris, 1922.
Dendias, Michael. *La théorie institutionnelle et le regime administratif.* Athens, 1939.
D'Entrèves, A. P. *The Notion of the State.* Oxford, 1967, pp. 124–131.
Despax, Michel. *L'entreprise et le droit.* Paris, 1957.
Desqueyrat, André. *L'institution, le droit objectif et la technique positif.* Paris, 1933.
Elders, J. S. *Staatsbegrip en institutionalisme.* Amsterdam, 1951.
Fabrèques, Jean de. *Les sillon de Marc Sangnier: un tournant majeur du mouvement social catholique.* Paris, 1964.
Faribault, Marcel. *Traité théorique et pratique de la fiducie ou trust de droit civil dans le province de Quebec.* Montreal, 1936.
Gaillard, Émile. *La société anonyme de demain: la théorie institutionnelle et la fonctionnement de la société anonyme.* Paris, 1932.
Geny, François. *Science et technique en droit privé positif.* Paris, 1914–1924, vol. 2, pp. 87–110.
Goretti, Cesare. *Il liberalismo giuridico di Maurice Hauriou.* Milan, 1933.
Gurvitch, Georges. *L'idée du droit social.* Paris, 1932.
Hallis, Frederick. *Corporate Personality.* London, 1930, pp. 217–238.
Hauriou, André. *Droit constitutionnel et institutions politiques.* Paris, 1966.

Haynes, Thomas Morris. *Institutional Theories of Law: Hauriou and Jordan.* Ann Arbor (University Microfilms), 1949.

Herberichs, Gerard. *Théorie de la paix selon Pie XII.* Paris, 1964.

Jeanneau, Benoît. *Les principes généraux du droit dans la jurisprudence administrative.* Paris, 1954.

Lefébure, Marcus. *Le pouvoir d'action unilaterale de l'administration en droit anglais et français.* Paris, 1961.

Lepaulle, Pierre. *Traité théorique et pratique des trusts.* Paris, 1932.

Loyer, Pierre. *L'entreprise, fondements de la profession.* Paris, 1938.

Marty, Gabriel, and Albert Brimo, eds. *La pensée du Doyen Maurice Hauriou et son influence.* With contributions by Lucien Siorat, Paul Ourliac, Georges Vedel, Lucien Sfez, André Hauriou, Jean Rivero, Paul Couzinet, Pierre Hébraud, André De Laubadère, Pierre Vellas, Luiz Legaz Lacambra, Roman Schnur, and Albert Broderick. Paris, 1969.

Orlando, V. E. *Santi Romano e la scuola Italiana di diritto pubblico.* Bologna, 1948.

Pierce, Roy. *Contemporary French Political Thought.* London, 1966.

Piot, Alice. *Droit naturel et réalisme.* Paris, 1930.

Platon, G. *Pour le droit naturel: à propos du livre de M. Hauriou.* Paris, 1911.

Pound, Roscoe. *Jurisprudence,* I, 340–342. St. Paul, 1959.

Prelot, Marcel. *Institutions politiques.* Paris, 1963, pp. 39–42.

———. *La science politique.* Paris, 1963, pp. 85–90.

Rigaud, Louis. *Le droit réel, histoire et théories, son origine institutionnelle.* Toulouse, 1912.

Rivero, Jean. *Les mesures d'ordre intérieur administratives.* Paris, 1934.

Romano, Santi. *L'ordinamento giuridico.* 1st ed., Pisa, 1918; 2nd ed., Florence, 1946, 1967.

———. *Principi di diritto costituzionale generale,* 2nd ed. Milan, 1947.

———. *Frammenti di un dizionario giuridico.* Milan, 1947.

———. *Lo stato moderno e la sua crisi.* Milan, 1969.

Rouast, André, and Paul Durand. *Droit du travail,* 3rd ed. Paris, 1963.

Roujou de Boubée, Gabriel. *Essai sur l'acte juridique collectif.* Paris, 1961.

Rousset, Michel. *L'idée de puissance publique et droit administratif.* Paris, 1960.

Ruiz Giménez, Carlos. *La concepción institucional del Derecho.* Madrid, 1944.

Schellekens, J. A. *De Leer over de "Institution" bij M. Hauriou.* Nijmegen, 1945.

Schnur, Roman, ed. *Die Theorie der Institution.* Berlin, 1965.

Schwinge, E., and Zimmerl, L. *Wesensschau und konkretes Ordnungsdenken im Strafrecht.* Bonn, 1937.

Stone, Julius. *Social Dimensions of Law and Justice.* Stanford, 1966.

Uhler, Armin. *Review of Administrative Acts.* Chicago, 1943.

Van Heemstra, Sixtra. *De Staatsopvating van Hauriou.* The Hague, 1954.

Waline, Marcel. *L'individualisme et le droit.* Paris, 1949.

Zangara, Vicenzo. *La rappresentanza institzionale,* 2nd ed. Padua, 1952.

ARTICLES

Archambault, Paul. "L'irreductible droit naturel," *Cahiers de la nouvelle journée,* no. 3 (1925), pp. 199–204.

————. "Qu'est-ce que la politique? Technique, art et mystique," *Politique,* 1929, pp. 331f.

————. "D'Hauriou à Gurvitch," *Cahiers de la nouvelle journée,* no. 27 (1934), pp. 190–194.

Arrighi, Pascal. "Hauriou: un commentateur des arrêts du Conseil d'État," in *Livre Jubilaire, Conseil d'État.* Paris, 1949, 341–345.

Aubry, Pierre. "La philosophie de M. Hauriou," *Annales de la Faculté de Droit d'Aix,* Jan.–June, 1911, pp. 3–15.

Bastid, Suzanne. "Place de la notion d'institution dans une théorie générale des organisations internationales, in *L'Évolution du droit public* (Mélanges Mestre). Paris, 1956, pp. 43–51.

Bobbio, Norberto. "Istituzione e diritto sociale (Renard e Gurvitch)," *Rivista internazionale di filosofia del diritto,* vol. 16, 1936.

Brèthe de la Gréssaye, Jean. "Institution," in *Encyclopédie Dalloz.* Paris, 1960, nos. 29f.

Broderick, Albert. "Evolving Due Process and the French Institutionalists," *The Catholic University of America Law Review,* vol. 13, no. 2 (May, 1964), pp. 99–135.

————. "Hauriou's Institutional Theory: An Invitation to Common Law Jurisprudence," *The Solicitor Quarterly,* vol. 4, no. 4 (Oct. 1965), pp. 281–308.

————. "Sociological Jurisprudence," in *New Catholic Encyclopedia.* New York, 1967, vol. 13, pp. 398–400.

————. "'Institutional' Theory and a New Private 'Club': Court Enforcement of Union Fines," *Nebraska Law Review,* vol. 47, no. 3 (1968), pp. 492–527.

————. "La notion d'institution de Maurice Hauriou dans ses rapports avec le contrat en droit positif français, *Archives de philosophie du droit,* vol. 13 (1968), pp. 143–160.

————. "L'influence de la pensée du Doyen Maurice Hauriou aux États-Unis et en Angleterre," *Annales de la Faculté de droit de Toulouse* (1969), pp. 271-280.

Clemens, René. "Hauriou," in *The New Catholic Encyclopedia.* New York, 1967, VI, 949-950.

Corts, Jose. "Georges Renard y su doctrina de la institución." *Revista de Derecho publico,* no. 3 (1934), pp. 97–108.

Cuche, Paul. "Manifestations nouvelles de l'autorité dans la vie sociale par le développement de l'institution," in *Semaine Sociale de France.* Lyon, 1925, pp. 349f.

————. "La législation du travail et les transformations du droit." *Cahiers de la nouvelle journée,* no. 4 (1925), pp. 165f.

Declareuil, Jacques. "Quelques remarques sur la théorie de l'institution et le caractère institutionnel de la monarchie Capétienne," in *Mélanges Maurice Hauriou,* Paris, 1929, pp. 164f.

Dengerink, J. D. "Hauriou and Dooyeweerd: A Comparison of Some Elements of Their Social Thought," in *Philosophy and Christianity.* Festschrift Herman Dooyeweerd. Amsterdam, 1965, pp. 334–366.

De Solages, Bruno. "L'institution, mode actuel d'adaptation de la morale à la vie des affaires, in *Semaine Sociale de France.* Mulhouse, 1930, pp. 316f.

Desqueyrat, André. "L'institution, sa nature, ses espèces, les problèmes qu'elle pose," *Archives de philosophie*, vol. 12 (1936), pp. 65–115.

Dooyeweerd, Herman. "De 'Theorie de l'institution' en de staatsleer van Maurice Hauriou," *Antirevolutionaire Staatkunde*. vol. 14, (1940), pp. 301–347; vol. 15 (1941), pp. 42–70.

Durand, Paul. "La notion juridique de l'entreprise," in *Travaux de l'association H. Capitant*. Paris, 1947, vol. 3.

———. "Aux frontières du contrat et de l'institution: la relation de travail," in *Jurisclasseur public*. Paris, 1944, vol. 1, pp. 387f.

Eisenmann, Charles. "Deux théoriciens du droit: Duguit et Hauriou," *Revue philosophique*, vol. 110 (1930), pp. 231–279.

Fournier, Jacques. "Maurice Hauriou, arrêtiste," *Études et Documents, Conseil d'État*, vol. 11 (1957), pp. 155–166.

Gooch, R. K. "Hauriou and the Separation of Powers," *Political Science Quarterly*, vol. 38 (1923), pp. 578–601.

Gurvitch, Georges. "Les idées-maîtresses de Maurice Hauriou," *Archives de philosophie du droit et de sociologie juridique* (1931), pp. 155–194.

———. "L'idée du droit social et l'objectivisme métaphysique de Maurice Hauriou," in *Éléments de sociologie juridique*. Paris, 1940, pp. 114f.

Hébraud, Pierre. "Maurice Hauriou et les civilistes," *Recueil de législation de Toulouse*, XCIII (1967), 13f.

Jarlot, Georges. "L'institution," *Archives de philosophie*, vol. 12 (1936), pp. 144–160.

Jennings, Ivor. "The Institutional Theory," in Jennings, ed., *Modern Theories of Law*. London, 1933, pp. 68–85.

Le Fur, Louis. "Le droit naturel et la théorie de l'institution," *Vie intellectuelle*, vol. 10 (Jan. 1931), pp. 76–102.

Lissarrague, Salvador, "El concepto de institución en el derecho publico de Hauriou: su alcance filosofico-social," *Revista de la facultad de derecho de Madrid*, 6-7 (1941), 197f.

Lucas Verdu, Pablo. "Sobre el concepto de institución politica," *Revista de estudios politicos*, vol. 108 (1959), pp. 25f.

Lucien-Brun, J. "Les sources du droit et du pouvoir politique d'après trois théories modernes," *Archives de philosophie*, 12 (1936), 159–184.

Maspetiol, Roland. "L'idée d'état chez Maurice Hauriou," *Archives de philosophie du droit*, vol. 13 (1968), pp. 249–265.

Mestre, Achille. "Discours à la séance solennelle de la faculté du droit de Toulouse, June 8, 1929."

———. "Maurice Hauriou (1856-1929)," *Annuaire de l'institut international de droit public*, 1929, pp. 269–279.

Millar, Moorehouse, F. X. "Hauriou, Suarez and Chief Justice Marshall," *Thought*, VI (1932), 588–608.

Monaco, Riccardo. "Solidarismo e teoria dell'istituzione nella doctrina di Diritto internazionale," *Archivo giuridico*, 4th Series, vol. 24 (1932), pp. 229f.

Morin, Gaston. "Vers la revision de la technique juridique—le concept d'institution," *Archives de philosophie de droit et de sociologie juridique*, 1931, pp. 73–85.

Plassard, Jean. Preface to Pierre Raynaud. *La nature juridique de la dot*. Paris, 1934.

Poloupol, E. A. "L'idée de liberalisme dans l'oeuvre de Maurice Hauriou, in *Mélanges Paul Negulesco*. Bucharest, 1935, pp. 587–607.

Prelot, Marcel. "Institution," in Raymond Odent and Marcel Waline, eds. *Répertoire Dalloz de droit public et administratif*. Paris, 1929, II, 273.

———. "M. Renard et l'institution," *Cahiers de la nouvelle journée*, no. 19 (1931), pp. 205–211.

———. "La théorie de l'institution et la technique juridique," *Cahiers de la nouvelle journée*, no. 20 (1932), pp. 207–216.

Rivero, Jean. "Hauriou et l'avènement de la notion de service public," in *L'Evolution du droit public* (Mélanges Mestre). Paris, 1956, pp. 461–471.

Ruiz del Castillo, Carlos. "Un schema de la doctrine de la personnalité de l'état selon la méthode juridico-psychologique d'Hauriou," in *Mélanges Maurice Hauriou*. Paris, 1929, pp. 95–109.

Saboia de Medeiros, R. "Ensayo de filosofia concreta social y juridica. Una socio-filosofia juridica: El derecho social de G. Gurvitch," *Stromata*, 1 (1938), 103–160.

Schneider, Peter. "Hauriou," in *Staatslexicon der Gorres-Gesellschaft*, Vol. 4. Freiburg, 1959.

Stone, Julius. "Two Theories of the 'Institution,' " in Newman, ed. *Essays in Jurisprudence in Honor of Roscoe Pound*. Indianapolis, 1962, pp. 296–338.

Timasheff, Nicholas. "The Sociological Theories of the French Institutionalists," *Thought*, vol. 21 (1945), pp. 493–512.

Viehweg, Theodor. "Husserl, Hauriou und die deutsche Rechtswissenschaft," *Archiv für Rechts-und Sozialphilosophie*, vol. 31 (1937), pp. 84–89.

Vignaux, Paul. "La théorie de l'institution," *Politique*, 1930, pp. 989f.

Villey, Michel. "Droit subjectif," in *Seize essais de philosophie du droit*. Paris, 1969, pp. 140–220.

Waline, Marcel. "Les idées maîtresses de Duguit et Hauriou," *L'année politique, française et étrangère*, Dec. 1929, Mar. 1930.

Weil, Prosper. "Note to Conseil d'État, Ville de Nice, April 20, 1956," *Actualité juridique*, no. 257 (1956), pp. 267ff.

GLOSSARY

Acte juridique. Juridical act. Hauriou defines a "juridical act" (in German, *Rechtsegeschaft,* which Pound has translated as "legal transaction") as an "action on the way to being accomplished that tends to a juridical result." It is a "juridical *act*" only while it is in the course of execution; thereafter he calls it a "juridical fact." Hauriou, "L'institution et le droit statutaire," *Recueil de législation de Toulouse* (1906), p. 142. The notion of a juridical act originated with nineteenth-century German jurists (Bernhard Windschied, Otto von Gierke) and was first stressed in France by Henri Capitant and Léon Duguit. The more traditional view of juridical act was expressed by Duguit as "declaration of will by a person with legal capacity, having for an object a thing that he can wish to be determined by a legal end and made with the intention of creating a juridical situation." Léon Duguit, *Le droit social, le droit individuel et la transformation de l'état,* 3rd ed. (Paris 1922), pp. 70–71.

Action d'état. An action tending to establish or modify a person's legal status, as revocation of adoption or nullification of a marriage.

Action publique. An activity that "belongs to the society for the maintenance of public order by the use of penalties for infractions." *Dalloz' Petit dictionnaire de droit* (Paris, 1954), p. 42. The activity is exercised in the name of the society by officials designated by law.

Administration. "When we speak in France of 'the Administration,' just plain, with a capital *A,* we mean the ensemble of organs that carry out public tasks . . . as distinguished from certain other forms of public activity: legislation, the exercise of justice." Jean Rivero, *Droit administratif,* 2nd ed. (Paris, 1962), p. 9.

Administrés. Those subject to the Administration.

Affectation. Dedication to a prescribed function or use.

Arrondissement. An administrative subdistrict of the *département,* under a subprefect. Before the Vichy regime it had an elected assembly.

Association. In French law an *association* is conceived of as "the convention by which two or several persons put their efforts (*connaissances*) to common use in an activity that has as its objective something other than the sharing of profits." Law of July 1, 1901, Art. 1. See Appendix. It is distinguished from a *société* (in its various forms) by this notion of non-lucrative purpose. Although the law permits *associations* to be formed freely without filing of any preliminary declaration (Art. 2), to have "juridical capacity" it must file the declaration prescribed by Art. 5.

Chose publique. "The ensemble of institutions, public services, public resources that the state puts at the disposal of the public, in which they
participate and cooperate. But the *chose publique* does not necessarily
absorb everything that is of public interest, nor everything that is of
general interest, nor everything that concerns the public." Hauriou, *Précis
de droit administratif,* 5th ed. (Paris, 1903), p. 7.

Circonscription. A territory forming a subdivision of the state, endowed
with the name of juridical personality, whose boundaries circumscribe
the existence of certain competences or the accomplishment of certain
electoral or administrative operations.

Civiliste. A jurist concerned with the study of *droit civil.*

Commerce juridique. See Hauriou, *Principes du droit public,* 2nd ed. (Paris,
1916), p. 174. "Juridical commerce is an ensemble of juridical forms produced by economic transactions. In the political society, men are kept
in a group by their submission to the discipline of a single institution
or by their participation in ceremonial procedures. In the economic society they are kept in relationship with one another by their collaboration
in the common work of satisfying human needs. The political and economic forces, battling against one another in the social mass, tend to
produce two forms of society and two forms of law: the political institution and the relationships of juridical commerce. The true way to look
at things is to consider the complete society as composed of the two
elements of political institution and juridical commerce. The combination
of these two elements appears as a balance of two forces with reciprocal
actions and reactions."

Conseil général. Elective assembly of a *département.*

Construit. "Sometimes the task to be done takes established natural givens
as a departure point and tends to put them to use, to transform them,
or to make them supple, so as to model them on the needs of the juridical
order for which they are destined. And the result of the effort pursued
in this way, which is a work of artifice and which acts upon nature by
means of proper procedures that are drawn from the personal powers
of man, can, it seems, be called the *construit.*" François Geny, *Science et
technique en droit privé positif* (Paris, 1914–1924) Geny, I, 97. Cf. *Donné.*

Contentieux. See *Recours de plein contentieux.*

Cour de Cassation. "The supreme court of the judicial order [i.e., of the
common law, as distinguished from *droit administratif*], which has the
mission to decide upon appeals (*pourvois*) taken against judicial decisions
[of the lower courts] and to overrule (*casser*) those characterized by
violation or false interpretation of the law (*loi*). Henri Capitant, *Vocabulaire juridique* (Paris, 1936), p. 164.

Decisions exécutoires. "Every declaration of will intending to produce a
juridical effect, expressed by an administrative authority . . . in an executory form, that is, in a form that envisions official execution." Hauriou,
Droit administratif, 9th ed. (Paris, 1919), pp. 459–460. In each administrative operation there is a prescribed order: "(1) a regulatory decision;

(2) the particular executory decision; (3) the executory measure or measures" (p. 461).

Doctrine. The writings containing the opinions of the principal legal authors. They are sometimes classed as a source of French law, improperly it would seem (See Rivero, *Droit administratif,* p. 67).

Domaine public. "The *domaine public,* composed of goods (*biens*) particularly indispensable to the public utility (the criteria of the public domain is somewhat disputed) and consequently submitted to an exceptional juridical regime that protects the affection of the thing to its destined public utility (inalienability, imprescriptibility, penal protection against usurpation and invasion, free of requirements of *voisinage* [G.]." Capitant, *Vocabulaire juridique,* p. 203.

Donné. "Sometimes we purely and simply verify what is revealed by 'social nature,' interpreted in itself or according to the inspirations of a higher ideal, in order to reach rules of action, whose foundation will be all the more stable as their content is less artificial and arbitrary. This is what I call the *donné,* which should formulate the juridical rule, as it comes from the nature of things and, insofar as possible, in the brute state." François Geny, *Science et technique,* I, 97. Geny enumerates these *donnés* in various categories: real (or natural) *donnés,* the fruit of factual observation; historical *donnés,* the relevance of the evolution or long existence of these facts; rational *donnés,* which will contain the principal direction that will assure, insofar as possible, the scientific elaboration of objective law; finally, ideal *donnés,* "*desiderata* that are postulated by public opinion or by the current state of civilization," which are not required by the other type of *donnés* (II, 37–384). Cf. *Construit.*

Droit. The word "droit" used without adjectival qualification can hardly be defined out of context. It may mean what in English would be "right" (*droit subjectif*) or "law." It may be used in distinguishing law from other means of social control, such as religion, custom and manners (*moeurs*), or morality (*morale*). Cf. Geny "Le notion de droit en France," It may in context connote "justice" or "the legal order." All these uses have occurred in the course of this work. But general usage in France seems to regard *droit,* unqualified, as relating more often than not to *droit positif.* As with one use of the English word "law," *droit* is often used confusingly to indicate what are more properly *sources de droit.* For the distinction of *droit* from *moeurs,* see Delos, "The Object of Sociology," above, n.14. See also *Morale* (G.).

Droit disciplinaire. "The ensemble of the rules that incorporate the point of view of the group and that have as their object the disciplinary powers exercised in the name of the group. It is penal in nature, but it is distinguished from penal law properly so-called in that it does not contain a precise determination of faults." Hauriou, *Droit administratif,* 6th ed. (Paris, 1907), p. 19.

Droit objectif; droit subjectif. This terminology originated in Germany in the nineteenth century. Duguit was prominent among those who early accepted it in France (see his *L'état, le droit objectif et la loi positif* [Paris, 1901]), and Hauriou followed. Duguit made *droit objectif* a synonym for his *règle de droit* (see his *Manuel de droit constitutionnel,* 2nd ed. [Paris, 1911], p. 1); the *droit subjectif* existed only if it conformed to the *droit objectif,* which had clear primacy. For Hauriou there were two elements in every right (see *Droit*): "A subjective element, which is the will to exercise a power in order to satisfy an interest of one's own; an objective element, which is a certain social conception determined either by law or by a certain universally accepted ideal of juridical commerce, and which regulates the manner in which the power in question must be exercised." Hauriou, Note sous l'Affaire Olivier et Zimmermann, Cons. d'État, 27 fevrier 1903, S.1905.III.17, *Notes d'Arrêts,* I, 563. See also Hauriou, "The Theory of the Institution and the Foundation," above. See Michel Villey, "Droit subjectif," in *Seize essais de philosophie du droit* (Paris, 1969, pp. 140–220.

Droit réel. "A faculty put directly at the disposition of the individual [which] is enforceable against all." Cf. a right *in rem.* Hauriou, *Principes de droit constitutionnel,* 2nd. ed., p. 637.

Droit statutaire. "The institution is not only the *juridical field* in which states of fact are transformed into states of law; it is also the source of two sorts of well verified juridical rules: *le droit disciplinaire et le droit statutaire* . . . As a counterpart to *droit disciplinaire* the institution engenders in quite as spontaneous a way *le droit statutaire* . . . What are the *statuts* of an institution or even of a stock corporation or an association? In what respects do they differ from contractual documents? Do the *statuts* give birth to the institution or, on the contrary, does the institution engender the *statuts?* . . . It is always the case that the *statut* does not reduce itself completely to contract, that the *statut* emanates progressively from living institutions, whether in the customs that are established by their functioning, or in the resolutions voted by the majority in the assemblies of their members; and if some *statuts* are prepared in advance in order that an institution may be created, the institution once created can modify them according to its needs, etc. And so the *statut* rests not on an exchange of consents, but on the adhesion of several to the same fact (*fait*). Furthermore, the *statut* does not proceed in the manner of a source of obligations; the *statut* is in the category of real rights (*droits réels,* G.); it creates or confirms, as such for the collectivity, statutory situations (*situations statutaires*), that is, situations which are analyzed as real rights . . . By *le droit statutaire* the institution engenders *le droit réel.*" Hauriou, *Droit administratif,* 6th ed. (Paris, 1907), pp. 22–23; "L'institution et le droit statutaire," pp. 136–137. Cf. *Droit disciplinaire.*

Équilibres. The concept of *équilibres,* or balances, is central in Hauriou's political and juridical thought. He sees social life as a constant conflict of forces among which provisional balances are established at every turn. In his final writing on the theory of the institution, he says: "To sum up, the form of the institution, which is its durable element, consists in a system of balances of powers and of consents constructed around an idea." Hauriou, *Droit constitutionnel,* 2nd ed. (Paris, 1929), p. 71.

Établissement d'utilité publique. An entity that is recognized as a legal person and as having benefited from the recognition of a certain "public utility" involved in its activities. Nevertheless, unlike the *établissement public,* it remains a "private" person and, as such, subject to private law and not to *droit administratif.* See Rivero, *Droit administratif,* 2nd ed. (Paris, 1962), p. 405.

Établissement public. "An administrative person that manages a special public service." Hauriou, *Droit administratif,* 3rd ed. (Paris, 1897), p. 527.

Excès de pouvoir. "A complex notion that is both juridical and moral . . . There is *excès de pouvoir* not only when the Administration exceeds the legal limits of its powers, but even when it uses its discretionary power of judgment for motives that are foreign to the good of the service. At the present time the moral element of *excès de pouvoir* is reflected in the proceeding that has taken the name of *détournement de pouvoir.*" Rivero, *Droit administratif,* p. 474. See also *Recours pour excès de pouvoir.*

Fond, principes de. Basic principles, fundamentals.

Fonds de commerce. A small business property, such as a shop or store.

Fond de droit. To Hauriou this term connotes the traditional system of adjudication according to rules of law, as distinguished from what he calls *police juridique* in which "standards" rather than formal rules are a chief resort as a means of "administration" of law. See Hauriou, "Police juridique et fond du droit," *Revue trimestrielle de droit civil* (1926).

Forme. See *Hylomorphiste.*

Gemeinden. Hauriou's use seems in accord with Barker's reference to "the *Gemeinde,* or local community, with a history running back to Teutonic antiquity, and with survivals of co-ownership, or something even higher than co-ownership, in its possession of forest and waste." Ernest Barker, Translator's Introduction to Otto von Gierke, *Natural Law and the Theory of Society,* in *Das deutsche Genossenschaftsrecht,* Part IV (Boston, 1957), p. lviii.

Hylomorphiste (la doctrine hylomorphiste). Hylomorphic theory. In its original sense this theory of Aristotle conceives of all sensible reality as composed of "matter" (matière) and "form" (forme). "All forms are either in matter or abstracted from matter in the human mind. Their being consists in informing or determining matter, just as the being of matter consists in the capacity to receive these forms." Mortimer Adler, William Gorman, eds., "The Great Ideas of the Western World—a Synopticon of the Great Books of the Western World," vol. 2, ch. 28, which constitutes vol. I of Robert Hutchins, ed., *Great Books of the Western World* (Chicago, 1952). The theory of form and matter was extended by analogy to apply to groups, their dominant ideas or objectives being conceived of as the "form" to be realized in the sensible elements that constitute, so to speak, their "matter."

Jurisprudence. "(1) In an old sense, which has almost disappeared today, the science of law. (2) The interpretation of law by the courts. (3) The ensemble of court decisions on a matter. E.g., the jurisprudence on the matter of accidents and automobiles." Capitant, *Vocabulaire juridique,* p. 322.

Légistes. Ministers of the Capetian kings, particularly Philip the Fair, who were the subject of great historical controversy in the nineteenth and early twentieth centuries, e. g., by Thierry, Michelet, Guizot, and Langlois. See Joseph Strayer, "Philip the Fair—a Constitutional King," *American Historical Review,* LXII (1956–1957), 18–32, and especially Pegues, *The Lawyers of the Last Capetians* (Princeton, 1962), which opens (p.x) by referring to the varied uses of *légiste:* "The technical problem of this study was the delimitation of the term *légiste.* It has been used indiscriminately by historians to refer to many civil servants who were supposedly influenced by the principles of Roman law and who played leading roles in Philip the Fair's reign. I have applied the term only to men for whom there is concrete evidence that they were lawyers and had legal training."

Masse des consciences. Duguit rejected Durkheim's notion that the juridical rule is conceived by the "collective conscience" of a society. Duguit's *règle de droit,* "born of social solidarity . . . is fundamentally social in the sense that it exists only because men live in society. It is also individual because it is contained in individual minds." Duguit, *Manuel de droit constitutionnel,* 2nd ed., pp. 10–11.

Matière. See Hylomorphiste.

Morale. In a balanced contemporary French distinction of *la morale* from *le droit,* Professor Henri Battifol of the Faculté de Droit of Paris suggests that "Morality (*La morale*) regards the human act insofar as it betters or degrades man taken as such; it is concerned with other acts besides those that concern the relation of man with his neighbor, and views the latter from the angle of the human consistency of the subject." On the other hand, "*Droit* considers the acts of man from the angle of the relationship that they establish with the other members of the collectivity: it is the exterior aspect which is dominant, 'bilaterality' characterizes *le droit.*" Henri Battifol, *La philosophie du droit* (Paris, 1960), p. 125.

Objectif. See Droit objectif.

Opération à procédure. Hauriou's analysis of the "procedural operation" is most fully set forth in "L'institution et le droit statuaire," pp. 134–182. The following excerpts are indicative: "Take for example the making of a law in our parliamentary regime; it supposes at least three successive acts: the vote of each of the two Chambers and the promulgation by the President of the Republic. We cannot claim that these are three acts of consent concurring with each other like a contractual agreement of authorities face to face . . . In my sense they constitute a statutory pact, that is, an operation bound together in which the consent of the second authority actually inheres in the decision already taken by the first, at a moment when the latter is no longer an act, but a fact, because it has been executed, and so on to the next" (pp. 145–146).

"The text of the law is constituted by the content of the deliberation of the Chamber. However this deliberation does not become executory with respect to the text of the law in the sense that this text will become obligatory for citizens, but simply in the sense that the bureau of the Chamber will be obliged to transmit this text to the Senate . . . It is only the promulgation by the chief of state that will make the content of the law obligatory upon citizens, that will give its content the value of an *act,* and then, in a roundabout way by enjoining all the agents of the public force to have it put into execution . . . Not only is the executory form an element separable from the content of the decision, but it is an element that is not necessarily attached to a phenomenon of subjective consent. The executory form can be attached to a ceremony, that is, to a purely objective circumstance" (pp. 148–149).

"In this theory of the complex act or juridical operation we see that the diverse particular elements concur in the final result only insofar as each of them has advanced the exterior procedure of the operation. These successive acts are phenomena of consent, since they are decisions. But these consents are neither fused nor simply added to one another: they are incorporated, the new into the old, by their adherence to the same procedure" (pp. 153–154).

"The complex act explained by the unity of an external procedure is by that fact solidarized with the social institution; not only because every organized procedure is in itself a social institution, but mainly because every social institution of the category of groups, bodies or establishments, can only live an organic life according to certain procedures, and only because these procedures, which are the rhythm of institutional life, engender in a continual manner complex acts, most of which are statutory acts. And so we must clearly note that it is not the collective moral person supposedly existing within the institution that decrees the complex act or the statute. It is an objective procedure which, in functioning, brings it about in the name of the objective discipline of the institution" (pp. 154–155).

Ordre public. See Appendix, art. 6. In public and private law, the "ensemble of institutions and rules ordained to keep the public services functioning in a country and to maintain security and morality in the relationships between individuals, who, in principle, cannot avoid the application of these rules in their agreements." In private international law, the "ensemble of institutions and rules that are so bound to a country's civilization that the judges of the country must apply them in preference to foreign law, even when foreign law would be competent according to the ordinary rules of conflicts of laws." Capitant, *Vocabulaire juridique,* p. 358.

Patrimoine. An ensemble of rights and obligations, appreciable in money, that can belong to or be received by a single person and that constitutes a juridical totality. The word is sometimes used as in the expression *patrimoine affecté,* to designate a mass of goods that is appropriated to a special use, such as a foundation.

Petitoire. One of the two actions in French law to recover interests in immovable property. Actions in which the plaintiff asserts a mere possessive interest in the property are *actions possessoires;* those in which the plaintiff seeks to establish his ownership of such property (or of a usufruct or a servitude) are *petitoires.*

Physique. The classical notion of "physics," deriving from Aristotle, is the study of "movable being," as distinguished from "metaphysics" (i.e., transphysics), which is concerned with "nonmovable" being (in the sense of being that is not empirically perceived).

Plan cadastral. A geographical unit established for tax purposes. The unit is established by evaluating its revenue potential, the view being toward a proportional contribution by individuals, as distinguished from a fixed, unvariable tax on immovable property. The *plan cadastral* grew out of the Revolutionary reaction against privilege of any sort.

Plein contentieux. See *Recours de plein contentieux.*

Pleine juridiction. See *Recours de pleine juridiction.*

Police, or *le droit de police.* The "preventive application of law. This police 'law' is achieved in the first place by systematic regulation (that is, by legal prescriptions and rulings) . . . then it is executed by judicial and administrative processes." Hauriou, Droit administratif, 3rd ed., pp. 559, 565.

Police juridique. See *Fond de droit.*

Possession d'état. The (subjective) right a person has to enjoy, as against another person, the privileges inherent in his particular social or civil status, e.g., as citizen or alien, married or single, legitimate or illegitimate.

Possession des choses. Possession in civil law conceived as a factual relation between a thing and a person.

Pouvoir. See *Excès de pouvoir.*

Pouvoir minoritaire. A political elite characteristic of an early stage of society, as contrasted with the *pouvoir majoritaire,* a legitimate power emanating from the people. The latter is an essential element of the democratic state.

Principes de fond. See *Fond, principes de.*

Privatistes. Jurists engaged in "private law," including both "civil law" (*civilistes*), and "commercial law" (*commercialistes*).

Publicistes. Jurists engaged in "public law," i.e., constitutional and administrative law.

Puissance publique. A concept of inherent public executive authority that Hauriou suggested was the foundation of *droit administratif,* as against Léon Duguit and his School of Bordeaux (which denied the existence of *puissance publique* and rested *droit administratif* on the foundation of *service public*). A. V. Dicey compared *puissance publique* to "the views of the prerogative maintained by Crown lawyers under the Tudors and the Stuarts." See Dicey, *Introduction to the Study of the Law of the Constitution,* 10th ed., ed. E. C. S. Wade (London, 1959), p. vi; Rousset, *L'idée de puissance publique en droit administratif* (Paris, 1960).

Recours de plein contentieux. The two chief categories of *recours* (administrative actions) in French *droit administratif* are (1) the *recours pour excès de pouvoir,* which asks the administrative judge to set aside an administrative act (here all the judge can do is affirm the action or set it aside); and (2) the *recours de pleine jurisdiction,* in which the judge is vested with full judicial powers and may also modify the action of the administrative official or grant damages. See Marcel Waline, *Droit administratif,* 9th ed. (Paris, 1961), p. 203; Jean Rivero, *Droit administratif,* p. 185; Heilbrinner, "Recours pour excès de pouvoir et recours de plein contentieux," *Recueil Dalloz* 1953, p. 183. See also Hauriou, *Les éléments du contentieux* (Toulouse, 1905).

Recours de pleine jurisdiction. Review on the merits. "A judge vested with *pleine jurisdiction* in an administrative suit has the power to resolve the suit, to substitute his decision for that of the administrative authorities who had acted in the case." Hauriou, *La gestion administrative* (Paris, 1899), p. 33.

Recours pour excès de pouvoir. An administrative litigative action (*recours*) brought to set aside the act of an administrative official for want of legality. This is the basic action in French *droit administratif* for the control of administrative activity. Although *l'excès de pouvoir* simply means "nonconformity to law," nonlegality is here taken in a broad sense and by this action the Conseil d'État "tends to a control of administrative morality and practicality." Rivero, *Droit administratif,* pp. 205, 208. See Hauriou, Note to S.1917.III.25, and Welter, "Le contrôle jurisdictionnel de la moralité administrative," thesis directed by Georges Renard (Nancy, 1929). But see Waline, *Droit administratif,* 9th ed., pp. 489–491.

Régime d'état. Hauriou conceives of governmental development as traversing three historical stages: an age of custom and of primitive institutions; a transitional stage of "nations," which has "an organization of public life that is decentralized, particularist, acephalous"; and finally the "regime d'état," which is "a certain form of a nation or, more exactly, the political and juridical centralization of populations that have arrived at the national stage." Constitutional government (*le régime constitutionnel*), one species of the régime d'état, "properly speaking is a late phenomenon of the periods of civilization in which the *régime d'état* has attained a maturity." Hauriou, *Droit constitutionnel,* 1st ed. (Paris, 1923), pp. 1–2, 20–39.

Règle de droit. As used by Hauriou, this does not mean "the rule of law" in Dicey's sense, or in any of the usual contemporary senses (see discussion by E. S. C. Wade in his Introduction to the 10th edition of A. V. Dicey, *Introduction to the Study of the Law of the Constitution* (London, 1959), pp. xcvi–cli). For such senses Hauriou uses *la règne de droit. La règle de droit* for Hauriou is the rightful legal rule, i.e., the juridical rule. He rejects Duguit's "pretended sovereignty of the juridical rule." Hauriou, *La souveraineté nationale* (Paris, 1912), p. 4. This was defined by Duguit as "a rule of conduct that imposes itself upon individuals living in society, a rule the respect for which is considered at a given moment by a society as a guarantee of the common interest, and a violation of which provokes a collective reaction against its author." Only to such rules, says Duguit, was obedience owed by citizens. "The reality is that obedience is due to rules formulated by the government when and in the measure in which these rules are the expression or the application of a *règle de droit.*" Duguit, *Manuel de droit constitutionnel,* (Paris, 1923), pp. 1, 29. See also *Droit.*

Règles de droit disciplinaire ou statutaire. Two bodies of rules that Hauriou held were created by each institution: "Disciplinary law, which represents the interest of the group expressed by the constraint of the power of domination, and statutory law, which represents the interests of the group expressed by the individual adherence of the members to the collective procedures of corporate life, counterweigh each other and this balance of juridical rules is an element of the total balance of the forces that sustain the institution . . . The disciplinary power in the institution is a power of constraint over individuals destined to assure the cohesion and welfare of the group. But this power should not be arbitrary; it should be limited: and the precise role of statutory law is to define this power, to define the end of the institution, and lastly to assure certain guarantees for the participants. Hence the balance between disciplinary and statutory law." Hauriou. *Droit public,* 1st ed. (Paris, 1910), pp. 135–137, See Roujou de Boubée, *Essai sur l'acte collectif* (Paris, 1961), p. 265.

Réglement. "A form of law that the government decrees or sanctions as being the expression of its own will." Hauriou, *Droit public,* 2nd ed., p. 28.

Réglementation. The traditional distinction between a law and a regulation (*règlement*) is that the first is enacted by a legislative (parliamentary) authority, the second by an administrative authority. For a discussion of the present status of the distinction under the French Constitution of 1958, see Rivero, *Droit administratif,* pp. 57–64.

Science. In the special sense used by François Geny, "science," or the data of the "scientific elaboration of law," consists primarily of the real, historical, rational, and ideal *donnés* (G.). As a complement, Geny added the physical, psychological, moral, economic, and social data. See Geny, *Science et technique en droit privé positif,* II, 369–371.

Scientisme. Total confidence in the infinite possibilities—theoretical and practical—of science.

Service vicinal. A rural service of the Administration, usually a road connecting villages or other rural roads.

Situations statutaires. Certain laws are designed to give rise primarily to individual rights; others are more directly designed to satisfy an interest of the common good. This latter type give rise to what are called "objective situations" or "situations of status." Renard gives as an example of the first, rules for the distribution of the property of a bankrupt, and as an example of the second, the *situation statutaire,* laws governing compulsory military service. Georges Renard, *La théorie de l'institution.*

p. 308. See Paul Roubier, *Droits subjectifs et situations juridiques* (Paris, 1963).

Société. A juridical person deriving from the contract of *société*: "a contract by which two or more persons agree to put something in common use with a view to realizing and sharing profits and considered as proprietor of the social patrimony." Capitant, *Vocabulaire Juridique,* p. 453.

Sociétés de commerce. Commercial companies. This is the generic term for profit-making business associations of any sort, including partnerships and unincorporated associations as well as corporations.

Sociétés par actions. Stock companies, including both corporations and partnerships with negotiable shares.

Sociologisme. A monist collectivist system, at the opposite pole from extreme individualism. In its broadest sense sociologism would reduce the individual to an organ in a social organism. See Renard, *La théorie de l'institution,* p. 314. Le Fur writes, "Sociologism would see society as a being endowed with a will and an intelligence of its own, the true creator of individuals as they exist today, instead of seeing that it is individuals, already existing with their nature of reasonable beings, endowed with intelligence and morality, who by joining together, have formed society." Quoted in Renard, *La théorie de l'institution* (Paris, 1930), p. 43.

Statut. "The *statut* [charter, constitution, fundamental laws] is the juridical form of the order established within a group, and this established order is the reality that subsists if the group is emptied of its present organs and members . . . It ranks above individual rights and above the government, but it admits the independent existence of these two elements, which even help to create it." Hauriou, *Droit public,* 2nd ed., p. 665.

Stipulatio. One of the two formal contracts of Roman law, the *stipulatio* "consisted essentially in a formal question and answer. For instance, one party (stipulator or reus stipulandi) said to another (reus promitendi), 'Do you promise to give me one thousand sesterces?' The other said, 'I promise.' This concluded the contract and gave rise to a legal obligation on the part of the promissor to do what he had promised. It was essential that there should be precise correspondence between question and answer." R. W. Lee, *The Elements of Roman Law,* 4th ed. (London, 1956), p. 298. There were other kinds of *stipulatio* that concerned security required by the judge or praetor to be given against possible damage in connection with certain activities. See Justinian, *Institutes,* Bk. III, Tit. XVIII, but the contractual type (elaborated in Tit. XV) was primary.

Subjectif. See Droit objectif; droit subjectif.

Sujet de droit. Since this French terminology is taken from German juristic thought, Maitland's explanation is apt: "Germans distinguish between the Subject and the Object of a right. If Styles owns a horse. Styles is the Subject and the horse is the Object of the right. Then if we ascribe the ownership of the horse to the Crown, we make the Crown a Subject; and then we can speak of the Crown's Subjectivity. And so in political theory, if we ascribe Sovereignty to the Crown or to the Parliament or the People,

we make the Crown, Parliament or People the Subject of Sovereignty."
Frederick Maitland. Translator's Introduction to Otto von Gierke, *Political Theories of the Middle Age* (Boston, 1958), p. xx, n.1. See also *Droit*.

Syndicats. Although usually referring to labor unions, *syndicat* embraces other professional groups. See the definition of Rouast and Durand, *Droit du travail*, p. 188: "A *syndicat* is a *group* in which several persons, engaged in a *professional activity*, agree to use their activities and a part of their resources in common, in a *sustaining way and by means of an interior organization*, in order to assure the *protection and the representation of their profession* and to *better their conditions of existence.*"

Technique. In the sense introduced to French jurisprudence by François Geny (contrasted with *science*), *technique* "specifies itself by its *constructive* character, striving to choose and organize, as kinds of devices (*trucs*), the most suitable means to attain the supreme ends of law (*droit*) . . . Juridical technique seems to me to represent the *artificial* side of the legal edifice, that part of it which is in a true sense *constructed* (*construit*), in opposition to that part which is *given* (*donné*)." Geny, *Science et technique en droit privé positif*, III, 18–19. Cf. *science, construit*, and *donné* in G.

Tutelle. In civil law, simply guardianship of minors, but in administrative law *tutelle* has a special meaning: "the decentralized administrations are subject to an administrative control of the central power, which bears the name of *tutelle administrative*. This is not in principle an official action of supervision like civil guardianship, but an a posteriori intervention by authorizations, approvals, or annulments." Hauriou, *Droit administratif*, 9th ed., p. 178.

Vitalisme. The late nineteenth and early twentieth centuries witnessed a lively revival of the ancient controversy concerning the explanation of living phenomena, between mechanism, which regarded all things as subject only to physico-chemical laws, and vitalism, which viewed processes in living things as not adequately explained in terms of processes in nonliving nature and emphasized the "independence, originality and irreducibility of the phenomena of life." Morris Ginsburg, "Mechanism and Vitalism," in *Encyclopedia of the Social Sciences*, V (1937), 267. The influence on Hauriou of the vitalist and neovitalist ideas of Aristotle (potency and act, matter and form), Claude Bernard (*idées directrices, forces évolutives*), Émile Durkheim (*conscience collective*), and Henri Bergson (*élan vital, évolution*) may be argued. His own special variety of "vitalism" may have borrowed something from each. He subtitled his chief work on the theory of the institution, "A Study in Social Vitalism." Renard rejected the vitalistic terminology. See Renard, "The Theory of the Institution," above.

Voie de fait. In general, a *voie de fait* is a civil wrong, or tort. The term has a special meaning in *droit administratif*. While it may be loosely considered an "administrative trespass," as in Armin Uhler, *Review of Administrative Acts* (Chicago, 1943), p. 138, it is, says Vedel, "one of the most subtle notions of French *droit administratif*." He suggests two criteria: (a) an administrative act that is "manifestly not susceptible of being connected with the application of a legislative or regulatory text," and (b) "the irregular forcible execution of a decision that is itself proper." Georges Vedel, *Droit administratif,* 3rd ed. (Paris, 1964), pp. 91–92.

Voirie. Literally, *voirie* connotes the system of public roads, and in law it embraces highways, waterways, and certain rights of way over public land. In *droit administratif* the term *contraventions de grande voirie* embraces "certain injuries or damage, voluntary or involuntary, to the *domaine public* that constitute a limited penal jurisdiction of administrative tribunals. In the area of administrative contracts, in the concession of rights of way for public services, such as railroads, certain standard provisions setting forth the obligations and rights of the concessionaires were developed and given standing by decree of the Conseil d'État. These clauses, known as *cahiers des charges,* could generally be adapted to particular situations only with the approval of a special decree of the Conseil d'État. Waline, *Droit administratif,* p. 703. Hauriou's reference to the *regime de la simple permission de voirie sans cahiers des charges* concerns special legislation (Law of February 27, 1925) giving rights of way to electric companies by a simple permit of right of way without binding them in the usual way to an administrative contract with a public collectivity. pp. 346, 672.

Voisinage. The Conseil d'État has evolved a theory of governmental liability when governmental activity creates "an exceptional risk for a neighborhood" (*le voisinage*), such as collecting a great quantity of grenades in an area that leads to an explosion. See C.E.28 March 1919, *Regnault-Desroziers* S.1918–1919. 3.25, note Hauriou, and Long, Weil, Braibant, *Les grands arrêts de la jurisprudence administrative,* 3rd ed. (Paris, 1962), p. 147.

Index